# No Less a Man

# No Less a Man:
# Masculist Art
# in a Feminist Age

## Doug Robinson

Bowling Green State University Popular Press
Bowling Green, Ohio 43403

## Acknowledgements

Lyrics from the following songs are reprinted with the permission of the Jon Landau Management Company:

"Promised Land"
"Darkness on the Edge of Town"
"Born in the U.S.A."
"Adam Raised a Cain"
"Independence Day"
"My Father's House"
"My Hometown"
"Walk Like a Man"
"The Long Goodbye"
"Mary Queen of Arkansas"
"Grownin' Up"
"For You"
"Wild Billy's Circus Song"
"She's The One"
"Racin' in the Street"
"Downbound Train"
"Brilliant Disguise"

"One Step Up"
"Valentine's Day"
"Cautious Man"
"With Every Wish"
"Leap of Faith"
"Living Proof"
"Souls of the Departed"
"My Beautiful Reward"
"Book of Dreams"
"Used Cars"
"Ain't Got You"
"Held Up Without a Gun"
"Local Hero"
"Shut Out the Light"
"Real Man"
"Real World"

Excerpts from Robert Parker's novels are quoted with the permission of Bantam Doubleday Dell.

Copyright © 1994 Bowling Green State University Popular Press

Library of Congress Catalogue No.: 93-72885

ISBN: 0-87972-638-7 Clothbound
      0-87972-638-5 Paperback

Cover design by Gary Dumm/Dumm Art

for Heljä, Laura, Sara, and Anna

and for Bill and Sherrie,
who were there too

# Contents

| | |
|---|---|
| **Foreword by Sherrie Gradin** | 1 |
| **Preface** | 5 |
| **Introduction** | |
|     Popular Culture and the Emancipatory Critic | 11 |
| **PART ONE: SPENSER** | 37 |
|     Chapter One | |
|         The Hardboiled Hero | 39 |
|     Chapter Two | |
|         The Liberal Hero | 60 |
|     Chapter Three | |
|         Violence and Need | 76 |
|     Chapter Four | |
|         The Missing Mother | 93 |
| **PART TWO: RAMBO** | 107 |
|     Chapter Five | |
|         From *First Blood* to *First Blood* | 109 |
|     Chapter Six | |
|         The Hurt, Betrayed Son | 129 |
|     Chapter Seven | |
|         Surrender | 147 |
| **PART THREE: SPRINGSTEEN** | 163 |
|     Chapter Eight | |
|         The Dark Street | 166 |
|     Chapter Nine | |
|         Healing the Father | 187 |
|     Chapter Ten | |
|         Displaced Mothers | 212 |
| **Conclusion** | |
|     The Hero Myth | 249 |
| **Notes** | 263 |
| **Works Cited** | 297 |
| **Index** | 307 |

# Foreword

Doug Robinson's *No Less a Man: Masculist Art in a Feminist Age* is a hard-hitting eye-opener for both feminists and profeminist men. When I first read this text I found myself in turmoil and conflict. Anger, sadness, joy and fear arose simultaneously as I read, and these sharp feelings did not abate until long after I had turned the last page.

My first responses were anxiety-ridden and kneejerk: how dare this academically and economically successful white male complain about the damage done him by the patriarchy he continues to uphold in innumerable ways? But also as I read *No Less a Man*, I had glimpses of insight and heard messages of great import. When I allowed myself to hear Doug's voice and his arguments, I began to feel his need for transformation as a man controlled by the patriarchy in all of its sickness as much as I feel my own needs for transformation as a woman. Through years of work, pain, and psychic disintegration, I have slowly come to see myself as a "survivor" rather than as a victim of patriarchal power. What Doug's book so painfully points out is that men are as much victims of the patriarchy as I have been. The sort of transformation that Doug enacts and reads through Spenser, Rambo, and Springsteen is also that of a victim becoming a survivor.

In the past few years I have come to realize that it is time for feminists to take bold new steps toward dialogue and work with profeminist men and men working within the men's movement. For many years I have wanted the feminist movement to be only for and about women, since it is women who are so clearly trapped by the patriarchy. While I feel this need for "women's own space" is crucial at both an individual and a collective level, I have come to envision a space within which women and men can work together as well as separately toward a dismantling of patriarchal control. In order to do this, feminists must realize the ways in which the patriarchy has programmed us, as mothers, sisters, aunts, wives, and friends of men, to manipulate men into remaining well-greased cogs in the patriarchy that we have tried so hard to transform. Likewise, profeminist men must continually guard against internalizing and recreating patriarchal roadblocks to women's liberation.

## 2  No Less a Man

Creating a dialogic space in which men and women can take action in loving, supportive and caring ways against patriarchal programming is essential to any such enterprise. In spite of the pain, frustration and unease it awakened in both of us, for instance, Doug and I were able to talk about the anger and anxiety his original subtitle—"Masculist Transformations in Post-Feminist Popular Culture"—caused in me. There is nothing "post" about my life and work, and it is only a false perception quickened by the backlash against feminism that suggests the feminist movement is over. If we had not been able to create—and then enter into—this dialogic space, I would have continued to be angry and Doug would have continued to believe that his word "post-feminist" merely suggested that the women's movement was in progress; he would not have recognized how he was unintentionally mouthing the rhetoric of the antifeminist backlash.

We must work through and past our deep resentment and blame, which only serve to bolster the patriarchy's control over both men and women. As uncomfortable as it may be for both genders, we must move toward dialogue and away from resentment. At the same time, we must make room for men to write and talk with men, not only about the ways in which they are representatives of the patriarchy, but about the ways in which we women too are puppets of the patriarchy who unconsciously reinforce the sickness we are trying to cure in the men we love and work with.

Forthright and risky books like this one are necessary if we are to see and enjoy any long-lived freedom from patriarchal domination. Many feminists scoff at the men's movement and fight hard to keep feminism free from male appropriation. Feminists must not let the patriarchy appropriate feminist studies and concerns—but neither must we continue to see men's attempts to transform themselves and their relationships with women as trivial and false poses of victimization.

*No Less a Man* is a brave book that envisions the possibility of radical transformation and change in men—a move from sickness toward health. It is a book primarily for and about men. It speaks to experiences and pain that only men can fully know. It is not exclusionary, however, and women and feminists need to find the strength to read and learn from it as well. In groups of men and groups of women gathering separately we can gain great power and enact important changes. But it is only together that we can arrive at revolutionary change and a better, healthier society for all of us.

If you as a reader, man or woman, can quiet yourself long enough to read, listen, hear and respond to Doug Robinson's anger, pain and joy, and ultimately the transformation he reaches through his readings of popular culture, *No Less a Man* will change your life, and our society, for the better.

Sherrie Gradin

# Preface

Writing this book was a labor of love—and pain, and trauma, and joy. It grew out of my love of popular culture, especially that popular culture that spoke and speaks to my pain and my joy as a man; and it grew out of my ongoing (*laboriously* ongoing) process of disintegration and transformation out of some of the more soul-destructive defenses of patriarchal masculinity, especially as those defenses and disintegrations were refracted through the lens of American popular culture of the past two decades.

The book is, in other words, thinly disguised autobiography—autobiography writ large, autobiography collectivized through the profeminist men's movement and various cultural expressions sensitive and sympathetic to that movement, and to men's need to be transformed. It rides somewhere out on the front lines of men's experience of the importance and possibility of change, radical change, traumatic change, breakdown and slow rebuilding.

Perhaps as a result of the personal and emotional spot from which it was written, the book has had a spotty history since I first wrote it in the fall of 1988: enthusiastically embraced by a series of editors at university presses (six or seven of them, I think), who sent it out for external evaluation to feminist scholars of American popular culture and social history; returned by almost all those scholars with recommendations not to publish, despite a determined sympathy with my project that was invariably eroded by anxiety, even anger. My own anxieties and angers are often too close to the surface here for traditional academic discourse, and that is unsettling enough; for a man to address himself to feminist and masculist allies about men's *and* women's programming for the patriarchal battle of the sexes (and potential for truce, and mutual love and respect) is far worse. Just as there are masculists who nurse ancient resentments against their mothers and sometimes project those resentments onto all women, so are there feminists who project their anger at their fathers, and at repressive patriarchal power and authority in general, onto all men—and whenever I'm guilty of the former, my feminist readers seem to respond with the latter.

## 6   No Less a Man

And why not? I do the same in reverse—with, socially and historically speaking, far less justification. That vicious circle is programmed into us by patriarchy. As long as we're at each other's throats, we're not moving toward health, which would pose a *truly* serious threat to the status quo.

So where does this leave us? Must this be a book for changing men—excluding women? I hope not, although my primary audience *is* male, other men like me who have begun to detonate the patriarchal walls that have hemmed us in. But as I have learned immensely and intensely from feminists who see themselves as primarily addressing other women, I hope women will find something to take away from this too. I have no idea what; perhaps confirmation of current stereotypes about whiny men jumping on the victimization bandwagon or playing cowboys and Indians at warrior weekends and beating drums in sweat lodges; perhaps some feel for men's hurt, some sense that all is not well in the land of patriarchy, some trust in men's growth toward health.

My early research into Spenser, Rambo, and Springsteen was aided and abetted by a host of fans, especially of Springsteen; some of their names I've forgotten, others I never knew. Our names were never important anyway; it was always "did you know?" and "have you heard?" A Dell publicist, upon request, sent me a wonderful packet of materials on Robert Parker. After dreaming about writing on *First Blood* the movie for a year or so I happened upon David Morrell's novel, which the movie was based on; immediately upon putting the book down I took a chance on finding his phone number listed, and it was. In that first phone call he directed me to all the published material he knew of dealing with Rambo, especially Pat Broeske's production piece in the *L.A. Times*, John Stark's interview piece on Morrell in *People* magazine, and his own article in *Playboy*; just how invaluable all three sources were is evident from chapter five. In later phone calls and a short visit to his house in Iowa he fleshed out more of his own history with Rambo, his father, his son, and his pain.

My first stabs at articulating any of this were conference papers, actually the same conference paper delivered twice: once at the 11th American Imagery Conference in New York in the fall of 1987, again at the 2nd Maple Leaf and Eagle conference in Helsinki in the spring of 1988. Both audiences, as I mention in passing toward the end of my Rambo section, responded powerfully to the material, especially Stallone's monologue that concludes the movie version, which, for lack of easily accessible video equipment (both times), I read aloud—and finished almost in tears. It had much the same effect on my listeners, which told me something about the movie's deep resonances with my own and other men's (and even some women's) experience, and I built a lot of that into the Rambo chapters. I also gave a talk on Reagan's appropriation of Springsteen in the 1984 presidential campaign at the 2nd Biennial American Studies in Tampere, Finland, in the spring of 1987; and some of that talk got reworked into the end of chapter nine, with help from audience response.

Then there was the talk on being "Politically Postmodern" at a postmodernism conference in Stockholm, in the spring of 1988, where I moved from Springsteen into the first public performance ever of a song I'd just written, "Reborn" (appearing here in front of the Rambo section), and screwed it up royally. Oh well. The songs, by the way, were written over a three- or four-year period during repeated revisions of the book, in an attempt to get at what I felt going on in me in a more powerful way, a more *physical* way, than just sitting at the computer and building sentences. My friend Tarvo Laakso helped me make demo-quality recordings of them on an eight-track deck in the Vaajakoski church in Finland, and has himself played and sung "Living in Paradise" and "Love Song" in concert. I have no delusions of grandeur, no dreams of becoming a rock star (honest); this stuff has been largely for my own enjoyment and growth. But I'll be happy to send interested readers a copy of the tape, at cost. Contact Bowling Green Popular Press.

Most of the friends, colleagues, and students who have read parts of the manuscript over the years since I wrote it have been fans of individual heroes: Liz Maguire read the Spenser section (twice, and kept calling me on the phone to talk about it); Robin Bodkin, Bill Kaul, and the participants in a graduate seminar Sherrie Gradin and I team-taught on gender theory in the spring of 1992 read the Rambo section (as did David Morrell); and Doug Branch, Billy Albright, and Mark Allister read the Springsteen section, a few weeks before some of us saw him perform in Atlanta and Minneapolis. David Nye, Debra Rae Cohen, and Daniel Herbst gave me good reads on the whole manuscript as students of American popular culture; Barbara Bancroft and Sherrie Gradin gave me even better, closer, more engaged reads on the whole thing as committed feminists, incest survivors, and above all close friends. Sherrie was the first to draw my attention to how outdated some of the anger of my 1988 draft had become by 1991 or 1992—how my own growth had outstripped my earlier articulations, so that some passages no longer felt like me—and helped me to revise. She was also the first to work out with me some of the buttons my claims pushed in her—a woman repeatedly traumatized by her father and still shafted over and over by male colleagues—and how other women like her were likely to respond. It was her determined resistance to the term "post-feminist," which I had been using to refer to what my subtitle now calls "a feminist age," that finally got me to recognize the term's harmful connotations and to change it. I was trying to say "after feminism *started*"; she got me to see that it was usually read to mean "now that feminism is *over*." It's not, and I hope it never will be.

My brother David has been crucial to the working through of my feelings about my mother; he and I also learned to play the piano together when we were kids, and his composing later inspired me (he's the musically talented one; I'm a hacker). Bill Kaul is more than my closest male friend ever; he's a soulmate and a helluva sick guy (as our kids say about both of us; I take it as an affectionate way of saying "nice"), and my partner in crime in a book we just completed called "Academic Addictions." My wife and life companion Heljä has loved me and yelled at me and supported me through all of these changes, never shying away from my angers or fears or needs, depressions or breakdowns, always reassuring me both verbally and nonverbally that it's okay to let go, be weak, be lost, always giving me grief when I start thinking I know it all again. The commonalities we've found in each other as the defenses start coming down—the terror of ridicule, the need to be loved—convince me that men and women *can* communicate, can understand each other, can grow out of the battle of the sexes, can find each other in love. This book is dedicated to that hope.

D.R.<br>
Vaajakoski, Finland<br>
Oxford, Mississippi<br>
Peoria, Illinois

# Love Song

For Heljä

2. I'd love you son if you'd just first love me
   That was my mother's fearful legacy
   I'm too afraid to throw
   My heart away on you
   How can I love you when no one loved me?
   How can I love you when no one loved me?

3. I guess it's kind of hard to be a man
   They bring you up to be a steely Dan
   Inside you're just a kid
   Yelled at for what they did
   Afraid their love will wash away like sand
   Afraid their love will wash away like sand

4. Please help me break out of my slavery
   Please help me shake my guilty loyalty
   Please help me love myself
   Help me find something else
   I need your love before I can be free
   I need your love before I can be free

**Copyright 1993 Doug Robinson.**

# Introduction

## Popular Culture and the Emancipatory Critic

### 1

In her recent book *The Remasculinization of America: Gender and the Vietnam War*, Susan Jeffords argues that the last two decades or so in American culture have been a period of masculine resurgence, a time when both men and the ideologically normal masculinity that defines and sustains them have regained ground lost from the 1950 to the 1970s to such cultural "others" as women, minorities, and the young. We have seen, she suggests, "a revival of the images, abilities, and evaluations of men and masculinity in dominant U.S. culture" (xii), and this revival is most clearly evident in American responses to the Vietnam War. More recently, Susan Faludi and Naomi Wolf and others have documented, with depressing precision and persuasiveness, a widespread societal "backlash" against feminism, "an attempt," as Faludi puts it, "to retract the handful of small and hard-won victories that the feminist movement did manage to win for women" (xviii).

Unfortunately, these writers are largely right. Hegemonic images of (white middle-class) men as stoic endurers, unemotional planners, aggressive doers, controllers not only of women, minorities, and the young but of all physical and cultural otherness (including, as I add this discussion of Jeffords to the book in January 1991, half a million Iraqi soldiers and their President, thematized as an Arab "Hitler")—these images, challenged and to some extent unsettled in the 1960s and 1970s, are currently undergoing a renaissance. In popular novels, movies, and songs we have seen a new determination to glory in the rock-hard male body (muscles and no feelings), in the symbiosis of man and machine, in masculine violence and silence—even in the humble work-a-daddy, as Tom Wolfe called him, who really asks little more out of life than that he be appreciated by a loving support group of wife and children when he comes home from a hard day at the office. U.S. military attacks on third-world countries like Grenada and Iraq have "restored" Americans' faith in the Armed Forces and the normative masculine values that inform them: heroism under fire, suppression of fear (and all other counterproductive emotions), strict hierarchical obedience to a chain of command, and the use of violence to achieve dominance over all otherness.

At the same time, women are being portrayed as "victimized" by feminism, with spurious statistics about the "marriage crunch" or "man shortage" (educated and competent and independent women supposedly have a diminishing chance of getting married), an "infertility epidemic" (women who postpone childbearing to start careers are supposedly waking up to find it's too late) and a "career burnout" afflicting highly successful professional women (they really want to be June Cleaver). When women challenge these bogus statistics and try to talk about continuing inequality in the work force and the home, they are called man-haters. The cosmetics industry, the dieting industry and the media have stepped up their assault on women's self-esteem by turning attention away from success in the public realm to failure in the private: on the scales, in front of the mirror. Public images of women on television, in the movies and in magazines portray an anorectic ideal designed to make even underweight women hate themselves for their obesity. As daily calorie intakes plunge dangerously, well below starvation levels, the statistics for anorexia, bulimia and other eating disorders soar.

And all this is themered, in politics, in popular art, in media reporting, as a return to normalcy—an overthrowing of the insidious legacy of the 1960s in order to bring about the resurgence of true biological masculinity and femininity, the aggressive, competitive male and the passive, submissive female. As the chief of Reagan's Census Bureau's fertility statistics branch, Martin O'Connell says in a passage Susan Faludi quotes, "People I've dealt with in the government seem to want to recreate the fantasy of their own childhood" (8). After a rather pointless episode (this conservative scenario runs) during which a few loud-mouthed radicals imposed their fanatical notions of political correctness on the mass of decent Americans, we're back to business as usual. For the rest of us, doubly depressed by the resurgence of conventional patriarchal values and the reassurance it brings to the large majority of a profoundly conservative country, these analyses conduce, precisely because they are so implacably accurate, to despair, even to fatalism. Can *nothing* be done?

I want to suggest in this book that things are at once considerably better and considerably worse (at least for us counterhegemonic few) than these writers claim—better, I suppose, because worse. More hopeful because more desperate. The very revival of masculinity that Jeffords, for example, traces through cultural images of Vietnam bespeaks an exacerbation of American men's fear, confusion, and desperation in the midst of ongoing social transformations that make the future look bleak. And while the bleakness men feel when they look at the future prompts much of the macho revival, this also entails the possibility, even the likelihood, that the very fear, confusion, and desperation undergirding that revival will eventually undermine it. The "center" of recent remasculinization, I am arguing, is no center at all, is decentered by the denied anxiety that drives it, and so cannot hold.

This may sound Pollyanna-ish (too "feminine" to be taken seriously, especially from a male scholar); maybe it is. But in a larger historical context, viewed in terms of the last three or four centuries of bourgeois social history, the current "remasculinization of America" is neither a new nor a particularly earth-shaking phenomenon. The emergence and establishment of the middle classes in the modern era has meant the progressive feminization of Western society, the gradual displacement of medieval masculinity, with its reptilian territorialism, by humanizing feminine voices and values. That history has been punctuated, however, by recurrent periods of remasculinization, periods in which patriarchy, as it were, has panicked at social change and slammed on the brakes. Our conventional literary periodizations reflect this jerky progress: romanticism is an attempt to feminize Enlightenment common sense, and classicism, realism, and naturalism are attempts to slam on the brakes; but classicism and realism give way to symbolism and modernism, where Ezra Pound finds himself too close to "Amygism" for comfort and again slams on the brakes (swears off effeminate imagism for a more masculine fascism).

More pertinently, Jeffords' book title responds silently to Ann Douglas' *The Feminization of America*, which traces the emergence of women, femininity, and what Jeffords would call the "feminine point of view,"[1] in nineteenth-century American culture—and, more generally, I would claim, in Western bourgeois society. But to the extent that Jeffords is implying that American culture is *just now* being remasculinized, after a century and a half of unbroken feminization, her implication is historically off-base. Robert Bannister has traced another remasculinization period in America in the first half of this century, a period in which prominent American men, alarmed at the impact on male adolescents of strong mothers, began to proselytize for manly organizations (like the Boy Scouts, founded in this era) that would protect young men against the feminizing influence of their mothers and

## 14  No Less a Man

a generally "effeminate" culture. Feminism suffered a series of setbacks during this period, but when it resurfaced in the 1960s, it did not have to start from scratch; indeed, it emerged stronger than ever. The advancement of feminism, or of the "feminine point of view," had proceeded apace, despite masculine retrenchment. If we are currently in another period of remasculinization, therefore, another patriarchal resistance to feminization, this does not necessarily mean that we are back to square one.

Most importantly for us men, I would argue, talk of remasculinization among both conservatives and feminists elides the frightening but also promising fact of our desperate confusion, our terror of the unknown that is already all around us, our sense that we have no solid inner core from which to face the future. If this is a time of remasculinization, it is also a time of what the media call "men's crisis." As conventional masculine values crumble—as wives and daughters and mothers and even other men ("new men," "changing men") begin to withdraw from patriarchal men the approval for conventional behavior that has helped maintain that behavior, as the denial of emotion and the instrumentalization of other human beings become increasingly self-destructive even for men who continue to receive that social support for repression and dominance—some men turn to machismo for relief; others turn to the men's movement, or to various incremental forms of men's liberation. By far the majority remain undecided, inclined to ridicule men's liberation, men's groups, male sensitivity training, but also uneasy around rank masculine violence in word or deed and uninclined to accede to pressures back toward territorial masculinity.

And it is heartening to hear the new voices of feminism affirming these changes. In a talk at the University of Mississippi, Naomi Wolf speaks of the damage done to men's psyches by pornography and other patriarchal tools, recognizes many men's desire and need to change, and calls on women to hate what men have done in the name of patriarchy while still loving and working with the men in their lives. After 456 pages of depressing and even terrifying documentation of the antifeminist backlash, Susan Faludi addresses in her conclusion the resistance of many women *and* men to these reactionary forces:

> It was in this period [since 1970] that favorable attitudes toward women's rights experienced their greatest growth among men, too, While many women in the backlash eras have feared "offending men" with feminist demands, women in the '70s who were assertive and persistent discovered that they could begin to

change men's views. By vigorously challenging the conventional definition of masculinity, these women allowed men to start to question it, too. After all, to a great extent so many men have clung to the sole-provider status as their proof of manhood because so many women have expected it of them. (In the Yankelovich poll, it's not just men who have consistently identified the breadwinner's role as the leading masculine trait; it has also consistently been women's first choice.) As much as men fought the female challenge in the '70s, they also absorbed and incorporated it into their private experience; and when they saw women wouldn't back down, many men started to make accommodations to keep the women they loved in their lives...For what has been largely forgotten in the backlash era—where women are encouraged to please men by their demeanor or appearance rather than persuade them by the force of their argument—is that men don't hold all the emotional cards. Men need women as much as women need men. The bonds between the sexes can chafe, and they can be, and have been, used to constrain women. But they also can promote mutually beneficial growth and change. (457)

Faludi is primarily using her perception of men's changes to encourage women, here—to keep the feminist age alive by underscoring men's healthy responses to feminism, our willingness to be transformed by feminist challenges rather than merely reacting in anger and fear. That willingness is often hard to detect, given the intensity and the ubiquity of the anger and the fear, the resistance that drives the antifeminist backlash; but it's there, and Faludi is saying that women can trust it, finally, to submit to, support and be transformed by their drive to independence.

2

I am, in other words, far more hopeful about men and masculinity than feminists like Jeffords—probably because I feel in myself and in men around me the impulse toward emancipation, and know that it is stronger than it may appear to women who despair of ever getting through to the men in their lives. This book is an attempt to explore that impulse—and to prod it, to advance it, to fan what embers of change men (and women) carry within them into a fire.

Such a project seems to me to require that I stroke contemporary American culture, specifically popular culture, against the grain—indeed, against several grains. Against the academic grain, first of all, I suppose, because I am interested in the most popular of popular culture—massmarket genre fiction, blockbuster movies, and multimillion-unit rock music. But also against the popular or populist grain, in that I do not take popularity to be a virtue in and of itself—do not assume, for example, that the bigger the market the better the art, and indeed consider a good deal of the most popular art to be exploitative trash. And finally, as my reading of Jeffords' book began to hint, against the feminist grain, in that I am interested in men, men's art, art about men and masculinity, art that often seems to glorify masculinity and thus, in Jeffords' terms, to participate in the project of "remasculizing" America—and my interest in that art is largely admiring and supportive. I do not, for example, propose to launch an attack on this art and the men it represents for its sexism (nor do I plan to defend or downplay its sexism). As a result, some readers have wanted to associate my claims with the antifeminist backlash Faludi and others have documented—an association I want to talk about a little later.

Neither feminist nor patriarchal, neither elitist nor populist: this is a pretty negative way to map out my project. It seems a useful preliminary mapping because popular men's art is one of the strongest ideological confluences in American culture, one of the cultural phenomena about which everyone has a deeply felt and strongly articulated opinion, and therefore a preconceived notion about what my concerns here will and ought to be. Popular men's art is, alongside an atavistic Christian fundamentalism and advertising, one of the most mythic vehicles of normative patriarchal ideology in contemporary capitalist society, and as such a prime target for feminist, Marxist and postmodernist deconstruction—three critical ideologies and methodologies that have powerfully shaped my own critical practice. To study popular men's art is, according to currently reigning assumptions, to study the patriarchal/capitalistic/metaphysical mainstream; to study it admiringly, therefore, to find things to praise in it, is to collaborate with reactionary forces within patriarchal society.

My choice of popular male heroes will probably be seen as more reactionary still. I will be dealing with three such heroes, two invented by novelists, one a breathing human being: Robert B. Parker's private detective Spenser, David Morrell's (and Sylvester Stallone's) Vietnam veteran Rambo, and Bruce Springsteen. All three are patently macho men, precisely the kind of men that have come under the heaviest feminist fire in the past 15 or 20 years. We might, of course, discriminate more subtly than that: Spenser is a liberal and apparently liberated tough guy, and Springsteen has soft, tender, vulnerable eyes. Rambo—or at least the myth of Rambo, which is all most people who use the name ever mean by it—is a different story. In conversation with colleagues who ask what I am working on, in fact, I find a vague intellectual resistance to the study of popular culture (an uneasiness about why anyone like me, who is also interested in high culture, would bother), but more specifically, and more intensely, an immediate emotional reaction against Rambo. "I *hate* Rambo!" one feminist colleague burst out recently, when I told her what I was working on. "Of course you do," I said. "You hate the mythic image of Rambo. So do I. But have you seen any of the movies? Have you seen *First Blood*?" "No," she replied, "and I don't want to."

This is, I think, indicative not only of academic bias (elitist and feminist, in this case), but of the power of myth to displace or dispel the very human textures of the stories that constitute it—to purify and universalize the ideal core of a story and relegate its rough edges *to* the edges, to the dark peripheries of collective experience. Without those rough edges, those peripheralized darknesses, the myth would never attain its explanatory power; but if the myth directed attention to the rough edges, if it encouraged self-consciousness, self-reflexivity, it would lose its esemplastic power, its power to shape readers and viewers and listeners into a uniform community of believers, "fans" as ideologically normal or normative fanatics, consumers as the individual "subjects" who, in Althusser's telling pun, are "subjected" by capitalism.

This "esemplasm" is, clearly, the remasculinization stratum of recent American popular culture; it is not the stratum or aspect I am interested in. The bloodthirsty sequels to *First Blood* do not appeal to me, and I have no desire, except briefly, in passing, to deconstruct them. The mythic image of Rambo is a defensive ideological structure that exercises me very little, and will concern me here even less. It is essential, certainly, as a first step in a project of emancipation, to identify the forces that hold you fast, to explore the prison block in which you are incarcerated; but to dwell on incarceration exclusively seems to me ultimately counterproductive, leading to an overwhelming sense of your powerlessness before the hegemonic forces of patriarchal society. I am interested specifically in the liberatory potential of the peripheralized rough edges of this art—the ways in which we as ideological discontents can seize upon powerfully or potentially emancipatory moments in popular art to facilitate our own resistance to dominant ideological inscriptions, our attempts to displace or replace those inscriptions in our lives, to reinscribe ourselves as men and women.

(The restrictions that last sentence places on the lectorial side of that "we," you as my readers, are deliberate: I do address myself specifically to ideological discontents, men first, perhaps, as the group

## 18  No Less a Man

most concerned with *men's* liberation, but also women as the interested onlookers and in some sense instigators of men's liberation.)

What does this mean in interpretive practice?

It is possible—and relatively easy, since our culture coaches us in this—to identify the ideological "centers of popularity" of the three figures I am concerned with:

Spenser is popular, in Parker's novels and on the now discontinued but widely syndicated network TV series *Spenser: For Hire* (starring Robert Urich), largely because of his liberal humanism, his "ethical" concern for the people he comes into contact with, perhaps also his careful "feminism"—his avoidance of terms and phrases that offend feminists, his awareness that women have been silenced and peripheralized, his willingness to give women a chance and a voice—and, of course, the sheer undeniable fact that he's a big strong fightin' man who has a gorgeous articulate woman friend with whom he has exuberant nondestructive sex and who (Spenser) regularly beats up the bad guys and puts them behind bars. Spenser, like other hardboiled detectives before him (though in a more "liberated" fashion than they), is a wisecracking tough guy who cares—a widely attractive masculine ideal in "post-feminist" America.

Rambo is popular, in David Morrell's 1972 novel *First Blood* and the 1982 movie version of it (starring Sylvester Stallone), in the movie sequels and their novelizations by Morrell, and in merchandising tie-ins (Rambo knives, T-shirts, dolls, etc.) because he acts out the idealized masculine fantasies of conservative America, single-handedly defeating the collective enemies of God's own country, everyone (the Russians and other godless communists outside America, cynical politicians within) who would destroy all that is pure and decent in the world—and because his shapely inarticulateness has an immense anti-intellectual (and implicitly antibourgeois, certainly anti-upper-middle-class) appeal. He is Superman as underdog, an unlikely but ultimately invincible warrior who represents a mythic or utopian ideal (freedom, democracy, the American Way) that the New Right perceives as in imminent danger, beleaguered, threatened from all sides.

Springsteen is popular on his 11 albums, on the radio, in concert, in rock videos, and in merchandising tie-ins because he transforms into charismatic rock music, the dominant form of musical expression in the West for the past 35 years, all of the deepest hopes and fears of contemporary culture. By drawing on the entire history of rock music in his own songs, from the 1950s to the 1990s, and by setting "great lyrics" to "catchy tunes," he also unifies his audience, breaks down generational, gender, and class boundaries (attracts 15- and 40-year-olds, men and women, white- and blue-collar workers—few minorities, however) and thus creates a kind of "true America," an idealized community of Springsteen fans, joined in their loyalty to and love of "the Boss" (the leader not as Jesus or Reagan but as Rock Messiah).

This is, give or take, the ideological center of these three figures, that which ensures or (in the technical sense) constitutes their runaway popularity, and which early manuscript readers of this book all expected me to be concerned with. But there is another side to all three figures—or rather an entire fragmentary array of other sides, out on the rough edges of their public existence—which at once (a) defines the center by exclusion (the totalitarian constitution of popularity), (b) enriches the center by complication (the pluralistic constitution of popularity), and (c) undermines the center by misdirection (the therapeutic or transformative reconstitution of popularity). My concern throughout this book will be with (c)—and with (a) and (b) only as the ideological backdrop or scene against or in which (c) is staged. Indeed my concern will be with actively *staging* (c), actively undermining the ideological centers of popular men's art, partly by showing how the artists in question are themselves engaged in a reconstitutive or transformative project, partly by going beyond the artists' projects to stage a therapeutic moment even when they lose heart.

I am interested in Spenser, for example, not as ideological icon (the quest for an adequate representation of American masculinity), nor as detective hero (the quest for a murderer or missing woman or child), but as a mirror of failed masculinity: as an identificatory reflection that will show us back our own crumbling gender identities and unproductive solutions to our distress. I am interested—perversely, it may seem to ideological critics who read him as an unfeeling ideological machine, a clone or cyborg of an imperialistic foreign policy—in Rambo's emotional traumas, his fears, anxieties, emotional needs, feelings of bitterness, betrayal, and abandonment throughout *First Blood*, and the stunning therapeutic moment that concludes the movie version. And I am interested in Bruce Springsteen's attempts through his songs and concert monologues of the late 1970s, 1980s, and early 1990s to reconstitute his own masculinity by liberating himself from his destructively "normal" (repressively angry, locked-up, defensive) relationship with his father.

## 3

One useful way of sketching out my approach to popular men's art might be through the distinction Fredric Jameson draws in the conclusion to *The Political Unconscious* between "negative" and "positive" hermeneutics—between ideological analysis and utopian visions. For the ideological critic, the pressing task is to map every square inch of the jailcells in which we are currently trapped; for the utopian critic, the crucial task is to engineer a jailbreak. The ideological critic's negative hermeneutic is an articulation of everything that is deadening and dehumanizing about the status quo; the utopian critic's positive hermeneutic is a reimagining of the status quo in revivifying and rehumanizing terms. Jameson argues that Marxist criticism, for example, has tended to lean too heavily toward the negative—toward attacks on capitalism, say—and in the process has often undermined its own claims to be a utopian or emancipatory hermeneutic. What we need, Jameson suggests, is an ongoing dialectic between negative and positive hermeneutics, between ideological analysis and utopian vision—a dialectic through which the utopian imagination takes on substance through its grounding in a realistic appraisal of the obstacles to be overcome, and the ideological imagination gains hope for the future by being charged with a sense that things might be different.

Jameson's critique of some Marxisms applies equally well, it seems to me, to some academic treatments of popular culture and to some feminist treatments of men: wherever the ideological negative leaves no room for dialectical engagement with the utopian positive, any positive hermeneutic is automatically branded as a reactionary celebration of the status quo. Any positive discussion of popular culture is an ode to exploitative consumer capitalism; any positive discussion of men is an ode to male supremacy, violence, and repression.

But consumer culture *is* exploitative, ideological critics protest; men *are* violently repressive power-mongers. True, much of it is; many of us are. These are facts that must be owned, admitted. We cannot escape the accusing fingers of ideological criticism, and should not try. But must we stop there? Is all popular culture capitalist exploitation—and must it always be? Are all men violently repressive power-mongers—and must they always be? Even if all popular culture is exploitative trash, the utopian imagination insists on envisioning a regeneration, and striving toward it; even if all men are violent male-supremacist oppressors, the utopian imagination again envisions a regeneration, a transformation from within. And once that transformation has been envisioned, the utopian imagination seeks out

**Introduction  21**

signs that it is already underway, even if only embryonically: seeks out the first harbingers of a utopian popular culture, a utopian masculinity, that might not be visible, might not even be *there*, if one didn't know how and where to look for it.

Wishful thinking, you say—and perhaps it is, in some of its aspects. The thing is, given the ideological forces that repress and suppress such utopian impulses, they might never surface at all were it not for the momentary spaces of trust and encouragement established by utopian critics—were it not for some observers' faith in their existence and practical viability. Hegemonic disbelief in utopian "what might be's" has the (intended) effect of enforcing "what is." Ridiculing the utopian imagination as wishful thinking, as a pipe dream, as puerile escapist fantasies, constructs and maintains an ideological prison from which the only escape *is* through fantasy.

My emancipatory reading of selected works of contemporary American popular men's art is utopian, then, in the sense of seeking to elicit in this art, from behind the facade projected by hegemonic social forces, a tendency toward a new masculinity, a reconstruction of men's gender identity along healthier, more life-affirming lines. This means moving through the "negative" ideological analyses of patriarchal masculinity launched so persuasively by feminists to a "positive" utopian vision of regenerated masculinity—moving "through" feminist analyses in the sense not of discarding them but rather of responding dialectically to them, taking them as the antithesis of our traditional training in masculinity and striving toward a utopian synthesis.

Not, however, a "synthesis" as a simple conciliatory mixture or amalgam: say, traditional machismo with a few rhetorical concessions to feminist critiques, the male feminism of many liberal men (e.g. Parker's Spenser). Rather, a transformative synthesis, a synthesis as transformation: a new masculinity jerrybuilt out of the exploding fragments generated in the collision between blatant self-satisfied machismo and feminist critiques. If the masculine "thesis" is the sick and self-destructive macho man who claims there's nothing wrong with him, and the feminist "antithesis" is a devastatingly painful diagnosis of his illness, the transformative synthesis is no uneasy mediation or compromise between those two positions but a cure, a restoration to health.

I have found, in discussing this project with feminist friends and colleagues who like and respect me and understand why it is important for men to undertake this synthetic step beyond feminism, that it still, despite all their sympathy and understanding, makes them profoundly uneasy. (Not that all feminist colleagues like and respect me; it's just that the unease this masculist project provokes in feminists is more obvious in women who feel comfortable with me as a person than in those who dislike or don't know me. In this latter group, as we'll see in a moment, the unease comes out as overt anger or defensive condescension.) Isn't this all just another rejection of feminism, another fine-tuning of misogyny? Or, worse, isn't it a subtle cooptation of feminism, an adjustment of feminist political and interpretive practices for appropriative use by men, who then continue to monopolize the goodies handed out by a male-dominated society?

There is a lot of this fear on both sides of the gender barricades. Men too, individual men as opposed to men in the aggregate, men as generalized emblems of "patriarchy"—often feel dismissed, peripheralized, deprived of various social goodies by women. Some of this may be a paranoid fantasy prompted by our socialization to gender, our training in the patriarchal battle of the sexes, which coaches each gender to blame the other for all (real and imagined) defeats and deprivations. Much of it is hard political reality, especially in what men have done to women: since patriarchy assigns men the political victory over women, we have been in a position to deprive them of a lot. Individual women have also victimized individual men. But what this insistence on the negative does is to perpetuate the battle of the sexes, and thus in some sense to perpetuate patriarchy: as long as we live in fear and loathing of the opposite sex, as long as men continue to blame women for everything and women continue to blame men for everything, we shackle ourselves with anxiety and insecurity and effectively block impulses toward liberation. Mutual mistrust is patriarchy's last best weapon against its discontents.

An emancipatory gender politics requires, it seems to me, a relaxation of the programmed suspicions that keep us in thrall to patriarchy. The sheer unconscious effectiveness of patriarchal ideology makes this possibility seem so utopian as to be virtually attainable, certainly—my feminist friends feel uneasy when I talk about men's studies, and I feel uneasy when they express their unease, and inwardly all of us feel almost as far from relaxation (mutual trust, love, acceptance), despite our outward friendliness, as ever did bitter foes—but without that utopian possibility I don't see any hope of real liberation, ever. If men can't relax the inner patriarchal voice that objectifies and demonizes women, and women can't relax the inner patriarchal voice that objectifies and demonizes men, we'll all remain caught in the same trap.

One of my main concerns in this book is in fact to deobjectify the male subject as portrayed in popular men's art, and as attacked (objectified as oppressor) by many feminists. I want to try to inhabit a utopian space of sympathy within each of the three male figures, Spenser, Rambo, and Springsteen, seeing in them more of the patriarchal oppressor identified by feminists than any of them can see but also, continually, crying out of their pain, fear, vulnerability, and surrender to change. I don't want to "disprove" feminist critiques so much as I want to move beyond them, through them, to a deeper and more inward perspective on the subjective impulses that drive men to act as we do—and, most especially, to a sense of the masculist transformations that are already undermining the old patriarchal masculinities, even, in some cases, devastating and regenerating those masculinities.

So: if I'm moving through and beyond feminism, is this book part of the antifeminist backlash? Let me try to formulate my response to this question as clearly as possible. I do argue that some feminists, even some feminisms, continue to be voiced by the patriarchy—especially when they uncritically and unconsciously adopt the patriarchal stance that everything harmful in gender relations is to be blamed *tout court* on the opposite sex. But I don't equate the speaking of patriarchy *through* some feminisms *with* feminism. I take feminism to be a transformative engagement with the patriarchal prison that attempts to liberate the women incarcerated there. I assume that a healthy feminism will naturally work to help men liberate themselves from the same prisons (possibly from trusteeships in that prison—we have more power and greater rewards, but we are no less incarcerated). I assume, in other words, that a healthy feminism will be promasculist, just as a healthy masculism will be profeminist. Conversely, I assume that blanket accusations of "all men" are patriarchal survivals within feminism (as blanket accusations of "all women" are patriarchal survivals within masculism), and that focusing critical attention on those survivals is, if anything, an *antipatriarchal* backlash that furthers the emancipatory aims of both the profeminist men's movement and the promasculist women's movement.

### 4

It is time, perhaps, to examine the unfamiliar term that appears in my subtitle and that last paragraph: masculist. *Masculism* and its adjectival form *masculist* are my coinages for the profeminist men's movement and its emancipatory ideology. The men's movement began as a response to feminism in the early 1970s in the form of men's groups and the odd conference, in an attempt initially to sensitize men to feminist critiques but also, increasingly, to become collectively aware of masculine gender programming and to instigate and provide social support for men's liberation from patriarchy. For the first 10 or 15 years of its existence, it struggled along with very little visibility, an embarrassment to most men who knew about it (and they were few) and the butt of even fewer feminists' scorn and contempt. Most of the writing done about men's liberation in the early years was restricted to men's conference manifestoes of one kind or another. Men involved in the movement either didn't feel ready yet to put their thoughts to paper or couldn't find publishers for the thoughts they did write down. In terms of books and articles published, the 1970s for the men's movement was like the 1960s for the women's movement: limited to a few isolated cases.

Still, those isolated cases broke important new ground, and are still worth reading. In 1975 three important books appeared: Jack Nichols's *Men's Liberation*, Warren Farrell's *The Liberated Man*, and Goodman and Walby's *A Book About Men*. Men's movement journals started to appear in the 1970s also: *Brothers*, *Changing Men*, and others. The National Organization for Changing Men was founded in 1983, the National Organization for Men Against Sexism (NOMAS), and the NOMAS-affiliated Men's Studies Association since that time. Gradually masculist scholars, first of all in social psychology, then in men's history, began to explore new avenues in masculinity, and thus to forge the academic discipline now called men's studies.[2] The first university gender studies program to include men, the Program for the Study of Women and Men in Society at USC, was founded in 1975; very few universities have followed suit in the almost two decades since, but the number of incidental men's studies courses offered around the country has been rising dramatically in the late 1980s and early 1990s. A collection of men's studies readings appeared back in 1977, edited by Jon Snodgrass, *A Book of Readings for Men Against Sexism*, and another, *The American Man*, edited by Elizabeth H. Pleck and Joseph H. Pleck, appeared in 1980; but it was not until 1987 that publishers and scholars alike began to show that they were taking the movement seriously by bringing out hefty essay collections: Michael Kaufman's *Beyond Patriarchy: Essays on Men on Pleasure, Power, and Change*, Harry Brod's *The Making of Masculinities: The New Men's Studies*, and Franklin Abbott's *New Men, New Minds: Breaking Male Tradition*. In 1987 and 1989, Klaus Theweleit's exciting two-volume dissertation *Männerphantasien* appeared in English translation (*Male Fantasies*) and offered what for me was the first truly dynamic synthesis of leftist, feminist, and masculist thought in an explosive reading of the German proto-Nazi Freikorpsmen.

Compared with the 1990s, all this remains a mere trickle. The big boom began with the runaway popularity of Robert Bly's *Iron John: A Book About Men* in 1990; it sparked a media blitz on the men's movement, usually (not always) having a few chuckles at the spectacle of men sitting around in sweat lodges beating drums and getting in touch with their feelings. In the fall of 1991 it seemed like every sitcom on prime-time TV had to have its own men's movement episode: the men at the station on "Murphy Brown" came back from a warrior weekend speaking of transformation but untransformed; HBO's "Dream On" explored Martin Tupper's (and through him male viewers') anxiety about open discussions of feelings and disgust at physical intimacy with other men; there were half a dozen lesser efforts. The mythopoeic men's movement was on everybody's lips—and the men who were involved in it walked around uneasily muttering things like "Well, it's not just drumming" and "It's easy to laugh at things you don't know anything about." Many academic men began to dissociate themselves from Bly and popular images of him, calling what they do men's *studies* rather than the men's *movement*—some even swearing off men's studies, for fear of association with drumming.

New scholarly journals appeared, especially *The Journal of Men's Studies* in August, 1992, edited by Jim A. Doyle. The publishers also began to get into the act. Many trade presses began to seek out books on men, and others became bestsellers as well, notably Sam Keen's *Fire in the Belly* (which inspired Alfred Gingold's satire on the men's movement in *Fire in the John: The Manly Man in the Age of Sissification* [1991]). University presses expanded their women's studies lists to include men's studies books, notably the University of Minnesota Press, New York University Press, and Oxford University Press.[3] Routledge started a men's studies series, and at this writing (February, 1993) they have brought out four interesting books and have yet another in press: Joseph A. Boone and Michael Cadden's *Engendering Men: The Question of Male Feminist Criticism* (1990), Kaja Silverman's *Male Subjectivity at the Margins* (1992), Peter Middleton's *The Inward Gaze: Masculinity and the Postmodern Subject* (1992), Ed Cohen's *Talk on the Wilde Side: Toward a Genealogy of a Discourse on Male Sexualities* (1993), and Stephen Cohan and Ina Rae Hark's *Screening the Male: Exploring Masculinities in Hollywood Cinemas* (forthcoming).

Masculism seems to me the obvious word to describe a movement and a political and ideological stance that conceives itself as allied to but not subsumed in feminism. It is the precise morphological equivalent of feminism, and should, it seems to me, be used in an similar positive sense. Largely due to a widespread "negative" or "ideological" association of patriarchy with *men*, however, and thus with the essence of masculinity, there has been little inclination to derive a positive term for the men's movement from "masculine." The only derivation currently in use is "masculi*ni*sm," a term of contempt used of patriarchal masculinity by some feminists; the implication is that, while women are liberating themselves from the traditional subservient femininity imposed on them by "men" (which is to say, by patriarchal society as transmitted and maintained by men *and* women), men and masculinity in general are to be linked exclusively with an oppressive system.[4] Masculism would be the positive counterpart to feminism: a movement dedicated to the liberation of men from patriarchal gender programming.

The current "positive" ism bandied about by many feminists and some men is "male feminism," a term that implies the primacy of feminism and its grudging extension to a few sympathetic males. (Male feminist is to feminist in feminist rhetoric what "wife-man" or woman is to man in patriarchal rhetoric: the marked extension of a universalized norm.) Male feminism has a long and often illustrious historical pedigree, dating back at least to Richard Hyrde's 1525 polemic in favor of women's education, and finding its perhaps most famous pre-twentieth-century articulation in John Stuart Mill's *The Subjection of Women* (1869); in its most benevolent form it is liberal men's rather condescending sympathy for women's ill-treatment in an inhumane social order and dedication to the redress of those ills. In its least benevolent form, however, it is a channel of male self-abasement, self-loathing: men repeating and confirming feminist attacks on a patriarchally programmed masculinity that is taken to be somehow essential and immutable, our pernicious "birthright" as males. A good (if extreme) example is the absolute self-denigration of the British "effeminist" John Stoltenberg, who writes in 1983: "To take seriously in one's 'consciousness' the fact of sexist injustice would have to mean for men, as it already does for many women, *a total repudiation of masculinity*. All 'Men's Liberation' that in form and content is masculinity-*confirming*, is thus an escalation and permutation of masculinist aggression" (qtd. in Rowan 53). Stoltenberg has since written a book called *Refusing To Be a Man*.

Male feminism has tended, in fact, to vacillate uneasily between these two poles: on the one hand assuming that everything is basically all right with men and will be all right with women, too, once we right a few social wrongs; on the other that everything is basically wrong with men and nothing will be all right until masculinity is utterly rent and assimilated to the life-affirming structures of femininity. On the one hand, men are subjective beings who have unfortunately objectified women and must stop doing so; on the other, men are objectified oppressors who must enlist the increasingly powerful subjectivity of women in the project of curbing our most destructive impulses. Liberal paternalism and liberal guilt; condescending panaceas and anxious self-abasement.[5]

Male feminism is, understandably, an attractive concept to some feminists. In her Presidential address to the women's breakfast at the 1987 American Studies Association Convention in New York, for example, Lois Banner took issue with the very idea of "men's studies," denying the need for men to study masculinity on our own terms. "I think it is time for all of us to use the term 'feminist'," Banner said. "This term encompasses the rest: thus we have the feminist study of women, of men, and of gender" (4). "From the beginning of the emergence of the new feminism in the 1960s, women feminists have always written about male roles" (4)—and why should men have to add anything to that? Banner speaks specifically to a fear that the "women-centered" analysis of feminism might be coopted by men, and offers a universalized feminism as a stay against that possibility. The implication, of course, is that men's analyses of gender must be women-centered as well. Men are not to develop independent viewpoints on our own masculinity; we are to take our cue from women.

When I first read Banner's speech in the *ASA Newsletter*, I thought my chest would burst with pent-up anxiety; I felt small, infantile, powerless, faced with an all-powerful mother who was telling me exactly how to behave so as to please *her*. I was five years old, about to burst into tears—or, since both of my parents always ridiculed me for crying, into a more "masculine" display of anger. I remember pacing restlessly around our bedroom with the text of Banner's speech in my hand, reliving all those childhood fears and frustrations, wondering what to do. Finally I sat down at my computer and started to write a response, speaking openly of my hurt and frustration when reading her piece and calling for a kind of truce, for the same relaxation of the polarized recriminations that drive the battle of the sexes that I've been calling for here.

And they published it—strangely, beginning at the back of the newsletter and moving forward—along with Banner's reply. But Banner's reply was more hurtful than her original speech. "Professor

Robinson's remarks sadden me," she wrote. "They seem hysterical and overblown and filled with ageism. I'm tempted to say that they sound like a small boy having a tantrum, but to do so would be only to engage in the kind of name-calling in which Professor Robinson indulges" (6).

*Hysterical*: because I admitted my feelings, I suppose. I had thought "hysterical" was patriarchy's name for women (especially, since the 1960s, feminists) who do not toe the official line by repressing rebellious impulses; now established feminists accuse "rebellious" men of the same? What does this say? *Overblown*: out of all proportion to the real hurt suffered, this seems to mean. Men can't be hurt; they're oppressors. Stop whining and melodramatizing your "plight." *Ageist*: because I spoke of her as an established feminist, someone my mother's age in a position of power in the academy. And then that last sentence, which really pulls the iron band tight around my chest—that subtly extended and quickly withdrawn insult, that infantilization that I can analyze, intellectually, as fear-driven maternal rhetoric, but without much impact on my somatic response: halfway into my analysis my neocortex is shut down by my own fear, that infantile terror of mommy's anger. In my response I had said how her defensive maternal rhetoric ("defensive" was the only "name" I called her) made me feel like a scared and cowed little boy; out of whatever need to defend against my confession, she escalates my self-description into a "tantrum" and then, as if magnanimously, as if with a calm maturity I can only dream of, withdraws her accusation.

Is this the kind of exchange we want? Is this a liberatory dialogue between men and women, masculists and feminists? Obviously not—but what are the alternatives? What could Lois Banner and I have done differently to break out of the mother-son impasse we found ourselves in? I needed to grow up, obviously, and not feel so terrorized by manipulative maternal rhetoric; but how could I do that when I felt surrounded by feminists who spoke of gender liberation for both men and women but continued, driven by their insecurities, to play the old patriarchal power games? Banner needed to relax her fears of male cooptation (and, perhaps, of men's feelings) long enough to hear what I was saying, to let me become a subjective being for her; but how could she do that when everything I said generated massive anxiety in her?

I suppose it is fair to say that this book was not written for defensive defenders of paternal or maternal authority (of whatever generation), but for men and women who are actively engaged in gender liberation. This will not be the last exposure of my personal vulnerability to emotional assaults in the book, and I would prefer to think that anxious, defensive readers inclined to lash out at me for "blowing everything out of proportion" or "overreacting" or "being over-sensitive" or "indulging in paranoid fantasies" or "throwing temper tantrums" or whatever were simply not interested in what I write, and put this book down shortly after stumbling upon these "uneasy" or "embarrassing" self-revelations in the introduction.

Emancipatory criticism, if it truly is that, seems to me exceptionally vulnerable to this kind of dismissive attack. I am convinced that whatever is easily articulable and intellectually obvious is likely to be counteremancipatory, ideologically hegemonic, normative; this means that the articulation of an emancipatory impulse invariably requires a shuffling and a stumbling and a stammering out of the well-lit mainstream of cultural life, or of a given text or cultural myth, into a shadowy realm where the way is not marked and the path is overgrown with brambles. This is a realm where the critic must find his or her way, and guide his or her readers, by the light of neither reason nor maps but by instinct, by a gut feeling for what comes next. As a result, it is also a realm where the critic will find it impossible to prove that he or she is not just making everything up—not just generating the "emancipatory undercurrent" in Rambo, say, out of his or her egregious desire to be saying something clever and new.

Above all, it seems to me, emancipatory criticism must emerge from the critic's own experience of emancipation—not some "plateau" of emancipation, certainly, on which the critic can sit back with a contented smile and declare, "*Now* I'm emancipated, isn't it wonderful!", but rather the somatic sense of what it feels like to go through a transformative process, even if that process is still ongoing. Without this sense the critic's faith in the very possibility of real change, of breaking out of destructive ideological inscriptions like traditional femininity or masculinity, will ring hollow (it may anyway, for readers with no experience of such change). This also means putting yourself on the line, exposing yourself—your experiential grounds for a reading or a belief, your deep-seated need to set an argument up in a certain way, your angers and fears, all the underlying emotional motivations that are traditionally supposed to undermine a critic's credibility—to readers who are likely to dismiss or ridicule you for such exposure. Self-exposure, the grounding of emancipatory claims in personal experience, is not merely some "trendy" new parasite in the critical text, some fad that will soon blow over, as it is often characterized by readers whose repressions it ruffles; it is an integral part of the critic's groping toward the truth that will set us free.

5

Just as the women's movement has generated among academic women a new critical look at women's writing—rediscovering those works that have been critically neglected, lost, or that were never published, and rereading and reappraising from a feminist point of view those works that were popular or critically acclaimed—so too has the men's movement recently begun to generate among academic men a new revisionary interest in men's writing. Here again men are about 15 years behind women. The male supremacists responded to feminist critiques immediately, of course, most notoriously, perhaps, Norman Mailer (to Kate Millett's *Sexual Politics*) in *The Prisoner of Sex* (1971). It is a relatively easy response to make, requiring only a new consolidation of age-old patriarchal attitudes. The male feminists were next: I think of Peter Schwenger's *Phallic Critiques: Masculinity and Twentieth Century Literature* (1984—13 years after Mailer), which mainly details a feminist critique of phallic literature (Mishima, Hemingway, etc.) from a male point of view. Masculist readings of literature are just now beginning to appear: the articles by James D. Riemer, John W. Crowley, and Louis Crompton in Harry Brod's 1987 collection, *The Making of Masculinities*, Frank Lentricchia's section on Wallace Stevens in *Ariel and the Police* (1988), David Leverenz's *Manhood and the American Renaissance* (1989), and my own *Ring Lardner and the Other* (1992).[6]

With the qualified exception of my *Lardner*, however, which broaches the possibility of and need for emancipation in alternating chapters without exploring it in detail, these are all reappraisals of canonized men's literature—which, while it is occasionally sensitive to the self-defeating dilemmas traditional masculine programming places men in, is almost never overtly emancipatory. F. Scott Fitzgerald, for example, in *The Great Gatsby* and "The Rich Boy" and other works, is by no means blinded by his well-documented sexist attacks on women to the debilitating effect of programmed masculine ideals on men. He knows, deep down, how profoundly patriarchal society (which he doesn't identify as such, of course) has damaged his heroes; he just doesn't know what to do about it, or who (or what) to blame it on. When Nathaniel Hawthorne imagines an emancipatory project in *The Scarlet Letter*, not only can he not extend emancipation from thought to action, he can only imagine it for his heroine, not for his hero: Dimmesdale is only liberated from the guilt that is destroying him an instant before his death, and he is never liberated from the ideological inscriptions that generated the guilt (and caused his death) in the first place. Noting these masculine failures to break out of destructive social inscriptions is an

## Introduction  31

important first step, but it is only a first step. We need critical work on actual literary emancipations of men; we need, in Jameson's term, a utopian masculist criticism.

I believe, in fact, that the best place to look for artistic representations and enactments of masculist transformation is precisely in the popular men's art of the last two decades. In *Time Passages* George Lipsitz notes his discovery that "Popular music and films seemed to resonate with the tensions of the time in a way that more formal academic texts did not" (x), and certainly it seems clear to me that popular men's art has proved far more sensitive than "serious" or "great" art to the social transformation melodramatized in the popular press as "men's crisis." Popular male artists have responded quickly and profoundly to the increasingly widespread feeling men have had in a feminist age of being cut off from the security and social approval of their fathers' gender programming, and also, partly as a result of that programming, from potential sources of help.

And it is popular male artists who have begun to articulate these repressed feelings, to dramatize them in their art. I have chosen three such artists; there are many others. A similar book to this one could be written on, say, the Travis McGee novels of John D. Macdonald, Stephen King's novel *The Dead Zone* and David Cronenberg's 1983 movie version, and the folk/rock music of Harry Chapin. A different sort of book, which I adumbrate at the end of chapter nine, could have been based around books, movies, and songs about the Vietnam experience: from the bitter ironies of Country Joe and the Fish playing "The Fixin' to Die Rag" at Woodstock, through the nightmares of John Prine's "Sam Stone" or Michael Cimino's *The Deer Hunter* (the Vietnam movie that hit me hardest), to potentially or problematically therapeutic tales of "coming home" like *First Blood*, *Born on the Fourth of July* in Ron Kovic's 1976 book and Oliver Stone's 1989 movie version, Jeremy Paul Kagan's 1977 movie *Heroes*, or Stephen Snow's play *Strange Snow* and David Jones's 1989 movie adaptation *Jacknife*. My explorations of the impact of Vietnam on American men (and ideologically "normal" masculinity) in part two are a beginning, but no more than a beginning.

A book could be focused around a single sport, like baseball: from the failed transformations of Bernard Malamud's *The Natural* (and the "normal" trivialization of that failure as heroic success in Barry Levinson's 1984 movie version, with Robert Redford as Roy Hobbs), through the nightmarish going-under of Frederick Exley's *A Fan's Notes*, to Donald Hays' *The Dixie Association* and W.P. Kinsella's breathtakingly therapeutic *Shoeless Joe* and Phil Allen Robinson's 1989 movie adaptation, *Field of Dreams*.[7] The mythic role baseball has played in American society suggests that much more is at stake in these works, and in the sport they depict, than the theme of games and play some critics have focused on. I study some of this in chapter four of my *Lardner*; it would be interesting also to look at baseball memoirs like Jim Bouton's *Ball Four* (1970), with its stories of Seattle Pilots kissing on the team bus and popping bennies to be "up" for games.

A book could be written on a single album, like Folkways' 1988 tribute to Woody Guthrie and Leadbelly, *A Vision Shared*, exploring the ways in which socially conscious singers and groups in the eighties musically recover and propagate an ongoing sense of oppositional history in a conformist conservative era. Bob Dylan sings Guthrie's "Pretty Boy Floyd" about how "You'll never see an outlaw drive a family from their home," and Bruce Springsteen, Arlo Guthrie, John Mellencamp, Emmy Lou Harris, and Willie Nelson sing Guthrie songs about people cut loose from conformist society. Emmy Lou Harris's contribution in particular makes me want to study what happens to the male listener when a woman with a hauntingly beautiful voice sings "Hobo's Lullaby"—it brings tears to my eyes, but why? It seems to me to combine the infantile power of maternal memory (the mother's lullaby) with a mournful sense of loss, absence, disintegration of "normal" ideological constructs, and to point through that combination to a transformation in and through sleep (the hobo sleeping to the sound of the train underneath him) and dream (the reconstruction of ideology). On other cuts Taj Mahal dismisses the governmental center of white conformist American society through Leadbelly's "Bourgeois Blues," and Sweet Honey in the Rock, Pete Seeger, and other assorted voices construct and confirm an oppositional community through Leadbelly's "Sylvie" and Guthrie's "This Land is Your Land."[8]

And, to suggest only one other fascinating possibility, a masculist study could be done of a single movie, such as Sam Peckinpah's *Pat Garrett and Billy the Kid*, paying particular attention to the Bob Dylan character, the somewhat effeminate "survivor" sidekick who survives precisely because he incorporates into a transformed masculinity some features traditionally associated with women, like the willingness to duck under the table when the bullets start flying. (This might send the writer and reader on a tangential exploration of the original sidekick, Sancho Panza, the cowardly, "effeminate," lower-class servant to Don Quixote who, from a masculist standpoint, reveals the destructive insanity of his master's [and his culture's] "chivalric" masculine ideal.)

Bob Dylan not only triangulates James Coburn as the steely paternal lawman and Kris Kristofferson as the boyishly irrepressible and irresponsible Billy, offering a dramatic third choice to the father-son dualism posited by those two; he also writes the wonderful score, including the haunting "Knocking on Heaven's Door," and that book would have a long section on Dylan's emancipatory music.[9]

These are the places, it seems to me, where men's growing anguish in patriarchal society is most powerfully and poignantly expressed. Think, for example, of the abyss that gapes in Kris Kristofferson as Billy the Kid in Peckinpah's movie, and of the overwhelming sense of loss, and of being lost, that paralyzes James Coburn as Pat Garrett after he has gunned Billy down. (This latter is an emotional state I associate with my father's generation, born in the late 1920s and early 1930s, but I still find it prevalent—though stoutly denied—in my 20-year-old male students.) Think of the confusion of Harry Chapin's male figures, the appalling sense so many of them have that the world is changing out from under them ("Halfway to Heaven," "On the Road to Kingdom Come"), and that no one ever loved them ("The Sniper"), and that "normal" parenting and pedagogical practices have destroyed them inwardly ("Flowers Are Red," "The Cat's in the Cradle"). Think of what happens to seemingly well-adjusted successful men in Stephen King's *Firestarter* when Andy McGee "pushes" them mentally, sets their "normal" masculine defenses or egos slightly off-kilter (the novel's objective correlative of the "push" feminist critiques of patriarchy have given men): the experimental psychologist Herman Pynchot becomes obsessed with the garbage disposal as a terrifyingly attractive symbol of his mother's vagina, and finally commits suicide by jamming his arm down it; Cap Hollister, director of the CIA-like "Shop," becomes so obsessed with snakes, reliving an incident when he was three and his brother was bitten by one, that he self-destructively instigates the final holocaust.

6

Feminists are often blamed for men's social disorientation, especially by male supremacists; but the feminist critique is in fact only the most articulate of the recent assaults on American (and other Western) masculinity. Specifically, in the context of the three figures I will be looking at here, men's current crisis seems to me to hinge upon three perceived demises or declines—three areas in which some social order that seemed solid and stable and secure in our childhood now seems to be disintegrating.

## 34 No Less a Man

Spenser: *the decline of the middle class*. In some ways, of course, the middle class is stronger than ever—taking over not just America, but the entire world. Consumer society, advertising, the commodification of the individual and his or her lifestyles and values, all the component elements of late-twentieth-century mass-production/consumption capitalism, are middle-class achievements. But in other ways the middle class is disintegrating. Hard middle-class work (in the form of technological advances and advertising) has made work increasingly obsolete. In the twentieth century (especially in the 1920s and the post-World War II period) leisure, not work, and consumption, not production, have been the keys to happiness—but the middle-class has never had an ideological rationale for enjoying the traditionally aristocratic ideals of leisure and consumption. The shameless plutocracy of the Reagan/Bush eighties eroded even this middle-class impulse toward leisure by undermining job security and purchasing power and allowing health care costs to skyrocket. Over the last century and a half middle-class (liberal) principles of individual autonomy have trickled down to women and children, with the result that the seen-but-not-heard service personnel of the family increasingly want their own piece of the middle-class cake too, and the hierarchical structure of the middle-class family is collapsing. The bourgeoisie, which has been the West's primary force of social stability over the past 300 years, is on the wane. What do we do now? What lies ahead? How do we go on day to day?

Rambo: *the decline of the United States as a world power*. As Morrell writes *First Blood* at Penn State in the late 1960s, his generation is in the process of placing the moral and political superiority of the United States under question. The demonic duo of Calvinism and capitalism are increasingly seen as the source of all evil. Vietnam helps the radical left cast America's historical sense of messianic mission—America as God's last great hope on earth, America as the world's policeman, appointed by God to usher in the capitalist millennium—in a horrific light. By the time the movie version of the novel gets made in the early 1980s, Americans have been through Watergate, the ignominious loss of the Vietnam war, and the Iranian hostage crisis; our two old enemies from World War II (now our close allies), Japan and Germany, have pulled ahead of us economically and technologically (and Germany is a socialist economy!). America is being beaten, hated, and humiliated all over the globe. This is especially disturbing for men, trained to identify with our country and to take collective slights personally (and to deny that we do this). Will no one stand up for America? And, secretly: will no one stand up for *me*?

Springsteen: *the decline of the sixties*. By the "sixties," of course, I mean a whole (partly mythologized) clutch of cultural events and values that seemed to offer a true and attainable alternative to the world we inherited from our parents. Flee the dying, polluted, overcrowded cities back to the land. Slough off the defensive, territorial mentality of the medieval warrior, stop fighting wars all around the world, and live in peace and harmony and brotherhood (sisterhood was still around the corner). Dump the arrogant and repressive absolutism of Christianity and merge with the universe, through Eastern religions and mind-expanding drugs. And, most important for Springsteen: save your own life through rock and roll; work selflessly through rock and roll to save others too, to overcome your programmed capitalist "enlightened" self-interest and *care* for others. As Springsteen himself told Kurt Loder of *Rolling Stone* in late 1984, after Reagan had tried to appropriate him in his presidential campaign: "I guess my view of America is of a real big-hearted country, real compassionate. But the difficult thing out here right now is that the social consciousness that was a part of the Sixties has become, like, old-fashioned or something. You go out, you get your job, and you try to make as much money as you can and have a good time on the weekend. And that's considered okay" (qtd. by Dave Marsh in *Glory Days*, 286).

It is significant, in fact, that the works of art I identify here as symptomatic of a new transformative approach to men in popular culture all span the two-decade period from the early 1970s to the early 1990s: David Morrell published *First Blood* in 1972; Robert Parker published his first Spenser novel, *The Godwulf Manuscript*, in 1973; and Bruce Springsteen released his first two albums, *Greetings from Asbury Park, N.J.* and *The Wild, the Innocent, & the E Street Shuffle*, likewise in 1973. It is precisely the period during which feminism begins to establish itself as a social movement to be taken seriously on a large scale (at least by women, who then promptly try their new ideas out in practice on their baffled husbands and male friends and colleagues); it is the period during which Americans' confidence in their country begins to crumble under the massive onslaught of the Watergate scandal, the loss of the Vietnam War, the Iranian hostage crisis, and Japanese economic superiority; and it is the period during which the utopianism of the sixties begins to be experienced as socially bankrupt, or perhaps just passé, and is gradually superseded (at least mythically, in the popular press) by the preppie/yuppie careerism of the 1970s.

My own feeling is that it is, and has been, an exciting time to be alive: that it is about time flag-waving Americans and the middle class and patriarchally programmed men began to take a long hard look at themselves, and that (as should be obvious from my tone by now) in many of us the spirit of the 1960s never really died. My general sense of what feminists have done for men is that they have opened all the doors wide, let the light into our terrified nightmarish darkness, and said "Come on, get going, we need your help." The nightmares have been theirs too—I have no illusions about the ease of women's liberation—but they took the lead, preceded us into the darkness and out the other side, and had initiated a social transformation before we had time to get our bearings and join them. This helped precipitate our "crisis"—but we were so ensconced in the seat of power that it took a crisis before we could begin to recognize the extent to which our power and privilege were destroying us from the inside. The dark path through the uneasy liberal guilt and self-denigration of male feminism to masculist liberation is not an easy one either; but we really have no alternative.

# Part One
# *Spenser*

# Living in Paradise

2. I speak the word
   The primeval word
   I give the sign
   Of democracy
   And the past and present
   Wilt into my hands
   I fill the future
   With blowing sands

   CHORUS

3. So we beat on
   So we beat on
   Boats against the current
   Back into the past
   How cold the world is
   Dreams burnt into ash
   How raw the sunlight
   On the unmade grass

   CHORUS

4. I've been a man
   I've been a son
   To be a god
   I made this song
   Do you think the world will hail me?
   A star that shines so bright
   Do you think my dad will love me?
   Say that I'm all right

   CHORUS twice

**Copyright 1993 Doug Robinson.**

# Chapter One

# The Hardboiled Hero

"What is it you want to know?"

"Why you engage in things that are violent and dangerous."

I sipped half a glass of beer. I took another bite of veal.

"Well," I said, "the violence is a kind of side-effect, I think. I have always wanted to live life on my own terms. And I have always tried to do what I can do. I am good at certain kinds of things; I have tried to go in that direction."

"The answer doesn't satisfy me," Rachel said.

"It doesn't have to. It satisfies me."

"What he won't say," Susan said, "and what he may not even admit to himself is that he'd like to be Sir Gawain. He was born five hundred years too late. If you understand that, you understand most of what you are asking."

"Six hundred years," I said. (*Looking for Rachel Wallace* 25)

I am not sure why, but the mystery or crime or detective novel has been the formula genre most sensitive to the new winds blowing in the most recent feminist era. The classic or "ratiocinative" or "parlor" detective novel has been wonderfully transformed over the last 15 or 20 years by writers like Amanda Cross (Carolyn Heilbrun, professor of English at Columbia), who throws a little Henry James and Edith Wharton into a pot with Agatha Christie and the campus novel and produces profound, and profoundly moving, feminist novels. In the hardboiled genre, long considered the exclusive domain of misogynistic macho men, Marcia Muller, Sara Paretsky, Sue Grafton, Lia Matera, Susan Dunlap, and others have carved out a brilliant new niche for tough, competent women who are vitally involved in a feminist community and have all the despair and courage and fear and intelligence of real women.[1] Joseph Hansen's detective Dave Brandstetter is tough and gay, and explores the politics of toughness along the interfaces between the straight and the gay communities of Los Angeles. Tony Hillerman uses the hardboiled detective genre to explore the marginality and the mysticism of the Navajo people in Arizona and New Mexico.

And then, of course, there is Robert B. Parker's Spenser. Of the new detectives just mentioned—Kate Fansler, Sharon McCone,

## 40  No Less a Man

V.I. Warshawski, Kinsey Millhone, Laura Di Palma, Kiernan O'Shaughnessy, Dave Brandstetter, Joe Leaphorn, and Jim Chee—Spenser stands the closest to the classic hardboiled heroes of Hammett's, Chandler's, and John D. Macdonald's novels. The Spenser novels are, as a *New York Times* reviewer wrote, "tough, wisecracking, unafraid, lonely, unexpectedly literate"; also politically liberal, deeply moral, ethically finicky. But, like Macdonald's Travis McGee novels beginning around the time Parker starts writing—the early 1970s—they also transcend that tradition in exemplary ways; complicate it, render it self-conscious.[2] Whether in response to the women's movement and the pressure it has brought to bear on traditional sex roles, or out of personal role-trauma and growth, or out of some combination of the two, Parker has created a hero who is not content to *be* tough, but must know why he is that way and what he can do about it. Parker's signal contribution to the hardboiled detective tradition, and more importantly to the profeminist men's movement (which has been historically concurrent and ideologically congruent with his own work as a writer), lies in his exploration of masculinity: his insistence on asking in the books, through articulate feminist characters like Susan Silverman and Rachel Wallace, "What is a man?" and "Why do men have to be so hardboiled?" and "What is this masculine obsession with violence?" and "Why is the macho man so obsessed with protecting others, being the knight in shining armor?"

Not surprisingly—whatever else they are, they are first of all formula detective novels—each of the Spenser novels is a quest for truth (what's happening) and justice (how can wrongs be righted and the good guys differentiated and rescued from the bad guys). But the series as a whole itself constitutes another and deeper kind of quest: a quest for self-knowledge and self-transformation, for who we are and why we do what we do and how we can move beyond our more self-destructive fixations.

I say a quest for who "we" are, though it is obviously first of all Parker's quest. Spenser is Parker's self-therapeutic tool. Parker is intensely concerned with men and masculinity—specifically with understanding the unseen substrata of men and masculinity, the emotional undergirding that supports and drives the hardboiled fronts traditional male heroes (in life and fiction) so insistently present to the outside world—and Spenser is his testing ground. His testing ground for understanding himself first, I suppose I should say; given Spenser's constant complaints about generalizing, I am not sure Parker would feel comfortable with my depiction of him as being intensely concerned with something as general as "men and masculinity." But Spenser is not a real person. He is a marker; a rather complex and changing marker, but a marker nonetheless: a kind of macho everyman who "stands in" for machismo in all of its guises, whatever Parker projects onto him. A concern for what drives Spenser is, at least potentially, a concern for what drives men, what constitutes masculinity.

More, once Parker has done his work, "we" are also Parker's readers, caught up in the lives of Spenser, his buddy Hawk, the love of his life Susan Silverman, his surrogate son Paul Giacomin. We too (not just Parker) project ourselves onto Spenser and Friends, and as we do, we make their explorations of Spenser's masculinity our own. We don't so much generalize from Spenser to all men as *apply* Spenser to ourselves—ourselves as men, or ourselves as women who, like Rachel Wallace, share Spenser's defensive tendencies toward self-control and the suppression of feeling.

As Parker sets up his dialogue with his readers (or perhaps as I imagine him setting up a dialogue with me), this self-conscious exploration of men and masculinity is neither passive nor static—no "scientific," academic, objective representation. Parker is determined to understand Spenser, and through Spenser himself, and through his self-understanding is determined to help us too to understand ourselves, to learn the "truth" about ourselves. But the "truth" is valuable for Parker not in its own right, not for its own sake, as in academic discourse—but only if will set us free. Understanding, for Parker, must be a path to self-liberation.

Another way of saying this is that Parker brings pressure to bear on his readers to read *actively*. The active reading that he encourages resembles (and takes impetus from) the active reading traditionally encouraged by mystery writers—trying to figure out "who done it" and how, trying to figure things out before the detective does—but at a deeper level. In the quest constituted by the series as a whole, active reading is encouraged to find out not who the bad guys are and how to stop them, but what is wrong with Spenser, and how he might learn to grow toward greater emotional health. "What is wrong with Spenser" is too strong a formulation, perhaps: the surface question is, what makes Spenser tick, why does he do the things he does. But the question is invariably motivated in the novels by failures or misfires in what he does. He does what he has taught himself (what the whole culture has taught him to teach himself) is the "right thing"; but he does it to people even when they don't want him to, when his interference is positively harmful; and he knows that he would do it again no matter what people say, knows that he would feel compelled to do it again—all of which suggests that somewhere his motives are twisted, that he has a compulsion to act as he does, that he is driven by an emotional need.

What need? What drives Spenser? What drives Parker? If we feel moved to identify with Spenser, what drives us?

My plan for this first section of the book is in fact to keep asking these questions that Parker insists we ask, keep tracing Parker's asking of the questions, and keep trying to answer them. Keep trying, perhaps, to do something with the materials Parker gives us. If nothing else, after 19 Spenser novels Parker himself still has mainly questions. He has hardly any answers yet. And, to the extent that we (Parker and you and I) begin to uncover some answers, they will probably only generate new questions. Parker will, in any case, take us only part-way into the argument of this book: one-third of the way, up to (not beyond) an increasingly lucid perception of the problems facing contemporary men. My sense of the importance of Parker's writing is that it charts the need for a transformation, even if he still has very little sense of how he might go about engineering one; even if he is not really sure he wants to engineer one.

This means that in order to take Parker's project seriously, we (you this book's reader, I its writer) must go beyond it—take what Parker gives us, his attempts to transform masculinity, for instance, but not be satisfied with what *he* gives us. Rather, we must try it on, test it against our own experience, feel where Parker goes wrong in terms of that experience, feel where he is still groping, and grope further in that same direction, or in whatever direction feels better, more valid for our own lives.

This suggestion flies in the face of much contemporary critical practice. One of the critical principles we have inherited from the New Critics is that the narrator is not the author and should not be equated with him; another is that fictional characters are not real people and should not be treated as such. The effect of both principles is, of course, as reader-response theorists like David Bleich and Norman Holland have made clear, to put distance between the "text" as an autonomous fictive creation and the reader's affective response to it—that critical bugbear declared "fallacious" and therefore off-limits by Wimsatt and Beardsley in 1954. This has the effect of rendering the "text" stable and safe; it can neither be transformed *by* readers nor wield any transformative power *over* readers.[3]

I would argue, in fact, that the New Critical reification of intention and response as text is finally a masculine defense against emotion and its power to bring about change—a defense that is very similar to, and indeed ideologically and emotionally related to, Spenser's own defensive insistence on rugged masculine autonomy. The interpretive porosity I am calling for, in which characters flow into authors and readers into characters (and authors), is profoundly threatening to the self-protective enclosures of traditional masculinity. This porosity is most familiar from emancipatory feminist criticism, in the determined resistance to authorial and societal intentions of Judith Fetterley, say; or, most powerfully for me, in the experimental work of Rachel Blau DuPlessis and the feminist reader-response work of Patrocinio P. Schweickart:

"addressing the reader, making herself and her reader part of the narrative...an offhand, conversational manner." [Julia Penelope Stanley and Susan J. Wolfe (Robbins)]

*I find myself more and more attracted to the porous, the statement that permits interpretation (penetration?) rather than positing an absolute. Not vagueness—I want each component to be clear—but a whole that doesn't pretend to be ultimate, academic.* [Anita Barrows]

Not positing oneself as the only, sol(e) authority. Sheep of the sun. Meaning, a statement that is open to the reader, not better than the reader, not set apart from; not seeking the authority of the writer. Not even seeking the authority of the writing. (Reader could be writer, writer reader. Listener could be teacher.) (DuPlessis 275)

Consider Lawrence's *Women in Love*, and for the sake of simplicity, concentrate on Birkin and Ursula. Simone de Beauvoir and Kate Millett have convinced me that this novel is sexist. Why does it remain appealing to me? Jameson's thesis [that we need a dialectic between negative and positive hermeneutics] prompts me to answer this question by examining how the text plays not only on my false consciousness but also on my authentic liberatory aspirations—that is to say, on the very impulses that drew me to the feminist movement.

    The trick of role reversal comes in handy here. If we reverse the roles of Birkin and Ursula, the ideological components (or at least the most egregious of these, e.g., the analogy between women and horses) stand out as absurdities. Now, if we delete these absurd components while keeping the roles reversed, we have left the story of a woman struggling to combine her passionate desire for love and for other human bonds. This residual story is not far from one we would welcome as expressive of a feminist sensibility. Interestingly enough, it also intimates a novel Lawrence might have written, namely, the proper sequel to *The Rainbow*. (Schweickart 43)

## 44  No Less a Man

There have been a few maverick attempts to open a porous critical interchange in masculist writing as well; David Leverenz's *Manhood and the American Renaissance* comes immediately to mind, and Frank Lentricchia's exchange with Sandra Gilbert and Susan Gubar in the pages of *Critical Inquiry* is not far behind. My dialogue with Ellen Gardiner in and behind the pages of *Ring Lardner and the Other* is another example. What I am hoping to do in this book is to enact in my interpretive practices the emancipatory surrender of control, the breakdown of barriers, which those practices uncover in recent men's art.

In pursuit of that project, throughout this first section of the book I am going to be equating Spenser with Parker, and treating Spenser as a real person. Not simplistically: my Spenser-Parker equation, for example, will not be statically one-to-one. Parker is also more than Spenser, understands more; Parker is also Susan Silverman and Rachel Wallace and Hawk and Paul Giacomin and the other people who force Spenser to look at himself from the outside. Nor should the equation be taken as representing an ontological truth claim (such as "Spenser is the 'true form' of Parker"). The equation is pragmatic, heuristic. Spenser serves important self-therapeutic functions for Parker. Parker creates his fictive images of Spenser as he would a character or role in drama therapy, a surrogate self or alter ego to use in the therapeutic process of dramatization. "Equating Spenser with Parker" is perhaps best understood as shorthand for saying that I imagine Spenser and Parker in a close dialectical relation, each generating the other as his other self or alter ego: Parker Spenser as the "man of his dreams" (in the full complex sense of "dreams"), Spenser Parker as the force (Freud would call it the unconscious) that shapes or directs his dreams. This dialectic will allow me to explore the ways Parker's masculine self-conception changes over the years of (and through) writing about and as Spenser, writing Spenser's first-person narratives—the ways in which Parker (conceived largely though not exclusively as the creator of Spenser, i.e. through the mediation of the novels) both puts into and takes out of Spenser insights into masculine transformation.

Treating Spenser as a real person, then, allows me to explore the ways in which we as Parker's readers use Spenser in the same kind of therapeutic process: by identifying with him we project ourselves, or certain parts of ourselves (our tough, would-be autonomous self-images), onto him and test the viability of those selves in imaginary action. Even when we distance ourselves from Spenser, when we pull away from the lure of identification and self-projection, Spenser takes on a kind of imaginary reality for us: he feels as real to us, while we're reading, as any friend. Perhaps even more real. The reality of other people *as* people, as thinking, feeling beings, is wrapped up in just this kind of image-creation: based on our observation of a friend's behavior and what he or she says, we generate an image of him or her as a person that is very like the image a writer generates of a character. The image is invariably simplified; even when we live with someone for years, our image of that person is less complex than the sum total of his or her "personality" (which is relational and faceted differently in relation to other people than ourselves). But by projecting ourselves empathetically into the behavior of a friend or a fictional character we can flesh out the "character" of that person in therapeutic ways.

The implication of all this is that, just as I assume Parker to be (at least partly) doing self-therapy by writing the Spenser novels, and encouraging his readers to participate in the same process, so too am I (at least partly) doing self-therapy by writing this book, and encouraging you to participate in the same process. My sense of what is "really going on" in Spenser is only partly based on my reading in the novels themselves, and in interviews with Parker; and, while the therapeutic process invariably involves some exposure to psychological thought, it is only partly based on my reading in the works of writers like Freud and Karen Horney and Alice Miller and Herb Goldberg.[4] It mainly comes from self-analysis, self-discovery, insights arising out of my own ongoing process of masculist transformation. This, it seems to me, is to respond in the spirit of Parker's own approach to Spenser. It is to leave behind traditional academic criticism—Old, New, and New-New (postmodern, deconstructive, etc.)—as Parker himself did in his move from a Boston University dissertation on Hammett, Chandler, and Macdonald to his first Spenser novel.[5] It is to move from "objective" accounts or factual descriptions of what someone else is doing—which tends to leave you, the describer, untouched, which in turn is probably your subconscious intention in the first place—to active self-liberation.

I want to begin my reading of the Spenser series by taking a fairly close look at Parker's first novel, *The Godwulf Manuscript*, in order to establish the foundation on which Parker constructs (and, increasingly, deconstructs) his increasingly self-conscious structure. There are signs in this novel of the innovations to come: an emergent self-consciousness; a strong, positive female character. But for the most part *The Godwulf Manuscript* could have been written by one of Parker's mentors, especially, perhaps, Raymond Chandler (whose Philip Marlowe series Parker has continued in some of his most recent work).[6]

The book's second chapter is a veritable treasure trove of these conventional elements. Spenser gets together with two members of the revolutionary student organization that the head of campus security Carl Tower suspects is behind the theft of the Godwulf manuscript, Terry Orchard and her boyfriend, Dennis Powell—a fairly contrived beginning, as it turns out, since Dennis is precisely the person he is looking for, the man who stole the manuscript, and his murder in the next chapter points him straight at the book's real villain, a medievalist in the English department named Lowell Hayden. Spenser goes to a pub with Terry, who at first remains uncooperative and defensive (Spenser represents the establishment, the older generation, etc.—we are, after all, in the early 1970s, which for all intents and purposes are the tail end of the 1960s). Her defense against him is mainly a revolutionary rhetoric pronounced in the tones, as Spenser says, of "the people who do telephone canvassing for dance studios" (19). Since Spenser has just been dealing out some tired private eye rhetoric about how "no one ever tells me everything he knows; it is the nature of the beast" (18), the horse he rides here seems a little high. (Terry sneers, "You must get a swell view of life looking at it through a keyhole half the time," and Spenser says archly, and rather unconvincingly, "I see what's there" [18]). Then Dennis shows up. When Dennis plops himself down at the table and drinks the rest of Terry's beer, Spenser becomes (only half-ironically) proprietary: "I bought her a beer and you drank it. On my block that entitles you to get your upper lip fattened" (20). Spenser has only just met Terry, and probably is not, in any sense of the word, trying to possess her. But when, two chapters later, Dennis has been shot and Terry framed for the murder, Sergeant Belson of Boston Homicide suggests that Spenser might have been hustling Dennis's girlfriend a little, and Dennis showed up and caught them at it, there is some deep emotional sense in which he seems to be on the right track. Spenser *is* an excessively proprietary man, a man overly given to protecting damsels in distress, from the mob, from the police, and even, as befits Sir Gawain, from their equally proprietary boyfriends ("Terry's my woman," Dennis says pugnaciously, to Spenser, and Terry replies, "I'm not anybody's woman, Dennis. That's a sexist statement. I'm not a possession" [21]). When Terry tells him that Spenser is a private eye, Dennis calls him a "freaking pig" and takes a swing at him. This seems to be just what Spenser has been waiting for: he dodges the fist, thinks "He was not planning to quit, so I figured it best end swiftly," and punches him out. Women he likes he likes to protect; men he doesn't like he likes to beat up. So far, we are strictly in the macho territory of the traditional hardboiled detective—and, more generally, in the macho territory of the traditional tough guy. Spenser leaves the pub and goes out to his car, which he has parked by a hydrant, throughout the series his favorite place to park. There is a ticket on his windshield, and he rips it up with a cynical thought about eternal vigilance being the price of liberty. Again, Spenser is more like these kids he is feeling superior to than he wants to believe: his rhetoric, like Terry's, is tired; his attitudes toward Terry are as paternalistic as Dennis's; and his individualistic rebelliousness, the petty gesture of parking in front of a hydrant and tearing up the ticket, is just as adolescent as Dennis's revolt against the system.

In good hardboiled detective novel tradition, Spenser walks away from the scene of another man's apparent possession of the damsel in distress (a man who is, of course, powerless to protect her), only to be called the next night to ride to her aid. Terry calls him in the middle of the night, and he drives over to find Dennis murdered (served him right, drinking Terry's beer like that!) in the apartment he and Terry shared, and a drugged Terry holding the smoking murder weapon. Two hitmen have just shot Dennis with her gun, which they brought with them, forced her to pull the trigger to put another bullet in him (and powder burns on her hand), and forcefed her an overdose of drugs. Spenser immediately starts doing what he does best, protecting the damsel in distress: puts her in the shower, pours coffee down her, walks her till she revives, gets her story, then calls the police.

Surprisingly—here is one fairly superficial divergence from the classic hardboiled detective novel—Spenser has a good deal of respect for the police. He used to be one himself; was dismissed for insubordination (which he likes to think of, he tells us in *God Save the Child*, as "inner-directed behavior" [43]). But while he feels the hierarchical structure of police forces to be limiting (he wanted to do what was right, not what someone told him to do), and feels also that he can bring criminals to justice much more effectively than the cops, he has no contempt for the police. Except at higher levels (Captain Yates here, who responds to political pressure) and in small towns (Chief Trask in *God Save the Child*, Chief Rogers in *Pale Kings and Princes*), Parker never portrays the police as either crooked or incompetent. Lieutenant Martin Quirk and Sergeant Frank Belson of Boston Homicide and Lieutenant Healy of the state police appear throughout the series, and are always treated with respect and admiration. All three do Spenser a good number of favors down the line, and Spenser returns the favors by catching the bad guys. Still, when he meets Quirk and Belson here in *Godwulf*, they indulge in a little conventional hardboiled cop-gumshoe repartee:

"If it seems pertinent, I'll tell you."
"If I want to know, you'll tell me." Quirk's voice squeezed out sharp and flat like sheet metal.

## 48  No Less a Man

"I'll tell you if you need to know it. I don't make a living telling cops everything they want to know about clients."

"I don't make a living taking crap from hole-in-the-wall shysters like you, Spenser."...

He turned to me. "You're not working for the D.A. now, boy, you're working my side of the street, and if you get in my way I'll kick your ass right into the gutter. Got that?"

"Can I feel your muscle?" I said. (33)

Terry is booked for the murder, and Spenser goes home to sleep. He is wakened by Terry's father Roland Orchard calling him to come up to the house and talk about being hired to clear Terry's name. The Orchards, it turns out, are Boston old rich; but Parker, at this early point in the series, is still so deep into the mythology of the hardboiled detective that he has Spenser portray them as new-rich insecure about their social status and power over underlings like himself—a portrait that seems to have more to do with class envy and hardboiled conventions than with reality. Roland tries ineffectually to impress Spenser with his senior partnership at Orchard, Bonner, and Blanch, and Marion Orchard tries to impress him with her body: "I felt as if I were walking into a window display" (50), Spenser says, and later, when she gives him an enticing side view, wonders whether he was "supposed to bark" (51).

This is all standard fare. "The real hostility of the hard-boiled story," as John Cawelti argues in *Adventure, Mystery and Romance*, "is directed toward women and the rich" (158). Invoking David Riesman's terms from the fifties, Cawelti persuasively identifies the aggressively "inner-directed" behavior of the hardboiled dick as a mask or fantasy cover for true other-directedness. His analysis is worth quoting at some length:

For the person who succeeds in responding to the cues and conforming to the demands of his various peer-groups the rewards are considerable: popularity and success, the sense of status and belonging. But anxiety still drives the other-directed character. He fears he will not continue to live up to the elusive demands of the group. This anxiety brings resentment that is intensified by the feeling of continual pressure to shift goals and values. Thus the other-directed person often feels that the pressures of conformity have somehow seduced or corrupted his inner integrity, that he has, as a favorite twentieth-century American phrase puts it, lost his identity. To compensate for this perpetual anxiety the other-directed person frequently develops a bitter cynicism and hostility toward the others whose expectations and judgments he fears. Since he feels that his own behavior and attitudes are forced upon him by social pressures to conform that he cannot escape, he is continually aware of a discrepancy between what he imagines as his true inner desires (to tell the boss to go to hell; to beat up his wife) and his actual behavior (deference to the boss and adjustment to his wife). This emotion is intensified when the other-directed individual believes that he is not gaining a full share of the rewards of the social system in terms of popularity, esteem, and consumption. To escape from this inner tension, the other-directed person projects his own sense of corruption and phoniness onto others, particularly onto those who control the central symbols of esteem and status in his world: the rich and successful who possess the power to consume with impunity; and women, whose sexual and emotional deference symbolize popularity and esteem....

This tension is further complicated by the new status of women as economic and social competitor as well as object of sexual desire and symbol of popularity. For the other-directed personality, success with women is a crucial index of status, and "making-out" one of the few tangible measures of the elusive goal of group esteem and popularity. The more economically and socially independent of masculine domination women become, the more male esteem and status are threatened. The only possible resolution to the insecurity caused by the conflict between the need for women as sexual and social fulfillment and the threat of feminine independence and domination is the simultaneous possession and destruction of the female, a goal that can hardly be achieved except in fantasy. (158-59)

Cawelti goes on to illustrate his analysis of the hardboiled detective's insecurities from Mickey Spillane, who is of course the most obvious example of hardboiled misogyny. But his analysis raises more questions than it answers. Even assuming, by way of getting started, that Parker too is other-directed and resolves his terrible personal tensions by making Spenser aggressively inner-directed (and hostile toward the rich and women), why should this be so? What is the social programming that makes "other-directedness" an anxiety- and tension-ridden state of being? Parker does seem to share with Cawelti and Riesman the liberal ideology of self-reliance that idealizes inner-directedness as the true nature of man (not woman), and renders "other-directedness" the simple monolithic opposite and diseased version of that nature; but what drives this ideology? What alternatives to it do we already have? What alternatives can we imagine, and perhaps bring into being in our own lives? (I will be returning to this question next chapter.)

Beyond that, Parker's portrait of Spenser doesn't really conform very well to Cawelti's pattern. In this same scene with the Orchards, for example, Marion asks Spenser, graciously but rather imperiously, to put another log on the fire, and he muses: "It was a way of establishing relationships, I thought, as I got a log from the basket and set it on top of the fire—get me to do her bidding. I'd known other women like that. If they couldn't get you to do them little services, they felt insecure. Or maybe she just wanted another log in the fireplace. Sometimes I'm deep as hell" (51-52). Not only does Parker give us Spenser's self-ironic realization that he might be reading too much into Marion's request; he specifically says that Spenser had known *other* women like that—not, in other words, that Marion's request was typical of women. Only of some women. It is only a short step from there, in fact, to saying that Spenser's "hostility," such as it is, is really directed not at women, but at traditional feminine programming, the early childhood coaching in indirection and manipulativeness that feminists have been fighting as much as (and more successfully than) men.

What's more, Marion Orchard appears only once more in the novel (Roland not at all), and then in a considerably more sympathetic role, one that clearly points ahead to the introduction of Susan Silverman in the next novel. True, Marion seduces the big strong handsome Spenser by way of satisfying her lust and getting back at her insecure husband—conventional hardboiled elements remain—but before that happens we find out more about Marion, some of her own anxieties and needs, her feeling of loss at having submerged herself in a successful man, for instance. She shifts slightly out of her earlier role as manipulative window dressing and into a tentative, burgeoning humanity. Parker also gives her some revealing insight into Spenser:

"Where's Mr. Orchard?" I asked

"At the office. Sitting behind his big masculine desk, trying to feel like a man."

"Does he know Terry's gone?"

"Yes. That's why he went to the office. It makes him feel better about himself. All he can cope with is stocks and bonds. People, and daughters and wives, scare hell out of him." She finished the drink, took mine, which was still half-full, and made two fresh ones.

"Something scares hell out of everybody," I said. "Have you any thoughts on where I should look for Terry?"

"What scares hell out of you?" she asked.

The bourbon was making a lot of headway against the coffee. I felt a lot better than I had when I came in. The line of Marion Orchard's thigh was right against the blue robe as she sat with her legs tucked up under her on the couch.

"The things people do to one another," I answered. "That scares hell out of me."

She drank some more. "Wrong," she said. "That engages your sympathy.

It doesn't scare you. I'm an expert on what scares men. I've lived with a scared man for twenty-two years." (103-04)

Actually, here, they're both wrong. The things people do to one another do engage his sympathy, Marion is superficially right about that; but it is a controlled form of sympathy, a sympathy that leads uneasily past frightening feelings of vulnerability and need into protective action (protective at once of himself and others). His is a traditional chivalric sympathy, a desire to protect others that comes, as Parker begins to realize about ten years down the line, more from Spenser's own defensive needs than from a godlike self-possessed altruism.

And the things people do to one another do scare Spenser, he too is superficially right about that; but it is a deeper and more specific fear than he will lay claim to, as we find out later in the series, when Susan leaves him. Spenser is afraid of the emotional neediness that would result from falling in love and being hurt—afraid of incompleteness. In fact, when Spenser says that the things people do to one another scare him, I don't believe he really even knows what he's saying. It *feels* wrong, empty, hollow; and certainly there is no evidence in this novel or any other that his reaction to what people do to one another is typically one of fear. It sounds suspiciously like a hardboiled detective cliche, and it functions here as what Rupert Wilkinson calls a "belying device":

> A belying device is a feature of the hero that superficially contradicts his admired qualities: in this case, his toughness and mastery. It underlines by contrast his possession of those qualities, and it humanizes them.... For individuals pressed into especially demanding roles, a staple belying device is the playful, unheroic posture: it accentuates the protagonist's real toughness in the eyes of others while providing a sense of escape and a release of tension for the protagonist himself. Most belying devices, however, are confined to fiction and myth. American popular novelists rely on them heavily to offset their heroes' tediously extensive competence. (22)

At the level Parker seems (here, in this first novel) to want us to understand Spenser's claim to fear, the idea would be that he is afraid of the emotional complexities of interpersonal relations—and maybe, more specifically, that he is afraid of what women like Marion do to him, their emotional manipulativeness. This is humanizing, in one sense: the fearless hardboiled hero is afraid of something after all. In another sense, of course, it is not humanizing at all; it just reduces Spenser to the controlled image of the tough guy, who as a man isn't *supposed* to be good at emotional complexities. As it turns out, however, Spenser is far better than your average macho man at emotional complexities—better for example at recognizing the origins of his own machismo in fear and need—and as the series progresses this belying device increasingly expands and displaces the conventions of the genre Parker's working in. The more Parker learns about Spenser, the more aware we all become (Spenser, Parker, and Parker's readers) that Spenser's sympathy is at least in part a defense against fear, and specifically against what people might do to him. This, in my view, humanizes him considerably more than his carefully controlled front of altruistic sympathy.

Parker takes another step away from the conventional hardboiled hostility toward women when he introduces Iris Milford into the novel, an overweight widowed black woman with four kids—precisely the kind of woman Spillane's Mike Hammer would love to despise. Spenser, however, takes an immediate liking to her. "She'd been there and seen it done," he says. "A tough, wised-up, honest broad" (123).[7] By "tough" and "wised-up" he seems to mean that Iris is like him, macha to his macho, and practical, hard-headed, realistic, unfooled by hype, impatient with hypocrisy. "Honest," in the context of Spenser's praise, is more complicated. Many people in Spenser novels are honest because they lack opportunities for dishonesty. Iris, again like Spenser himself, is honest in a stronger sense: responsible, ethical, dedicated to doing the right thing, which is, by and large, helping people, caring for and about them, protecting the defenseless. A macha black woman, Iris is in some ways a precursor of Hawk, Spenser's "tough, wised-up, honest" friend and macho mirror, who will not enter the series for two more novels.

This could, of course, be a calculated move on Parker's part: Spenser as liberal hero of the 1970s. We could imagine Parker saying, "Let's see, I don't want Spenser to be seen as a sexist or racist, gotta be sure and distinguish him from Mike Hammer, so hm, maybe I'd better introduce a positive black woman into the novel, that ought to cover my rear end." But the book doesn't read that way to me. Parker's introduction of Iris Milford doesn't feel opportunistic or calculating or self-protectively liberal. As I read the book, anyway, Iris is quite simply the strongest, most positive, most obviously sympathetic secondary character in the novel—Spenser's peer and unofficial associate in virtually every sense. Here, I think, Parker is beginning to find his own vision, beginning to feel his way to an articulation of his world. Like his creator, Spenser *is* a liberal, certainly, and therefore ideologically predisposed to be sympathetic to the victims of social oppression, like blacks and women. But his gut reaction to Iris Milford (or rather my gut reaction to his) is more than an ideological predisposition. He finds in her someone like himself; she him likewise. They hit it off.

These swerves from the classic hardboiled detective novel are really only adumbrations, however, foreshadowings of things to come, in this first Spenser novel. The biggest shift—the difference that is clearest without recourse to retrospect, based on the later novels—is Parker's redirection of the conventional detective's hatred of the rich to academia, where Parker was himself employed while he was writing *Godwulf*. I said earlier that Roland Orchard, who might well have been the bad guy in Hammett or Chandler, never reappears in the novel—not even in the end, when Terry is cleared of all charges and needs Spenser to pick her up at the police station. By having Spenser pick her up and drop her off outside her parents' house Parker misses an ideal opportunity to rub Roland's nose in his selfish attitude toward his daughter—his desire to have Spenser clear the *family* name of the murder charge of murder, *his* name, Orchard, of which Terry is only the marked extension (Orchard Female Child).

But Parker has other fish to fry: he shifts his attack from the Orchards and the world they represent to the university, a world of willful flight into abstraction and knowledge for knowledge's sake. Spenser goes to talk to the chair of the English department at Terry's university, the university whose fourteenth-century manuscript has been stolen (and, presumably, in Parker's imagination the university and department he was teaching in at the time, the Northeastern English department); while he talks about Terry, the chair talks about academic freedom, which he seems to interpret to mean freedom from accountability to the outside world. In a 1981 *Boston Globe* interview with Maria Karagianis, Parker says he was "always sort of a square peg in the round academic hole," and characterizes academics as "the worst people I know. They know more and more about less and less, and they come to think it really matters" (43). In Parker's vision academics flee real people, real issues, real responsibility to the real world:

"Listen [Spenser says to the English department chair], there's a twenty-year-old girl who is a student in your university, has taken a course from your faculty, under the auspices no doubt of your department, who is now out on bail, charged with the murder of her boyfriend. I think she did not kill him. If I am right, it is quite important that we find out who did. Now, that may not rate in importance up as high as, say, the implications of homosexuality in Shakespeare's sonnets, or whether he said *solid* or *sullied*, but it is important. I'm not going to shoot up the place. No rubber hose, no iron maiden. I won't even curse loudly. If the student newspaper breaks the news that a private eye is ravaging the English department, the hell with it. You can argue that it's an open campus and sit tight." (80)

## 54  No Less a Man

"The freedom I'm worried about is not academic," Spenser says, "it's twenty and female" (80). But this formulation is uncomfortably reminiscent of Terry's father; "twenty and female" suggests that Spenser might not be quite as focused on Terry the real person as he claims. It suggests, in fact, that Spenser, like Roland Orchard, is mainly interested in his own freedom—or rather, that his concern for Terry's freedom is a mask for a concern about his own integrity and autonomy as a man. By defending and protecting Terry, he satisfies his own need to protect and defend people; and by satisfying that need he convinces himself that he is autonomous, that he controls his own fate, that he is in fact free. The need is deep inside him; it is a compulsion, one that he is powerless against, even when he knows intellectually that he should suppress it, as in *Looking for Rachel Wallace*. He must protect and defend. If someone or something in the outside world prevents him from acting on that need, he feels unfree. But whence stems the need? Why does he feel compelled to act as he does? Parker doesn't even think to ask, here in *Godwulf*, and while he asks the question more and more insistently in the novels that follow, he still hasn't found a satisfactory answer.

Even if both Spenser and Roland Orchard treat Terry as a projection of their own needs, however, in the emotional hierarchy underlying this novel Spenser is better than Roland, because Roland doesn't act on his need (he retreats to his office to try and feel masculine) and Spenser does (he saves Terry from the mob who is trying to frame her for murder). Acting on a need is better than running from it. Roland Orchard, in turn, is better than the English chair, because while both retreat to their work and the abstractions that work revolves around (stocks and bonds for Roland, philological problems like *solid* and *sullied* for the chair), Roland still retains a passion, a strong feeling for or about or regarding his daughter (even if it is only an embarrassment about her divergence from his ideal image of her), while for the English chair Terry is just a name, a pure abstraction very much like *solid* and *sullied*, except less interesting. In Parker's attack on academia, this protective disinterest among the faculty is uppermost: an academic is someone who cannot deal with the real world, real people, and especially real feelings about people and the world, and so withdraws into the safe intellectual world of abstractions.

But even the English chair is better, in that emotional hierarchy, than the novel's real villain, Lowell Hayden. He is behind the theft of the manuscript; he is also connected to Joe Broz, a local and highly successful mobster who appears in several of the Spenser novels, and for ideological, Timothy Leary-type reasons ("I don't use drugs, but many people need them...to elevate their perceptions and free them from the bondage of American hypocrisy" [189]) has recruited Dennis Powell to deal heroin for Broz on campus. Dennis has been demanding better-quality heroin, which annoys Joe Broz; when Broz's threats have no effect, Hayden helps Broz's men hit Dennis and frame Terry. Hayden gets his girlfriend Cathy, Terry's ex-roommate, to give him Terry's gun, and passes it on to Broz to use in the hit; when he then realizes that Cathy can tie him to the murder, he and his wife kill Cathy.

But this is only a bare plot summary. The real emotional impact of the novel, especially as Spenser begins to discover the extent of Hayden's perfidy, lies in Parker's merciless vilification of his chosen bad guy, the English professor. First Hayden calls down a hit on Spenser, but instead Broz tries to hit him: Hayden stands in the same relation to Broz as Cathy did to Hayden, the person who can connect him to the murder. Spenser doesn't know much yet and is harder to kill, so Broz goes after Hayden. Spenser saves his life, gets badly wounded in the process, and Hayden leaves him to die. Hayden is totally narcissistic; totally wrapped up in his own fears, anxieties, and insecurities, and has no concern left for other people, such as the man who just saved his life.

When Spenser (who in good hardboiled tradition has left the hospital still groggy from painkillers and against doctor's orders) gets Hayden's wife, Judy, to take him to her husband's hiding place, so as to be able to protect him from the mob, the vilification intensifies. Parker makes Hayden utterly and irredeemably stupid, for starters—smart about the fourteenth century, perhaps, but stupid about the twentieth. Even when Joe Broz's hit man Phil comes in to kill all three of them, Spenser, Hayden, and Hayden's wife, Hayden refuses to believe that Broz wants him dead: he first chooses to believe that Phil has come to rescue him from his wife and Spenser; then, when Phil says he too is going to die, decides that Phil must be acting on his own and threatens him with Broz's anger. This is a desperate delusion of power in a powerless academic—one that is not all that far, in fact, from Parker's own apparent hope that writing this novel will give him, the powerless newcomer in an academic world, some kind of moral revenge on his colleagues. Next Hayden sicks Phil on his wife, whom Parker portrays as possessing the moral courage her husband lacks:

"And you know how angry Joseph Broz can be. I'm on your side. I want to change all of this. I want a world where you won't have to work outside the law. I'm not your enemy. Shoot them. He's your enemy and she is, too, she betrayed me. She led him here. She led you here. Kill her. Don't kill me. Please don't. Please don't."

His legs went out from beneath him, and he dropped to his knees and back onto his heels. "Please don't. Please don't. Please don't."

Phil liked it. He cackled to himself. (194)

This is degrading, of course, embarrassingly unmanly behavior, and as such the best way—if, like Parker and Spenser, you believe in the macho code—to humiliate a brainy wimp like Hayden. The one worm in Parker's apple at this point is Phil's cackle: Phil too believes in the macho code, for which Spenser has respected him throughout; and the proper response to Hayden's degradation from a macho man Spenser respects would be embarrassment, not cackling. In any case, Judy leaps on Phil, takes several bullets in her stomach, but keeps holding on (by her teeth to his arm), absurdly sacrificing herself to save her worthless husband. She is a traditional wife, schooled well and effectively in the virtues of submerging herself in her husband—and strong enough, also like the traditional wife, to bend her will to self-sacrifice. Judy's altruistic act gives Spenser a chance to strangle Phil, and the two men are saved. Spenser pushes the two dead bodies off him and goes looking for Hayden, who is cowering behind the shower curtain in the bathtub: "I reached down, took the front of his shirt in both hands, and yanked him up out of the tub. There was a peculiar smell about him and I realized he'd wet himself. I was revolted" (197). Worse and worse. Perhaps worst of all, from a macho point of view, is that Hayden has no grief or remorse for the enormity of his wife's self-sacrifice or the devastation his aggressive narcissism has brought about, but immediately turns the novel's events into more empty rhetoric, lecturing the police on the social and political implications of what has just happened.

Why this frenzied attack on an English professor? The scene reads like a scapegoat ritual, in which self-revulsion is projected fiercely outward onto a surrogate. But what is Parker projecting? What is he trying to deal with here?[8]

It is significant that Hayden shares certain features in common with his creator: both are English professors at large Boston universities; both are reformers, men who want to change the world, men who are dissatisfied with the academic extension of the Kantian principle that art (now knowledge too) should be perfectly purposeless. Hayden, like Parker, is something of a crusader; and unlike Spenser, who takes his crusade out into the world and does physical battle with the bad guys, both Hayden and Parker wage their crusades with words, Hayden in his teaching and revolutionary rhetoric, Parker in the liberal rhetoric of his novels. In fact, Hayden works more in the "real" world of politics than

Parker does, taking risks with mobsters, betting his life on his convictions—another reason to make the distinction between him and Spenser, and by implication between him and Parker, crystal clear. Hayden works with the abstractions of Marxism, while Parker sees himself as working with individuals, "real" people. But of course a Marxist is trying to deal with the real world too, and uses abstractions (class struggle, superstructure and base, labor, profit, alienation, etc.) only in order to get a handle on complexity that seems to defy articulation; and Parker's characters are the same kind of handles, simplified fictions that give Parker some kind of inroad into the world.

There is this, then: Parker is worried that his assistant professorship at Northeastern University is going to identify him with, and ultimately assimilate him to, the scared, self-protective academics he despises; and he is worried, further, that writing the Spenser novels, which he hopes will take him out of academia, will do little to counteract the debilitating effect of academic abstraction and withdrawal. He is still really only reading and writing! Not only that, he is writing books that can be taught in college courses (which I have done) and written about in scholarly treatises (which I am doing right now). Will people (will mommy and daddy, in the introjected family romance) assume he is just wasting his time like the other academics, playing with words rather than engaging the real world? Will they assume he is as self-indulgent as Lowell Hayden? Then it is important to put as much space—emotional space—between himself and Hayden as possible.

The other side to this coin is that, despite his sneering at academia—or perhaps even because of it—Parker is immensely popular among academics. Part of it is the fact that his hero is well-read in English and American literature, and quotes frequently from Shakespeare, Donne, Keats, Whitman, Thoreau, Frost, Stevens, and other "literary" writers; also makes a habit of correcting thugs' grammar and pronunciation. Spenser too, like academics, does research (even library research) in search of the true nature of a case. Like most academics, Spenser and his creator are dyed-in-the-wool liberals who feel uncomfortable with radical politics; it is therefore altogether congenial to feel superior to a wimpy radical like Hayden (especially a medievalist, although in current institutional politics a radical medievalist is something of an oxymoron). More generally, many academics feel quite comfortable, even self-congratulatory, about dissociating themselves from the idealized purposelessness of academic pursuits, and reading Spenser novels is a good way of confirming that dissociation (I am like Spenser, not like Hayden) without actually having to do anything purposeful about it. As I suggested above, this makes

Parker's attack on academia *attractive* to academics. Even the attack on the department chair can be explained in similar terms: most scholars have no interest in chairing their department and feel superior to the kind of administrative wizards (defensively branded "drudges") who enjoy it and do it well. On the whole, Parker doesn't really hit very many academics very close to home.

But of course it is more complicated than that. After all, academics reading Parker are mainly *playing*, not working—they are taking time off from philological problems like *solid* and *sullied* to read a detective novel. Formula fiction: not "serious" literature. No chance of becoming a classic. There are those of us who write professionally about detective novels, but most academics don't; mainly it is a vacation from work. Reading an entertaining book like *The Godwulf Manuscript*, a formula book about academia, is a kind of busman's holiday for the academic reader. What makes the busman's holiday seem like a real holiday, however, is Parker's portrait of "real" academic work (literary criticism, literary theory) as idle "play," a playing with words while real people are out there suffering in the real world; and, by contrast, his portrait of what Spenser does as, in the Frost poem he quotes in several of the novels, work that is also "play for mortal stakes." By reading Spenser novels, therefore, the academic reader too can believe that she or he is playing for mortal stakes—that *this* playing with words is somehow more important, more "work-like," than the playing with words that she or he is paid to call work.

On the other hand, why is all this important? Why am I going on about Parker's complex attitudes toward academia? Aren't I just playing with the words "work" and "play"? Is this any more significant than whether Shakespeare said *solid* or *sullied*? It is significant, or can be, only if we grant that reading and writing can be powerfully transformative ways of participating in the real world. It is significant only if we grant, say, that we are programmed by our culture to populate our worlds with social fictions (men are strong, women are weak; detectives are tough, academics are wimpy) that seem very like reality but will in fact yield, if pressed hard enough and long enough and effectively enough, to the kind of rethinking, refeeling, reprogramming that reading and writing can engender.

As Parker portrays him, Lowell Hayden is a miserable, pathetic character, scared of his own shadow but programmed to act like an autonomous superhero (a traditional man), and defensively locked into his revolutionary rhetoric as the only conceivable stay against his inner divisions. But Spenser too is scared of his own shadow, in many ways, and so is Parker: scared of the shadow of his deepest needs, for instance, and the childhood experiences that feed them. Parker has still not found the courage to make Spenser confront the scary things inside himself. Few people do have that courage, in fact; this is no adverse reflection on Parker. It is only in the novels of the middle 1980s that Parker even becomes aware that Spenser's strength is just as much a defensive prison as Hayden's rhetoric, just as much a frightened stay against inner division. What makes Hayden pathetic is not that he is an academic, nor that he deals mainly with words rather than with guns and fists. It is what makes most of us pathetic: that he is, and we are, unable to deal with the internal monsters. Parker too uses words (rather than guns and fists) to start dealing with those monsters, but that doesn't necessarily make him pathetic. Hayden, given half a chance (given a sympathetic creator, say) might well do the same. Parker the liberal and Hayden the radical both believe that words—writing and lecturing—can change the world.

# Chapter Two

# The Liberal Hero

If the world Parker wants to change in *The Godwulf Manuscript* seems to be the academic one in which he feels incarcerated, by *God Save the Child* (1974, the second in the series) his focus is already on the world that will concern him most centrally throughout the series: the ordinary domestic world of the white American middle class, its crises and failures, its confusions. The trouble Spenser is hired to solve typically revolves around a middle-class couple's confusion about traditional liberal values: individual autonomy vs. collective duty and responsibility; personal expression and fulfillment vs. self-sacrifice and self-submergence in the family. These are key Spenser issues too, especially at this early juncture in the series; Parker seems to be exploring his own attitudes toward the middle-class domesticity in which he finds himself lodged, especially things like his duty toward his wife and children, his "rights" to "self-indulgence," etc. Spenser starts off these novels in a position or stance of strength and certainty, full of impatience with his mixed-up clients who seem to have no idea about correct behavior. But as the series progresses he becomes less and less certain, less and less inclined to solve complex problems from behind a rigid screen.

Parker does, certainly, expand the novels beyond the domestic realm; these are not middle-class Agatha Christie novels, but fairly broad social canvases that incorporate such diverse elements as the gay body-building scene and drugs (*God Save the Child*), professional sports and prostitution, (*Mortal Stakes*, 1975), land development, loan sharking, and armed feminist revolution (*Promised Land*, 1976), international terrorism (*The Judas Goat*, 1978), radical lesbianism and right-wing politics (*Looking for Rachel Wallace*, 1980), investigative journalism (*A Savage Place*, 1981), political blackmail (*The Widening Gyre*, 1983), militant sub-Christian cults (*Valediction*, 1984), arms smuggling and the exploitation of illegal aliens (*A Catskill Eagle*, 1985), drug-smuggling (*Pale Kings and Princes*, 1987, and *Pastime*, 1991), serial murder (*Crimson Joy*, 1988), intercollegiate sports and illiteracy

(*Playmates*, 1989), television stardom (*Stardust*, 1990), inner-city gang warfare (*Double Deuce*, 1992) and dirty politics (*Paper Doll*, 1993). But of the 20 Spenser novels to date, 12, or almost two-thirds, are emotionally centered around bewildered middle-class couples and their neglected children: five (*Mortal Stakes, Promised Land, The Widening Gyre, Pale Kings and Princes,* and *Paper Doll*) around marital difficulties, another four (*God Save the Child, Early Autumn* [1981], *Crimson Joy,* and *Pastime*) around the effect of parental neglect or engulfment on a son, three others (*Ceremony* [1982], *Taming a Sea-Horse* [1987], and *Stardust*) around the effect of neglect on a daughter, and the twelfth (*The Judas Goat*) around a self-made man's implacable desire to avenge the death of his wife and children.

(Three of the other seven, *Looking for Rachel Wallace, A Savage Place,* and *Valediction*, revolve around unmarried "new women," women determined to make their own way in a man's world; only one of the three, Rachel Wallace, the hard, humorless radical feminist, is portrayed as successful, able to rid herself of traditional feminine wiles, and she is the only one to survive the novel she appears in and become a kind of series semiregular. A fourth, *Double Deuce*, focuses on the drive-by shooting of a teenage mother and her infant child by a druglord.)

Parker's repeated return to themes of middle-class confusion and crisis is clearly a response to a social transformation or transition that is all around us—a transition that arises out of liberal ideology, largely, but is also corrosive of liberal values, liberal traditions and assumptions, all the traditional supports of middle-class life. A class dedicated in its deepest historical origins to hard work, thrift, and common sense increasingly (from the mid-nineteenth century to the twenties, first, then again and more intensely after World War II) finds itself thrust into a rampant prosperity earmarked by advertisers for leisure. The commodification of leisure provides new jobs and new prosperity for the rising middle class; but it also deprives the middle class of one of its central ideological stays, the value placed on hard work. Middle-class men are now regularly chastised for being workaholics, and sternly admonished to spend quality time with their children.[1] Middle-class women, even before feminism transforms their attitudes toward domestication and self-submergence, are increasingly alienated from traditional housewife-roles by advertisers, who foster dissatisfaction in order to sell their product. Consumer capitalism sells leisure in the familiar terms of liberal autonomy, the self-possession of the bourgeois subject (women too, now, not just men)—be your truest self, be all that you can be, get the most out of your life—but what is being sold, as John Berger makes clear, is an idealized image (the sizzle, not the steak, as Spenser is told in *Taming a Sea-Horse* [183]) that makes reality pale by comparison:

Publicity is effective precisely because it feeds upon the real. Clothes, food, cars, cosmetics, baths, sunshine are real things to be enjoyed in themselves. Publicity begins by working on a natural appetite for pleasure. But it cannot offer the real object of pleasure and there is no convincing substitute for a pleasure in that pleasure's own terms. The more convincingly publicity conveys the pleasure of bathing in a warm, distant sea, the more the spectator-buyer will become aware that he is hundreds of miles away from that sea and the more remote the chance of bathing in it will seem to him. This is why publicity can never really afford to be about the product or opportunity it is proposing to the buyer who is not yet enjoying it. Publicity is never a celebration of pleasure-in-itself. Publicity is always about the future buyer. It offers him an image of himself made glamorous by the product or opportunity it is trying to sell. The image then makes him envious of himself as he might be. Yet what makes this self-which-he-might-be enviable? The envy of others. Publicity is about social relations, not objects. Its promise is not of pleasure, but of happiness: happiness as judged from the outside by others. (Berger 132)

Television, America's (and increasingly the world's) dominant cultural medium, sells glamorous self-images not only in commercials, but in its regular programming as well: the soaps, the sitcoms, the cop shows and talk shows all sell lifestyles, the lifestyles of the rich and famous, even when their success consists entirely in being considered worth immortalizing on TV. (Even failure, or the kind of constant verging on failure explored in *Roseanne*, can be glamorous, and thus a kind of normative success, if it makes enough Americans laugh or cry: *that* is the proper way to fail! Those are the proper emotions to feel, the proper things to say, when you fail.)

Parker records and responds to this crisis, perhaps even decay or disintegration, of the middle class throughout the Spenser novels. Everywhere in the series there are people like Harry Kyle from *Ceremony*, who have "moved away from the old neighborhood," as Susan Silverman says, "both literally and figuratively. The old rules from that neighborhood don't apply here. Or people like Harry Kyle don't think they do. They don't know the new rules, so they latch on to the conventions of the media and the assumptions of the magazine ads and the situation comedies. They try to be like everybody else, and what makes it so hard is that everyone else is trying to be like them" (17). By far the most devastating of the social changes Parker records and sets Spenser the task of dealing with, however, are the shifts in sex roles brought on by the women's movement.

In some sense the right-wing alarmists are exactly right when they claim, like the born-again Christian politician Spenser works for in *The Widening Gyre*, that "the family, the nucleus of civilization, is under attack from the spread of feminism" (12). Feminism is indeed a radical critique of patriarchal society, of societal structures like the family and government and business and the ideologies that underlie them; and feminists are typically no passive academics, content to describe, but political activists who work to dismantle and remake society. What's more, feminists have been spectacularly successful in even initiating, over a period of 150 or so years, a major social transformation—in even beginning to upset the patriarchal apple cart.

Parker is liberal enough to be sensitive to feminist critiques and sympathetic with feminist projects; but he is also honest enough, true enough to his own experience, not to bury his misgivings about them in liberal rhetoric. He is sensitive to the confusion wrought by feminism among both men and women: a little liberation, as Spenser implies in *Promised Land*, can be a dangerous thing. His client in that novel, Harvey Shepard, wants him to find his wife, and Susan Silverman asks whether he expects it to be difficult:

"No. Sounds like she's simply run off. If she has she'll be easy to find. Most wives who run off don't run very far. The majority of them, in fact, want to be found and want to come home."

"That doesn't sound particularly liberated."

"It isn't particularly liberated but it's the way it is. For the first time the number of runaway wives exceeds the number of runaway husbands. They read two issues of *Ms.* Magazine, see Marlo Thomas on a talk show and decide they can't go on. So they take off. Then they find out that they have no marketable skills. That ten or fifteen years of housewifing has prepared them for nothing else and they end up washing dishes or waiting table or pushing a mop and they want out. Also lots of them get lonesome."...

"You...make it sound, oh I don't know, trivial. Or, commonplace. As if you didn't care. As if they were only items in your work. Things to look for."

"I don't see much point to talking with a tremor in my voice. I care enough about them to look for them. I do it for the money too, but money's not hard to make. The thing, in my line of work at least, is not to get too wrapped up in caring. It tends to be bad for you." (15-17)

But this already begins to sound defensive. Spenser's problem, as Parker has by now shown us in *Mortal Stakes* (of which more in a moment), is that he tends to care too much about his clients; that he does get "too wrapped up in caring." He is trying, here, not very successfully, to maintain a light, easy tone, a controlled tone, the sound of caring just the right amount, not too much, not too little. His cynicism about women getting a little exposure to feminism and dumping everything is a fake; and when Susan gets angry at him (saying she too has read *Ms.* Magazine and been married and gotten out and knows more about what it feels like than he does) and pushes on him, a deeper source of his caring comes out:

She looked at her menu. "Smug," she said. "That's the word I was looking for, a kind of smugness about the woman's silly little fling."...
"I don't buy smug," I said. "Flip, maybe, but not smug."
"Condescending," Susan said.
"No," I said. "Annoyed, maybe, if you push me. But not at her, at all the silliness in the world. I'm sick of movements. I'm sick of people who think that a new system will take care of everything. I'm sick of people who put the cause ahead of the person. And I am sick of people, whatever sex, who dump the kids and run off: to work, to booze, to sex, to success. It's irresponsible." (17-18)

Spenser is annoyed at the silliness of a world where the middle class is falling apart, where the stable old liberal ideology, which was good enough for three or four hundred years, is disintegrating and being replaced with a succession of new "systems," like feminism. Spenser places the blame on the movements, the causes, the new systems, or on the people who invent and maintain those things; but in fact he is standing in the midst of a massive social transition, witnessing the breakdown of the old liberal system that he finds attractive and reassuring, and must deal with people who quite simply don't know what to do or where to turn.

His solution, here in the early novels of the series, is aggressively liberal in both the pluralistic/progressive and the authoritarian/reactionary political guises liberalism takes. On the one hand, everybody is free to do his or her own thing, he is not going to dictate anybody's life; on the other hand, everybody should do the right thing, which is to say, the *old* thing. The liberal thing. The rugged, individualistic ethos of early liberalism: possess yourself, be your *own* self, and take sufficient strength from self-possession to do your duty to those given into your care, your spouse, your children, your aging parents, your friends, whomever. Just as Jonathan Edwards, facing the demise of Puritanism, responded by being more ardently Puritan than the Puritans ever were, so too Spenser, facing the demise of liberalism, responds by raising liberalism to a holy crusade.

In *God Save the Child*, for example, he engineers things so that the reunion of runaway Kevin Bartlett with his narcissistic parents Roger and Marge makes all three of them aware of what "matters"—in other words, of what is manifestly the right thing to do. It is, unsurprisingly, to sacrifice your selfish desires for those you love. In *Promised Land* he concocts and executes a daring scheme that solves the Shepards' pressing legal problems and practically (emotionally) coerces them into giving their marriage another shot.

But by the books of the early eighties, these tried-and-true solutions are beginning to feel hollow and unlikely to Parker. In *Early Autumn*, for example, he rewrites *God Save the Child* so that, instead of rescuing the runaway son from the brutish body-builder/lover who has helped stage the kidnapping and restoring him to his parents, Spenser himself becomes the body-builder/kidnapper (no longer thematized as brutish) who helps the son run away from his viciously selfish parents, and blackmails them to stay out of their son's life. The answer, at some level, remains the same: Paul Giacomin must create himself as Spenser once created himself, "by effort, one brick at a time" (161), as he says in *The Widening Gyre*. But now, instead of trusting the family to do the job of shaping children into autonomous adults—instead of trusting the social unit, liberal society—Spenser begins to feel compelled to intervene personally. He takes Paul into the woods, teaches him to jog, lift weights, and build a house; brings him back into the city, teaches him to eat out, dress up, and know what he wants (helps him create himself as a dancer). If society won't do it, Spenser will. If liberalism is disintegrating in America as a whole, Spenser will revive it in small individualistic enclaves. Paul becomes Spenser's most important experiment in creating a self-creating liberal hero.

That is paradoxical, of course. If Spenser creates Paul, Paul doesn't create Paul. "Autonomy," Spenser tells Paul at one point in the novel, "means self-reliance, not changing your reliance from your mother and father to me" (176). Autonomy is probably Parker's favorite word for the individualistic ideal of liberal masculinity; Susan is always saying that Spenser is the most autonomous person she knows. And emotionally, in English, autonomy is an autonomous sort of word: it buries the insecure "self" that must be pumped up to maintain appearances in the Greek root "auto," making it seem as if personal autonomy were a thing to be possessed, and a most simple and natural thing at that. The other word in Spenser's prescription for Paul (and himself), Emerson's word "self-reliance," is more anxious. There is a lack, a failing, a weakness, that needs a foundation or support to rely on; and the "self" is now openly recruited as the place or agency of that support. But the "self" is also the agent that requires support, which implicates "self-reliance" in self-division.

And in fact there is an emotional double-bind built into liberal "self-reliance." It is already evident in Spenser's manifest desire to convince Paul that he (Paul) is doing the self-creating, not Spenser: creating Paul gives Spenser a strong sense that he is himself self-created and is contributing to the liberal ethos of self-creation on a larger social scale; but it also situates Paul's self-creation in the interdependent context of Spenser's help. "Self-made man," the historian Francis Parkman sneered back in the age of the robber barons, the late nineteenth century. "Show me a self-laid egg!"[2] Another way of coming at the double bind is by seeing in self-reliance its conflicting calls to responsibility to others and self-containment—to duty and independence. If I am complete and whole in myself, why do I need others? Why should I do things for others? If I feel driven to do things for others, and to receive love and other goods and services from others, am I still complete and whole in myself?

Like Emerson in "Self-Reliance," which he quotes in *Paper Dolls*, Parker senses that the double bind has something to do with adolescence and adulthood: Susan is constantly chiding Spenser for his adolescent attitudes, and also accusing him of being *too* mature and self-contained. But neither Emerson nor Parker can quite put his finger on the problem. Here, for instance, is Emerson:

> The nonchalance of boys who are sure of a dinner, and would disdain as much as a lord to do or say aught to conciliate one, is the healthy attitude of human nature. A boy is in the parlor what the pit is in the playhouse; independent, irresponsible, looking out from his corner on such people and facts as pass by, he tries and sentences them on their merits, in the swift, summary way of boys, as good, bad, interesting, silly, eloquent, troublesome. He cumbers himself never about consequences, about interests; he gives an independent, genuine verdict. You must court him; he does not court you. But the man is as it were clapped into jail by his consciousness. As soon as he has once acted or spoken with *éclat* he is a committed person, watched by the sympathy or the hatred of hundreds, whose affections must now enter into his account. There is no Lethe for this. Ah, that he could pass again into his neutrality! Who can thus

avoid all pledges and, having observed, observe again from the same unaffected, unbiased, unbribable, unaffrighted innocence,—must always be formidable. He would utter opinions on all passing affairs, which being seen to be not private but necessary, would sink like darts into the ear of men and put them in fear. ("Self-Reliance" 48-49)

This is, of course, one ideal of liberal masculinity, or one part of the ideal: complete independence, complete autonomy, complete freedom from the "feminine" bonds of responsibility, duty, other people. Emersonian self-reliance is a godlike state of total self-sufficiency—a state, in other words, of *no needs*. "You must court him; he does not court you." He doesn't need you, your approval, your support, your love. He is "unaffected" in every sense of the word: not affected by your loving demands, affectless, and *not* pretending.

In *Manhood and the American Renaissance* David Leverenz takes a slightly different tack on this passage: "Yet the boys' breezy freedom, like the line's jaunty stride, depends on being 'sure of a dinner,' not sure of themselves. And what about the girls? One can picture them in the kitchen with the angels of the house, getting more faceless and sexless by the minute while they put out the meals for their lounging brothers. To achieve a bold male self-reliance presumes a depersonalized female support system" (63). Parker's liberalism and male feminism, significantly, only succeeds in extending this virtue to girls (and women) as well: in expanding the sphere of male self-reliance so as to obviate the need for a female support system (Spenser is a good cook, neat housekeeper, etc.), and thus to "liberate" women from prescribed patriarchal facelessness and sexlessness into full-fledged self-reliant "masculinity." This was in fact one of the transitional achievements of 1970s feminism: "freeing" women to enter the work force and the heart attack statistics, "liberating" women into the dubious freedom of patriarchal masculinity, with its emphasis on the management of emotion and stress for purposes of hierarchically defined "success."[3]

The difficulty, as Emerson's negation of what he obviously takes to be the normal state of affairs suggests—his negation of affect, bias, and fright—is that need seems to be emotionally prior to and foundational for autonomy. Need comes first; autonomy, or its controlled image, is built upon it. This is made even clearer by Emerson's elevation of male adolescence as the human ideal: the little boy needs love, needs his mommy and daddy; the adolescent boy still needs them, still needs parental love and support, but feels increasingly compromised by his need, and so works to separate himself from it. He affects nonchalance, which is etymologically a lack of warmth: he neither needs nor feels warmth. He aspires to total disdain for conciliation. He longs for freedom from his deepest emotional inclinations, toward dependence and responsibility: dependence on his parents' love and approval, responsibility as an inward compulsion to respond to their demands. The "healthy" man Emerson paints for our emulation is a kind of monster, a man who is utterly blind to the sources of his nonchalance, disdain, independence, and irresponsibility in emotional need, utterly dedicated to repressing need in himself and others; and bourgeois society's idealization (egged on by Emerson himself) of this repressive illusion of health has cloned the monster a million-fold. The man who utters opinions on all passing affairs in the blithe conviction that his opinions are not needy but necessary is an all too familiar figure, from both our social experience and feminist critiques.

Parker seems to be sensitive to the complexities of liberal self-reliance. He is, for example, inclined to reject Emerson's blithe idealization of nonchalant male adolescence in more or less the same terms I have used here: adolescent nonchalance (as evidenced in Paul Giacomin's shrugging indifference before Spenser takes over, say) is a cover for something, a defense. Reading Parker, whose emotional roots seem to be in the working class, or in the hard-working lower middle class, it becomes clear that Emerson's nonchalant male adolescent can be sure of a dinner in large part because his family belongs to the leisure class; through Parker's eyes also, then, it begins to seem as if the "healthy" man's adolescent nonchalance for Emerson may be a defense against the patriarchal association of leisure with femininity. I must look nonchalant to prove my toughness—I have no hard physical labor to prove it for me, no work-hardened muscles to display my machismo. In a journal entry from 1838, Emerson writes:

> The effeminate rich man says in his shrug, in his gloves & surtout on the cold spring day, that he fears the earth will not yield to man bread this year. The hard visaged farmer looks contented & fearless. He has fronted the year cold & grim. He has embraced the shovel & the ox yoke & ploughtail long ago & knows well that the hardest year that ever blew afforded to such straining & sweating as his, milk, rye, potatoes...and he does not think of famine. (JMN 5:470)[4]

The difficulty is that Emerson is himself, by now, the "effeminate rich man"—always given more to thought than to hard physical labor, he has been left a small fortune by his dead wife, placing him comfortably in the leisure class in economic fact as well as emotional inclination[5]—but he still idealizes the hard-working farmer, "nature's" macho man. To be a "healthy" human one must be a man, a real man, tough, self-reliant—which is to say, in the capitalist iconology, a working man, a laborer. To be rich, even well enough off not to have to work for a living, therefore, is to be effeminate. Placed in the ideologically awkward position of belonging to a social class branded as effeminate (and therefore unhealthy) while propounding a doctrine of manly health, then, Emerson tries to solve his dilemma in "Self-Reliance" by offering his own insecure adolescent self (the self he still feels in his body, in his muscle memory of youth) as the healthy human norm. The unspoken implication—that the self-reliant man of intellect (and incidentally of leisure) is more manly and therefore healthier than the brutish farmer—is left for Emerson's disciple Thoreau to spell out in the first chapter of *Walden*:

Most men, even in this comparatively free country, through mere ignorance and mistake, are so occupied with the factitious cares and superfluously coarse labors of life that its finer fruits cannot be plucked by them. Their fingers, from excessive toil, are too clumsy and tremble too much for that. Actually, the laboring man has not leisure for a true integrity day by day; he cannot afford to sustain the manliest relations to man; his labor would be depreciated in the market. He has no time to be any thing but a machine. How can he remember well his ignorance—which his growth requires—who has so often to use his knowledge? We should feed and clothe him gratuitously sometimes, and recruit him with our cordials, before we judge of him. The finest qualities of our nature, like the bloom on fruits, can be preserved only by the most delicate handling. Yet we do not treat ourselves nor one another thus tenderly. (6)

Integrity requires leisure. It also requires labor, but not too much: just enough to harden a man, not enough to dull him. The laborer who only labors becomes a machine. Growth requires enough leisure to realize your ignorance; too much labor forces you to overuse your knowledge, to place your knowing and knowledgeable doing under the constant strain of *need*. In order to find the breathing space to become truly self-reliant the laborer must be fed and clothed gratuitously, recruited with cordials, handled delicately—treated, in other words, like a rich man. Not a lazy, self-indulgent, decadent rich man who whittles away his leisure in pastimes that bespeak "quiet desperation" (8)—rather, a principled, self-reliant rich man, or perhaps even a man with little money who simply *acts* like a rich man, and by careful self-control and image-management is able to combine labor with leisure, work with play. Someone, in fact, a lot like Thoreau: an insecure lower-middle-class intellectual, say, whose protective ability to act self-reliant and articulate his actions endears him to a rich patron like Emerson. A surly, intractable man with the studied adolescent nonchalance—"You must court him; he does not court you"—to write a classic of American self-reliance while living on land owned by his patron, like a sinecured poet-laureate, at Walden Pond.[6]

When Parker has Spenser defend Emersonian self-reliance, he typically alludes not to Emerson directly, but to Thoreau. His most pervasive Emersonian quote, however, is from neither of these two writers, but from that devoted modern follower of both, Robert Frost. I refer to the famous last four lines of Frost's "Two Tramps in Mud-Time," a powerfully Thoreauvian poem about two tramps approaching the poet while he is out chopping wood, and looking at him as if he were taking food from their mouths: "As that I had no right to play / With what was another man's work for gain" (359). It is early spring—mud-time—and the middle four stanzas unmistakably recall Thoreau at Walden Pond, moving through nature description to philosophical reflection; also like Thoreau, Frost ties his philosophical reflections to hard-headed things like unemployment and social class. "My right might be love but theirs was need" (359), Frost notes: they need the work to live, to eat, and I am only out here chopping wood because it feels good, because I love the feel of the ax coming down and splitting the wood so cleanly. This is leisure for me, "play"; for them it is "work for gain." Like Thoreau, however, Frost is at some pains to transcend the leisure-labor dualism, to combine the manliness of labor with the energizing relaxation of leisure. ("A stereotyped but unconscious despair is concealed," Thoreau wrote, "even under what are called the games and amusements of mankind. There is no play in them, for this comes after work" [111].) Here, then, is the famous ending that Parker keeps returning to, the passage I referred to earlier, in my discussion of Parker's complex attitudes toward academia—the lines Parker takes as epigraph to, and title source for, *Mortal Stakes*, and has Spenser and various other characters quote throughout the series:

> Only where love and need are one,
> And the work is play for mortal stakes,
> Is the deed ever really done
> For Heaven and the future's sakes. (359)

In the context of the whole poem, "love" and "need" are specifically references to motivations for working: you either love to work, and work for the sheer love of it (the gentleman farmer), or you need to work, and work to meet your financial needs (the migrant worker). Taking these lines out of context, as Parker typically does, has the salutary effect of tying social and economic relations to emotional relations: leisure-class "playful" work like chopping your own wood is implicitly linked with a giving to others out of the fullness of personal integrity ("love"), and working-class financial duress is linked with the terrible pressure of emotional lack ("need"). The leisure-class man is "self-possessed" in both senses of the word: he possesses both the material and the emotional resources to give to others from a position of strength (think of Spenser helping people out of a sense of "honor," without financial remuneration, all through the series, most strikingly in *Ceremony*). The working-class man is "broke" in both senses of the word: lacking money and forced to work to make ends meet, and broken in spirit, lacking the serene strength of the "autonomous" liberal hero.

Thus goes the idealized liberal version, anyway. Tying economic need to emotional need gives Frost's insistence on unifying love and need, work and play the power to deconstruct the traditional division: the leisure-class man *needs* to appear autonomous, self-possessed; which is to say, he needs to seem unneedy. Emerson's ideal, certainly, would be love without need—providing we agree to mean by love not eros but the mystical vision of oneness with the Beautiful that tops Socrates' hicrarchy in the *Symposium*, an unaffected sharing out of perfect self-containment.[7] Not feeling. Not affect. Not longing or lack. This, as I said before, doesn't solve the problem of motivation: if the lover were truly self-contained he would have no reason (no need) to give of himself. If he needs to give of himself he has a lack (a need for praise, say) that compromises his self-containment. (Theologians ponder this paradox in connection with why, if he was self-contained and self-sufficient, God created the heavens and the earth. One common answer is that he did it in order to multiply the beings who will sing his praises, a common enough desire among would-be self-reliant men as well.) The human impossibility of love without need makes this problem of motivation translate finally as a problem of image-management: the real question is not how to love without needing, but how to appear to love without appearing to need.

Need without love would be Emerson's anti-ideal, the man "watched by the sympathy or the hatred of hundreds, whose affections must now enter into his account"—a man so entirely governed and imprisoned by his need for other people's feelings that he has nothing to give back. Need without love is an anxious, defensive state that resembles Riesman's "other-directedness" and often masquerades as love—clinging, demanding, insatiable love.

As Emerson's gender assignations remind us (masculine for the healthy human nature, feminine for the unhealthy), of course, love without need (inner-direction) is the patriarchally programmed masculine ideal, and need without love (other-direction) is the patriarchally programmed feminine ideal. To lack and thus to need is a frightening state that patriarchy projects insistently onto women.

But it is also more than that. The leisure classes associate financial need with emotional need, and envision those who have to work for a living as somehow emotionally deficient, driven by their needs, their longings and lacks. This is clear enough from Thoreau's patronizing deprecation of the "laboring man." But since, as Emerson's journal entry makes equally clear, we are also trained to image the "laboring man" as masculine and the rich man as effeminate, the confrontation of love and need, work and play that Frost portrays in his poem suggests a whole network of emotional defenses. The working man associates the rich man's leisure and resulting soft muscles with femininity, and thus defends himself against the "emasculation" of economic disenfranchisement; the rich man associates the working man's economic disenfranchisement with femininity, and thus defends himself against the "effemination" of leisure. Both men are specifically driven by emotional need (fear of dependency, fear of vulnerability, fear of need itself) to project need onto women first and feminized men at the opposite end of the social scale second.

Frost's utopian vision of unifying love and need and work and play in a bid for Heaven and the future, then, translates finally as an attempt to transcend gender and class in a kind of liberal apotheosis. Where Emerson idealizes leisure-class masculinity (his own enviable state) as the model for healthy human nature, Frost insists that "man" incorporate into a healthy human nature both masculine love and feminine need, and both the leisure of the rich and the labor of the masses. So constituted, the superhuman (or superliberal) hero would be ideally impervious to the vulnerability, weakness, defenselessness, and neediness he most fears.

This need to defend against need also explains the high premium Emerson, Thoreau, Frost, and Parker all place on self-control. They feel a pressure to let go, to break down, to give in, to be everything a self-reliant man isn't supposed to be—vulnerable, needy, afraid, "affected"— and meet that pressure with a constant counterpressure. "Nothing is at last sacred but the integrity of your own mind," Emerson says. "Absolve you to yourself, and you shall have the suffrage of the world" ("Self-Reliance" 50). But if integrity is sacred, it is also taboo: work to absolve yourself so that nothing can damage your untouchable inner self. Control yourself. "I went to the woods because I wished to live deliberately," Thoreau says, "to front only the essential facts of life, and see if I could not learn what it had to teach" (90). To live deliberately is to prune your life of everything that is "inessential," Thoreau says, implying that self-reliant deliberation is a core from which all dross must be cleared away; a less idealizing formulation would be that self-reliant deliberation is a protective enclosure from which everything uncontrolled, especially everything that threatens control, must be driven away. Frost too defines the "love" he feels for his wood-chopping in terms of a careful management of self:

> The blows that a life of self-control
> Spares to strike for the common good
> That day, giving a loose to my soul,
> I spent on the unimportant wood. (357)

Giving a *cautious* loose to his soul, which he equates with self-control: sometimes a few impulses escape the iron bars of his soul's cage, and must be directed somewhere; normally he directs them "for the common good," like Spenser out saving the weak and the helpless, but today he takes them out on the "unimportant wood." His "right" to be chopping wood is the love he feels at being able to channel his uncontrollable impulses in harmless ways—which is to say, at being able to control himself perfectly, without residue. The lines just preceding the four that Parker likes to quote make it clear that the unity of love and need and work and play Frost prescribes is no mystical oneness achieved through the surrender of self, but precisely something Frost is *working* at, striving for, an "object" he feels he needs to attain:

> But yield who will to their separation,
> My object in living is to unite
> My avocation and my vocation
> As my two eyes make one in sight. (359)

Astigmatic, I wouldn't know about that last line; maybe some people's eyes do make one in sight. It seems obvious, in any case, that Frost's deepest need is not to "yield."

Spenser too works very hard at achieving Frost's utopian superliberalism. In *Early Autumn*, while he is "raising" Paul by teaching him to lift weights and build a house (in Maine, on land Susan received from her ex-husband as part of her divorce settlement), Paul wonders why they have to dig the postholes by hand; it would be so much easier to rent a machine to do it. Spenser answers in the spirit of Frost chopping wood or, better, of Thoreau building a house at Walden Pond:

"We do it to get the pleasure of making something. Otherwise we could hire someone. That would be the easiest way of all."
"But this is cheaper," Paul said.
"Yeah, we save money. But that's just a point that keeps it from being a hobby, like making ships in a bottle. Only when love and need are one, you know?" (118)

He and Paul are working, and by not renting a gasoline posthole digger they constantly remind themselves physically that this is *work*, not leisure (and that they are workers, not Emersonian nonchalant boys, leisure-class boys like pre-Spenser Paul who are sure of a dinner). But they don't have to be working—like his mentors Emerson, Thoreau, and Frost, Spenser could afford to hire somebody to do the work[8]—so the work is also leisure. He does it out of love, not financial need: he doesn't need to build the house in order to earn money to live on, and he doesn't need to save money, either; he only saves money to keep it from being a hobby. It is an odd explanation, in fact—for the life of me I cannot imagine how saving money keeps a project from being a hobby—but the ruling idea is clearly the same as Frost's: the need to direct his uncontrollable blows onto the "unimportant wood" fills the work with the pleasure of "making something."

Like Thoreau, in fact, whose sojourn at Walden Pond (and, in "Resistance to Civil Government," his sojourn in jail) was largely an attempt to prove his self-reliance, Spenser is constantly going out of his way to engage in action that will enable him to push his behavior into Frost's categories. He deliberately raises the stakes of whatever he is doing so as to bring work and play, love and need into some kind of intense but precarious balance. In *Ceremony*, for instance, Spenser feels driven to find April Kyle, no matter what it takes, and Susan asks him "How much is it for April? How much for you?" "Doesn't matter," he says. "It's a way to live. Anything else is confusion" (134). It does matter, of course, very much, to Spenser most of all: doing it for April is love, doing it for himself is need, and he is concerned to stave off confusion by making love and need one. By *making* them one: by carefully controlling his desires and his environment so as to bring the two into as close a proximity and balance as possible. It is not just *a* way to live; for Spenser it is the *only* way to live. Spenser is a liberal hero not out of autonomy, out of the completeness of a fully realized self; he is a liberal hero out of terrible, driving emotional need, out of a fear of letting go. And as the series progresses, that need increasingly rises to the surface.

# Chapter Three

# Violence and Need

Beginning in *A Savage Place*, the novel in which Spenser's client is murdered, Spenser's need to control himself becomes more and more intense and evident, as his ability to control himself becomes more and more questionable. By *Valediction*, the most desperate novel in the series, the line between self-reliance and self-destruction has become almost imperceptibly fine. Spenser tries to keep going, tries to live his life normally and go on loving Susan and not mind her sleeping with another man, and Hawk comments that would "take some balance.... Be like carrying a glass of water filled right to the top and not spilling any. Be a bitch" (30). Spenser later remarks that Hawk "knew things you wouldn't think he'd know. He seemed immune to pain, yet he knew about trying to balance it. He seemed immune to affection, too, except with Susan...I tightened my arms across my chest and got my mind back into its blank balance" (105).

But the operative word there is *seemed*: Hawk is able to seem immune to pain and affection precisely because he knows so much about balancing, about careful self-control. Hawk is like Spenser before he fell in love with Susan, as Spenser himself has begun to realize in *Ceremony*, where at one point Susan suggests that they invite Hawk over for Thanksgiving dinner. Spenser flat-out refuses: " 'Suze,' I said. 'You just don't have Hawk for Thanksgiving dinner.'" He can't explain why; he just knows that it is true, and that Hawk would know exactly what he meant. He says Hawk would be compromised.

Susan was quiet, her hand in mine, our bodies close together. Then she said, "It's where you lose me, this arcane male thing. It's like a set of rituals from a religion that no longer exists, the rules of a kingdom that disappeared before memory. It can't be questioned or explained, it simply is—like gravity or inertia."

"I know," I said.

## Violence and Need 77

"I realize it's a source of strength for you," she said, and turned her head from profile to full face, lying close to mine on the pillow, "but you pay a high price for it too, and so does Hawk."

"Hawk higher than I do," I said.

"Because of me?"

"Yes. I have you. He has no one."

"He has you," she said.

I said, "He and I are part of the same cold place. You aren't. You're the source of warmth. Hawk has none. You're what makes me different from Hawk." (126-27)

The "same cold place" of masculinity is the place of careful self-control, the rigidified set of rituals or norms from an extinct religion that still provides a cold sort of strength for Spenser and Hawk; Susan is the threatening external force that undermines Spenser's self-control, the outside source of warmth that keeps Spenser more or less human, but that also leaves him vulnerable to collapse, the loss of "nonchalant" control, the surrender of rigid, defensive ego.

In the next novel, *The Widening Gyre*, Susan leaves him, and the true test begins. Paul notices that Spenser has been hitting the bottle, and forces him to face up to some things:

"What's happened to you is that you've left Susan inside, and you've let me inside. Before us you were invulnerable. You were compassionate but safe, you understand? You could set those standards for your own behavior and if other people didn't meet those standards it was their loss, but your integrity was..."—he thought for a minute—"...intact. You weren't disappointed. You didn't expect much from other people and were content with the rightness of yourself."

I leaned my forehead against the cold window glass. I was drunk.

"And now?" I said.

"And now," Paul said, "you've fucked it up. You love Susan and you love me."

I nodded with my forehead still against the window. "And the rightness of myself is no longer enough."

"Yes," Paul said. He took a large swallow of whiskey. "You were complete, and now you're not. It makes you doubt yourself. It makes you wonder if you were ever right. You've operated on instinct and the conviction that your instincts would be right. But if you were wrong, maybe your instincts were wrong. It's not just missing Susan that's busting your chops." (72-73)

## 78  No Less a Man

As Susan herself says over the phone in *Valediction* (1984), "Everything you've achieved you've achieved through strength, through force, through will. This you can't force. This you have to permit" (217). A simple little word, "permit"—but how difficult for a man like Spenser to accept. Mitigating the strength, the force, the will that (he thought) held the whole world together; tampering with his self-control, self-containment, all the protective barriers he has raised against a random and arbitrary world; letting the hard edges of his inner categories go soft, permeable, letting love and need, work and play, interpenetrate any old which way, without forcing them into a formula or mold—that is frightening. But that kind of letting go is the release Spenser needs from his need-driven adherence to the traditional macho code. He has to get past Emerson *and* Frost—past all formulas, past all prescriptions for happiness or integrity. He has to learn how to slip back into life.

Spenser's love for Susan and Paul is a step in the right direction: he has let go of a little control, and pays a salutary price, a potentially therapeutic price, for it when Susan leaves him. The problem is, of course, bigger than Paul understands: before Susan and Paul, Spenser was by no means invulnerable. The high stakes he placed on balancing and self-control made (and continue to make) *any* sympathetic response to another person—not just his love for Susan and Paul—a potent threat to his masculine defenses. But this also means that the potentially therapeutic effect of "invasion"—someone breaking in past his defenses, leaving him vulnerable to the terrifying feelings he is repressing—is closer and more powerful than he thinks too. Susan and Paul are not the only ones who can devastate him, break through his walls, smash his defenses, and leave him vulnerable to change.

Back in *Mortal Stakes*, for example, before he had fixated on Susan, he found himself powerfully drawn to the predicament of Marty Rabb, after Sandy Koufax the second-best major-league pitcher he had ever seen. Marty is caught in a bind: to protect his family from a blackmailer who threatens to go public with a skin flick his wife Linda acted in when she was a prostitute, he has to throw games, give a slugger a fast ball at just the right moment, say, to let the other team win, or even to let the other team score a certain number of runs in a certain inning. This is not only against baseball rules; it breaks the macho code to which Marty has dedicated his life. Spenser tries to play the pragmatist, the relativist, the mature advocate of compromise with ideals—he wants Linda to go public, confess to having been a prostitute and a porn actress—but is utterly caught up in Marty's situation, identifies so thoroughly with Marty that Linda screams at both of them, several times, as "goddamned game-playing children" (118).

As the novel develops, Spenser begins to show signs of wear: wholesale identification with Marty, who is (or feels) caught between a rock and a hard place, is emotionally exhausting for Spenser, and he begins to lose control. "I was getting sick of people yelling at me" (142), he says, modulating his tone carefully. And when he finally comes down to it, when the confrontation he has been spoiling for throughout the novel becomes a reality, he does lose control, beats and nearly kills a man, a tae kwon do black belt named Lester:

A kind of pressure was building in me, and I saw everything indistinctly. I slammed him on the wall and then stepped back and hit him left, left, right, in the face. I could barely see his face how, white and disembodied in front of me. I hit it again. He started to sag. I got hold of his collar with my left hand and pulled him up and hit him with my left and hammered him with my right. His face was no longer white. It was bloody, and it bobbled limply when I hit him. I could feel my whole self surging up into my fist as I hit him. The rhythm of the punches thundered in my head, and I couldn't hear anything else. I was vaguely aware of someone pulling at me and I brushed him away with my right hand. Then I could hear voices. I kept punching. Then I could hear Linda Rabb's voice. The pounding in my head modified a little.

"Stop it, Spenser. Stop it, Spenser. You're killing him. Stop it." (183)

The "whole self" that surges up into his fist probably is not his whole self, but it is a good deal more whole than the carefully controlled wisecracking self-image that has skittered uneasily across the pages of the series so far. When he loses control, a peripheral part of him surges upward, an excluded part, a repressed part, and he is, for a second, more whole than he had been. Because the cold place of masculinity was kept cold by the forcible exclusion of anger, however, that wholeness has to explode past the idealized barriers erected and maintained by self-control, and it finds expression in the form of murderous violence.

This may be the place to address the feminist critique of masculine violence, since this is one of the primary areas in which I want to move through feminist critiques to a profeminist but deeper masculist understanding. Despite the undeniable fact that women too are violent—that female perpetrators commit a substantial number of crimes against persons, for example, and lead the child abuse statistics—it is also unquestionably true that there is an impulse toward violence built into patriarchal masculinity. Susan Brownmiller articulates this masculinity =

violence equation most strongly in *Against Our Will: Men, Women, and Rape*, where she quotes Genghis Khan on a man's "highest job": "'A man's highest job in life,' said the man who practiced what he preached, 'is to break his enemies, to drive them before him, to take from them all the things that have been theirs, to hear the weeping of those who cherished them, to take their horses between his knees, and to press in his arms the most desirable of their women'" (290). "This remains, I think," Brownmiller comments, "the definitive statement of heroic rape: woman as warrior's booty, taken like *their* proud horses. We owe a debt to Genghis for expressing so eloquently the direct connection between manhood, achievement, conquest and rape" (290).

This is a "definitive statement" of the masculinity = violence equation only, it seems to me, for a largely unconscious man like Genghis Khan intent on idealizing and universalizing his desires as "natural" or "normal," or for an angry woman like Brownmiller intent on objectifying men in terms of that universalized "ideal." Neither Genghis Khan nor Susan Brownmiller seems interested in why men do these things, what drives men to violence (and drives them to repress the fact that they are indeed *driven* to it). It is a bare fact, a behavioral pattern like the shrike's habit of impaling its victims on twigs, to be "understood" (if one can call it that) not in the inward terms of motivation but in the purely outward terms of observed repetition.

To say this is not to "blame" either Genghis, who lived in twelfth-century Mongolia, where the quest for inward motivation was not a going concern, or Brownmiller, who is not a man and cannot be expected to know what is going on inside a man's head; if anyone is to blame, it is all of us twentieth-century men who have refused to ask this question with any kind of courage, with any willingness to strip away the protective layers of repression and explore what is really going on inside. But in fact it's not men's "fault" either; it is a function of a repressive social system that systematically encourages repressive idealization, universalization, and objectification, and taboos inquiries into true inward motivations.

Male violence is another function of that system, of course—both violence and its restraint. As I argued in *Ring Lardner and the Other* (chapter six), patriarchy double-binds us, gives us mixed messages: be violent, be nonviolent. Leash and unleash your anger. Destroy and preserve. Rape and do not rape.

In sexual relations, these mixed messages intertwine with the messages patriarchy whispers to women: be sexy and antisex; promise everything, give nothing. The sickening shadow dance of patriarchal sexual skirmishing: the woman promises, the man wants, the woman denies, the man withdraws; the man wants, the woman promises, the man presses, the woman withdraws. Anything to contaminate sexuality with power and fear, dominance and submission. Sexuality is too powerful for patriarchy, too explosive, so it works to defuse it, to mire it in subtle terrorisms that strip it of caring and joy. Rape is in one sense the *failure* of this insidious system of double binds, the breakdown of this delicate balance of pushes and pulls; but it is, of course, implicit in the system. In this sense Genghis Khan's idealized self-description is no longer true of patriarchal masculinity, which is programmed to *control* the impulse to rape; but the monstrous self-control that thwarts rape *contains* in negated form the denied impulse, and so perpetuates it.

Here is where a systemic analysis is liberating, it seems to me: by assigning blame not to the opposite sex, as patriarchy teaches us to do, but to the patriarchal system, to the self-perpetuating ideological socius that programs all of us, men and women alike, in self- and mutually destructive ways, we can begin to move beyond the debilitating recriminations of the battle between the sexes and recognize that we—feminists and masculists—are fighting the same enemy. Patriarchy perverts feminine sexuality by teaching girls and women to use it for conquest without liking it: to lure men to them with the promise of sex, with "sexiness," while taking no pleasure in it and withholding it as long as is practicably possible. Patriarchy perverts masculine sexuality by teaching boys and men to (think we) want it constantly, and to feel anger at any obstacle to the satisfaction of our omnipotent desires: to transform sexual desire into carefully controlled violence. The two undesirable extremes of patriarchal sexuality, the carrot and the stick of our sexual programming, are loving touch and murderous rape; patriarchy's sexual ideal is the middle ground between those two, somewhere in the vicinity of date or spouse rape: just enough violence so that nobody enjoys it. If this sounds extreme, consider that marital sex, the official sexual ideal of Christian patriarchy, was long a form of spouse rape, since women were programmed not to enjoy and never to initiate sexual relations. Husbands were "required" by their patriarchal programming to rape their wives ("just a little") in order to satisfy their all-powerful "desires"— their physical (not emotional) "needs."

Between men, where violence most commonly occurs in the Spenser novels, the patriarchal impulse to violence takes a rather different form. For the macho man, violence is part of the ethos of "self-creation." As Spenser says in the passage from *Looking for Rachel Wallace* that I quoted at the beginning, "the violence is a kind of side-effect, I think. I have always wanted to live life on my own terms" (25), and that means, among other things, being able to fight for what you think is right, and for the right to *do* what you think is right. The macho assumption is that there is a certain right way to do things, but not everybody knows what it is, and those who do don't always act on it, so you have to be prepared to use whatever force you have at your disposal—rhetoric, fists, guns, whatever—to ensure your ability to act right, to "be yourself."

But it is more than that. As Hawk says in *Promised Land*, when Susan claims that Spenser tries to help people and Hawk only wants to hurt them, "Maybe he aiming to help. But he also like the work" (88). He likes the physicality of violence. He likes beating people up. The difference between Hawk and Spenser at this point is mainly that Hawk works for mobsters and beats up normal people who get in debt to the mob, while Spenser works for the normal people who are being pushed by the mob. As Spenser would put it, Hawk works for the bad guys and he works for the good guys. But that moral distinction (which is often difficult to make with any certainty) doesn't change the fact that Spenser *enjoys* violence.

Violence is, after all, a time-honored masculine channel of self-control, a kind of emotional fine-tuning that requires no actual attention to feelings. Spenser and Hawk both used to be boxers and soldiers; and boxing and soldiering are both ways of reducing violence to a science, which is to say, controlling and directing it in the most efficient way possible. If you lose your head in a fight, you cannot fight effectively. Therefore, the usual reasoning runs, to fight effectively you must control yourself. The deeper emotional thinking is just the reverse: to control yourself you need to be able to fight effectively. You need to feel your fists slamming into the other guy's body, to feel the effect of violence, which is to inflict pain on a body that resists your control (your own *and* the other guy's). That is why the thud of fists, or any kind of hand-to-hand combat, is much more satisfying than shooting a gun or, worse (more distanced, more abstracted), dropping napalm. In all forms of violence you are attempting to bring bodies into conformity with controlled mental images, to impose, paradoxical as this sounds, an intellectual order on what you feel is emotional chaos. But only in hand-to-hand combat do you get the satisfaction of feeling the blows strike home with your body, which is the part of you that needs reassuring, needs confirmation of its self-control.

And the paradoxes of this convoluted situation, the need to feel intellectual order imposed physically, also leave room for potentially

## Violence and Need

therapeutic failure: because the body is needed to impose order on itself, because physical violence is needed to quell physical chaos, men get locked into a macho circuit of violent repression and rebellion that can all too easily short itself out. Thus the man who, like Spenser, uses physical violence to impose intellectual order on his own and the world's body leaves himself vulnerable to the body's *escalation* of violence. Spenser tries to control his anger by beating Lester up; but the anger is too powerful to control, and the very same physical and emotional impetus that was directed to the control of anger is suddenly and imperceptibly transformed into the release of anger:

His buddy said, "You are very close to getting yourself in some real hot water, pal."
The anger had enlarged and was working its way up from the pit of my stomach, spreading along my back and shoulders and down my arms. I could feel my face getting hot. I was careful with my voice, easing it out so it was steady.
"This is different business," I said, "from pumping iron. It's a business I'm almost sure to be better at than you are. Don't make a mistake." The muscles in my neck and shoulders were starting to bunch on their own. My whole upper body was tense.
The crew-cut deacon said, "You are going to have to be taught a lesson."
He put his left hand out toward me and I hit him with the back of my right hand as I unfolded my arms. I hit Baldy with the front of the same hand. His sunglasses flew off and the genie was out of the bottle. The energy release was immediate and large. It fed itself and intensified as it enlarged so there was only the welter of fists and elbows and knees and feet and forearms. Only butting heads, only gouging and biting, only force expanding in a kind of ecstasy, a frenzy released.
It was over too soon. A shame in a way to waste the energy. The deacons weren't that good. (*Valediction* 73-74)

That last paragraph is misleading: it was over too soon not because it "wasted" energy, but because it had not yet sufficiently channeled it. All through this novel Spenser has been depressed, clinically depressed, at Susan's absence; and he hopes, as patriarchy teaches him to hope, that violence will bring his inner balance back, his carefully maintained equilibrium between "energy" (Spenser's word here for the passions he needs and fears) and self-control. With low energy, he has no desires, no needs, cares about nothing, and so has nothing to control. He hardly even feels he exists. He *needs* his passions, and passionately needs to control them, to feel a corresponding balancing force. In no sense was it a shame to "waste" the energy; it was an attempt, hugely but only temporarily successful, to *regain* the energy. And restrain it. He breaks one of the deacons' arms and shatters a kneecap, which is fine, just the right intensity of violence—he didn't lose control, didn't almost kill them, as he did Lester in *Mortal Stakes*. It was a controlled frenzy, a carefully balanced ecstasy. The right kind. The macho kind.

The problem is, as Spenser begins to suspect in *Valediction*, this is an unlivable sort of life. Balancing passion and restraint brings order to life; but that order is destructive. If it succeeds, it kills inwardly; if it fails, it explodes and kills outwardly. The macho circuit of repression and rebellion converts all passion into a potential for violence, so that, in place of the mystical slipping into love-and-need oneness that Spenser claims to be striving for, he is pushed ever more irresistably into the self-escalating use of violence to control violence. In the aftermath of *Mortal Stakes* Parker has Susan Silverman try to get Spenser to work it out, understand it, but he gets no further at this point than an awareness of the double-bind that is built into the masculine ideal:

> "I know what's killing him. It's killing me too. The code didn't work."
> "The code," Susan said.
> "Yeah, jock ethic, honor, code, whatever. It didn't cover this situation."
> "Can't it be adjusted?"

"Then it's not a code anymore. See, being a person is kind of random and arbitrary business. You may have noticed that. And you need to believe in something to keep it from being too random and arbitrary to handle. Some people take religion, or success, or patriotism, or family, but for a lot of guys those things don't work. A guy like me. I don't have religion or family, that sort of thing. So you accept some system of order, and you stick to it. For Rabb it's playing ball. You give it all you got and you play hurt and you don't complain and so on and if you're good you win and the better you are the more you win so the more you win the more you prove you're good. But for Rabb it's also taking care of the wife and kid, and the two systems came into conflict. He couldn't be true to both. And now he's compromised and he'll never have the same sense of self he had before."

> "And you, Spenser?"
> "Me too, I guess. I don't know if there is even a name for the system I've chosen, but it has to do with honor. And honor is behavior for its own reason. You know?"
> "Who has it," Susan said, "he that died a Wednesday?"
> "Yeah, sure, I know that too. But all I have is how I act. It's the only system I fit into." (188-89)

To protect yourself against randomness and arbitrariness you have to fit yourself into a system. And to make sure that you are good and protected you have to make the system rigid and unbending: if you adjust it, then it isn't a code any more. "Honor is behavior for its own reason," Spenser says, idealizing. Actually, it is behavior for self-protection, for protection against the inner horror, the monsters of uncertainty and self-doubt, ultimately of infantile emotional needs. Making it seem like its own "reason" is only one way of making it seem inviolable, immutable, a hard-and-fast given.

The problem is, of course, that life is too complicated for any system. It overflows any focus you bring to it. So you have to have, say, two systems: the jock ethic and protecting your family. And they are too simple, too: they overlap, conflict, place each other in question. Men are supposed to be successes at work and good fathers too—and each takes time and mental energy away from the other. At home our wives and children say, "You don't love us, you only love your work, you're never here when we need you." At work our boss and fellow workers say, "If you want to make good here you're going to have to get your priorities straight. You can't stay home with a sick child and be a good employee too." Both demands seem justified; and yet they are often incompatible.

More: this business about "loving" your wife and children. What is love, and how do you know when you've got it? Taught to focus life into codes of behavior, men tend to think of love too as a set of behavioral norms. If I put food on the table, work myself to death to earn a living so my family can eat and live comfortably, then I love them—that is what my father's generation believed. Nowadays it is more complicated. Wives work too, so putting food on the table isn't my job alone. To fulfill my obligations—to prove my "love"—I have to share responsibility with my wife, pick up around the house, fix food, wash dishes, wash and fold clothes, listen to the children's problems, plan social events, etc., etc. "Love" is a collection of demands placed on a man's behavior.

It is facile to say love isn't like that at all—facile, because there is a sentimental tradition that provides us with counterimages of love, images dealing in softness and cuddliness and so on, all images that we associate with women and children. Not with men. It is easy, too easy, to appeal to that other tradition, that feminine tradition, and attack men for not being soft and cuddly—for thinking that love is like success, something you can check off on a checklist—because that other tradition is just another code, another internalized system, one that women have been trying to fight their ways out of for centuries, and are just now beginning to succeed. If men could truly make the shift to that system they would be no better off than before; they would be equally trapped. What is needed is not a counterimage, a countersystem, but a getting-lost, a slippage, a drifting into the periphery where new solutions are to be found.

But that feels profoundly frightening. Self-control may not work perfectly, but it feels like the only solid footing in a slippery, treacherous terrain. And given a choice between uncertain defensive security and an unknown that awakens deep-seated fears, most men will, of course, choose security. Not that they would think of it that way: security is for women and children, not for men. Men don't *need* security; we are strong, autonomous, independent. Survivors. But of course the very need to think that way is motivated by a need for security. Masculine self-control, control of the body against and through violence, is a stay against anger, fear, need—all the feelings that might threaten hard-won stability and security.

Somewhere early on in the series, Spenser seems more or less convinced that it is all working, that he has actually reached that utopian place where he can live life on his own terms. But in the midst of Spenser's overweening self-confidence, in the midst of his attempts to convince himself and others (including us) of his self-reliance, Parker grows gradually aware of this deeper current of failure and need, a scarier current charged with anxiety, insecurity, depression. Spenser has successfully repressed this current, of course, covered it over with such overwhelming certainty that Susan feels suffocated. But awareness of the repressed begins to float to the surface, in Parker's growing sense both that referring right behavior to utopian dreams only moves the central question to a deeper level—why do I feel compelled to do the deed for heaven and the future's sakes?—and that the impossibility of the romantic union of love and need, work and play bespeaks an idealization that is motivated by emotional need (which in turn skews the love/need equation).

Parker begins to explore that current in the three novels where Susan is gone—the time when Spenser is most vulnerable to his anxieties and insecurities. This is also the time, significantly enough, when Parker becomes most intensely interested in *The Great Gatsby*. Not only does he allude to Fitzgerald's novel throughout the three Spenser books that relate Susan's defection (and here and there before them, as in *Mortal Stakes*, where Linda says Marty has "lived too long believing in do-or-die for dear old Siwash" [144]), but, in between *The Widening Gyre* and *Valediction*, he rewrites it in a non-Spenser book, *Love and Glory*.[1]

Here, for example, is a passage from *The Widening Gyre*, which begins with a near-quote from Nick Carraway's eulogy to the dead Gatsby and ends by reasserting the impossibility of deviating even slightly from Gatsby's self-destructive course:

"You pay a very high price, as I said last time, for being what you are." [Paul is trying to get Spenser to lighten up.]
I nodded.
"It makes you better than other men," Paul said [a reassurance that Parker is always having Paul and Susan give Spenser]. "If you hadn't been what you are, where would I be? But it also traps you. Machismo's captive. Honor, commitment, absolute fidelity, the whole myth."
"Love," I said. "Love's in there."
"Of course it is, and, if need be, to love pure and chaste from afar. But, damn it, I'd like to see you get more back."
"Me too," I said.
"I don't mean from Susan. I mean from life, for chrissake. You deserve it. You deserve everything you want. You have a right to it." [Every liberal hero does; deserving everything you want is part of the myth.]
I drank the rest of my drink and made another one.
"I am what I am, kid. Not by accident. By effort, a brick at a time. I knew what I wanted to be and I finally am. I won't go back." [How about going forward?]
"I know," Paul said. "You can't even talk about things like this unless you're drinking."
"I can," I said. "But unless I'm drinking, talking about things like this seems pointless. I can't be what I am and love Susan differently."
"And you won't be something else?"
"I worked too hard to be this," I said. (160-61)

Like Gatsby (and Boone Adams), Spenser not only invests but *incarnates* himself in a woman: for all three the beloved woman is the significant scene and occasion of self-creation, the screen onto which the motivation, execution, and validation of Platonic self-incarnation is projected. "He talked a lot about the past," Nick says of Gatsby, just after Gatsby has declared his intention to repeat it, "and I gathered that he wanted to recover something, some idea of himself perhaps, that had gone into loving Daisy. His life had been confused and disordered since then, but if he could once return to a certain starting place and go over it all slowly, he could find out what that thing was...." (113), a quest not unlike Parker's in these novels. Nick, the voice of responsible adulthood in Emerson's formulation (split off from Gatsby, the Emersonian adolescent), will not go as far as Gatsby, or Spenser: Gatsby, he says, only wants to recover some idea of himself. For the self-creating liberal hero, it is much more than that: it is rebirth from the womb of the beloved-as-symbolic-mother.

The important first step in trying to understand this romantic automaieusis, this liberal self-incarnation in and from the body of the beloved, is a feminist critique such as the ones launched by Susan Silverman and Rachel Wallace. It is only a first step, and must be followed by a masculist critique that explores why the woman takes on such importance for the macho man; but as a first step a reading like Judith Fetterley's of Gatsby is trenchant:

> This investment of self in Daisy means, of course, that Gatsby needs Daisy to validate him. Since everything is done for her, she must be worthy of this investment in her and she must provide a response commensurate to it. The ritual of validation is the last of the symbolic functions Daisy performs for Gatsby. Gatsby will have his great reunion with Daisy only at his house or, if that is impossible, then next door to it, for he does not wish to see *her* but rather for her to see what he has done *for* her, as if only through her eyes will his vision of himself be made real. The same implicit demand is there when he spills out before her his wealth of gorgeous shirts: they are deployed to exact tribute from her. It is no wonder that Daisy cries. What response could possibly be adequate to this demonstration? Her tears are an understandable reaction at once to the pathos in the demonstration and to the pressure on her to be valuable enough to validate the identity so painfully set before her.
> But it is impossible for anyone to be this valuable, and so Daisy is inevitably inadequate to Gatsby's vision. Daisy can't help but fail Gatsby, because such failure is inherent in the terms of his quest; or, to put it in terms of the pattern I am developing, the investment of the romantic imagination is prelude to the divestment of moral indignation because the one creates the conditions for the other. (76-77)

If, as I am going to suggest, the romantic investment and indignant divestment of masculine self in the woman is a response to the man's fearful and needy (and therefore thoroughly repressed) sense that he has lost his mother—the all-powerful figure from childhood who seemed to promise all but could not deliver—then perhaps the tone of moral indignation toward men that characterizes Fetterley's book, and much feminist rhetoric, is caught up in the same emotional dynamic, but in reverse. The woman who as a child invested herself romantically in her father grows up to find him woefully inadequate and divests herself indignantly from him, attacks him as cold and distant and unloving, or as an oppressor. Thus such tonal polemic as Fetterley's claim that Gatsby shows Daisy his shirts in order to "exact tribute" from her. My own reading of the passage, as a man, is that Gatsby is *begging* tribute from her (actually, he is begging for love), like a little boy from his mommy. But, just as Fitzgerald projects a distant, love-withholding mother-image on Daisy, Fetterley projects an aloof, authoritarian, judgmental father-image onto Gatsby. The dynamic of romantic investment and indignant divestment that Fetterley so brilliantly explores plagues both genders, and the resulting hostility that appears as misogyny among men often masquerades among women as radical feminist rhetoric.

I am not, let it be noted, arguing here that feminist attacks on cold, aloof, authoritarian men are invariably motivated by women's divestment from the father: certainly under conditions of patriarchy men often are cold, aloof, and authoritarian, partly because they are programmed to live up to that sort of ideal, partly because patriarchy gives them no emotional tools for dealing with the impossible demands emotionally deprived women make on them. I will be looking at some authoritarian fathers in my sections on Rambo and Springsteen, and exploring the emotional reasons behind authoritarianism and some possibilities for breaking out of it there. All I am really saying at this point is that the tendency of some feminists to associate *all* masculinity, all men, with patriarchal authoritarianism is a defensive reaction that is probably related to the tendency of some men to associate all femininity with impossible emotional demands.

In any case, the congruence of Fetterley's feminist critique of Gatsby with Rachel Wallace's feminist critique of Spenser shows clearly that in writing the Spenser novels Parker is aware not only of the immense attraction the Gatsby figure holds for him as a macho man, but also of the frightening validity of feminist attacks. Here, for example, is Rachel Wallace's articulation of Spenser's macho pride after he has beat up some men that were harassing her:

"Back there you embodied everything I hate," Rachel said. "Everything I have tried to prevent. Everything I have denounced—machismo, violence, that preening male arrogance that compels a man to defend any woman he's with, regardless of her wishes and regardless of her need."

"Don't beat around the bush," I said. "Come right out and say you disapprove of my conduct."

## 90  No Less a Man

"It demeaned me. It assumed I was helpless and dependent, and needed a big strong man to look out for me. It reiterated that image to all those young women who broke into mindless applause when it was over."

We were in front of the Ritz. The doorman smiled at us—probably pleased that I didn't have my car.

"Maybe that's so," I said. "Or maybe that's a lot of theory which has little to do with practice. I don't care very much about theory of the long-range consequences to the class struggle, or whatever. I can't deal with that. I work close up. Right then I couldn't let them drag you out while I stood around."

"Of course from your viewpoint you'd be dishonored. I'm just the occasion for your behavior, not the reason. The reason is pride—you didn't do that for me, and don't try to kid yourself."

The doorman's smile was getting a little forced.

"I'm sure you would," Rachel said, "but you'll have to do it with someone else. You and I are terminated. I don't want you around me. Whatever your motives, they are not mine, and I'll not violate my life's convictions just to keep your pride intact."

She turned and walked into the Ritz. I looked at the doorman. He was looking at the Public Garden. "The hell of it is," I said to him, "I think she was probably right."

"That makes it even worse," he said. (82-83)

As Spenser discovers in conversation with Susan Silverman in the next chapter, his problem was that he simply *could not* let Rachel be dragged out. His body wouldn't let him. It was not an intellectual or reflective decision. It had nothing, or very little, to do with what people would think. It was a deep-seated impulse. It probably, in fact, despite what both Rachel and Susan insist, had little to do with vanity, or pride. Spenser tentatively accepts the pride diagnosis at this point, but it doesn't ring right. There might have been pride in beating up a physical equal, a sense that Spenser had proved his toughness; but the men he throws around are nothing like his physical equals. He removes them from Rachel like children, and there is no pride in beating up children. There might have been pride in defending Susan Silverman against a slur that somehow implicated him, like Vic Harroway's saying "Take your slut and get your ass out of here, or I'll bend you into an earring" (87), in *God Save the Child*. Not only is Harroway Spenser's physical equal, he is implying that Spenser runs around with sluts, and *that* hurts Spenser's pride.

There is none of that in the scene with Rachel Wallace. Neither Spenser's competitive spirit nor his vanity is involved. What drove him

## Violence and Need 91

to do what he did? The only adequate explanation is that it has something to do with *need*—emotional and physical need, an emotional need that is expressed somatically (a felt impulse to act) and must be released physically. A fear of some sort, a fear of losing something important if he doesn't act in a certain way. This tentative interpretation is given added credence when Spenser rescues Rachel Wallace from her kidnappers (see? the threat was real! I *was* right to respond as I did!) and bursts into tears. Pride is surface: how do I look in the mirror? This, Spenser's emotional investment in Rachel's well-being, is deep shit.

And if we bring this idea that Spenser is afraid of losing something that is vitally important but deeply repressed to bear on the whole Spenser series, the deep shit starts turning up everywhere. The death of Candy Sloan in *A Savage Place* is the most obvious place: her murder, which Spenser was powerless to prevent, devastates him almost beyond repair. In *Valediction*, while Susan is away, he falls sort of in love with Linda Thomas, and is at the movies with Linda when the mob try to hit him:

> "I'm scared," she said. "I'm so scared I can barely stand up."
> "I'm sorry," I said. "But I want to keep you with me."
> "Because why?" she whispered.
> I shook my head. I remembered another rainy day. In Los Angeles. When I had blundered through an oil field. Looking for Candy Sloan.
> Linda's voice became more insistent, and her whisper was louder. "Because *why*?" she said.
> "I'm not going to lose you too," I said. (180-81)

Note the intensity of Spenser's fear. This is not pride. It is gut-level terror, a terror of loss. He is afraid he has lost Susan, which forces him to direct all his emotional energy into balancing, staying on a more or less even keel. When the mob strikes in *Valediction* and Linda is present, therefore, he is unusually vulnerable to his fears—and the first thing he thinks of is the loss of Candy Sloan. Why was losing her so important? In *A Catskill Eagle*, after Spenser has rescued Susan from Russell Costigan, she tells him what drove her over the edge, made her leave:

> "When you came back from California and asked more from me, needed me to help you recover from failure, needed the support of a whole person, there wasn't enough of me for the job."
> I sat without moving in the imitation leather armchair across from her.

She stood again and went to the kitchen and got a glass of water and drank a third of it and put the partly full glass on the counter. She came to the entry between the kitchen and the living room and leaned against the entry wall and folded her arms.

"You did help," I said.

"No. I was the thing you used to help yourself. You projected your strength and love onto me and used it to feel better. In a sense I never knew if you loved me or merely loved the projection of yourself, an idealized..." She shrugged and shook her head. (261-62)

Another way of saying that would be: "I never knew if you loved me or just needed me, needed the certainty of my love, my being-there." The idealized projection of himself that Spenser needs is an image of himself as loved by Susan: a man who doesn't *need* love, doesn't *need* the comfort of a woman's support and affection and companionship, because he already *has* it.

Something like this need to deny need seems also to underlie Spenser's self-image as a "catcher in the rye," as he describes himself to Susan in *God Save the Child* (128), when they hardly know each other. He is a middle-aged Holden Caulfield, anxiously standing in the rye field, trying to rescue a few of the children who are running desperately over the cliff. The superficial explanation of this need is paternalism, which Susan accuses Spenser of, and which, as Spenser himself says in *Promised Land*, is "hard to shake" (162). "You also can't be everybody's father" (80), Susan tells him earlier in the novel.

But being an over-protective father is only the adult male's way of coping with the inner feeling of being an anxious, insecure son—a son afraid that mommy is going to go away. There is very little textual evidence to go on here, but what evidence there is suggests that Spenser is driven by a need for his mother—a need to find his missing mother and protect her forever from the forces that once made her go away. This speculation takes us well past Parker's own fictive self-analysis— perhaps too far. My last chapter in part one, like my last chapter in part three, delves into the most heavily guarded depths in any man's soul, the land of the strongest and most frightening taboos: the mother. If I have to rely almost entirely on speculative reading here, that is largely because Parker (like Springsteen in part three) respects the maternal taboos too well to chart out a textual path past them—but also, inevitably, because I too am a man and must overcome my own maternal taboos in order to write anything at all.

# Chapter Four

# The Missing Mother

In *A Catskill Eagle* Parker adds a new wrinkle to the Spenser story. After knowing Susan for over a decade, Spenser finally gets around to telling her a rather significant fact about his childhood: he never knew his mother. She died in an accident, he says, when she was nine months pregnant with him, and he was removed from her womb surgically shortly after her death. He was raised by his father, who never remarried, and his two uncles—the three of them owned and ran a carpentry shop.

This is a bizarre story. In fact, considering that back in *God Save the Child* Spenser keeps "thinking about the American chop suey my mother used to make and how I felt after I had eaten it" (140), one is almost tempted to dismiss it, to discount it as typical hardboiled detective patter, as a cynical or flip or even defensive (but untrue) remark. This won't work. Spenser tells Susan the story in a context of extreme seriousness. He also tells Hawk earlier that he doesn't remember his mother, that he was raised by his father and uncles (99), and confirms and exfoliates the story throughout *Pastime*, several novels later. The missing mother is an authentic addition to or amendment of Spenser's biography.

My guess is, however, that it is defensive at another level: that it somehow reflects, and perhaps attempts to at once hide and explore, Parker's own anxious feelings of need for his mother.[1] The claim that Spenser was torn from his dead mother's body reads to me like a kind of traumatic ideal, an extreme fictional enactment of Parker's feeling that his mother was absent or distant, that he didn't get enough of his mother's love. Susan says, "So in some sense you never had a mother," and Spenser replies, "Un huh. Not of woman born" (335).

That might, in fact, be reassuring: if you never had a mother, you would feel no need for one. On the other hand, consider the circumstances. Spenser was raised by three men—a purely masculine upbringing. All three were carpenters, lower-middle-class craftsmen-entrepreneurs, men who worked with their hands, men who filled their work with the playful pleasure of making things. His father never remarried, which, in the absence of other information, implies one or more of several possibilities. (1) He didn't like women, their manipulating, engulfing ways, their emotions, their demands on time and feeling. (2) He idealized his dead wife and could never find another woman who could match his ideal image. This is perfectly compatible with 1, in fact; idealizing a dead person is, as Parker reminds us in *Pale Kings and Princes*, a common way of dealing with the guilt of never having liked him or her. (3) He finds the company of men, his brothers and only son, sufficient and satisfying. This is similarly compatible with the other two; finding complete satisfaction in the company of men is a traditional masculine way of withdrawing from the oppressive company of idealized but demanding women. (4) He was the kind of man who was too passive to pursue a woman, and didn't happen to get pursued by one himself. This too fits: the idealization of women does make men timid around them, and timidity can be a powerful ally of dislike in motivating the idealization in the first place.

Suppose, then—and this is all speculation, following my own instincts past the actual information Parker gives us—that Spenser was raised in roughly this environment. His father's defensive idealization of his wife, Spenser's dead mother, would have created a hole in Spenser's perception of the world, a negated image called "mother" that he would have to spend his whole life trying to fill, with girlfriends that he loves too much but doesn't want to marry (because marrying them as his father did his mother would leave him vulnerable to losing them through death?), and with female clients that he needs to find and rescue and protect too intensely, so that he goes to pieces if he fails, and almost goes to pieces if he almost fails. That hole would generate a pressing need to "find" his mother, "rescue" her from the dark place she has gone. If his father was in fact passive and timid, that would add intensity to Spenser's desperate search: his father didn't look hard enough; he, Spenser, will have to look even harder.

In addition, though this ventures onto hotly disputed ground, it is at least plausible to insist that Spenser had already bonded with his mother in the womb, through a somatic introjection of her emotional states (fear, anxiety, happiness, etc.). If our experience of the world begins not at birth but at conception—or at some magical point between conception and birth—then Spenser is born with a somatized sense of loss. What is less open to dispute is the birth trauma Spenser must have suffered: being removed surgically from the womb of a woman fatally injured in an automobile accident would have left massive emotional scar tissue in

# The Missing Mother 95

Spenser's psyche. Medical science is just now, as Thomas Verny shows in *The Secret Life of the Unborn Child*, beginning to explore the impact on later affective life of this sort of natal and prenatal trauma; it is simply not the case, as we have believed until very recently, that the fetus enters the world a blank slate, unwritten on by experience. Spenser would have entered the world shaped powerfully and indelibly both by his intrauterine bond with his mother and by the violent severing of that bond in the car crash that killed her.

It is significant, in fact, that the literary text Spenser starts quoting obsessively in *A Catskill Eagle* and the next two novels is Wallace Stevens's "Sunday Morning." His favorite image for what Susan is to him also comes from Stevens, in "The Anecdote of the Jar"—reality always coalesces around her for him, another indication that she is an attempt to fill the hole left in him by his lack of a mother[2]—but "Sunday Morning" is a rather more anxious affair. In *A Catskill Eagle* he quotes the famous line that Stevens gives us twice, "Death is the mother of beauty" (258), and in *Pale Kings and Princes* Susan quotes it back at him just after alluding to the Frost poem about mortal stakes (169); in *Double Deuce* Susan uses it to deconstruct Spenser's cautious argument in favor of them living apart ("'That's an intellectual conceit and you know it,' Susan said. 'No one ever espoused that when death was at hand'" [44]). Earlier in *Pale Kings and Princes* (140-41) Parker quotes the first five lines:

> Complacencies of the peignoir, and late
> Coffee and oranges in a sunny chair,
> And the green freedom of a cockatoo
> Upon a rug mingle to dissipate
> The holy hush of ancient sacrifice. (66-67)

In *Ariel and the Police*, Frank Lentricchia offers a persuasive reading of this poem in terms of Stevens's fear that writing poems feminized him—his anxiety at not doing something more masculine with his life, like making money. Or rather, not *only* doing something more masculine with his life: his work as vice president of a bank in Hartford, Connecticut, was, Lentricchia argues, an attempt to please his father, a "successful lawyer, small businessman, and a poet himself (the first Wallace Stevens, as it were)" (140). Here is part of Lentricchia's reading of the lines that Spenser quotes (while relaxing from his frustrating work in the comfort of Susan's apartment):

## 96 No Less a Man

A pet cockatoo (whether female or male, the sound of freedom is phallic, cocky: it will become transformed, later in the poem, into the sound of men chanting naked in a ring), a pet cockatoo upon a rug is a bought bird in captivity. Not so much an ironic bird as a pathetic one. The pet cockatoo, like those roses in the rug, is a sign of a relation to nature that expresses androgynous desire (peignoired and pipe-smoking Wallace Stevens) for the green freedom of an impossible natural autonomy. In Stevens' middle-class settings of freedom, "green freedom" represents maximum desire. (153)

Spenser's too: not only is he sick of the small-town industrial wasteland in which *Pale Kings and Princes* is set, and powerfully drawn to visions of natural autonomy, green freedom; he associates the maternal comfort he feels in Susan's apartment *with* that green freedom. It is Sunday, they sleep till 10:30, make lazy love, wonder what to do with the rest of the day. But in order to make the connection between natural autonomy and his bondage to Susan in love, he has to keep doing his careful balancing act:

"One of the best things I like best about you," she said, "is how earnest you are about your work. You pretend to be such a wise guy, and you are so rebellious about rules; but you are so careful to do what you say you'll do."
"There's not much else to be careful about," I said.
"Post Christian ethics," she said.
"I'm careful about you," I said.
She cut a wedge of cornbread and transferred it carefully to her plate.
"Yes," she said, "about me, and about us."
"You too," I said.
"We've both learned to be careful of us," she said.
We looked at each other. The connective force of our gaze was palpable.
"Forever," I said finally.
Susan nodded. (142-43)

Five *carefuls* in the time it takes to turn the page: *this* is freedom? This is the mystical unity of love and need? Lentricchia notes the way the woman of "Sunday Morning," like Stevens himself, is "surrounded by things that have been refined, picked, caught, shipped, fashioned: representations of nature drained of their naturalness," and comments:

In "Sunday Morning" Stevens imagines two forms of liberation from that kind of production, both forms perfectly suited to the needs of a secular middle-class poet. His first imagination of liberty is offered in the second section of the poem

## The Missing Mother 97

under a definition of "divinity" [cf. Emerson's and Frost's formulas for right action]; the second is offered in the seventh section as a vision of community. The first form of liberation is offered as resolution for the peignoired woman; the second is offered presumably for the peignoired woman's desire for paradise, but the community imagined is homogeneously male [like Spenser's household as a child] and in some sense homosexual. Both forms of liberation are utopian: they are offered as the possible, in future tense; both imagine perfection in sensuous, erotic, and natural settings, which make some sense as an American aesthete's religion of nature, but even better sense if read as visions of return to the physical world from an impoverished, oddly unreal, sometimes neurasthenic, and oddly uncomfortable Prufrockian middle-class existence. (154-55)

Spenser's utopia, my guess is, would be a return to his mother: her recovery from the dark place to which she has been taken before Spenser's birth, and perhaps even his restoration to the dark place from which he was taken after her death, her womb. This is the physical world of natural autonomy Spenser secretly longs for: union with his mother. Transformation of the "impoverished, oddly unreal, sometimes neurasthenic, and oddly uncomfortable Prufrockian middle-class existence" that he had with his father and uncles into a "ring of men" who, "supple and turbulent," "shall chant in orgy on a summer morn / Their boisterous devotion to the sun" (69-70), is one answer, but for Spenser not a very good or lasting one. The companionship of men (Hawk, for instance), with all its barely suppressed homoerotic overtones, is good, but insufficient. The only satisfactory solution is recovery of the dead mother. As Stevens says in section six of the poem, in the lines just preceding the vision of the naked ring of men:

Death is the mother of beauty, mystical,
Within whose burning bosom we devise
Our earthly mothers waiting, sleeplessly. (69)

When Spenser quotes those first six words in *A Catskill Eagle*, he glosses them thus: "The possibility of loss is what makes things valuable" (258). I read this as an anxious translation of: "The fact of loss—the loss of my mother—is what makes things frighteningly fragile, and therefore *too* valuable to sustain my need." Significantly, Stevens's own mother died three years before he wrote the poem in 1914; and Lentricchia comments on the three lines above in terms of a biographical "eruption" into the poem:

Stevens' biography here erupts into the poem, making him speak against his poem's male/female contest of voices, making him conceive his readers as radically like him—an audience composed wholly of bereft children, specifically of bereft males, sons who have all lost their mothers and who are all projecting their mothers on the other side of death waiting for them in transcendental space, worrying, refusing to sleep until they (we) come safely home. I read the aphorism "Death is the mother of beauty" in its second appearance this way: My mother's death is the mother of beauty, my mother's death is itself a mother—a substitute mother that shocks me, as all death must, into cherishing the earth. My mother's death is therefore the birth of my imagination, the necessary angel of earth, yes, but I have only one mother and this substitute does not suffice. I need to see her again, my real mother, whose death enabled the birth of my poems, knowing that I cannot. So I will invent her there, "devise" her waiting for me—in heaven, site of all enduring love. The full-throated phallic song of earth (section 7) follows, now all the more powerfully when we see what it is that Stevens is trying to forget. (175-76)

Stevens has the advantage over Spenser of having lost his mother only three years before, at the age of 33; he can deal with his mother's death as an adult, with the intellectual (and poetic) tools of an adult. Spenser lost his mother before he was born, and looking for her means, at some deep level of his imagination, breaking taboos, crossing uncrossable lines, pushing deep into his earliest memories, and beyond, before his birth. No wonder his search for Susan in *A Catskill Eagle* is increasingly suffused with a pervasive feeling of dread, culminating when he walks down the pitch-dark tunnel into the remodeled mine where Russell Costigan's father Jerry is hiding. Killing Jerry, the monster at the center of the labyrinth, doesn't restore Spenser's mother, or give him peace of mind; in *Taming a Sea-Horse* he retains only a nagging guilt at all the killing he had to do to rescue Susan, and the carefulness about their love that I discussed before. This is not much return on a dangerous journey into a mythically laden symbol for the uterine place his mother disappeared.

In the two novels that follow that descent, in fact, Spenser's strongest feeling is of frustration, a sense of being shut out, locked out of the community of knowledge: April Kyle disappears again and her disappearance is shrouded in a mystery that reeks of taboo (anyone Spenser asks about her gets killed); the town Spenser is investigating the murder of a reporter in snubs him so thoroughly that he feels like a leper: "Everybody knew me. Nobody liked me. Nobody talked to me.

Everybody avoided me. I'd been unpopular before in my life, but never with this kind of heady pervasiveness. People who'd never met me disliked me" (51).

This is, in fact, precisely how the middle-class child feels, surrounded by adults who all know something but refuse to tell him (like the fact that his mother is dead). It is also how the patient in therapy feels, trying to dig past the taboos of resistance to the earliest memories. Parker does no Spenserian self-analysis in these two novels; in fact, they are almost aggressively formulaic. But the *feeling* of both novels, their emotional undercurrent or mood, is revealing: it is the dread that comes from having approached too close to a taboo. It is, I am guessing, the dread that comes from having realized the importance, in *A Catskill Eagle*, of never having had a mother. Parker got close to the mystery, but his very proximity scared him and he backed off.

In *Crimson Joy*, which for me is his most courageous novel to date, Parker pushes back into the vicinity of the dark land beyond the taboos. The novel is really about mothers, overwhelming, engulfing mothers, and their effect on their sons: the villain of the piece, the serial killer who abducts middle-aged black women, ties them up, masturbates, kills them, and leaves a rose between their breasts, is emotionally tied to a demanding but ungiving mother named Rose Mary Black, nicknamed Blackie (to whom his father always used to bring red roses after he had been with a black prostitute; his father took him once to a middle-aged black prostitute who intimidated him so much he couldn't get an erection, and she teased him for it). When he was small his mother molested him, and warned him against girls: they would eat him alive, take him for everything he had (which is to say, as Susan, his analyst, makes him see, take *him* away from *her*).

The novel is really more a psychological thriller (as *A Catskill Eagle* was more a political thriller) than a hardboiled detective novel: the main detective work done is literally psychoanalytic, as Susan tries to figure out which of her clients it might be, and, since she refuses to tell Spenser the results of her ruminations, as Spenser tries to figure out why Susan is being so stubborn. The one psychological question that doesn't get asked, however—and would have been asked relentlessly back in *Mortal Stakes* or *Promised Land* or *Looking for Rachel Wallace*, when the answers Parker was finding to his questions concerned fairly safe things like paternalism and pride, or even as late as *The Widening Gyre* and *Valediction*, before the discovery of the significance of the mother in *A Catskill Eagle*—is the one that interests me most: What does Gordon Felton's fixation on his mother tell us about Spenser himself?

We learn from Felton's ex-wife, for instance, that he wouldn't go anywhere alone, without her—he was intensely fixated on her, like a mother (145). This most obviously recalls Aaron Newman of *Wilderness*, and Boone Adams of *Love and Glory*, before he restores his self-control; but it unmistakably recalls Spenser as well. Spenser can function without Susan, but not very well; it takes all his concentration and self-control to keep from falling apart during the two years and three novels Susan is away. Felton kills the women he selects to symbolize his mother, while Spenser saves them; but the intensity of their involvement with the women is almost identical. Felton is a security guard who dreams of being a cop; Spenser is an ex-cop who dreams of absolute freedom. When Spenser and Susan burst in on Felton and his mother, Felton finally confesses to being the Red Rose killer, and finally also gets the courage to tell his mother off, prompting in Spenser a telling response:

"Just fuck off, will you. You been saying how you stood on your fucking head for me all my fucking life and I don't want to hear it anymore. Dr. Silverman knows. You stood me on my head. You didn't love me. You never loved anybody. You loved me when I did stuff you liked and didn't love me when I did stuff you didn't like, and none of it had any logic. You frigid bitch, you ruined my life, that's what you did."

I felt like cheering, except it was too late. (193)

Too late to be therapeutic—Gordon has already killed four women. But the liberating act of confronting and releasing his anger toward his mother strikes a powerfully sympathetic chord in Spenser: is it too late for him too? He has killed no women, but the rage Gordon feels for his mother is in Spenser too; it is only through iron self-control that he keeps it in, keeps it under restraint. Gordon too works at self-control, and knows all too well the high price of losing it. Here, for example, is one of the italicized passages that Parker writes to give us the killer's thoughts, the first time another narrative consciousness has ever been introduced into these novels alongside Spenser's (a technical parallel that also links Felton and Spenser):

*"...I was hers all the time I was a kid," he was saying.*
*"Her what?" the therapist [Susan] said.*
*"What do you mean, 'her what'? I was her son."*
*The therapist nodded.*

*He wanted to say more about what he was.* "I was her only child, you know, she worried about me all the time."

"How do you know she worried?" *the shrink said.*

*Christ, couldn't she figure anything out?* "She said so," *he said,* "and when I did stuff that worried her she'd get, like, sick."

"Sick?" *the therapist said.*

"Yeah, she'd lie on the couch and not talk all day and her face would have this look, like she was having cramps or something. You know, like broads get when they're having their period." *He felt the tingle of daring and guilt when he said it.*

"Like mean, you know. Bitchy."

"What does bitchy mean to you?" *the shrink said.*

"It means crabby, it means, you know, not talking to you, being mad at you, not...not loving you. Not being nice to you."

*The shrink nodded.*

"If I'd come home late for supper or hang around with the guys or go out." *He could feel the tightening in his throat and the way his nose began to tingle.*

"Go out?" *the shrink said.*

"With girls," *he said. His eyes were filling. He felt himself burning with frustration and shame.* "She told me that every girl was going to take me for all they could get." *He fought the hot crying. He turned his head.*

*The shrink said,* "Let it come. Let's see what comes with it."

*Like hell. He wasn't going to cry here. His mother had never caught him crying. He held his head down and forced his breath in and out. In his groin he could feel the pressure.*

"I can control myself," *he said.*

"Always?" *the shrink said.*

*He felt a trill of fear.*

"Absolutely," *he said.*

"You lose control," *he said,* "you lose yourself."

*The shrink waited.*

"You get controlled," *he said.* "You don't control yourself, people control you."

"Then they could take you," *the shrink said,* "for all they could get."

*He wanted to speak and couldn't. He felt as if he'd pushed something aside. He felt shaky now. Deep breath. Let it out. His arm muscles were bunched, and he pressed with his elbows against the arms of the chair.*

"My mother always used to say that," *he said.*

*The shrink nodded.* (50-51)

## 102   No Less a Man

The only significant difference between Gordon's self-control here and Spenser's in *Valediction* is that Gordon is more willing to talk about his mother. In one sense, of course, his problem is easier: he had an overwhelming, engulfing mother to talk about. How do you talk about a mother you never knew? But in another sense it is more difficult. The tabooed double binds of love and fear, incest and sexual loathing, build the walls higher than any mere absence. The telling point is that it is easier to see the connection between *someone else's* fixation on his mother and self-destructive behavior than it is to see your own: the taboos that obscure that fixation in your own head reveal it, by projection, in another man.

Parker is coming right up to the problem, here, standing right next to it, closer than he has in any of the previous novels—his creation of Gordon Felton signals that he is subliminally aware of the striking parallels between Spenser and Gordon—but then backing away again. At the end, for example, Spenser has chased Felton down the beach, finally caught up to him, and submitted to being *embraced* by him: Felton holds him tight and cries, sobbing "Papa, Papa." This is something like the longing for a paradisical community of men that Stevens wrote into "Sunday Morning"—and it is something that, thinking back, Spenser probably wanted to do with Hawk in *Valediction*, but was too embarrassed to. In any case, in the rehash with Susan, Spenser expresses some sympathy for Felton, and Susan fails to pick up on it:

When she was gone I said to Susan, "I feel kind of bad for Felton."
   Susan said, "Yes."
   "I feel even worse for the women he murdered."
   "Yes," Susan said again. "How about his mother?"
   "That's hard," I said.
   "But not impossible," Susan said. "Think how desperately she's had to manipulate her life without any power but the uses of love."
   "And all for naught," I said. "Her reputation will be smirched anyway."
   "Cruel," Susan said.
   "Well, I never had a mother," I said. "Probably makes me insensitive."
   "Probably," Susan said, "but you've got strong loins. It makes up for a lot." (207-08)

Susan and Spenser's sexy-cutesy repartee has never been less funny than that last remark. Spenser's skill or strength at lovemaking, or whatever the "strong loins" is supposed to refer to, only makes up for his "insensitivity" about Felton's mother if Susan is willing to help Parker unsee the monsters that are here raising their ugly heads. Spenser feels sympathy for Felton for the same reason he cheers when Felton tells his mother off: because he too feels anger at his mother. His mother was absent, dead, Felton's all-too-alive, all-too-present; but Felton's mother punished him with emotional withdrawal, which is just like dying. Only a little less permanent. Parker-as-Susan is able to feel sympathy for the mother, which Parker-as-Spenser finds hard to do; but Parker-as-Susan is not able to draw the obvious conclusion from Parker-as-Spenser's insensitivity and cruelty.

Still, it seems clear to me that Parker comes closer to the "problem of Spenser" in this novel than he's ever come before. Emotionally the novel is so highly charged that on my first reading I found the suspense almost unbearable. It was like the terrible intensity of sex the moment before orgasm. The orgasmic or, in this case, therapeutic moment in which Spenser comes face to face with what he is most scared of, confronts it, owns it, makes it his, and relaxes into his life, is still deferred; but Parker leaves us with the sense that we are on the very verge: that fulfillment is very near.

It is significant, I think, that Spenser's (and the reader's—at least my own) intensity throughout the novel is largely motivated by Felton's threat to Susan's life. Complexly significant: one way of coming at it would be to see Felton's threat as a symbolic enactment of Spenser's desire to kill his dead mother for leaving him alone, and thus as a reenactment of *Valediction*'s displaced anger at Sherry Spellman, who was foil for the absent Susan Silverman, who was foil for the absent mother. All this is there, surely, and comes under Judith Fetterley's discussion of the romantic investment and indignant divestment of women. But another and I think equally important way to come at the threat against Susan would be to read it as a sign that Parker is contemplating having Susan die. He toyed with the idea of having her just leave, back in *The Widening Gyre* and *Valediction*—walk out of Spenser's life forever, leave him alone with his mother-fixation, leave him to come to grips with his obsession without the support of a focal woman, a woman around whom all reality for him coalesces. But then he brought her back. Even without Susan gone he couldn't bring Spenser across the crucial threshold, the healing threshold of ego-surrender, the letting go of self-control. So maybe, he may have thought, if Susan *died*...

But no. That would be too risky for Parker, who in the four novels since *Crimson Joy* (as in the two before it) has shown no sign of willingness to push Spenser beyond the safety net of his self-control. *Playmates* (1989) and *Stardust* (1990) are potboilers, full of Parker's "resignation" as Spenser's creator, in both senses of the word: resigned to churning out new Spenser novels every year, and resigned from the task he set himself back in the 1970s, to find out what's wrong with the man (and men).[3] *Pastime* (1991) shows some signs of life, but very listless ones: he has Paul Giacomin (now 25) thinking about getting married, worried that he doesn't love Paige as obsessively as Spenser loves Susan, and worried (this is the plot) that his mother has apparently disappeared. Paul and Spenser go looking for her, just as Spenser had apparently gone looking for his mother in *A Catskill Eagle*—a chance to move beyond the terrified displacements of that novel and *Crimson Joy* and deal with "past time," with his birth trauma. But he doesn't, and the past becomes a mere "pastime." No doubt chided by his wife or agent or editor or best friend for not revealing more about Spenser's childhood, Parker segues lamely over and over again into reminiscences of Spenser's rearing by four men; in the process he delivers up some interesting detail but never comes close to the problem of the missing mother. We do get an announcement of the connection between Paul's search for Patty and Spenser's nonsearch for his mother, which is more, really, than we got in *A Catskill Eagle* or *Crimson Joy*—

> "His mother really is missing," I said.
> "His mother has always been missing" [Susan said].
> "Mine too," I said. (49)

—but that is about all it amounts to. Spenser and Paul find Patty, Paul talks to her about his feelings of abandonment, which is probably the real issue here, and she evades his questions—with Spenser standing silently by, neither asking his own questions of Patty nor strong-arming her into answering Paul's (nor, for that matter, reflecting on his own investment in the case, if any). Nor does Susan, the psychotherapist, force Spenser to confront his own fears, his own emotional neediness. Nor is this novel, outwardly at least, in any way fearful or needy. It is very low-key, very offhand. There are only a few pages of suspenseful action, and even then Spenser is pretty casual about the danger he is in. Paul's quest for his mother having ended badly, he comes to Spenser for advice, and gets it more in the form of macho silence than in words:

> "You mean *will*, don't you?" Paul said.
> "Yeah."
> "You mean self-control."
> "Yeah." (116)

And the novel ends with Susan's ritual blessing and absolution of Spenser: "You are the most self-sufficient man I have ever known" (218).

Has Parker failed, then? Has he turned into just another formula writer? Perhaps not; certainly *Double Deuce* breaks some of the stagnant post-*Catskill Eagle* patterns, not only letting Spenser move in with Susan (*very* temporarily—out again by the end of the novel) but providing Spenser (and Hawk) with a new hard questioner to replace the guarded and timid Susan and defunct Rachel Wallace as feminist challenger of macho heroes—Hawk's broadcast journalist romantic attraction, Jackie Raines. As Jackie forces Spenser and Hawk to examine their own motives, especially their defenses against emotion and self-disclosure, the tired formulas start to crumble, and the series wobbles unevenly to its feet. By the end of the novel, however, Jackie has had enough of Hawk's taciturnity, refuses to fall in love with a man who gives so little of himself, and walks out of the series. *Paper Doll*, his most recent novel at this writing, is a crackling good Chandler or Hammett novel, alive with suspense and crisp dialogue; but it has none of the self-exploration, self-awareness of the earlier novels.

Even if the series is losing steam, however—even if Parker has not yet found, and now probably never will find, an answer to the question "What's wrong with Spenser," he is certainly no failure. The Spenser series is a salutary exploration of machismo from the inside, a tentative and hesitant but more or less persistent attempt to crack open the vault that protects the terrified man within. Parker has not "healed" Spenser by any means, and the novels of the late eighties and early nineties seem to be attempts to idealize his sickness by repressing the symptoms; but one man need not have all the answers. Not only do we know more about machismo and its emotional underpinnings for Parker's persistence; we have some idea of the direction in which self-transformation, self-liberation is to be sought.

# Part Two
# *RAMBO*

# Reborn

1. If you don't stop the Com-mies in Vi-et-nam next year they'll be in L. A.

You got-ta stamp out e-vil in the jun-gle son Be a

man and save the U. S. A. Our way 2. Well I

2. Well I proved my manhood on the barricades
   When I was eighteen
   But the walls I manned became the iron cage
   Of my self-esteem
   So clean

3. To be a man, to be yourself
   You fight to keep control
   And the people flock to your success
   But in your gut there's a black, black hole
   No soul

4. Dad fought the Commies, I fought my dad
   But we both fought the same old fight
   We fought to keep a lid on the world
   And stand in a hand-held light
   So bright

5. But what do you do when the ache keeps aching
   And the darkness won't go away?
   What do you do when the black hole keeps on gaping
   In the deadness of the day?
   You pay

6. You pay till there's nothing left to own
   No lid to put on that hole
   You pay till you're broke and on the street
   Cleansed of self-control
   Grown old

7. Now the fog hangs thick like God's confusion
   Before the sky was torn
   But I know in the waters of this decreation
   Something will be reborn
   Forlorn

Copyright 1993 Doug Robinson.

# Chapter Five

# From *First Blood* to *First Blood*

It is easy to forget, in these days of the Rambo myth, associated in every corner of the world with the magnificent physique and droopy eyes of Sylvester Stallone, that Rambo was created in the late 1960s by a skinny graduate student of American literature. The author, David Morrell, was researching a dissertation on John Barth, which was published in 1976 as *John Barth: An Introduction* (and remains today one of the best source books on Barth's work), but he wanted most of all to be a novelist. Morrell and Barth were both at Penn State, and while Morrell was interviewing Barth for the dissertation, he was working at writing fiction with another Penn State professor who wrote science fiction under the pseudonym of William Tenn, Philip Klass. "My stories were very literary and not very good," Morrell told *People* magazine reporter John Stark. But then he tried an action story, and Klass loved it: "That son of a bitch went home and brought me a story that really banged! I was astonished at his talent" (107).

Well, this is commonly known as "lowering your sights." You start off trying to write "serious" fiction, Literature with a capital L, immortal stuff, find you are no good at it, or are afraid you will never make a living at it, so you lower your sights. You "settle" for writing genre fiction instead. Barth told me—another Barth scholar—that he envied Morrell his addition of a new character to the American mythology, but when I told Morrell that over the phone he laughed and said that was ironic, because Barth really didn't think very highly of his action fiction, his thrillers. When Morrell wrote *First Blood*, Barth had already written two reasonably good (and "serious") apprentice novels, *The Floating Opera* (1956) and *The End of the Road* (1958), and two big fat experimental novels that were to become classics of postmodern fiction, *The Sot-Weed Factor* (1960) and *Giles Goat-Boy* (1966). *Lost in the Funhouse* (1968), a collection of experimental short pieces, came out while Morrell was working with Barth on the dissertation; *Chimera* (1972), a collection of three experimental novellas, while he was revising it for publication. By the time *First Blood* appeared Barth had, in other words, already established his reputation as one of the most brilliant new postmodern novelists, and has continued to expand that reputation with big novels like *LETTERS* (1979), *Sabbatical* (1982) and *Tidewater Tales* (1987). Morrell "settled" for writing thrillers.

That, at least, is the usual way of looking at it, at least in English departments, where Morrell and I were both trained. Now suppose we look at it the other way. Barth is right: Morrell has, with the help of Sylvester Stallone and half the movie industry, truly added a new character to the American mythology, another Paul Bunyan, Daniel Boone, Kit Carson, Davy Crockett. This is no mean feat. I also believe that Barth's admiration was sincere: to me he sounded neither patronizing nor pompous, but honestly admiring and envious. Barth is on record as wanting to write more simply and more popularly, for a larger, less academic and specialized audience—and certainly his novels of the 1980s, *Sabbatical* and *Tidewater Tales*, show signs of Barth's attempts to write for a large popular audience.[1]

The usual defense of popular fiction (genre fiction, formula fiction) is, in fact, that it is more "mythic" than elitist fiction; that its popular appeal lies precisely in its ability to tap the deepest mythic experiences of a culture. Hence the myth of Rambo, this line of defense might go. By "settling" for writing thrillers, Morrell was able to tap a mythic vein in the American imagination, and is now 10 or 15 million dollars richer for it.

But this strikes me as only half a defense—the indulgent half, invented and propagated by academics trained in the numbing "science" of literature and nostalgic for a Golden Age of myth. So what if popular fiction is mythic? What good does that do anybody? The myth of Rambo has a good deal to do with American insecurity and self-hatred, with a desire to recover a sense of empowerment after the debacles of Vietnam and Watergate: Sylvester Stallone dropping into Vietnam in *Rambo: First Blood Part II*, all alone against the Vietnamese and the Soviets, salvages some measure of American self-respect. Of course it is a fragile sort of self-respect, really only a fearful defense against anxieties about failure, weakness, and vulnerability, so it has to be propped up again in *Rambo III*, where the American hero goes into a demonized Afghanistan (which looks like Arizona but feels like Nazi Germany) and beats the Russians *again*. Ironically, this movie is released just as Gorbachev is pulling Soviet troops out of Afghanistan; but the historical irony is really irrelevant in the face of mythic American insecurity. The Rambo myth is a shot in the American arm, which is the arm of a junkie hopelessly addicted to hope.

So what good is a myth, I repeat, if it only helps a culture defend itself against growing up? What good is "mythic" popular fiction or cinema if all it offers is a fix for the collective junkie? The other half of the "mythic" defense of popular fiction, it seems to me, must go something like this: the popular writer, in exposing him- or herself to the mythic undercurrents of a culture, opening his or her emotional set to the profoundly frightening things down there, the anxieties and the insecurities of all social life, is placed in roughly the same relation to the culture that a psychotherapist occupies in relation to a patient. A therapist too, like a popular writer, can work to impose traditional, reassuring, i.e. defensive and repressive solutions on the patient—can offer pills or implants to the impotent, sure-fire sexual fantasies to the frigid, Oedipus to the father-tormented son, feminist rage to the father-tormented woman. This sort of therapy is very popular, and the self-help books based on it make a lot of money for their publishers and writers. But like the therapist, the popular writer can also work through the wild things lurking in the emotional dark, engage them directly, smash through culturally sanctioned defenses and confront them therapeutically, and thus begin to work toward a cure.

This therapeutic perspective will allow us, in a moment, to explore the American public's need for a mythic savior like Rambo—someone to help them deal with their feelings of abandonment and betrayal, someone to act out those feelings and then to triumph over them in significantly openended ways. But before I turn to this collective need for and use of Rambo, let me backtrack to his creator, David Morrell, and to the self-therapeutic needs Rambo was an attempt to meet.

In my discussion of the Spenser novels I ended on a note of longing for the absent or distant mother—an unusual, though certainly not unprecedented, note in patriarchal society, where the mother is assigned the role of overwhelmingly and self-sacrificingly present caretaker. These programmed patriarchal roles, absent father, present mother, are no doubt one source of that sense of strangeness I felt in Spenser's story, in the image of Spenser ripped from his dead mother's womb: what lengths must a boy's imagination go to, to explain the absence of the parent he too has been programmed to believe should be overpoweringly there!

If it sounds strange to read that Spenser never knew his mother, however—that she died before he was born—it sounds almost natural to read that David Morrell never knew his father. His father died in his early infancy—was killed in Europe, in World War II, in 1943, before his first birthday. The "naturalness" of this scenario is partly biological, of course: it has its roots in the physiological separation of insemination and parturition. Some societies have never made the connection between genital intercourse and pregnancy. But for whatever reason—it is tempting but perilous to speculate about the origins of patriarchy—this biological gap has almost invariably been widened by society and entered as a norm in the cumulative somatic database of ideology. The father is not needed for childbirth. The father is not needed for childrearing. If the father is needed at all, he is needed to stand outside the tent and guard the precious life within; preferably to hunt far from the hut in order to provide food for the hungry mother and child. He is needed, in other words, to stay away. The bond between the mother and her child is sacred, and therefore taboo, as powerful and terrifying a taboo for modern men as it must have been for primitive men—so powerful, in fact, that the therapeutic breaking of that taboo is for the destructively trained patriarchal son the most difficult step in his gender liberation.

So the patriarchal father is absent, almost by definition; what difference, then, if he is dead? His absence is only more permanent. His absence is normal; indeed, as Morrell suggests in his novels and private conversation, his absence is a blessing for the mother, for it allows her to idealize him, to elevate him above all other men, to make of him the man she wished he had been.

But it does make a difference for his children. Especially the son of an idealized dead man is damaged by his absence. Morrell certainly was; in a 1988 interview he told John Stark of *People* magazine that "The trauma of having my father die has been all through my fiction.... In *Rambo III* the character only springs into action after someone has posed a threat to his foster father, the Green Beret colonel who trained him" (104).

The writer as neurotic: this is the Freudian reading that has proved so attractive to a culture impatient both with art and with therapy. The important point about Morrell's writerly relation to the trauma of having his father die, however, is not that he was damaged by it, but that he has spent his professional life as a writer dealing with it. His claim about the omnipresence of his absent father in his fiction is true, and it is one of the features of his work that lifts it above most formula writing in the genre: Morrell, like Parker in the hardboiled detective novel, uses his work in the thriller as a vehicle for an ongoing process of self-discovery, self-therapy, self-healing.

It is also almost invariably literally true: in virtually every novel he writes Morrell creates male protagonists who have lost their fathers, and whose quests, whatever their ostensible objectives, are at some level always for the lost father. In the recent "Brotherhood" series, for example, a trilogy moving toward a tetralogy,[2] Morrell creates three central male characters who either never knew their fathers or lost their fathers at an early age. In *The Brotherhood of the Rose* (1984), Saul

Grisman and Chris Kilmoonie are orphans: we never hear what happened to Saul's parents, but Chris's father is a military intelligence pilot who is killed on a mission in 1948, five years after Morrell's father's death and three years after Chris's birth. Chris is also abandoned by his mother and placed in an orphanage, as Morrell himself was for a time. In *The Fraternity of the Stone* (1985) Drew MacLane sees his parents killed by a terrorist's bomb at the age of ten, and dedicates his life to avenging that loss by assassinating other terrorists. In the third book in the series, *The League of Night and Fog* (1987), Saul and Drew meet and pursue two groups of missing fathers, one of ex-Nazis, the other of Jews who once escaped from concentration camps. The Jews have abducted the ex-Nazis and are terrorizing their prisoners' sons, in retribution for the *Nacht und Nebel* terrorist tactics practiced by the Nazis in the 1940s, when thousands of Jews simply disappeared into the "night and fog."

*The Fifth Profession* (1990) reads like a book in the same series, begins with the same kind of historical events that set the stage for the novel's action and deals centrally with problems of identity and betrayal; it only lacks the something-of-the-something title and, like *The Covenant of the Flame* (1991), the carry-over characters from the earlier books. In the novel the man we know as Savage is an executive protector whose father committed suicide when he was young, and who got into intelligence and protection as a defense against this early loss of his father. As the novel progresses, we learn with Savage that shadowy forces (who by the end are revealed as Japanese nationalists working in conjunction with the CIA) have performed neurosurgery on him in order to introduce false memories into his mental makeup: he remembers two Japanese men being brutally murdered, but discovers that they are still alive; he remembers himself being beaten so severely that he was nearly killed, and taking six months to recover, but discovers that his surgical scars are only skin-deep. By making every memory unreliable, this neurological reconstruction of Savage's past and present effectively destabilizes his entire sense of self and drives him near madness. And significantly enough, his tormentors "give" him his father back: horrified to think that his memory of his father's suicide might have been another simulated memory (or *jamais vu*), Savage drives to his mother's house, which he remembers perfectly, enters and greets his mother, whom he also remembers perfectly—and she doesn't recognize him, screams, calls the police. Her screams bring his "father" into the room—his father as he would have looked had he lived—and he doesn't recognize Savage either. Savage flees in terror; and while he is later told by one of the principals behind his torment that both "parents" were in fact carefully made-up and trained actors, this does not restore him to solid, stable reality. In fact, the tell-all denouement seems woefully inadequate; Morrell wants to bring his character (and his reader) into something like his own nightmarish sense of destabilized fathered/fatherless reality, and even in tying together the loose ends of his story can't bring himself to dispel the nightmare.

In a less well-known novel, *Blood Oath* (1982), Morrell explores his longing for the dead father explicitly, giving us a hero who, like himself, is a writer (not a professional in intelligence or guerilla warfare, like the Brotherhood heroes and Rambo), and whose father, like his own, was supposedly killed in World War II the year he was born. (Morrell dedicated the book to "George Morrell...the father I never knew.") Pete Houston and his wife Jan have traveled to France on vacation, and while there have stopped off at the military cemetery where his father is supposed to be buried—but his grave isn't there. At first they assume the military screwed up, or else that Houston simply remembered wrong, but then Houston remembers his mother speaking about a man named Pierre de St. Laurent, who had written to say he was caring for her husband's grave. They start looking for St. Laurent, and almost immediately their lives are threatened: they are run off the road, and Jan dies; Houston narrowly survives this and several later hits. There is, in fact, at this point very much the same air of taboo surrounding Houston's quest as surrounds Spenser's in the novels following *A Catskill Eagle*: Houston, like Spenser, and like their two creators, is approaching too close to the secret of his birth—for Houston the secret of his paternity, for Spenser the secret of his maternity. Unlike Spenser, Houston refuses to back off, follows the trail doggedly until at last he comes face to face with his still-living father. This is, as Morrell cagily makes clear, the working out of a childhood fantasy of his:

Houston nodded. "You have to understand. I never knew my father. He was killed about the same time I was born. My mother glorified him. She told me how smart he was, how handsome, how he loved us. He was tall and strong, and he was good at fixing cars, and he could sing like an opera star. He was a saint to us. But all the time I was growing up, I saw the fathers my friends had, and I envied them. I knew those fathers couldn't be as wonderful as mine had been, but they were living, and I wished with all my heart that one of them was mine. I asked my mother if she ever planned on marrying again. She told me, 'I'll never find a man to match your father.' And she didn't. To her death, she stayed unmarried."

He blew smoke. Simone picked up the bottle and drank. Her brow was furrowed.

"Kids are so inventive," Houston said. "Let's call it fantasy, a child's suspicion based on insecurity. Or maybe we should call it hope." He shook his head. "But I began to have this daydream. Soon it came to me when I was sleeping. I invited it. I analyzed it. I imagined different—I don't know—scenarios I guess adults would call them. What if he had never died? Supposing he had lost his memory and didn't know he had a wife and son. Or let's try this. Supposing he'd been mutilated, scarred so badly that he couldn't bring himself to let us see his ugliness. Or worse, the blackest possibility [the one that Morrell enacts in this novel]. Supposing he was perfectly all right, but he'd decided that he didn't want to come back home. That he'd abandoned us, that he had turned his back on me and left me to grow up alone."

Houston felt his sudden tears. (72)

The "scenario" Morrell invents in this novel to explain his father's absence is precisely a "child's suspicion based on insecurity." It is a lurid tale of hugger-mugger, stolen billions in Nazi gold, false identities, an evil half-brother (who arranged the hit in which Jan Houston died), all the elements of suspense. What makes it more than empty formula fantasy is Morrell's insistent focus on the emotional insecurities that motivate the concoction of such fantasies, his patent attempt throughout the novel to come to grips with the absence of his own father.

This sort of imaginative exploration of childhood traumas is often dismissed as escapist, unrealistic, or else as morbid or paranoid, precisely because the ideological norm for our adult memories of childhood entails an easy (repressive) idealization that we are coached to call "putting the past behind you," "letting bygones be bygones," and so on. Someone like Morrell who insists on stirring up the past, on recognizing that bygones have almost never gone by, therefore constitutes a potential threat that must be defended against. But as artists have always known, and as psychoanalysts are just beginning to realize, an openness to childhood experience—what really happened, but also, en route to that hazy realm of systematically repressed and tabooed real experience, what might have happened, what feels real—is the key to therapeutic liberation.

Psychoanalysts since Freud have always placed great stress on childhood, of course; but as Alice Miller makes clear in *Thou Shalt Not Be Aware*, that stress has typically been defensively mechanistic (psychic "mechanisms," mechanical "drives," fixed, static "phases"—oral, anal, genital—and universal biological "complexes") and repressive (geared toward reconciling the patient with his or her childhood rather than accessing his or her true feelings about and experiences of that time). Miller's requirements for psychoanalysts who

## 116   No Less a Man

would facilitate patients' cures by respecting and eliciting their childhood experiences are germane to the business of analyzing art as well, and critics who would facilitate artists' and their audiences' moves toward self-understanding and self-liberation would do well to take them to heart. It is essential, Miller says:

1. To be sensitive to the child's narcissistic needs for echoing, mirroring, understanding, respect and support, and to the ensuing traumatizations if these needs are not met.
2. To have understanding, proceeding from the foregoing sensitivity, for the reactive significance of the child's narcissistic rage.
3. To know that even unintentional cruelty hurts and that the patient must experience in analysis the anger and pain of his or her early childhood in order to be set free, even though as an adult the patient knows that the parents were victims as well.
4. To realize that children will pay for their parents' silence with pathological symptoms.
5. To recognize that grief leads to reconciliation, whereas guilt feelings are divisive.
6. To make the conscious decision not to assume a judgmental role, which would be colored by the moral precepts of our upbringing.
7. To identify the patient's taboos, peculiar to his or her country and family. (182-83)

Do not (we might paraphrase and consolidate Miller's requirements for emancipatory criticism) demand of writers repressive strength but seek out their half-hearted willingness to be weak, their regressive explorations of childhood, their hesitant transgressions of deep-seated taboos. Identify the taboos against which they struggle, and flesh out a sense of the resistance they must overcome in order to transgress them. Do not judge them for what seem like failures (especially normative "aesthetic" failures; even failures to liberate themselves), but show how those "failures" are themselves potentially instructive gestures in the direction of success. Be sensitive to the psychological costs of even these partial successes, and with those costs firmly in mind (preferably in connection with your own personal experience of such costs), encourage the writer (and his or her readers) to take ever greater risks in future. Remember the loneliness of the artist and the analysand and anyone else who is swept up in the turbulence of emotional transformation, anyone who is in the process of transgressing ideological norms and taboos and reconstituting the social self, and seek always to create a supportive community of understanding and encouraging readers.

For example, in the context of Parker's and Morrell's work, I would add to Miller's fourth point that idealization of an absent parent is itself a form of parental silence for which children will later pay: Spenser, like Morrell's Pete Houston, must experience the anger and pain of being deprived not only of a parent but of an open, honest channel of exploring the emotional cost of his or her absence. This deprivation is always traumatizing, even when the child copes with the trauma in "socially successful" (i.e. repressive) ways, and always generates narcissistic rage, which may surface (as it does here and there, without therapeutic issue, in Spenser, and more concertedly, consciously, directedly in Houston, with—as a result—intense emancipatory release) in the supposedly successful adult subject. Thus the therapeutic impact of Houston's recovery of his father at the end of the novel and ensuing discussion with him about the circumstances of his conception and birth:

> Then Houston squinted, turning to confront his father. "*Why?*"
> His father studied him. "I don't know what she said about me?"
> "You were wonderful."
> His father shrugged. "We didn't get along."
> The courtyard seemed to tilt. "You're lying! To her death, she claimed to love you!"
> Houston's father gaped. "You mean she's...Carol's *dead?*"
> A block of ice sank in Houston's stomach.
> "*When?*" his father said.
> "Two months ago. A stroke."
> "But she was only fifty-eight!"
> "You still remember?"
> "Certainly. I think about her all the time. I wondered what her life was like, what *you* were like, what you and she were doing."
> "*But you said you didn't get along with her.*"
> "That doesn't mean I didn't love her."
> "I don't understand."
> "A special pain," his father said. "To love a person and to know that you in turn aren't loved. She didn't get along with *me* would be more accurate. You were an accident."
> Houston paled.
> "You didn't know?" his father said.
> "I thought you wanted me."
> "Please, understand. In those days, sex was not the easy thing that it became. And birth control was not as common. I had friends who carried contraceptives, but I wasn't either confident or cynical enough to have one. Both your mother and I agreed to wait, but one night passion overpowered us.

## 118  No Less a Man

That one time. Only once. You were the consequence. Abortion was unthinkable in those days. Morally and legally. The people who performed them could be butchers. We had planned to marry when I finished school. Instead we were married one month after Carol learned she was pregnant. For myself, I loved your mother so much that our early marriage was a privilege. I was happy. But your mother was more sensitive to scandal, to the frowns of friends and neighbors and her parents. She had planned one kind of life, and now she had a different kind, less proper, less respectable. She blamed me for the pregnancy. Eventually she hated me."

"Then why did she describe you with such love?"

"To hide the truth. She could have taught you bitterness. She could have made you hate me. But she chose instead to teach you love, to make your origins seem good and decent."

"But I asked her why she didn't marry again. She said that, having known the best, she'd never find your equal. How could she be satisfied with someone less? she said."

"She hated sex. She lied to hide her bitterness."

Houston felt a hollow freezing in his stomach.

"Carol wanted a divorce. In those days that too was a scandal. But the military drafted me, and we agreed that when the war was over I wouldn't come back to her. The separation saved her from the scandal. I suppose I could have argued with the draft board, pointing out I'd soon be a father. But the war was getting worse. They needed every soldier they could get. And I doubted I would win. Your mother made me feel so worthless I let the Army take me. I sent letters, but your mother never answered them. If I survived the war, I hoped I could persuade her to think differently. But deep inside I knew she wouldn't change. When St. Laurent approached me, I felt so demoralized I took the chance he offered. See, I didn't have anything to lose. I thought if I was suddenly rich I could persuade her."

"Did you try to get in touch with us?"

"I couldn't. Afterward, I realized I'd trapped myself with my own logic. St. Laurent insisted we stay in hiding. 'One mistake,' he told us, 'one step toward our former lives, a message sent to those we knew, and we'll all go to jail. The military will be watching all our relatives.' He vowed to kill whoever talked. From the moment we deserted, we were forced to realize that what we once had been was dead. Believe me, I was tempted to risk everything and try to contact Carol. Then I asked myself if she was worth the risk—a woman who repeatedly had done her best to let me know how much she hated me. In the end I was a coward." (192-94)

This is a fascinating fantasy of recovering the absent father, one that deidealizes and humanizes both the father and the mother: the little orphaned boy's deep feelings of anger at the father for leaving him and at the mother for smothering him here surface (signaled by a coldness in the stomach, the body part that was warmed by the mother's food in childhood, and by the emotional "food" she fed him about his father's wonderfulness) in the form of the father's desertion and the mother's lies. Morrell, who revealed in the interview with John Stark in *People* Magazine that his mother put him in a Catholic orphanage when he was four, and only returned to get him when she remarried a year later, vents his suppressed anger at his mother in the form of Carol Houston's dislike for sex, her obsession with propriety, and the hostility toward her husband that drove him away from her and, more importantly, from her son.

This sort of attack on the mother by the adult son is often decried by feminist critics as misogyny—even though women's liberation generates in the daughter an immense amount of anger at the domesticated, guilt-inducing mother as well. Following Miller, I would insist that it is crucial "to have understanding, proceeding from the foregoing sensitivity, for the reactive significance of the child's narcissistic rage"—that we should not judge Morrell (or any other man angry at women in general or his mother in particular) for his sexism, but rather seek to understand the significance of that anger for his attempts to free himself from her power. This should be true, it seems to me, even when the angry man's enactment of his narcissistic rage is physically brutalizing or even life-threatening: the wife-batterer, the rapist. While neither condoning nor physically allowing misogynist violence (we will, for example, want to lock some angry men up to protect the women onto whom they project their narcissistic rage), we should not simply condemn them as woman-haters, or, worse, condemn all men (by angry feminine/feminist extrapolation) as woman-haters. Condemnation only drives narcissistic rage inside, behind carefully maintained social barriers—which it then crosses with redoubled ferocity. The daughter's anger at her angry, abusive father may be one step in her own liberation as a woman; but that anger is already built into patriarchal ideology in repressed and displaced form (the wife's anger at her husband and the mother's anger at her son, for not giving her the love her father never gave her), and simply validating feminine anger at men as a programmatic part of feminism changes nothing—indeed, only perpetuates the vicious patriarchal circle. What all of us, men and women alike, need is neither a repressive controlling nor a systematic theorization of anger at our parents, but a therapeutic release of that anger, a working through anger to the hurt and need and fear that lies behind and drives it, and ultimately to a liberated sympathy for the angry parent.

Morrell doesn't really deal with his feelings about his mother in any of the novels; we will see Bruce Springsteen repeating the same pattern in part three, dealing with his paternal introject but shying away from the considerably more terrifying project of engaging the maternal introject. In *Blood Oath* Pete Houston's father is a traitor to his family, to the son who worships him; but by the end of the novel Pete does make therapeutic progress with him. The father is weak, but weak in a way that Houston (himself a man who has been forced to confront his own weakness in the course of the novel) can understand. And the father is allowed to redeem himself somewhat for his betrayal: "I want to save your life. You're everything I wish that Charles was. I can't be the father to you—it's too late for that—but I can treat you as the son I should have raised. I can protect you. Hate me as you will, but also trust me. Let me save your life" (195).

And he does. Pete lets his father save him; his father does save him, dying in the process. This resembles, in fact, and in some sense restages, the regressive imaginative recovery of the repressed angry or absent parent in therapy: the "lost" because actively denied parental introject is forcibly brought to reconstitutive consciousness and transformed, de- and reformed so as to render it powerless to lock the subject into destructive behavior patterns, and then dismissed, remanded back into the darkness from which it was taken (with the significant difference that now the patient knows where it is, and can recover it him- or herself if need be). Having cured the patient-as-child, the parental introject can now "die" again, and this time rest in peace.

The implication of all this, clearly, is that Morrell is doing self-therapy in the novel, and, I will claim, all through his fiction: that his writing is at least in part an attempt to understand and cure himself. The enormous popularity of his novels, however, is evidence that (perhaps fortuitously) they do something for millions of readers as well; and I want to argue that what they do is precisely to access the American public's feelings of betrayal and abandonment in the post-Vietnam, post-Watergate, feminist era. The world hates us! We hate ourselves. And why shouldn't we? There is, as President Carter said, quoting Christopher Lasch, a malaise in America. We are sick, diseased, gasping our last. Everything is going to hell. Democracy is on its last legs, society's morals are in the gutter, nobody cares about anyone any more—why go on? Why not end it all in one big bang?

As long as it was possible for the American people to repress these feelings successfully, to go on saying and believing that America is the greatest country on earth, that there is nothing wrong with us that a little good ole American ingenuity can't fix—say through the late

1960s or early 1970s—Rambo was not only not needed, he was irrelevant, even perhaps somewhat frightening. As long as repressive self-congratulation "worked" (staved off the nightmares during waking hours), it was possible for John Wayne to be our hero: the man bothered by nothing, touched by nothing; the man with no dark fears, no inner divisions, no conflicted desires. Rambo, especially in *First Blood* but in the sequels as well, is no John Wayne. He is the inwardly divided man, the fearful, conflicted man, who in the myth is able to overcome his fears and conflicts long enough to fight and prevail—but who actually (at least in my reading) is driven into battle by those fears, by those inner divisions. Rambo is precisely as frantic as the American people were through the dark seventies and early eighties—before the great white hero Reagan (a defective but still effective John Wayne clone) returned to rescue us from our fears, to restore order to the world, to wave his hand and sow freedom and peace in the Soviet Union (Reagan as the Holy Ghost-writer of perestroika), in Eastern Europe (Reagan as the Joshua who, even after leaving office, blows his own horn and brings down the Berlin Wall), even in Nicaragua (Reagan as the David who picked up five smooth billions and hurled them at the evil Philistine giant, Daniel Ortega, and installed the good President Chamorro in his place). Morrell's frantic nightmare of Rambo precedes Reagan, indeed builds a highway for him; Reagan returns the favor for Stallone's Rambo, who rides to mythic glory out of the dawning of morning in America.

One of the most interesting aspects of *First Blood* in this context is that its therapeutic effect on America has really been double. When the novel appeared in 1972, we were still at war in Vietnam. The bombs were still dropping, the boys were still dying, the students were still protesting. I was turning 18 and worrying about my draft number and what I would do if drafted. (My number was 83. I would have been drafted. Whether I would have gone, I don't know.) I got lucky: Nixon, as part of the de-escalation of the war he had promised four years earlier, ended the draft shortly after my birthday. Morrell himself described his inspiration for the novel in a 1988 *Playboy* article:

> By chance, I watched a television program that changed my life. It was the *CBS Evening News*, and on that sultry August evening, Walter Cronkite juxtaposed two stories whose friction flashed like lightning through my mind.
>
> The first story showed a fire fight in Vietnam. Sweaty American soldiers crouched in the jungle, shooting bursts from M-16s to repel an enemy attack. Incoming bullets kicked up dirt and shredded leaves. Medics scrambled to assist

the wounded. An officer barked coordinates into a two-way radio, demanding air support. The fatigue, determination and fear on the faces of the soldiers were dismayingly vivid.

The second story showed a different sort of battle. That steamy summer, the inner cities of America had erupted into violence. In nightmarish images, National Guardsmen snapped bayonets onto M-16s and stalked the rubble of burning streets, dodging rocks, wary of snipers among devastated vehicles and gutted buildings.

Each news story, distressing enough on its own, became doubly so when paired with the other. It occurred to me that if I'd turned down the sound, if I hadn't heard each story's reporter explain what I was watching, I might have thought that both film clips were two aspects of a single horror. A fire fight outside Saigon, a riot within it. A riot within an American city, a fire fight outside it. Vietnam and America.

What if I wrote a book in which the Vietnam war literally came home to America? There hadn't been a war on American soil since 1865. With America splitting apart because of Vietnam, maybe it was time to write a novel that dramatized the philosophical division in our society, that shoved the brutality of war right under our nose.

I decided my catalytic character would be a Vietnam veteran, a Green Beret who, after many harrowing missions, had been captured by the enemy, had escaped and returned home to be given America's highest distinction, the Congressional Medal of Honor. But he would bring something back with him from Southeast Asia, what we now call post-trauma stress syndrome. (It's an overused term these days, but it wasn't in 1969). Haunted by nightmares about what he had done in the war, embittered by civilian indifference and hostility toward the sacrifice he had made for his country, he would drop out of society to wander the back roads of the nation he loved. He would let his hair grow long, not bother to shave, carry all his possessions in a rolled-up sleeping bag slung over his shoulder and look like what we then called a hippie. In what I loosely thought of as an allegory (don't forget, I was a professor in training), he would represent the disaffected. (89, 134)

Simplifying, Morrell's novel idea might be called pacifist, antiwar. The plan was to *show* Americans the Vietnam war. Morrell's sympathies were clearly with Rambo, the disaffected, and against the establishment that conducts both the war in Southeast Asia and the hunt for Rambo in Madison, Kentucky.[3] He continues in his *Playboy* article:

While Rambo would represent the disaffected, I needed someone to embody the establishment. Another news report, this time in print, aroused my indignation. In a Southwestern American town, a group of hitchhiking hippies had been picked up by the local police, stripped, hosed and shaved—not just their beards but their hair. They had then been given back their clothes and driven to a desert road, where they were abandoned to walk to the nearest town, 30 miles away. I remembered the harassment that my own recently grown mustache and long hair had caused me. "Why don't you get a haircut? What the hell are you, a man or a woman?" I wondered what Rambo's reaction would be if he were subjected to the insults those hippies had received. (134)

Simplifying still further, *First Blood* might be described as a fictional participation in (not just allegorical depiction of) student antiwar violence: Morrell was not merely making a connection between the war in Vietnam and the war at home; he was throwing the war in conservative America's face. You like the war so much, here, taste a little of it.

The movie version of *First Blood* did not appear until almost exactly ten years later, in 1982. There were numerous reasons for the delay, which Pat H. Broeske traces in fascinating detail in a production piece in the *L.A. Times* called "The Curious Evolution of John Rambo." Lawrence Turman got Columbia Pictures to buy the film rights to the novel almost immediately upon its release in 1972, but in a now-legendary series of second thoughts and changed minds and personality clashes and film company changes (Warner Brothers bought it from Columbia in 1973 and Carolco, the company that ultimately produced it, bought it from Warners in the late 1970s), it didn't get filmed until 1981.[4] David Morrell summarizes some of the production problems ("how to match actor and role," 135), but adds: "Part of the reason was the mood of the Seventies. America's involvement in Vietnam had ended badly, and feelings about the war were bitter. The few films that referred to Vietnam reflected that attitude. *Coming Home* is a good example" (135). But then, "A new decade arrived. Now Reagan was in the White House. America was feeling optimistic again. The defeat in Vietnam seemed long behind us" (135).

Beyond that, the psychological cost of the Vietnam War to Vietnam vets was just beginning to seep into the collective consciousness. Post-trauma stress disorder, as Morrell says, became a buzzword. More and more Americans were feeling sympathy for the vets: both the conservatives, who had been pro-war and therefore pro-soldier, but who had wanted to forget all about the vets when we pulled out so ignominiously, and the ex-protestors, the people like Morrell (born 1943) and me (born 1954) who had lived through the late 1960s and early 1970s with a terrified hatred of everything that had to do with Vietnam, including the men who fought there. Now, all of a sudden, the time was ripe for a movie that would dramatize the Vietnam vets' plight:

plagued by nightmares, unable to take civilian life seriously, therefore unable to hold fast to jobs or relationships, and above all totally ignored by a society that wanted to forget.

One way of explaining the shift in *First Blood*'s therapeutic effect would be to claim that Morrell was ahead of his time: he was ready to talk about the vets and PTSD a decade before anybody else was. I think that is probably true, but trivially true. The reason Morrell was ready to deal with the vets so early is that, while the war was still going on, he found in their plight, abandoned by a society that wanted to forget about their very existence, an external mirror or enactment of his own feeling of abandonment, his loss of his father—found in them an objective correlative for his own emotional set. In other words, it was not that he was just a better liberal than everybody else, more sensitive early on to a mistreated group of fellow citizens; it was that he was more aware of his own need for paternal love and attention, less able to repress his inner feelings of abandonment. The rest of America was not yet ready to feel like abandoned children—isolated, neglected, defensively defiant about their own self-worth—about Vietnam. Two years before Morrell started writing *First Blood*, in 1967, Norman Mailer had offered as explanation for *Why Are We in Vietnam?* the insecure American male's need to prove his machismo; and as long as we were still there, that seemed a good enough diagnosis, even for the (male) student protestors, who proved their machismo not in the jungles, but on the barricades. The Vietnam war was a rite of passage for many young American men at both ends of the political spectrum—or, perhaps, in both the middle class (who stayed and protested) and the working class (who went and died, or returned, traumatized, to general cultural hostility).

But that was an idealization based on an unchallenged set of assumptions about traditional masculinity: for example, that patriarchal gender programming in men was a biological imperative, a genetic code that must be obeyed for emotional health, and that simply excluded (rather than being a defense against) terrifying feelings of vulnerability and need. Before Morrell's deep sense of abandonment and defensive defiance could strike a chord in the American imagination of Vietnam, we had to lose the war, leave the country, watch Saigon fall to the Viet Cong. We also had to experience the setbacks of the late 1970s, the Iran hostage crisis, and the defeatism of our leaders. And, by no means least significantly, we had to be educated by a generation of feminists about what gender programming is, what femininity and masculinity have been and might be, even, in the fiercest of feminist rhetoric, what hideous oppressive tyrants we men were. Instead of proving their manhood in the jungles and on the barricades, in other words, the men of the late 1970s

# From *First Blood* to *First Blood* 125

and early 1980s felt humiliated by the Viet Cong, the Ayatollah Khomeini, and American women. This meant being symbolized as the oppressor, of course—as the United States of America and the Patriarchal Father, the number one bad guy writ large both geopolitically and familially—but what that did to men was to make them feel like naughty little boys, punished by mommy with emotional withdrawal (which feels, as we saw last chapter, exactly like abandonment). American men were ripe for an underdog who fights back, asserts his right to be himself, maybe even, as the condition on which he is allowed to live, breaks down and cries, releases all the pent-up anguish his heroic macho-warrior fathers had taught him to repress. Let me quote Morrell again, from *Playboy*:

> I know it's fashionable for authors to complain that their work has been bastardized by Hollywood. The fact is, I like the movie, even though changes were made from my novel. The locale was shifted from Kentucky to the Pacific Northwest (to avoid harsh weather; ironically, the production was shut down by a blizzard). Rambo's Green Beret instructor, Samuel Trautman, was upgraded from major [actually, captain] to colonel. Rambo acquired the first name John ("When Johnny comes marching home"). Also, he was made less angry, less violent (he's far more savage in my novel). On the screen, he kills one man by accident (a rock thrown at a pursuing helicopter causes a vicious deputy to lose his balance and fall to his death in a gorge). Later, Rambo bumps a stolen truck against a pursuing car filled with gun-blazing deputies. They veer off the road and fail to avoid a car parked along the road. That's the total body count in the film (the police chief—now, I'm afraid, a stereotypical redneck—though badly wounded, lives). But in my novel, the casualties are virtually uncountable. *My* intent was to transpose the Vietnam war to America, where the *film*'s intent was to make the audience cheer for the underdog.
>
> The most important change between my novel and the film almost didn't occur. In a vault in L.A., there's a film clip in which Rambo shoots himself. But second thoughts prevailed. Another ending was filmed, and Rambo lived.
>
> I don't object, though I would never change the ending of my novel, in which Trautman is Rambo's executioner. The reason I don't object is that Rambo in the novel causes so much destruction that the authorities would hunt him down, even if they had to use a Nike missile. But Stallone's revision of the script makes Rambo so reluctant to use force, so sympathetic a victim, that his survival seems justified. (135)

Those are the plot changes in a nutshell. But of course novels and movies are more than plot. The plot changes the movie people made in Morrell's novel are only inert signs, as it were, indicators of deeper

## 126  No Less a Man

changes, changes in something that is hard to articulate but that might be called undercurrent, mood, maybe even, tritely, "style."

Some of these are technical and medium-bound: it is hard to do internal monologue convincingly on the screen, and Stallone has to convey Rambo's inner divisions and uncertainties with his body, his bearing, his eyes. Andrew Laszlo's camera crew has to dramatize his intensity, his anger and fear, with color and camera angle. Jerry Goldsmith's music has to make two-dimensional images on a white screen feel like real life, has to make a projected pattern of light breathe like flesh and blood. On the other side, print cannot hold a candle to film's total audiovisual experience, and after the movie Morrell's prose feels even harder, flatter, balder than before. Here, for example, is the first paragraph of the novel:

His name was Rambo, and he was just some nothing kid for all anybody knew, standing by the pump of a gas station at the outskirts of Madison, Kentucky. He had a long heavy beard, and his hair was hanging down over his ears to his neck, and he had his hand out trying to thumb a ride from a car that was stopped at the pump. To see him there, leaning on one hip, a Coke bottle in his hand and a rolled-up sleeping bag near his boots on the tar pavement, you could never have guessed that on Tuesday, a day later, most of the police in Basalt County would be hunting him down. Certainly you could not have guessed that by Thursday he would be running from the Kentucky National Guard and the police of six counties and a good many private citizens who liked to shoot. But then from just seeing him there ragged and dusty by the pump of the gas station, you could never have figured the kind of kid Rambo was, or what was about to make it all begin. (11)

From just seeing him you could never guess all that, and from the novel's point of view all the movie audience can do *is* see him. Movies lack the analytical capacity of novels. Morrell can anticipate the whole novel in his first paragraph, but all the movie viewer does is see Rocky Balboa walking down a back road near Vancouver, British Columbia, with a two-day beard and wearing an Army jacket. Morrell can make subtle analytical points like "he was just some nothing kid for all anybody knew," first telling us what Rambo was—nothing, a nothing kid—then hinting that we would be wrong to take that characterization at face value. (And it is an extremely attractive hint for the moviegoer, sitting there in darkness, feeling very much like a nothing kid or a nothing husband or a nothing mother or a nothing boss or whatever, and daydreaming of being—"for all anybody knew"—a superhero with secret powers.)

## From *First Blood* to *First Blood* 127

The flat, laconic tone of Morrell's first paragraph also hints at something else: the book is going to end badly. Don't get too attached emotionally to this nothing kid. I am probably making this up, reading it in (but what else *is* reading but "reading in," reading with empathy?). I hear Morrell saying, through this first paragraph: "I'm leaving no room for sentiment here. I'm not going to cater to your desire for a hero. Don't glorify Rambo; he's no savior. He's not going to save himself, much less you and me. He's going to have the cops and the National Guard and umpteen private citizens on his trail, and he's *not* going to get away. He's not going to turn into James Bond or John Wayne. There is no miraculous heroic way out of this for him. Set your emotional thermostats on 'stoic'."

The movie opens on a totally different note—and, while film can't explain or comment or analyze as effectively or subtly as print, it can convey a different note or mood much more powerfully. Part of the difference between the two openings is carried over from previous Stallone movies: I was not being entirely facetious when I said our first sight is of Rocky Balboa walking down the road. Especially in 1982, movie audiences seeing Stallone walking down the road saw Rocky Balboa, a sympathetic underdog, and would bring those assumptions to the new movie as well—which would be exactly right, as Andrew Vajna and Mario Kassar saw from the start.[5] But most of it is carefully crafted. Stallone wears a friendly, open face, a bit sleepy and diffident, like Rocky, but well-meaning and fundamentally well-adjusted. The message is: this is no psycho. He is a guy that may get pushed the wrong way. The sun shines on him and the lush green Canadian landscape as he walks—the only time the sun shines in the entire movie. (The rest of the time, true to the Pacific Northwest, where the movie is set—in a fictitious town ironically called Hope, Washington—and to British Columbia, where it was filmed, it is dismally cold and wet, misty or rainy or threatening to snow.) As Stallone walks down to Delmar Barry's house, the sun glints off the lake like a mystic bridge of light—an overblown romantic phrase that I think is just right for the image we're given to start with. The birds twitter happily. All is at peace in God's country. Jerry Goldsmith's lyrical composition "It's a Long Road," which Dan Hill will sing Hal Shaper's words to over the closing credits, sounds now over the opening credits, in a soft romantic tone carried successively by trumpets, violins, and French horns. Sung by Hill, with a piano accompaniment, the song has a mournful catch to it; it sounds like a rueful 1960s folk ballad.[6] Played here by strings and horns, it sounds precisely like movie, or maybe TV, theme music.

## 128  No Less a Man

I'd like to think, in fact, that this resemblance is deliberate: that the producers are intentionally invoking the safe, sheltered world of television, where you always know that the hero (Davy Crockett is who I think of in the opening frames of *First Blood*) will come through everything all right. They want to set up those expectations in order to play off them, explode them. The world is not nice. It is full of frightened little souls with the power to hurt and the defensive desire to hurt *you*, if that will make their lives a little more secure. The sharp contrast between the bulk of the movie and these opening moments brings this lesson home. At the same time, by invoking a sheltered middle-American TV world the producers provide a subliminal reassurance that, no matter how nightmarish things get, everything will be okay in the end. The opening frames of the movie, in other words— even before Stallone says a word, while the credits are still running— already set up a very different story than the opening paragraph of Morrell's novel.

Rambo has come to Washington to see Delmar Barry, who is, he thinks, the only other member of his Special Forces team to survive the war.[7] Rambo finds Delmar's mother, is told he's gone, misunderstands her to mean he's out, away, and finally, after he shows her a picture of the team, with him and her son in it, is told that he is dead—that he died the previous summer of Agent Orange-caused cancer. As he tells Col. Trautman later, over the radio in the mine, "He's gone too. He got himself killed in Nam and didn't even know it." Almost before our eyes (and behind Rambo's, which glaze over with shock) the Washington sky goes gray and rainy, and the idyllic movie music is shattered with a foreboding drum roll that aurally anticipates both the drizzle that will dampen everybody's spirits and clothing throughout the movie and the sound of automatic rifle fire that will pursue Rambo deep into the woods. Until now Rambo has been Davy Crockett; now suddenly he is the hero of Bruce Springsteen's "Born in the U.S.A.," which was written around the same time the movie was being filmed (and released two and a half years later, in 1984):

> Ten years burning down the road
> Nowhere to run, ain't got nowhere to go

With the closing down of his face and the clouding over of the Washington sky, the romantic American wandering hero becomes a driven victim, pushed by an indifferent and hostile world beyond social self-control. And the movie can start.

## Chapter Six

## The Hurt, Betrayed Son

The open, friendly face Stallone wears in the opening frames of the movie tells us that his closed face now is only a reaction to bad news, specifically a defensive reaction, a pretend indifference that says: I don't care that my friend died. Please don't let me care. The thing is, and this is a sign of Stallone's much-maligned artistry as an actor, we *know* he's pretending. We know he cares. Stallone is often criticized for being an expressionless actor; but while it is true that the emotional range his face can express is fairly narrow, he works that narrow range with a highly charged subtlety. The macho mask that Rambo puts on when he learns his buddy is dead and wears for most of the rest of the movie is shot through with a characteristic Stallone sadness, a mournfulness, an emotional sensitivity that in some sense will save him from the death Morrell envisaged for him. In Stallone's face a battle is being waged between conditioned masculine control and an overwhelming impulse to give in, let go, release pent-up emotion. His violence throughout the movie will be an ongoing attempt to maintain control that will culminate in a redemptive "failure": in the end he will lose control, break down, cry, need consolation.

The novel Rambo is different—on the edge, boiling with resentment, spoiling for a fight:

Rambo knew there was going to be trouble, though. Big trouble, if somebody didn't watch out. The car he was trying to thumb a ride with nearly ran him over when it left the pump. The station attendant crammed a charge slip and a book of trade stamps into his pocket and grinned at the tire marks on the hot tar close to Rambo's feet. Then the police car pulled out of traffic toward him and he recognized the start of the pattern again and stiffened. "No, by God. Not this time. This time I won't be pushed." (11)

Morrell's Rambo has only been home from Vietnam six months, and has already been run out of 15 towns. With long, greasy hair and a thick greasy beard, he looks like a hippie, maybe, as Morrell himself says, but even more like a bum, a drifter. Sheriff Will Teasle is protecting his decent middle-class town's "aesthetic" sense—their unease with dirt, their cleanliness obsession, whose personal expression (a rigid dress code) and political expression (law and order) converge in Teasle's determination to "clean him up," to bathe, barber, and shave him. The relaxation of middle-class dress codes in the ten intervening years, combined with the movie producers' desire to make Rambo a sympathetic victim, together make Stallone look much less offensive: with his rumpled hair and fashionable stubble, he looks like anybody else in the eighties, at least anybody who would be walking around in rural Washington State. (He couldn't pass for a Wall Street stock broker, or even a Seattle lawyer. He might pass as a small-town lawyer in the Cascades.) This has the effect of making Teasle's determination to railroad him out of town unconvincing: what could the sheriff possibly have against him?

The actual confrontation between Teasle and Rambo here in the beginning, Teasle's attempt to get Rambo out of town and Rambo's stubborn attempt to come back in, is roughly the same in the novel and the movie, the major difference being that in the novel we know what Rambo is thinking:

> His clothes were filmed yellow with dust, his long hair and beard were matted dirty, and all the people driving by took a look at him, and nobody stopped. So why don't you clean up your act? he thought. Shave and get a haircut. Fix up your clothes. You'd get more rides that way. *Because. A razor's just one more thing to slow you down, and haircuts waste money you can spend on food, and where would you shave anyhow; you can't sleep in the woods and come out looking like some kind of prince.* Then why walk around like this, sleeping in the woods? And with that, his mind moved in a circle and he was back to the war. Think about something else, he told himself. Why not turn around and go? Why come back to this town? It's nothing special. *Because. I have a right to decide for myself whether I'll stay in it or not. I won't have somebody decide that for me.*
>
> But this cop is friendlier than the rest were. More reasonable. Why bug him. Do what he says.
>
> *Just because somebody smiles when he hands me a bag of shit, that doesn't mean I have to take it. I don't give a damn how friendly he is. It's what he does that matters.*
>
> But you do look a little rough, as if you might cause trouble. He has a point.

### The Hurt, Betrayed Son 131

> *So do I. In fifteen goddamn towns this has happened to me. This is the last. I won't be fucking shoved anymore.*
>
> Why not explain that to him, clean yourself up a bit? Or do you want this trouble that's coming? You're hungry for some action, is that it? So you can show him your stuff?
>
> *I don't have to explain myself to him or anybody else. After what I've been through, I have a right without explanation.*
>
> At least tell him about your medal, what it cost you.
>
> Too late to stop his mind from completing the circle. Once again he returned to the war. (21-22)

The problem with the circle he wants to avoid completing is that it is vicious. Thoughts of the war make him think of what "they" (the symbolic fathers who ran the war) *made* him do, the horrors he was trained to perpetrate and withstand; and so he turns to civilian life to take his mind off the war. But thoughts of civilian life make him think of what "they" (the symbolic fathers who run the towns he travels through) *won't let* him do, the humiliations he is forced to suffer; and so he turns back to the war. It is a vicious circle of paternal oppression: the fathers get him coming and going.

Note, though, in that internal dialogue, that some voice inside Rambo keeps offering an out, an escape from the vicious circle, or at least a consciousness that is not trapped in the vicious circle, an outside voice (like Susan Silverman's for Spenser) that tries to force him to work through his emotional fixations: "Then why walk around like this, sleeping in the woods?" The only answer Rambo can think of to this is the war, which he doesn't want to think about; like Scarlett O'Hara, therefore, he tells himself to think of something else. He thinks he is trying to repress the circular logic in which he is trapped; but all he is really successfully repressing is the possibility of escape. At some deep emotional level, he has trapped himself, and doesn't know how, doesn't *want* to know how, is afraid to know how, to untrap himself.

I don't mean to say that he is clinically paranoid—that he is, say, only imagining the hostility civilians, especially their law enforcement officers, feel toward him. That hostility is there. But he is, as his inner voice of self-conscious admonition knows, also provoking it, precisely by not shaving, not taking baths, not cutting his hair, not fixing up his clothes. Not getting a job and a wife and a ranch-style house and two-point-one kids. Sleeping in the woods is a defiant act that is *designed* to stir up civilians' hostility toward him.

The problem is, the military used him in the war as a tool to do terrible things, dehumanizing things: he was appreciated, esteemed, "loved" by his military "fathers" only insofar as he was useful to them, only insofar as he was skillful at doing their dirty work for them. This is bad enough: like everybody else, he wants to be appreciated for who he is, loved as himself, not as a killer, not as a tool. As he says explicitly at the end of *Rambo: First Blood Part II*, when Trautman urges him not to hate his country, he wants "*once* for our country to love us as much as we love it."

But however dehumanizing this "instrumentalization" by the Special Forces was, at least he could feel it was marginally worthwhile: he was good at it, he served his country, and received recognition for it, the highest recognition of all, the Congressional Medal of Honor. When he returned to civilian life he got no recognition at all. He was just a nothing kid. Overnight he went from feeling used to feeling abandoned, and the transition made him feel betrayed.

This is a familiar feeling in Morrell novels, and it will recur in the second Rambo film when Murdock, the government heavy played by Charles Napier (who looks remarkably like Brian Dennehy as Will Teasle), gives the order to abort the mission and leave Rambo to die.[1] The feeling has something to do with the insecurity of a boy in a "fatherless" world: because there is no father to love him, and by loving him to stabilize his world, his human worth is forever up for grabs, definable by the highest bidder. Bidding for the little boy's human worth (self-esteem) is conducted in the currency of kindness, affection, appreciation, respect, recognition; but the very use of these emotional expressions as a currency empties them out into sheer abstract markers, like dollar bills, which can be taken away as easily as they are given. The fatherless boy feels absurdly grateful for any attention at all from a father-figure, and devotes himself body and soul to the man who seems to love him; but the very intensity of his gratitude and devotion reveals its source in insecurity, in the fear of abandonment. That precarious balance between devotion and anxiety makes even the smallest sign of conniving or calculation on the father-figure's part a mortal offense, and sets the avalanche of feeling used, abandoned, and betrayed into motion.

And all that needs to be added to this analysis is the observation that, under conditions of patriarchy, which imposes and enforces the myth of the absent father, it is not just literally fatherless boys like David Morrell who suffer from this insecurity; it is all of us. Boys who grow up with fathers who are physically present but emotionally absent

# The Hurt, Betrayed Son   133

themselves become fathers who are afraid to be emotionally present for their own children, and the patriarchal cycle continues.

Morrell develops the used-abandoned-betrayed dynamic most explicitly in *The Brotherhood of the Rose*, where Saul and Chris discover that their foster-father Eliot never loved them:

> "He made us. Yes." Chris pursed his lips in anger. "And these other men as well [Eliot has "adopted" a total of eighteen boys in nine different orphanages and brought them up to be intelligence agents]. He programmed us to be absolutely dedicated to him."
>
> "Never to question anything. Like the Paradigm job," Saul said. "I never dreamed of asking him why he wanted it done. If he ordered something, that was good enough."
>
> "We were so naive he must have been tempted to laugh. When we snuck from school that night and the gang beat us up..." Chris glared. "I only now realized. Something about them always bothered me. They looked too neat. Their leather jackets were new. They drove an expensive car." He shivered. "They must have been operatives. He sent them to work us over, to make us angry so we'd grab the chance to learn [self-defense] at the *dojo*. God knows how many other ways he manipulated us."
>
> "Those Baby Ruth candy bars. He gave me one in Denver when he set me up to be killed."
>
> "The same when he asked me to hunt for you," Chris added. "We're Pavlov's dogs. Those candy bars are the symbol of his relationship with us. He used them to make us love him. It was easy. No one else showed us kindness. An old man giving candy to kids."
>
> The rain drummed harder on the roof.
>
> "And now we find out everything he said was wrong. A trick. A lie," Saul said. "He never loved us. He used us."
>
> "Not only us," Chris seethed. "These other men must have felt he loved them too. He lied to everyone. We were all just part of a group. I could almost forgive his lies—the things he made me do!—if I thought we were special to him. But we're not." He listened to the storm, his words like thunder. "And for that, I'll see him die." (202-03)

"I could almost forgive his lies—the things he made me do!—if I thought we were special to him." Rambo too was made to feel special, by his Green Beret instructor Captain Trautman, and is betrayed by him, eventually killed by him, later in the novel. But Morrell has not yet developed his finely honed sense of being used, abandoned, and betrayed in *First Blood*. Rambo reacts, and tries futilely to figure out

## 134   No Less a Man

why he's reacting as he does. At some point in the novel, fairly early on, he stops trying to understand—just acts. Acts as he was programmed to act: kills as many of the enemy as possible. For the Rambo of Morrell's *First Blood* there is no escape from programming, no escape from Pavlovian killing, as the heroes of the Brotherhood series start to hope, and as Rambo himself, brought back to life in the movies and in Morrell's novelizations of the sequels, begins to hope. Chris Kilmoonie, Drew MacLane, and Rambo III all retire to monasteries to find peace, to work through the programmed need to kill with professional coldness, to work down past the coldness to the deepseated needs for paternal love and approval and fears of paternal abandonment and betrayal that drive them. None of them finds peace, probably because their creator hasn't found peace and doesn't know what it feels like—although he claims Rambo does at the end of *Rambo III*. It is the dubious peace that comes from conforming yourself to your programming, doing what you were programmed to want to do:

> Yes. It was clear now. He finally did what Trautman had wanted.
> He accepted his destiny.
> The thought surprised him.
> Destiny?
> But what exactly *was* it?
> The answer came at once. God had fated him to be a warrior. As long as innocent people were brutalized, he had a meaning. He served a purpose.
> To protect. To suffer so that others would not.
> He smiled as he stared toward the draw into Pakistan, toward the future and, God willing, salvation. (242)

His destiny is to be the Incredible Hulk, a superhero in rags.[2] The thing is, this is somebody else's destiny *for* him, Trautman's, and beyond Trautman patriarchy's. Men shall protect. Men shall suffer so that others will not. Salvation and peace of mind lie in accepting that programmed patriarchal imperative.

But if this appears to be the "goal" of the Rambo series, Morrell's *First Blood* exploration of the circumambient path to that goal leaves room for another kind of hope, another kind of peace, another kind of salvation. Like Chris in *The Brotherhood of the Rose* and Drew in *The Fraternity of the Stone*, in *Rambo III* Rambo brings monastic discipline to bear on his unruly self: a *con*formative ending, an attempt to conform to social norms. But back in *First Blood* Rambo's self-control fails in ways that are destructive but also potentially *trans*formative. Just before he breaks in the police station, Morrell gives us a glimpse of the defensiveness of Rambo's intense need to keep himself in check:

> He was determined to keep control. There would be just the next five minutes and the continual touch of the scissors, and then it would be over, he would be all right.
> He started toward the chair, his feet slick in the water, and behind him Shingleton said, "Good God, where did you get all the scars on your back?"
> "In the war." That was a weakness. He should not have answered.
> "Oh sure. Sure you did. In which army?"
> Rambo almost killed him right there. (52)

His fear of being weak is mainly a fear of letting his tough image slip—the image of a man, a superhero, self-sufficient, unneedy, indifferent to sympathy or kindness, unaffected by others' claims on him. To admit that he had been wounded in the war is first of all to try to impress these men, to brag about being tough in an area they will admire; but it is also, more profoundly, a play for their sympathy. Look what I suffered in Vietnam. Look how badly I've been treated. Don't be mad at me; understand me. Love me. Care for me. Pamper me, cuddle me, make me feel safe again. In other words, make me feel like a baby being loved by his mommy. But infancy is the time of total vulnerability, total defenselessness, and that makes it frightening. Rambo, like most of us programmed for traditional masculinity, feels compelled to defend against defenselessness, to muster a defensive strength against weakness.

But he can't. By *Rambo III*, he can—he has internalized the self-discipline of four different religious traditions in support of his defenses, and it seems to be working—which makes that novel, and the movie it exfoliates, much less interesting to me than *First Blood*. Here in the first installment of the myth his needs and fears are stronger than his defenses, and he moves toward what he knows with a terrible certainty is trouble. Trouble is what follows from losing self-control. And my guess is that he senses the trouble will not only be with the police. Losing self-control means psychological trouble too, the incursion of all the frightening monsters from the locked chambers deep down inside:

> What the hell did you expect? he told himself. You asked for this, didn't you? You wouldn't back off.
> Damn right I wouldn't. And I still won't. Just because I'll be locked up, doesn't mean I'm finished. I'll fight this as far as it goes. By the time he's ready to let me out, he'll be fucking glad to be rid of me.

> Sure you'll fight. Sure. What a laugh. Take a look at yourself. Already you're shaking. Already you know what this place reminds you of. Two days in that cramped cell and you'll be pissing down your pantlegs.
> 
> "You've got to understand I can't stay in there." He could not stop himself. "The wet. I can't stand being closed in where it's wet." The hole, he was thinking, his scalp alive. The bamboo grate over the top. Water seeping through the dirt, the walls crumbling, the inches of slimy muck he had to try sleeping on.
> 
> Tell him, for God's sake.
> 
> Screw, you mean beg him. (39)

The reason torture and murder are so powerfully traumatizing and dehumanizing is that, whether you inflict them or suffer them, you are brought face to face with your own deepest and most terrifying impulses: the subliminal desire to escalate self-hatred into self-torture and suicide, or to escalate anger at a recalcitrant outside world into total destruction. Being locked up in the "hole" in Vietnam meant, in the economy of Rambo's psyche, being locked into the hole of his own worst nightmares. All the desires "decent" citizens successfully repress are now reality, a horrifying, mind-numbing reality that doesn't seem possible. How can a nightmare be as real as a ride in a car or a conversation with a cashier at the grocery store? How can I deal with what I fear most on that level? Once those monsters are let loose, there is no putting them back. They must either be frozen, stunned, shunted off to some holding tank of the imagination, by strict discipline—the road Morrell's most sympathetic heroes tend to take—or they must be befriended, transformed into acquaintances, familiars, and so rendered harmless.[3] The latter is the path to health; but it leads through a cathartic release of the monsters that is potentially very dangerous indeed: it is, in fact, the path that Rambo takes in *First Blood*. In the novel, the dangers inherent in the path are realized, and Rambo self-destructs. In the movie, Rambo manages to veer just this side of self-destruction, and (perhaps) is saved.

In any case, here in the prison block in Teasle's police station, Rambo feels forced into too oppressive a proximity to his own nightmares, his terrible memories of torture in Vietnam: the wet floor, the hostile male bodies crowding him, the razor brought too close to his throat. Sensitized by his Vietnam experience to the fluidity of nightmare in the world and in his head, he loses the ability to impose rational, logical distinctions on the world, and the prison block, the hole in Vietnam, and the nightmares in his head all fuse in one mystical moment of total terror, and he explodes with violence. He kills Galt—by slicing open his belly, not, as in the movie, by hurling a rock at the helicopter from which Galt is trying to shoot him—and the manhunt is on.

The movie Rambo is pursued by the same nightmares as the novel Rambo, and reacts to Teasle's pushing in much the same way, exploding with violence and escaping the prison block into the woods. But Stallone has made important changes in the character. He is, for one thing, no longer so intensely driven as his predecessor in print. Self-control seems to come easier to him, and yet he is also closer to his fears, less fearfully shut off from them. Since we don't know what Rambo is thinking on the screen, this is a feeling I at least get from Stallone, from the body signals Stallone conveys with his acting—which is, as I say, Stallone's many detractors to the contrary—extremely subtle. Stallone draws powerfully on his own personal access to failure and weakness and vulnerability and need, his own ability to slip back and forth across the patriarchal barrier between defensive hardness and terrified softness.

Much of this is Stallone's ability to access the conflicted, angry, lost, frustrated, and defensively self-destructive feelings of his childhood. Born in the charity ward of New York Hospital in 1946, Stallone spent the first five or six years of his life (neglected by his American mother Jacqueline, terrorized by his Sicilian father Frank) on the streets of Hell's Kitchen, an ugly nothing kid; and, even after his parents were divorced and his mother was remarried to a wealthy pizza manufacturer, Sly clung to his street-urchin ways, his working-class mannerisms. (He still sounds working-class, despite his later private education in Leysin, Switzerland.[4]) This is self-destructive behavior in an upper-middle-class family, as Spenser discovered in his dealings with the Orchards back in *The Godwulf Manuscript*; it does, however, yield some tiny measure of embattled integrity, even of self-definition, in and through the very fury it arouses in your parents. And some of that hurt but pathetically (and hopelessly) defiant little boy plays across Stallone's nerve-damaged slab of a face still today, whenever he plays the part of a man thwarted by the superior force of patriarchal fathers (Teasle in *First Blood*, Murdock in *Rambo: First Blood Part II*, his father-in-law in *Over the Top*). Even when he is acting his toughest, when he is portraying a character defensively given to macho blankness, there is an overwhelming sense of the little boy inside crying "Please don't do this to me! Don't hate me! Don't torment me! Please love me!"[5]

My guess is, in fact, that the critics' hostile reaction to Stallone is at least partly itself a defense. The vulnerability of a macho man is embarrassing to almost everybody, and Stallone reeks of both machismo and vulnerability. Thanks largely to Stallone, Rambo has become a byword for personally focused but professionally unfeeling American imperialism, SS tactics—torture and murder and destruction. Stallone himself is attacked as Mr. Expressionless. But one wonders. There is an intensity to these attacks that cannot be explained away as mere ideological repugnance, mere liberalism, mere middle-class distaste for violence. Could it be that male critics insecure about their own masculinity (and female critics insecure about their fathers' masculinity) react subliminally to that element of emotional frailty that is always just under Stallone's macho surface, and are so afraid of what they feel that they must escalate the attack on the safest, most predictable, most easily explainable part of Stallone's act? Certainly it is easier emotionally to criticize Stallone for being too tough than for not being tough enough. Machismo is too heavily under attack anyway, these days, for a critic to hold it up uncritically as an ideal; to admit that Stallone feels not too strong but too weak, not too impregnable but too vulnerable, would be to admit one's own fears of being weak and vulnerable, and that would be frightening.

Because the movie Rambo is less eager for action than the novel Rambo, shifts had to be made in the other two main characters as well, Teasle and Trautman. Teasle had to become more of a caricature, more of a cut-out figure (color me Oppressor)—more, in other words, of the heavy father. In order to be the sympathetic underdog, Rambo cannot push Teasle; Teasle must push him, out of some inexplicable inner rage. When Rambo walks back into town, he must do so not because he is looking for a fight, but because he is hungry (in the novel, Rambo makes it into town, gets a hamburger and eats it, and *then* is escorted out of town, for the second time, by Teasle). The novel Rambo has no external excuse for his stubbornness; his only excuse is that he is been pushed around one too many times. In the movie Teasle, not Rambo, feels like the man who has been pushed one too many times:

> Rambo: Why are you pushing me?
> Teasle: What did you say?
> Rambo: I said, why are you pushing me? I haven't done anything to you.
> Teasle: First of all, I ask the questions around here, you understand? Secondly, we don't want guys like you in this town. Drifters. First thing you know we got a whole *bunch* of guys like you in this town. That's why. Besides, you wouldn't like it here. This is a quiet little town. In fact you might say it's boring. But that's the way we like it. And I get paid to keep it that way.

## The Hurt, Betrayed Son 139

This kind of print rendition of the exchange between Stallone and Brian Dennehy doesn't do justice to the movie's visual dynamic. Stallone is calm in his vulnerability, if that makes sense: so comfortable in his vulnerability that he doesn't have to play the rebellious son. Dennehy is the insecure, driven one. When Stallone asks why he's pushing, Dennehy gives us the scared authoritarian father, his lip and cheek muscles twitching nervously, his eyes shifting as he struggles to keep himself firmly under control, the anger rising but being carefully transformed into authoritarian rhetoric. He comes up with a two-point list of reasons why he is pushing: the first is insecure, the uneasy claim made by a father unsure of his authority. The gist is: you shut up and let me talk, which translates as, you scare me, your defiance is profoundly threatening to me, so if you don't shut up and behave yourself and do exactly what I say, I don't know what I'm going to do. By the second point he has got himself more under control; and as he works out the details of why the town doesn't like drifters, he gradually relaxes into his benevolent sheriff's role, joking humorlessly about how he is paid to keep the town boring.

This is, in fact, the father seen from the outside: the father as inscrutable tyrant, irrationally rational in his determination to use any and every means to keep the unruly son in line. This is the novel Teasle too, up to a point. But, perhaps surprisingly, given Morrell's declared intention to make the novel an allegory in which Rambo would symbolize the disaffected and Teasle the establishment, he also makes Teasle sympathetic. Some readers, he tells us in the *Playboy* article, even thought Teasle was the hero of the novel. As the story progresses the Oedipal battle increasingly becomes, in fact, a kind of brother-battle, a battle between two rough equals who begin to intuit the other's position, to know, in some extrasensory way, where the other is and what he is doing and thinking and feeling. Morrell makes Teasle a Korean war hero, winner of the Distinguished Service Cross; and, though fat and out of shape and out of practice, by the end of the novel he has virtually become Rambo's military peer. The movie people make Teasle a fat, blustering, insecure, incompetent bully who survives the novel only because Rambo really doesn't want to hurt anybody, and takes every chance he gets to spare lives and even feelings. The movie Rambo is the victimized son who could kill the father but doesn't want to; the novel Rambo is the conflict-locked son who wants to kill the father and does, but only when he is next to death himself.

Morrell also goes inside Teasle's head, and gives us the inner torment of an insecure man whose father was killed in a hunting accident (here, in Teasle, even more than in Rambo, is Morrell's fictional version of his own fatherless childhood) and was raised by a foster-father whose expertise in hunting matters always made him feel inadequate. In the movie Orval Kellerman (John McLiam) is just some old fart with a bunch of trained Dobermans who gets shot in the leg by Rambo; in the novel he is Teasle's foster-father and Oedipal foil:

> "The dogs," Teasle called. "Did you bring the dogs?"
> "Sure, but I don't see the use of sending that deputy to help rush them into the van," Orval answered at the top, slowing. "Look at that sun. It'll be dark in an hour."
> "Don't you think I know it."
> "I believe you do," Orval said. "I didn't mean to try and tell you anything."
> Teasle wished he had kept quiet. He could not afford to let it start again. This was too important. Orval was always treating him like he was still thirteen, telling him everything to do and how to do it, just as he had when Teasle lived with him as a boy. Teasle would be cleaning a gun or preparing a special cartridge load, and right away Orval would step in, giving his advice, taking over, and Teasle hated it, told him to butt out, that he could do things himself, often argued with him. He understood why he did not like advice: there were teachers he sometimes met who could not stop lecturing once they were out of class, and he was a little like them, so used to giving orders that he could not accept someone telling him what to do. He did not always refuse advice. If it was good, he often took it. But he could not let that be a habit; to do his job properly he had to rely on himself alone. If Orval had only on occasion tried to tell him what to do, he would not have minded. But not every time they were together. And now they had almost started at each other again, and Teasle was going to have to keep himself quiet. Orval was the one man he needed right now, and Orval was just stubborn enough to take his dogs back home if they got into another argument.
> Teasle did his best to smile. "Hey, Orval, that's just me sounding miserable again. Don't pay attention. I'm glad to see you." He reached to shake hands with him. It had been Orval who taught him how to shake hands when he was a boy. Long and firm, Orval had said. Make your handshake as good as your word. Long and firm. Now, as their hands met, Teasle felt his throat constrict. In spite of everything, he loved this old man, and he could not adjust to the new wrinkles in his face, the white hair at the sides of his head that had become thinner and wispy like spider strands.
> Their handshake was awkward. Teasle had deliberately not seen Orval in three months, ever since he had walked yelling out of Orval's house because a

simple remark he had made had turned into a long argument over which way to strap on a holster, pointed forward or back. Soon after, he had been embarrassed about leaving the house like that, and he was embarrassed now, trying to act natural and look Orval straight in the face, doing a poor job of it. "Orval—about last time—I'm sorry. I mean it. Thanks for coming so quick when I need you."

Orval just grinned; he was beautiful. "Didn't I tell you never to talk to a man when you're shaking hands with him? Look him straight in the eyes. Don't jabber at him. I still think a holster should be pointed backward." He winked at the other men. His voice was low and resonant. "What about this kid? Where's he gone to?" (64-66)

Teasle is as quick to react to the slightest hint that Orval doesn't love him for *himself* as Rambo is to the slightest hint that he is being denied his rights as an American citizen. Both men, like Spenser parking in front of hydrants, are insecure about their "integrity," their masculine autonomy, their power and ability and space to "rely on themselves alone," and invariably overreact in any situation in which they feel that their "freedom"—the freedom to exert their will unhampered—is being curtailed. (Will Teasle's name is itself a complex miring of "autonomous" masculine will in childhood teasing and tousling, and in the anxious cunning that we proverbially associate with weasels.) Rambo and Teasle are not only made *for* each other, in some sense they are made *by* each other: they occupy the mutually activating father and son roles in the vicious patriarchal circle of emotional withdrawal and the repressed demand for love, the circle that leads to feeling used, abandoned, and betrayed.

Trautman too, in both the novel and the movie, plays his part in this patriarchal drama: he is a kind of father-figure to both Rambo and Teasle, and invokes variations on the same feelings of uneasy respect and resentment in both men. Teasle's resentment is the strongest: he is the local sheriff and is jealous of his jurisdiction, both when Dave Kern the state cop comes in to take over and when Trautman the Green Beret comes in to help out. In the novel, however, Teasle's insecurity around Trautman is muted, and linked specifically to his ambivalent feelings about Orval Kellerman:

"You've pointed out enough faults. Can't you offer something positive?"

He said it stronger than he intended, so that when Trautman answered "Yes," there was something new, resentment, hidden in that even voice: "I have a few details to settle on yet. I don't know how you run your police department, but I like to be sure before I go ahead on something."

## 142  No Less a Man

Teasle nodded his co-operation and immediately tried to ease off. "Sorry. I guess it's me who sounds wrong now. Don't pay attention. I'm just not happy unless I get miserable once in a while."

Again it came, that strange intense doubling of past and present: two nights ago when Orval had said "It'll be dark in an hour," and he himself had snapped "Don't you think I know it" and then had apologized to Orval in almost the same words he had just said to Trautman.

Maybe it was the pills. (173)

The pills are, of course, a convenient scapegoat: always better, for a traditionally programmed man, to blame uncontrollable behavior on something chemical or mechanical than something emotional. In any case, the novel Teasle is half-aware of his father-problems and backs off. (It is enough, maybe, for us to know his twisted inner feelings. Morrell doesn't have to hit us over the head with Teasle's insecurity, the way the movie does.) When this same scene is transposed to the movie, Trautman is assigned more or less the same lines, but Teasle's response is escalated to a paroxysm of insecure bullying; and the same relationship recurs throughout the rest of the movie, Trautman the calm, condescendingly conciliatory father who rests secure in his superior knowledge and skill, Teasle the touchy, anxious, resentful son. This is perhaps nowhere clearer than in the woods in front of the mine entrance, where everybody thinks the National Guard have just killed Rambo with a rocket:

Teasle: Buried in a hole by weekend warriors. I thought he was the best you ever trained.

Trautman: However he ended up, there was a time when he was very special.

Teasle: Special my ass. He was just another drifter who broke the law.

Trautman: Vagrancy, wasn't it? That's going to look real good on his gravestone at Arlington: "Here lies John Rambo, winner of the Congressional Medal of Honor, survivor of countless incursions beyond enemy lines, killed for vagrancy in Jerkwater, USA."

Teasle: Aw, don't give me any of that crap, Trautman. Do you think Rambo was the only guy who had a tough time in Vietnam? He killed a police officer, for Christ's sake!

Trautman: You're goddamned lucky he didn't kill all of you.

Again, Teasle's insecurity is mainly conveyed by Dennehy's body language: his restless stamping about in the woods like a wounded bull around Richard Crenna, who does Trautman as serene matador; his anxious mouth, his need to thrust his jaw in Trautman's face to make a point. Trautman is shown gazing speculatively at the smoking ground over the mine, guessing correctly that Rambo is still alive, and this has the effect (especially on a second viewing) of rendering Trautman even more superior, distant, and autocratic: he can afford to let little-boy Teasle rant and rave, because he possesses paternal knowledge that he is not imparting. The conversation continues in a bar back in town, where Trautman is having a drink surrounded by a carnival atmosphere of laughter and lights (Christmas, maybe? Morrell's novel is set in October) and Teasle comes up to apologize.

>   Teasle: Aw, I dunno, I just feel—
>   Trautman: Like you were cheated out of your chance?
>   Teasle: I wanted to kill that kid. I wanted to kill him so bad I could taste it.
>   Trautman: That doesn't sit well with that badge...It can get confusing sometimes. In Vietnam you can bet that Rambo and I got pretty confused. We had orders: When in doubt, kill. What the hell, you're a civilian. I mean, you can go home to your wife and your house and your little flower garden. You're under no pressure to figure all this out.
>   Teasle: Yeah, what about you, Colonel, what did you figure out from all of this, huh? I mean, what would you have done with him, if he came in? Would you have put your arms around him, given him a big, sloppy kiss, or would you have blown his brains out?
>   Trautman: I couldn't answer that until I met him face to face.

Here Trautman remains the cold, aloof, authoritarian and somewhat patronizing father—jabbing at Teasle about going home to his wife and house and "little flower garden," but also trying, like an uneasy father trying hard not to antagonize a difficult son, to put Teasle at his ease by admitting his own confusion in Vietnam. But the last couple lines of that exchange begin to point ahead to a significant shift in Trautman's role: the choice between giving Rambo a kiss and blowing his brains out is in one sense a choice between the movie's ending, where Rambo survives to cry in Trautman's arms, and the novel's ending, where Trautman does blow Rambo's brains out with a shotgun. In another and deeper sense, however, what Teasle is giving Trautman is a choice between being a traditional mother and a traditional father. A mother would have put her arms around Rambo and kissed him: that is the loving role we assign, almost exclusively, to women in our society. A father would blow his brains out.

## 144  No Less a Man

The implications are initially horrifying: that is what being a father is. That is what being a man is. Being hard, unforgiving, unloving and ready to blow your son's brains out if he doesn't knuckle down to your law. But the horror depends on our willingness to knuckle down to another "law," the felt compulsion of patriarchal programming. Paternally aloof as he is through most of the movie, Trautman here fights that programming by remaining flexible, willing to read the situation in its complexity rather than blindly applying a fixed principle; and in the end he shifts even further out of the traditional father-role by "mothering" Rambo, showing him love and kindness, throwing up a magic shield of protective warmth, as it were (telling the police to hold their fire), which gives Rambo the security he needs to release the fears he has been carrying around inside him for seven years.

This shift is anticipated in the movie in Trautman's relationship with Rambo early on. In the novel Trautman is a captain who had trained the men who trained Rambo; when he contacts Rambo over the radio of the police car he steals, Rambo remembers his voice over the loudspeakers at Special Forces training camp, cold, metallic, distant, disembodied:

"Rambo."
The voice startled him, coming from the car radio.
"Rambo. Listen to me. I know you can hear me."
The voice was familiar, years off. He could not place it.
"Listen to me." Each word smooth, sonorous. "My name is Sam Trautman. I was director of the school that trained you."
Yes. Of course. Never in sight. The persistent voice over the camp's loudspeaker. Any hour. Day after day. More running, fewer meals, less sleep. The voice that never failed to signal hardship. So that was it. Teasle had brought in Trautman to help. That explained some of the tactics the searchers had been using. The bastard. Turning on his own kind.
"Rambo, I want you to stop and surrender before they kill you."
Sure, you bastard.
"Listen to me. I know this is hard to understand, but I'm helping them because I don't want you killed. They've already begun to mobilize another force ahead of you, and there'll be another force after that, and they'll wear you down until there's nothing left of you. If I thought there was the slightest chance of your beating them, I'd gladly tell you to keep on the move. But I know you can't get away. Believe me. I know it. Please. While you still can, give up and get out of this alive. There's nothing you can do."
Watch me. (227-28)

## The Hurt, Betrayed Son 145

Used, abandoned, betrayed. Morrell will have Eliot say almost exactly the same thing as Trautman to Chris and Saul in *The Brotherhood of the Rose*—you can't get away, give yourself up—and will let them prove him half wrong: Eliot kills Chris, Saul kills Eliot. Trautman is completely right in *First Blood*: Rambo can't get away. But that still doesn't change Rambo's feeling of betrayal, his anger at Trautman for "turning on his own kind." That feeling is, in fact, only exacerbated by the disembodied coldness by which Rambo knows Trautman: like Morrell's own father, absent in body and present only in his impoverished mother's stories about him, Trautman was present for Rambo only in "the voice that never failed to signal hardship."

In the movie Trautman is promoted to a colonel, but also made Rambo's personal instructor and team leader, a man who fought alongside him in Vietnam. Despite his higher rank, in the movie he is closer to Rambo when the action starts—a mate, a trusted buddy, not just an impersonal voice. In a modification of the novel's car radio conversation scene added to the Sackheim-Kozoll script by Larry Gross, Trautman contacts Rambo in the mine by radio and gets Rambo to break radio silence (thus allowing the police to get a fix on his position) by invoking military hierarchy. He pretends to be with Rambo back in Vietnam, calls him by his code name, calls off the roll of Baker-team. There is a warmth to their conversation that clearly anticipates the ending: when Trautman says "Look, John, we can't have you running around out there killing friendly civilians," for example, and Rambo replies laconically, and famously, "There are no friendly civilians," one senses that Trautman and Rambo agree on this. There is a shared body of experience between them. But Trautman's next line rings false: "Well, I'm your friend, Johnny." Trautman is trying too hard to be the paternal pal. There is a lot of this falseness in Crenna's voice as he talks to Rambo, saying "Let me come in and fly you the hell out of there," and Rambo quite rightly says "I can't do that, sir." Trautman does seem to be a kind of stable authority figure for Rambo, someone he can trust, someone he can tattle on the cops to ("They drew first blood, not me"). But he is specifically a distant authority figure, an absent father ("I tried to get in touch with you," Rambo says, "but the guys at Bragg never knew how to find you") who can't resist adding his own little reproach:

Rambo: There wouldn't have been any trouble if it hadn't been for that king-shit cop. I just wanted to get something to eat, but he kept pushing.
Trautman: Well, you did some pushing of your own, Johnny.

## 146  No Less a Man

Did he? Maybe he did. Trautman is, of course, in a delicate position: by virtue of his friendship and war experience with Rambo, and their joint contempt for incompetent civilians, he is largely on Rambo's side (he says he has come to protect the cops from him), but he is also constrained to help the police find him and bring him in. Making contact with Rambo over the radio that Rambo stole off Galt's dead body is a way of reestablishing their friendship, of stroking away the effect of absence; but it is also a ruse to give the police a chance to find out where he is. Trautman would like, one gathers, to fly in and take Rambo out; but since he has no authority to make that kind of decision (as Teasle points out, Rambo is a civilian now, and a criminal in his jurisdiction), offering to do so must be understood by both Teasle and Rambo as just another ruse. If for both Teasle and Rambo Trautman feels like an authoritarian father, he probably thinks of himself as a sympathetic mediator, an uncle, maybe, or a much-older brother, caught awkwardly *between* father and son. It is not until the ending that Trautman meets Rambo face to face, without Teasle consciously present (when Rambo and Trautman meet in the police station, Rambo has just shot Teasle through the ceiling and he, Teasle, is lying unconscious on the floor), and is able to work through the father-son conflicts to an empathetic, egalitarian embrace.

# Chapter Seven

# Surrender

Morrell ends the novel darkly, tragically, in one sense: both Rambo and Teasle die. But the death of the two men is not the whole story. In a first stab at father-son reconciliation, Morrell develops an undercurrent of male bonding that harks rather uncomfortably back to the macho privitivism of Hemingway or Mailer. It amounts to a kind of ESP, or what Teasle calls "a kind of extra sense I've been having after what he put me through" (162). In part three Teasle begins to "know" where Rambo is, and what he will do next. At first this "knowledge" is vague: he only knows that Rambo hasn't left the hills where he was last seen. But as Rambo arrives back in town this "extra sense" focuses, and Teasle knows that Rambo will be blasting through town at a certain place and time, and goes there to head him off. He knows that Rambo has "crawled through the playground and pushed himself over the fence there and he's in the wild raspberries, the brambles. I got away from him through brush like that, and now he's trying it, but he's wounded too bad. You can't believe the pain in his chest" (243). "You have to be in his place," Teasle says. "You have to pretend that you're him" (243). He knows that Rambo "wants it to be me" (246), wants to be killed by Teasle, who is dying himself, wants to bond himself to Teasle, and Teasle to him, in death. Trautman ends up blowing Rambo's head off with a shotgun, but the bonding happens anyway. "He thought about the kid, and flooded with love for him, and just a second before the empty shell would have competed its arc to the ground, he relaxed, accepted peacefully. And was dead" (256).

The implication is this is the only way a father can learn to love his son, by killing him, by fighting him to the death. Anything less than that will not be true love, true surrender to the other in love; there will always be a residue of anger and fear, anxiety about being used, abandoned, and betrayed. Morrell gives us the patriarchal myth of fatherhood taken to its ultimate extreme: the son is a threat, a challenger, and must be destroyed. His will must be conformed to the father's, that is essential, but that alone is not enough; there is never any certainty that this conformation will be permanent. The son *will* rise up against the father. The father can never rest easy until he has destroyed the son—and only in the act of destroying him can he find perfect "love" for him. Because what he then comes to love is the perfected *image* of the son, the son made over into the idealized image of the father, the man the father never was and now, in the act of killing the son, becomes.

Rambo too enacts his part of the myth, killing the father (inflicting wounds that kill him slowly enough so that the father's death coincides with his own) and then, after a symbolic Act of Contrition (self-purification), symbolically kills himself:

What about God?

The idea embarrassed him. It was only in moments of absolute fear that he had ever thought about God and prayed to him, always embarrassed because he did not believe and felt so hypocritical when he prayed out of fear, as if in spite of his disbelief there might be God after all, God who could be fooled by a hypocrite. When he was a child, then he believed. He certainly did believe when he was a child. How did it go, the nightly Act of Contrition? The words came hesitantly, unfamiliarly to him. Oh my God, I am heartily sorry for—For what?

For everything that happened the last few days. Sorry that it all had to happen. But it all did have to happen. He regretted it, but he knew if this were Monday again, he would go through the next days the same as he had up to now, just as he knew Teasle would. There was no avoiding any of it. If their fight had been for pride, it had also been for something more important.

Like what?

Like what a lot of horseshit, he told himself: freedom and rights. He had not set out to prove a principle. He had set out to show a fight to anyone who pushed him anymore, and that was quite different—not ethical, but personal, emotional. He had killed a great many people, and he could pretend their deaths were necessary because they were all a part of what was pushing him, making it impossible for someone like him to get along. But he did not totally believe it. He had enjoyed the fight too much, enjoyed too much the risk and the excitement. Perhaps the war had conditioned him, he thought. Perhaps he had become so used to action that he could not ease off.

No, that was not quite true either. If he had really wanted to control himself, he could have. To live his way, he had been determined to fight anyone who interfered. So all right then, in a way he had fought for a principle. But it was not that simple, because he had also been proud and delighted to show how good he was at fighting. He was the wrong man to be shoved, oh yes he was, and now he was dying and nobody wanted to die, and all that he was thinking about principles was a lot of crap to justify it. To think that he would do everything again the same was just a trick to convince himself that what was happening right now could not have been avoided. Christ, it *was* right now, and he could not do one damn thing about it, and neither principle nor pride had any matter in the face of what was to come. What he should have done was cherish more smiling girls and drink more icy water and taste more summer melons. And that was a lot of horseshit too, what he should have done, and all that about God was merely complicating what he had shortly decided: if the numbness creeping up his thighs and forearms was an easy way to die, it was also poor. And helpless. Passively defeating. The one choice left to him was how to die, and it was not going to be like a holed-up wounded animal, a quiet, pathetic, gradually senseless deterioration. At once. In a great burst of feeling. (248-50)

Rambo is an astute self-commentator, here, and I have only two things to add. First, thinking about principles is a way to justify his filial resentment, his overpowering emotional need to resist being pushed, not just now, when he is dying, but all through the book, and probably all through his life. The principles he is thinking about are precisely the liberal principles of rights and freedom of choice and personal autonomy and integrity that men have worked into and borrowed from patriarchal ideology in order to defend themselves against emotional need—or rather, against awareness of emotional need, against having to come face to face with it.

And second, his desire to avoid an easy, helpless, passively defeating death is specifically an attempt to reassert his masculine autonomy, his strength, his power to decide rather than submit to others' decisions. Earlier he had been tempted to give himself up, get medical treatment: "No more running, no more pain in his chest, they would take him to a doctor, feed him, give him a bed. Clean clothes. Sleep" (196). But all that is feminine, or associated with femininity, with the little boy being taken care of by his mommy, being watched over by female angels: being deliciously passive, surrendering the watchful, fearful ego up to protected sleep.[1] He brings his gun up to shoot himself, but then sees Teasle, and realizes that there is a better way: to shoot and be shot by Teasle. He wants either to kill Teasle outright, or miss and give himself away, reveal his position to Teasle by the flash of his gun, and be blown away. He aims, but his body is so numb and his vision so blurred that he only wounds Teasle further. At this point Trautman raises his shotgun and executes Rambo, but we are inside Rambo's dying head and do not know exactly what hits him:

## 150  No Less a Man

Then death took him over, but it was not at all the stupefying sleep, bottomless and murky, that he had expected. It was more like what he had expected from the dynamite, but coming from his head instead of his stomach, and he could not understand why it should be like that, and it frightened him. Then since it was the total of what remained, he let it happen, went with it, erupted free through the back of his head and his skull, catapulted through the sky, through myriad spectra, onward, outward, forever dazzling, brilliant, and he thought if he kept on like this for long enough he might be wrong and see God after all. (254-55)

This is the surrender he has been resisting—postponing—all through the novel. The deadliness of traditional masculine programming is that, because the only surrender you can legitimately allow yourself is death, death comes too soon. You get killed trying to prove your autonomy on the field of battle or in dangerous sports; or you die of a massive coronary (the result of repressing your feelings and resisting your desire for sleep, healing, recuperation) in your 50s. And better the former than the latter: better to die in a "great burst of feeling" than to die poorly, passively, letting the numbness overtake you. The dazzling brilliance Morrell gives Rambo after death—the hope that he will see God—is little consolation. There must be a better way to live than merely choosing the best way to die.

I said earlier that the ten years during which *First Blood* lay fallow, as it were, waiting to be rendered in celluloid, were difficult years for American men, humiliated by the Viet Cong, the Iranians, and American women. But if those humiliations generated in American men a desire to get their own back, to prove their toughness—Carter's failed mission into Iran, Reagan's successful mission into Grenada, Bush's video-game war on Iraq, the resurgence of a male supremacy movement, *Rambo: First Blood Part II* and *Rambo III*, everything Susan Jeffords rightly calls the "remasculinization of America"—it also generated in us a new familiarity with pain, frustration, weakness, and failure, and a new need to come to terms with those feelings.[2] Alongside the male supremacists and the great masses of confused, secretly resentful men there arose during that ten-year period a new pro-feminist men's movement: a movement of men dedicated to understanding and overcoming the masculine gender programming that feminists had been attacking, but from a *male* point of view.

And I want to suggest that the new ending to Morrell's novel that Sylvester Stallone wrote into the Sackheim-Kozoll script comes out of something like this new "masculist" mentality. Not that Stallone was or is consciously affiliated with the men's movement, or that he has even expressed a concern with liberating men from traditional gender programming. I am not making a claim for Stallone as "men's libber." His conscious desire in writing that concluding monologue for Rambo, he told Pat Broeske for her production piece in the *LA Times*, was specifically to give the ignored Vietnam vets a voice: "I thought, what would it be like if a person hadn't been able to talk for five years, and then someone said, 'OK, you've got one minute to sum up everything you've gone through.' What would come out would be something like an abstract feeling—random thoughts overlapping, jumping for position, coupled together with stuttering...at the end Rambo is so angry he can't articulate fast enough" (37-38).

Stallone was worried about vets, not men in general. But in some ways the Vietnam vet is the supreme example of the contemporary American man for whom the old masculine way no longer works, the man to whom the aridity and emptiness of traditional masculinity have been most devastatingly exposed. Here is a group of several hundred thousand men who have been at best studiously ignored and at worst actively despised by an entire society—*precisely for being good macho men*. And what I claim happened to Stallone when he sat down to write that last monologue (which David Giler cut from eighteen pages to one) is that, in drawing from his own experience of failure and weakness and vulnerability and anxiety and fear and anger at betrayal and neglect, he articulated and enacted the cleansing rage and fear and need not only of the vets, but of all humiliated American men.

Embarrassing as male critics have almost invariably found Stallone's monologue,[3] it is, I believe, one of the most moving and potentially liberating events in contemporary American art. When I have talked about the artists I discuss in this book, Parker, Morrell/Stallone, and Springsteen, at academic conferences, I have always read the monologue aloud, and have invariably found myself so caught up in the emotions Stallone is purging that I finish it almost in tears. It tends to have the same effect on the audience, crusty, cynical academics though they are: the men come up and say with a little embarrassment, "Boy, that's powerful stuff," and the women, especially my feminist friends, say things like "You son of a bitch, you had me crying over *Rambo*, what are you trying to do to me?" Well, nothing really, just showing you what is there, what is inside all of us:

Trautman: It's over, Johnny. It's over!

## 152   No Less a Man

Rambo: Nothing is over! Nothing! You just don't turn it off! It wasn't my war. You asked me, I didn't ask you. And I did what I had to do to win, but somebody wouldn't let us win! Then I come back to the world, and I see all those maggots at the airport, protesting me, spitting, calling me baby-killer and all kinds of vile crap. Who are they to protest me, huh? Who are they? Unless they've *been* me, and been there, and know what the hell they're yelling about?

Trautman: It was a bad time for everyone, Rambo. It's all in the past, now. [Read: let bygones be bygones; put the past behind you; grow up; be a man.]

Rambo: For you! For me civilian life is nothing. In the field we had a code of honor: you watch my back, I watch yours. Back here there's nothing.

Trautman: You're the last of an elite group. Don't end it like this.

Rambo: Back there I could fly a gunship. I could drive a tank. I was in charge of million-dollar equipment! Back here I can't even hold a job parking cars! [Hurls M-16 at the wall.] Fuck it! [Collapses to the floor in tears, which he just barely chokes back until the end of the scene.] Oh God...Where is everybody? Gosh...I had a friend. It was Danforth. I had all these guys, man. Back there I had all those funky guys, who were my friends. Come back here there's nothing. Remember Danforth? He wore this black headband, and I took one of his Magic Markers and wrote on it, "If found, mail this to Las Vegas," 'cause we were always talking about Vegas, and this fucking car, this red '58 Chevy convertible, he was talking about this car, he said we were going to cruise till the tires fall off... We were in this bar in Saigon, and this kid comes up, this kid carrying a shoeshine box, and he says, "Shine, please! Shine!" I said no, he kept asking, yeah, and Joey says yeah, and I went to get a couple beers, and the box is wired, you open up the box, fucking blew his body all over the place. And he's laying there, and he's fucking screaming, and there's pieces of him all over me, and [wrestles off a gunbelt] like this, and I'm trying to pull him off, you know, and then—my friend, it's all over me! it's got blood, and everything, and I'm trying to hold him together, and put him together, and his fucking insides keep coming out, and nobody would help! Nobody would help me! He kept saying "Please help me go home, I want to go home," he keeps calling my name, "I want to go home, Johnny, I want to drive my Chevy!" I said, "Well, why? I can't find your fucking legs! I can't find your legs!" I can't get it out of my head. I carried it seven years. Every day it happens. Sometimes I wake up and I don't know where I am! I don't talk to anybody, sometimes a day, sometimes a week. I can't put it out of my mind.

The camera cuts to Trautman, whose steely macho lip is trembling; Trautman takes two steps toward Rambo, stops just in front of him, and Rambo reaches out, clutches his pantleg, then gradually pulls the stiff

Colonel down to floor-level, buries his head in Trautman's chest and sobs. It is, it seems to me, an immensely courageous scene for Stallone to write for himself: certain to embarrass every man in the audience; likely to stain his macho image for good. (In fact, he never went back to that surrender to weakness: in *Rambo: First Blood Part II* he ends the movie not with weakness but with the traditional masculine rage at betrayal, and in *Rambo III* he leaves us with a paternal gesture of friendship toward the surrogate son, and a classic exit into the sunset.)

What Stallone has done is to shift Rambo's surrender from the hopeless death-scene at which Morrell situated it to a redemptive moment *before* death that saves him from death. It is important to remember that even here, even when Trautman appears (out of nowhere, it seems) to encourage him rather paternally to give up, he could have refused. Morrell's Rambo did, and died. He could have kept fighting the police to the death. Trautman appears just as the wounded Teasle is egging him on, telling him to pull the trigger, enact the book's (and the traditional patriarchal father-son relationship's) ending by exacting revenge for humiliation. There is a subtle turning point somewhere in this scene, a point at which Rambo teeters on the verge and could go either way: back into inflexible, self-protective, self-destructive traditional masculinity, or ahead into a black hole of surrender that leaves everything open and uncertain. (It may well be the moment when Rambo slips back from macho action to *words*—when he responds to Trautman's repressive instruction to forget the past with the liberating cry, "Nothing is over! Nothing!") For whatever reason—the producers' decision to let Rambo live, Stallone's desire to give the vets a voice—Stallone hovers on that verge, and then moves forward, allows his character to confront the most terrifying things he can imagine, the nightmares of his past and the uncertainty of the future.

The act of kindness that makes it possible is not, after all, the paternal command to give himself up, Trautman's shout not to end it like this, but the protected moment of respite that Trautman secures him by telling the police to hold their fire. Now it is just Rambo and Trautman: Rambo the hunted warrior and Trautman the man who fought beside him in the jungles of Vietnam and successfully made the transition back to peacetime America. Trautman is the first person in the movie who is in a position to understand what Rambo is going through: he has seen the vets suffer, he has probably suffered himself, although he seems to have the kind of iron self-control that "successfully" represses suffering rather than facing up to it. In any case, once Teasle is shot and the police outside are momentarily pacified, the world shrinks to these two men, fighting mates, instructor and prize pupil, father-confessor and penitent, parent and child.

And what comes out first is all the suppressed rage: "I did what I had to do to win, but somebody wouldn't let us win! Then I come back to the world, and I see all those maggots at the airport, protesting me, spitting, calling me baby-killer and all kinds of vile crap. Who are they to protest me, huh? Who are they? Unless they've *been* me, and been there, and know what the hell they're yelling about?" "Back there I could fly a gunship. I could drive a tank. I was in charge of million-dollar equipment! Back here I can't even hold a job parking cars! Fuck it!" I thought I was important, respected, even admired—and now I'm not. Now I'm nothing, just a nothing kid. Men are not supposed to get angry about this, or about anything: giving in to your anger is feminine, especially when it involves whining about nobody loving you. You're supposed to suppress your anger and get on with the business at hand, which usually involves proving your worth to the people who neglect you. Don't whine, *do* something about it! *Win* their respect! And what happens if they still don't respect you, of course, if they go on refusing to respect you no matter what you do, is that you self-destruct: you keep escalating your attempts to prove your worth until they have to kill you or you have to kill them. So the first thing Rambo does here is to surrender to his anger, releasing it precisely as he is not supposed to, by "complaining," "whining" about being protested and misunderstood. This is the first step to health.

The second is to surrender to fear. The macho man is afraid of nothing. Women and children experience fear; true men never. This was, in fact, one of the most difficult dilemmas faced by the vets: they were terrified of their nightmares, and not only was there no social support system to help them deal with their fear—no hero treatment, say, as in previous wars, and precious little psychiatric help—their masculine programming made them afraid even to admit their fears.

Rambo's fear is first of all a fear of being left alone, being abandoned, isolated from a community of friends: "Where is everybody?" But once he gets started he quickly moves deeper, down through the fear of abandonment to the worst nightmare of all, the violent death of Danforth. Danforth's death deprived him of a friend, left him alone in that sense; but even worse, it left him with an overpowering image of friendlessness, or of the loss of friends, the explosion of friends into irrecoverable pieces. The nightmare he carries around in his head, the vision that he can't get out of his head, the image that organizes his world for him, is an *exploding* image, the image of his friend exploding into pieces. That bomb exploded all coherence in Rambo's mind into incoherence, all solidity into ephemerality, all completeness into fragmentation, all focus into periphery. And he is stuck out there now, stuck in the nightmarish inscape of incoherence, ephemerality, fragmentation, periphery. That is why he is a drifter; that is why he can't hold a job: there is no focus, no solid, coherent image of completeness. The only image he has is an anti-image, a black hole of an image that sucks emotional reality into nothingness.

The power this anti-image has over him is the terror that Rambo can't face up to till the end of the movie: the horrific knowledge not only that he harbors in his body a hole that can't be filled, but that he can't control his attempts to fill it, can't stop pulling himself apart at the seams in search of a solidity or a focus that will bring his life back onto a stable basis. His inability to manage even the barest conformity to society's expectations, even if only to keep insecure small-town cops off his back, is powered by this frantic repression of what he fears. But Rambo's very "wildness," his constant, terrifying access to what he most fears, is itself potentially redemptive. He is, to put it mildly, worse at self-control than Spenser—his anti-image of exploding emptiness is infinitely more vivid than the hole left by Spenser's absent mother (or, for that matter, Morrell's absent father)—but self-control is precisely the wall that separates Spenser from peace of mind, and that Spenser finds too high to climb. Rambo's wall is too low, and the slightest provocation escalates his response dangerously close to murder; but crossing that wall is the only path to health.[4]

So what am I saying? Since self-control keeps us all from going out and murdering people, we should all indulge our secret penchant for killing, and so achieve emotional health?

No. The killing comes not from letting loose, but from self-control: not from surrender, but from the density and the intensity of the barriers raised against surrender. The more you think you have to lose by letting go, the more likely it is that letting go will express itself in violent, destructive ways. Letting go of those barriers, releasing what Freud called resistance, in a safe, protected context is what therapy is all about; and Rambo's tête-à-tête with Trautman at the end of this movie is precisely a therapeutic encounter, a transformative relaxing of the barriers against feeling fear in a safe, protected context. If he had managed that release earlier—if, say, the VA had been properly sensitive to the nightmares vets were carrying around inside them, and had been properly trained to help the vets do something about it—there would have been no need to kill anybody. Rambo might never have become a good "decent" middle-class citizen—he has seen and experienced too much for that, could never force himself into that narrow confine—but he would not have felt compelled to force a conflict with an insecure cop.

Now, in the course of my evangelizing for *First Blood*, I have heard three different objections to this approach to Rambo. One is liberal and elitist: "Aren't you assuming an awful lot of sophistication in Rambo fans? You seem to be saying that people go to Rambo movies to educate themselves, to grow emotionally, to work through emotional blockages and fixations, to do self-therapy. But don't most people just go for the violence? Aren't they just there to see a tough guy like Stallone beat up, kill, and generally humiliate authority figures like cops and demonically portrayed 'enemies' like the VC and the Russians? Where is the therapy in that?" This kind of person is at least potentially sympathetic to the idea of therapeutic art, but thinks I have chosen a most peculiar example of it.

The second objection is populist, anti-elitist: "How boring the Rambo movies would be if Rambo didn't have the 'problems' you keep harping on! There would be no conflict, no drama, no violence either, and say what you like, violence is an immensely satisfying form of entertainment. You seem to want to play shrink to Rambo, to cure him, but why should any Rambo fan want him cured? He's already just the way we want him!" Here the antipathy is obviously at therapy, or at the kind of preachy, wholesome, "educational," good-for-you art that is usually thought of as therapeutic—made-for-TV movies with a message, say.

The third is anti-academic: "Isn't this just a lot of academic hype? Aren't you trying to package a B-grade action movie as high art by claiming that it can change our lives? Aren't you just trying to prove how clever you are by 'discovering' academically respectable elements in a movie that has been perceived in academia as irredeemably masscult?"

Well, that last charge is partly true, I suppose: whatever else I am, I am also an academic, and I suppose there is no getting around it. I am not sure that the therapeutic effect of a movie is academically respectable—academics tend to respect structural complexity, irony, self-consciousness, and the like more than therapeutic effect—and I am certainly not interested in packaging anything as "high art." High art reeks of high school classrooms and upper-middle-class pretensions to me, both of which give me the shudders. But I am trying to see *First Blood* as something like "worthwhile" art, art worth paying serious attention to, and that is, I suppose, at least traditionally, an academic pursuit.

But it seems to me that the third objection is finally just an expression of world-weary cynicism, and thus less weighty than the other two. Anything anybody does can be ridiculed—including being cynical. What I see myself doing in this book, and in all my writing and teaching, is pushing myself and the people around me—my readers, my students—toward a liberating confrontation with the monsters inside. Thus my answer to the first objection is that, while it may be true that many Rambo fans watch *First Blood* to strengthen their defenses, not to engage them, it does not have to be that way. The emotional power of the movie, including the emotional and physical violence, can be used for growing past defenses as well as for solidifying them. Nor do I think, in answer to the second objection, that this requires sappy, saccharine, preachy art. I am not saying that Rambo should be cured (especially before the movie starts!), but that Rambo's engagement with his own worst fears can help *us* be cured. I am not really talking, in other words, about either the empirical facts of audience response (how the statistical majority of Rambo fans respond to the movie) or the aesthetic facts of plot structure or characterization. I do think that the powerful audience response to the movie is an important factor in what I am saying, and that the *First Blood* producers, writers, directors and actors have worked to create a piece of art that is potentially very therapeutic indeed. But I am not interested in making static, descriptive, "objective" remarks about who watches the Rambo movies and why, or how it is structured artistically. I am interested in what we as viewers can do with the movie—how we can use it to change ourselves. I personally find it a powerful tool for self-transformation. All I am really doing is offering it to you too, and making a strong case for its use in your self-transformation.

More than most "masters" of American literature, Robert Parker has pushed back the shrouds of programmed resistance and discovered not only a good deal about what makes men tick, but also a good deal about how to hook male readers into the same growth process he himself is involved in. Morrell and Stallone are involved in the same quest, for power over the resistances to knowing who you are, for knowledge about yourself, and for ways of bringing other men into the quest too; but it seems to me that both Morrell and Stallone, and perhaps particularly Stallone, surpass Parker in their willingness to let their hero break down, surrender self-control, surrender ego, even, and thus to be transformed. When Boone Adams breaks down in *Love and Glory*, the effects are purely destructive, purely to be overcome by the sheer force of controlled will. When Rambo breaks down, it is a therapeutic moment, a moment not to be overcome but to be held onto, prolonged, expanded into the foundation for a new, self-accepting personality.

True, Rambo doesn't prolong the moment—he dies in Morrell's novel, and in Stallone's movie is hauled off to Fort Bragg, where he is recruited by Sam Trautman for his suicide mission into Vietnam in *Rambo: First Blood Part II*. If he expands it into a foundation for anything, it is for self-acceptance as a suffering warrior. But again, the point is not what the artists *give* us, but what we *do* with it. We can take Rambo past the ending of *First Blood* by taking him into ourselves, into our body response, into the way our bodies feel about the world, and act out a different Rambo there: a Rambo, say, who does not need to sacrifice his own comfort and kill bad guys and protect good guys (does not need to become the chivalric hero, the ideal patriarchal man) before he can feel good about himself.

We can also find that internalized self-healing Rambo in other works of art: in John Nichols's novel *American Blood* (1987), for example, as Vietnam vet Michael P. Smith, who works through his nightmarish impulses toward random destruction with the help of a woman, Janine, whom he loves with the uncontrollable passion for getting his way that led to Rambo's battle in *First Blood*. When he gets himself invited to her house for dinner, he tries to rape her—she fights back, successfully, but in the battle between the two of them her arm is broken, her house is demolished, and she and her teenaged daughter Cathie (who stops the destruction by shooting and almost killing Michael) are both severely traumatized. In order to prevent the rape attempt leaving emotional scars on the two of them (herself and her daughter), in order to work it through, Janine decides not to let Michael go—not to let him walk away from the scene of his destruction:

"I'll make it up to you both," I whispered.

"How?"

"I don't know, but I will."

"Maybe you could attack *her* next time, Michael. It's such a wonderful experience. Just what us cock-teasing women adore."

"I'll try to love you, Janine."

"Oh?" She really arched. "How do you plan to do that? Slit our throats, cut off our lips, jam rocks into our vaginas?"

"I don't know. I'll just try to love you."

" 'Love'." She groaned, pressing her hands to her face. "Boy does that sound vulgar coming from your mouth. Shall we get married? I'll wear a white

## Surrender 159

dress to prove I'm a virgin. Cathie can be the flower girl. Instead of champagne we'll drink human blood. Ought to get us off on the right foot together. You know something—?"

I closed my eyes. I sure didn't want to hear it.

"I can't get the feel of your grubby hands off my tits," she said. "I can't seem to scrub your filthy punches off my body." As I opened my mouth to protest, she cut me off. "And don't tell me one more time that you're 'sorry.' You do that, and I'll yank out all those tubes, I'll find a razor, I'll slit your throat."

"Big talk from a little woman."

Her head jerked sideways, and she stared infuriated out the window. Things hummed, bleeped, dripped; laugh tracks from rerun sitcoms gabbled down the hallway.

"Why take it out on me?" she pleaded at last. "Am I such a nasty person?"

No response to that. No answers to any of it. I made a hopeless gesture. Rain pelted down while a big hog gobbled human entrails. I kicked and stabbed and trampled dead VC. Dozens of diminutive gooks on fire zipped around frantically like dying fireflies.

"All right," she said at last. "I think something decent has to happen out of all this. You can't just go your way, and we'll go ours. Neither me or Cathie can continue living in this town, knowing that you are out there. And I aim to live in this town." She stiffened a bit, resolving to be strong again. "I got no place to make my stand at. I'm too tired to head on."

"I don't think I understand."

"We have to deal with this, you and me and her. For your sake, for my sake. For Cathie's sake. Plus I'll admit, crippled as it seems, I feel downright sorry for you, Michael. Maybe you could use somebody on your side if you'd only let them."

"How do we deal with this?" My forlorn voice could not rise above a whisper. How did you deal with those Vietnamese prisoners in the Conex box? How did you deal with hospital rooms full of gorks and bleeders and crispy critters? And how did you deal with a man who loved to fuck communist skulls?

"I think we have to keep knowing each other." She was hesitant, fearful, uncertain if her plan held water, or merely assured a kind of communal suicide. "We have to develop a relationship, and try to work it up to something decent. Otherwise—"

She halted, uncertain, unhappy. So I prompted: "Otherwise, what?"

"Otherwise, it's just like...just like a horrible act of God that doesn't make any sense. Otherwise, it's just crazy," she said exhaustedly. "And Cathie won't ever understand. And you'll just find another stupid woman to attack who won't have half the gumption to resist that I did, and you'll wind up in the electric chair."

"What are you suggesting?"

"I'm not sure." But haltingly she attempted to spell it out. "The three of us have to learn about each other. We have to find a way to care about each other. We have to make it turn into something...positive." (163-65)

And they do. And as they do, we too, Nichols's readers, fight to make "it"—whatever it is in our heads that has us identifying with all this—into something positive too. Nichols opens his novel with 40 pages of the kind of horrors Rambo can't get out of his head—40 pages of exploding images that undermine all attempts at maintaining internal coherence. Michael Smith can't get his images out, either, until Janine forces him to hold on to them, and to her—forces him to hold fast to the nightmares and not run away from either them or the person who is forcing him to look at them. There are more horrors ahead: Tom Carp, the man who loved to fuck communist skulls (the worst psycho in Michael's squad) also lives in town, and for whatever reason—he visits Michael in the hospital after Cathie has shot him and promises to "grease" her for him (ostensibly to avenge his war buddy, but he also just likes to maim and kill)—brutally and horribly murders Cathie. Michael and Janine track him down and go after him, and find him dead, a suicide. But the therapeutic work they have done all through the novel makes it possible for them to survive this new horror too, and the novel ends with a cautious hope for the future.

Or we can find the Rambo inside us in Alan Parker's movie *Birdy* (1986), a movie about childhood friendship, Vietnam, and extreme (psychotic) PTSD that also works through to a cautious hope. The movie, which is based on William Wharton's novel of the same name, is about two very different boys, Al Columbato and Birdy, who become rather unlikely friends and grow up to live through the Vietnam war. Al is straight, macho, an athlete, the right kind of boy, son of a bitter, hostile father (a garbage collector in Philadelphia); Birdy is sensitive, strange, withdrawn, son of a harridan mother and a soft, sensitive father (onetime wicker-chair maker, now janitor at the boys' high school). Despite his machismo, Al is completely intimidated by his father; despite his physical fragility, Birdy stands up to Mr. Columbato.

Birdy has a dream: to become a bird, to be able to fly like a bird, and when his attempts to fly in reality fail (he falls off a roof, builds a set of wings that don't work) he tries in his dreams, gradually moves more and more into a dream world. This is precisely *not* the direction a good man should be going, and the Vietnam War comes along supposedly to make a man out of him. It is not made clear, but Al gets drafted or (more likely, given his machismo) enlists, comes to say goodbye to Birdy, and Birdy's canary Perta follows Al down the street, then comes back to Birdy and crashes through the window and dies. Birdy enlists too, then, in what seems to be a complex sort of grief-stricken death-wish: Perta died flying after Al; I should too. In the war he does re-enact Perta's death: he is in a helicopter that gets shot down, and while he survives physically, to deal with the trauma of crashing he withdraws into psychosis. Al, called by the VA hospital psychiatrist Dr. Weiss, comes to help him, but fails to get through. Dr. Weiss comes on as the heavy father, hostile and suspicious like Al's father—yells at Al for his anti-authoritarian impulses, treats Al like a potential loony—until Al finally gives up and decides not to leave, to stay and be crazy with Birdy:

Al: Don't worry, Birdy, they can't make me leave you. I can't go out there. I couldn't make it. They got the best of us, Birdy. We're both totally screwed up. I mean we haven't had anything to do with making our own lives. Fuck! I was always so goddamn sure about being myself, and how nobody was going to make me do anything I didn't want. And now here I am. They either finish you off with a discharge or put you on a casualty list. It doesn't matter how special you are or were. I feel like one of those dogs nobody wanted, remember? You know, when that shell went off in my face, I could smell burning flesh. And it was crazy, 'cause the smell was so sweet—so familiar. And then I realized it was my own skin that was burning. And I couldn't even touch the pain! [He's sobbing by now] I don't even know what I look like any more, Birdy! I don't know if it's me underneath these bandages, or what some Army cutter thinks is me! Jesus Christ! I don't want some pathetic instant-pity excuse for a face! I just want it to be Al under here! Not some sewn-together freak mask! Shit! What's so great about the fucking world, anyway? We'll just stay here and keep the hell out of it. I don't have to go and get these bandages off. You see, I figured out what you're doing, Birdy. You're right. We should just hide out and not talk with anybody. And every so often, go crazy and run up the wall, and spit, and throw shit at them like the loony across the hall! Yeah! That's what we can do! That's what we can do!

Birdy: Al, sometimes you're so full of shit.

Al: W-was that you? It was! You talked! It's really you! I can't believe this! Say something else!

Birdy: Al...

Al: I can't believe it, it's really you! How come you decided to talk?

## 162   No Less a Man

Birdy: I didn't decide. It just happened, I don't know. You needed me, didn't you?
Al: Yeah!

Al helps Birdy to escape to the roof, pursued by the VA hospital staff, and while Al is making an obstacle for their pursuers Birdy goes to the edge of the roof and jumps off. Al sees at the last moment what Birdy is doing, thinks he is trying to commit suicide, cries "No! No!" and runs to the edge, where he discovers that it was just a 15-foot jump down to a lower roof, and Birdy is standing there unharmed, all innocence, saying "What, Al?" End of movie.

Or—and this points us onward, to part three—we can find Rambo in the songs of a man who, like Al Columbato and Birdy, grew up in a depressed working-class family in the industrial Northeast (New Jersey instead of Philadelphia), and like them has worked through his adolescent deviance, his difference from the social norms that guaranteed acceptance and approval, to a confrontation with the ideal of escape ("flight" in the literal sense for Birdy) into paradise and with the inevitable failures of that ideal. I am referring, of course, to Bruce Springsteen—one of the most successful questers after self-transformation in recent popular art.

# Part Three
# *S*PRINGSTEEN

# Breathing Again

2. But my enemy crawled out of the night
   When I killed him he devoured the light
   The cold black waters rippled slow
   His dark shark's body slid below
   When I saw his blood I thought I was dead
   His red tears numbed me with dread
   I caught my breath and eased out a sigh
   I gulped for air and started to die

3. I die in order that I might live
   I take in order that I might give
   I cry in order that I might laugh
   I answer that I might ask
   Will you never fill up my mouth?
   Will you never caress my pout?
   Will you never let me weep?
   Will you never let me sleep?

   CHORUS

4. My mother rattles vessels of dark
   Her gloved hand squeezes my heart
   Her nightmares stifle my dreams
   Down here nothing's what it seems
   The fetus hides in his fleshly cage
   Pounding on his bars in a rage
   His knees beat time on my chest
   Is there no place we can rest?

   CHORUS instrumental

5. The prison door erupted in blood
   The shark slithered white as a dove
   In death he was a fingerling
   Through my sobs I started to sing
   I sang of all his pain that was mine
   I sang of fear and love intertwined
   I sang of how he saved me in death
   I sang till I'd won back my breath

   CHORUS twice

Copyright 1993 Doug Robinson.

## Chapter Eight

## The Dark Street

On September 20, 1981, while Stallone was in the middle of revisions of the *First Blood* script and the film crew was setting things up in Vancouver, B.C., to begin shooting, Bruce Springsteen played a benefit concert in Los Angeles for the Vietnam Veterans of America, a group formed in 1978 by a former Marine named Bob Muller. After three years of hard work, Muller's group was still operating on a shoestring budget and, despite a massive response from the vets and some cautious recognition from the press, was still being stonewalled by the government. As Dave Marsh tells the story in *Glory Days*, the second volume of his excellent Springsteen biography, Springsteen wanted to do something to help the vets and asked his manager Jon Landau to set up a meeting with Muller:

Of all the shut-out groups of Americans he knew, Bruce was most moved and intrigued by the plight of the Vietnam veterans. He was no Rambo, and he frankly admitted doing everything he could to avoid being drafted. "I had no real political standpoint whatsoever when I was eighteen. And neither did any of my friends," he said. "The whole draft thing, it was just a pure street thing. You didn't want to go. You didn't want to go because you'd seen other people go and not come back. The first drummer in my first band, the Castiles, enlisted and he came back in his uniform and he was 'Oh here I go, I'm goin' to Vietnam.' Kinda laughin' and jokin' about it and that was it. He went and he was killed. There were a lotta guys from my neighborhood, guys in bands.... One of the best singers in the neighborhood, he was drafted and he went and he was missing in action.

"And so it got to be a thing. We didn't even know where Vietnam was when I was eighteen, seventeen. We just knew we didn't want to go and die. It wasn't until probably later in the Seventies that the awareness of the type of war it was, what it meant, the way it felt to be a subversion of all the true American ideals, twisted the country inside out—it wasn't until then that we had any what you would call political awareness about it."

Springsteen was 4-F because of a brain concussion received in a 1968 motorcycle accident in which he also badly injured his leg. Getting out of the draft wasn't that simple though. Springsteen filled out forms crazily, didn't take tests, did his best to get out of serving. But he never forgot how near he'd come.

"When I got on the bus to go take my physical, I thought one thing: *I ain't goin'*. I had tried to go to college, and I didn't really fit in. I went to a real narrow-minded school where people gave me a lot of trouble and I was hounded off the campus—I just looked different and acted different, so I left school. And I remember bein' on that bus, me and a couple of guys in my band, and the rest of the bus was probably sixty, seventy percent black guys from Asbury Park. And I remember thinkin', like, what makes my life, or my friends' lives, more expendable than that of somebody who's goin' to school? It didn't seem right."

By 1981 Springsteen's position on the war hadn't changed and neither had his feelings for those who couldn't escape fighting it. The war had been wrong and worse, and the men and women who fought it had been badly betrayed—not by "lack of national will," but by a government that was eager to use them to carry out pernicious foreign policy objectives and then discarded them without thanks when they returned defeated. (March *Glory* 66-67)

He read Ron Kovic's 1976 memoir of the war, *Born on the Fourth of July*, and a few months later found himself on stage at the LA Sports Arena addressing 20,000 rock fans, including a lot of vets, some of whom had to be brought to the show on their hospital gurney tables. Despite his nervousness about making a political speech to a rock audience—his first—Springsteen's introductory words were intense, focused around a powerful metaphor of seeing and not-seeing:

And it's like when you feel like you're walkin' down a dark street at night and out of the corner of your eye you see somebody gettin' hurt or somebody gettin' hit in the dark alley but you keep walkin' on because you think it don't have nothin' to do with you and you just wanna get home.

Well, Vietnam turned this whole country into that dark street. And unless we're able to walk down those dark alleys and look into the eyes of the men and the women that are down there and things that happened, we're never gonna be able to get home…and then it's only a chance. (qtd. in March *Glory* 72)

What is striking about this metaphor is that, as Springsteen presents it, it cuts two ways: onto the broad, collective, national level, where all America is the dark street and the willingness to walk down it and "look into the eyes of the men and the women that are down there and things that happened" becomes a radicalizing political awareness; and also, carried by the opening hint that "it's like when you *feel* like you're walkin' down a dark street at night," down into the dark street of the soul, where the willingness to walk with your eyes open means leaving yourself vulnerable to an even more frightening emotional awareness.

Here, I think, in Springsteen's imagistically grounded dialectic between the collective and the individual, between the public and the private, between external and internal forces and resistances, is the best place to begin my "reading" of his music. Unlike the solid Boston liberal Parker and the conservative Morrell and Stallone, Springsteen has openly espoused—if hesitantly, and only in the past ten or so years— radical working-class politics. The frequent contributions he has made to left-of-center political organizations; the increasingly articulate and pointed speeches he has made onstage and in interviews for the forgotten and neglected (the Vietnam vets, the unemployed, the homeless) and against smug American chauvinism; the benefit concerts he has played for the VVA, the Harry Chapin Foundation (December 1987), Amnesty International (September 1988), and others—all this attests to a dedication to radical social change, through the medium of music, primarily, but also through an appropriation and redirection of public speech and coin.[1] Springsteen is, after all, one of the richest and most popular rock stars in America today, and if the monetary rewards that have accrued to him from "hustlin' for the record machine," as he sang back in "Jungleland" (*Born to Run,* 1975), can be a powerful weapon *against* the record machine and the dehumanizing capitalist system it represents, so too can the sought-after words of a major cultural hero, a star, be effectively turned against the hegemonic institutions that conspire to *give* him that voice.

And Springsteen has worked hard, all through the 1980s and early 1990s, to redirect the flow of money and public voice to those impoverished and silenced by this land of opportunity. On the other hand, he could have worked harder. To take only one monetary example, where Springsteen typically donates $10,000 per concert to some local political or charitable organization, Harry Chapin typically donated half his concert proceeds to similar organizations. And money is, of course, only a rough and perhaps misleading indicator. More important than the smallness or largeness of Springsteen's donations is the type of verbal support or contextualization he gives his songs. Like his music it is, almost invariably, grounded in image and story. "And it's like when you feel like you're walkin' down a dark street at night"—there is a story there, and a powerful image that grounds the story he is going to tell in everyone's private but significantly collectivized nightmares, each individual fan's ideological nightmares: the law-abiding citizen's fear of the dangers that lurk on dark streets (murder, robbery, rape), the collectively instilled fear of darkness that keeps people law-abiding, keeps them from straying from the well-lighted path of decency and righteousness, keeps them also from exploring the darkness inside themselves.... This grounding of radical politics in image and story is one of Springsteen's greatest strengths as a rock star (both as singer-songwriter and as public figure), for it makes the things he has to say immediately accessible to tens of millions; but it is also (to the extent that he wants to change the world, as he says he does) his greatest weakness, for it makes his words and tunes easily reappropriable for reactionary purposes. After all, what is to be done if the streets are too dark and dangerous to walk? More light. More law and order. Break some heads (the conservative answer). Or: more education. More responsibility. Do your civic duty (the liberal answer). Springsteen's images typically radicalize the imagination by bringing us face to face with shadowy border areas, the dark streets just beyond the glow of the streetlights, and insisting that we explore them; but something always seems to remain unarticulated, a mythic and therefore potentially reassuring residue of some sort, caught in between myths of radical change and secure havens, that allows Springsteen fans to back away, retreat and regroup, patch up the torn clothing that tells of the assault from the darkness, and go on believing that everything is still fundamentally all right.

What I hope to do in this concluding section of the book is to push on into those dark areas of Springsteen's artistic work—to follow him into them, through an attention to the radicalizing effect of his images and stories and tunes, without backing away. Given the limitations of space and my own imagination, I will in fact be backing away from a good deal; I make no claim to exhaustive coverage, even of the very few songs I have the space to deal with. As in my reading of *First Blood*, my concern will be with setting up a certain kind of interpretive alignment or stance, a willingness "to walk down those dark alleys and look into the eyes of the men and the women that are down there and things that happened"—even a willingness to question the immensely attractive nostalgia of Springsteen's warning that otherwise "we're never gonna be able to get home."

Just a few weeks after playing for the VVA in Los Angeles, in fact, Springsteen returned to New Jersey and began to pour himself into precisely the sort of project I propose here, fleshing out his sense of inner and outer darkness (musically instead of critically, of course), incarnating it in what may be the most searching and personal album of his career, *Nebraska*. He later described the process of writing and recording *Nebraska* to Dave Marsh in terms unmistakably reminiscent of his speech to the benefit audience in LA: "So I just dove into it. I decided to look around. I decided to move into the darkness and look around and write about what I knew and what I saw and what I was feeling. I was trying to find something to hold onto that doesn't disappear out from under you" (*Glory Days* 95).

Judging from the incredible barriers Spenser and Rambo have to smash through in order to "move into the darkness," Springsteen's blithe "I decided to look around" is probably a little understated. It's not something you just "decide" to do. "I just *dove* into it" is closer; but my sense of what really happens is that you feel driven to dive, compelled to move into the darkness by things in your head, in your life, the failure of your defenses to keep the outer monsters out and the inner monsters in, and you withstand the pressure to do so for a long time, because you're afraid of it. But finally you give in and say, "Okay, okay, I'll do it." Or you find yourself already in the middle of it, whether you want to be or not. Springsteen had been feeling the pressure to move into the darkness since his incredible success with *Born to Run* (1975), and his next album after that was titled *Darkness on the Edge of Town* (1978); but it really wasn't until late 1981, sitting in his New Jersey house in a rocking chair in front of a four-track cassette machine with a guitar in his hands, that he was ready to plumb the depths, go down deep and look the inner monsters in the face.

The result was an album that diverged sharply from the rambunctious rock sound Springsteen had been developing ever since he played with the Castiles in high school. The recordings he made on the four-track board weren't originally intended to be released as an album—they were demos for the band to rehearse from—but everybody, in the band and the production team alike, quickly realized that the demos had a haunting, lonely sound to them that was much more moving than anything the band could do. Not only had he cut away the excess noise of the earlier records, the defensive noise, the noise that hid the monsters from view; he had simplified the music to the barest minimum, a voice (sung soft and low, as if to himself) and a guitar (plucked or strummed simply, with simple major chords—A, D, and G on a surprising number of bleak, dark numbers). Dave Marsh says, "He'd stripped his music until he laid bare the folk roots of rock and roll itself" (129), and I'd paraphrase: he had stripped himself until he laid bare the inner soul of rock and roll.

All of the songs he recorded between October and December of 1981 were charged with an intense awareness of that "quiet desperation" Thoreau says the mass of us live our lives in; unlike Thoreau, however, and his mentor Emerson, and his followers the Roberts Frost and Parker, all of whom did and do their best not to confront the desperation and deal with it but to control it, suppress it, bring it to heel, Springsteen allows himself to live it, feel it fully, opens himself up to it, lets it fill his body and his music.

This is, of course, one of the things music does to you: along with dance it is the most physical of all the arts, the most in tune with the rhythms of the body, the beat of the heart, the expansion-and-constriction of your breathing, the surging of your blood through your veins, the pulsing of alpha waves in your brain. Music dances the tensions in your neck and chest and stomach; it captures the desperate breakaway movement of your shoulders and arms and legs as they shrug off chains, and releases your desire to be wrapped up tight in a secure embrace. To feel the music is to feel the life of your own body. To write music well—deeply, powerfully—as Springsteen does is to plumb the life of your body. "I decided to move into the darkness and look around and write about what I knew and what I saw and what I was feeling"—*musically*. Think of the tools Spenser and Rambo bring to bear on their dilemmas: violence and intellect, the deadening, destructive extremes of body and mind that become men's last recourse when the extremes are pushed too far apart, kept too separate from each other. Springsteen has a much finer, subtler, and enormously more effective tool: rock music.

In two of the songs he wrote late in 1981, what was to become the album's the title song "Nebraska" and "Johnny 99," the desperation he is feeling explodes outward in Rambo style, in the form of violent murder, fiercely, intensely, in the spirit of the man who's been driven too far to turn back, in "Johnny 99," and flatly, resignedly, in the spirit of a man who's too far gone even for intensity, in "Nebraska." "Johnny 99" has a driving, nervous beat that is tinged with fear and anger—a lot like "Born to Run" from seven years earlier, in fact, but without the Phil Spector wall of sound to shore up Springsteen's defenses against fear—and while it's written in a major key (using only two chords, B and F#), Springsteen spends most of his melodic time on the third, second, and first of the B chord, hovering just short of triadic completion. And the lyrics give specificity and direction to this sense of frustration, falling short of goals, not even high, idealistic goals, either, just the desire to live a decent life, to have a job, to feel even halfway good about yourself. Ralph loses his job at the Mahwah auto plant when they close it down; in a depressed economy in the depressed Northeast there are no jobs to be found; the bank threatens to foreclose on his mortgage if he fails to make all outstanding payments; finally in frustration he "came home too drunk from mixin' Tanqueray and wine / He got a gun, shot a night clerk, now they call him Johnny 99."

## 172 No Less A Man

It is the desperate deed of a desperate man, a man pinned down very much like Rambo, in fact, by a depersonalized and dehumanizing economic/military/legal system that regards the working class as a reservoir of expendable soldiers (Rambo) and wage-slaves (Ralph), to be used as long as they are needed and then discarded. Needless to say, the system that reifies Ralph—treats him like a thing—reacts without mercy when he insists on his injured humanity: since the press has for some reason branded him "Johnny 99," the judge sentences Ralph to 99 years in prison. The figure is as arbitrary as the name, which in turn is as dehumanizing for a man who wants to be called by his "true name" ("Adam Raised a Cain," *Darkness on the Edge of Town*, 1978) as the loss of job and house for a man taught to equate those things with dignity and self-worth. Like Morrell's Rambo, however, Ralph can't see himself wasting away in jail for the rest of his life, so he begs to be executed:

> Well your honor I do believe I'd be better off dead
> So if you can take a man's life for the thoughts that's in his head
> Then sit back in that chair and think it over judge one more time
> And let 'em shave off my hair and put me on that killin' line

This is, as Morrell discovered in his first novel, one way to push yourself into contact with the nightmares inside: to imagine yourself driven beyond control, beyond even the primal human instinct to survive, to protect yourself against dying, and to *let go*.[2] Like Morrell's Rambo, who wants to go out in a great burst of feeling, Springsteen's Ralph pushes himself toward death with intense, explosive drama: the song progresses through the stale cliches of courtroom movies (the girlfriend being dragged away, the mother pleading with the judge) in a kind of frenzied double-time, a surrealistic speeding up of the projection system until the figures blur together and your eyes and ears cry for relief.

"Nebraska" is calmer, more reminiscent of Morrell's deadpan prose than of his frantic hero. It's a flat country tune that is absolutely devoid of excitement, unless each verse's eighteenth-bar shift up out of the song's tired A-D cycle into G can be counted as excitement. Here, as in many of the other *Nebraska* songs, Springsteen's usually nervous high tenor voice is pitched low, at the very bottom of a tenor range, and that sucks all force out of it: the song lacks all vestiges of the charismatic energy Springsteen usually brings to his singing. It's the flatline deadness of a man who has given up on life, even on death—a man who can no longer look forward to *anything*, even his own execution, with interest, much less excitement. The song is the first-person memoir of Charles Starkweather, who killed ten people on a senseless eight-day rampage in 1958; Springsteen had just seen Terence Malick's 1974 movie about Starkweather, *Badlands*, with Martin Sheen and Sissy Spacek, on TV, and found the Martin Sheen character powerfully attractive as a dramatic enactment of the deadness he was so scared of inside himself. And in his lyrics he didn't flinch from that deadness, but stood square in the middle of it, let it swirl around inside his body, let it deaden his limbs and infect his voice:

> I saw her standin' on her front lawn just a-twirlin' her baton
> Me and her went for a ride sir and ten innocent people died

Rock critics have noticed the frequent use of "sir" all through this album, pointing to a kind of flat deference in Springsteen's characters—they're too exhausted to rebel against authority. But what this song lyrically (or euphonically) makes clear is that the "sirs" are part of a larger pattern, in which all the ugliest sounds in the English language—er, uh, aa—are given particular stress. In the first line alone "her" appears three times, once (before "front") stretched out, as is the same sound in "twrrlin'." Springsteen hits the aa of "staandin' " and the uh of "front" and "buh-ton" hard too, with all the dead weight of a backwoods country drawl. If you listen to it this way, the song becomes almost a parody of country-Western singing, but Springsteen isn't trying to ridicule anybody; he's "dead" serious, literally serious about that deadness he finds in himself, which is, I think, the feeling he means by "meanness" in the last verse:

> They declared me unfit to live said into that great void my soul'd be hurled
> They wanted to know why I did what I did
> Well sir I guess there's just a meanness in this world

In other words, there's just a deadness in this "wrrrld," as the lyrics and the flat country twang and the uninflected music all confirm. The world feels mean in the sense not of nastiness but of stinginess: something is being withheld, some spark of joy, some gift of life that we grew up believing was coming to us, but *isn't*. One response to discovering that we're not going to get what we keep believing is coming to us is to go wild, let loose, kill people more or less at random, like Morrell's Rambo and Springsteen's Johnny 99 and Charles Starkweather. Another is to write a novel or compose a song or make a movie about going wild, and so confront that wildness therapeutically.

It may be wrong to say that Springsteen had been working up to this moment for almost 15 years, since he first started playing in a high school rock band at the age of 14. It may be better to say he had been working *back* to it, *down* to it, ever since he first started to make it big in rock, when he was discovered by John Hammond of Columbia Records (legendary discoverer of Billie Holiday and Bob Dylan) in 1972: back from the heights of success (on the covers of *Time* and *Newsweek* simultaneously after the release of *Born to Run* in 1975) to the humiliations of his childhood, the dehumanizations of a man-in-training by his emotionally withdrawn father, of a citizen-in-training by the nuns and his peers at a Catholic school:

I hated school. I had the big hate. I remember one time, I was in eighth grade and I wised off and they sent me down to the first grade class and made me sit in these little desks, you know, little chairs. And the sister, she said, "Show this young man what we do to people who smile in this classroom"—I was probably laughing at being sent down there. And this kid, this six-year-old who has no doubt been taught to do this, he comes over to me—him standing up and me sitting in this little desk are about eye-to-eye—and he slams me in the face. I can feel the sting. I was in shock.... In the third grade a nun stuffed me into a garbage can she kept under her desk because she told me that's where I belonged. (qtd. by Gambaccini 8-9)

"We learned more from a three-minute record," he would later sing—boastfully? no, bitterly—"than we ever learned in school" ("No Surrender," *Born in the U.S.A.*, 1984). But if his first three albums are any indication, what he learned from a three-minute record (one by Elvis, in fact) was mostly escape. On his first album, for example, *Greetings from Asbury Park, N.J.* (1973), he talks about "Growin' Up" in a circular piano tinkle (Csus/F—C/E—C9/D—C/E—Csus/F) that takes him on "month-long vacations in the stratosphere" in his jukebox "B-52," which he uses both to strafe his old high school and to resist the temptation to "land," settle down, get a job, get married, become an upright citizen. What makes the song circular, both in its chord progression and its vision of life in society, is that Springsteen is unable to imagine a real alternative to that ideological norm. You go up and you come back down. You leave and you return home. Home is the place of repression, but it is also the only place of community; to have community, a sense of belonging, you must accept and adapt yourself to repressive social norms. So you conform outwardly and only dream of escape.

In his second album, released later the same year, *The Wild, The Innocent, & The E-Street Shuffle* (1973), and the big one that came after that, *Born to Run* in 1975, Springsteen explores a new solution: get your girlfriend to come with you. That way you can have both freedom and community and sacrifice nothing. It is not, of course, a novel project; it is one of the deepest dreams of capitalized manhood, masculinity bound to the capitalist machine with the finest gossamer strands of what is euphemistically called love but deep down means possession and incarceration. The myth of the mysterious stranger—the Western hero who travels alone, appears from nowhere, turns outlaw or defender of the innocent as he chooses, and vanishes without a trace when his "work is done," or when civilization begins to cramp him—is one escapist dream that simultaneously sustains and contains the economically and emotionally incarcerated worker: like Walter Mitty, one survives an unbearable existence by dreaming about escape from it, reading popular novels of escape, watching movies and TV shows of escape, listening to songs of escape on the radio. "Growin' Up" both offers an escapist daydream of this sort to its listeners and finds it impossible to imagine anything more for its speaker; songs like "Sandy" from *The Wild, The Innocent* and "Thunder Road" and "Born to Run" from *Born to Run* still offer nothing more than this sort of escapist dream to its listeners, but now the speakers imagine something more: community *on the road*. "Ya oughta quit this scene too," the Springsteen hero tells Sandy in the song named after her, and in "Thunder Road" and "Born to Run" he devotes all his energy to persuading the girlfriend (Mary, Wendy) to leave with him. These are the songs that made Springsteen rich and famous, in fact; they are extremely lyrical utopias of a life of both love and freedom, togetherness and isolation, belonging and escape: "the night's busting open," he tells Mary in "Thunder Road," "these two lanes will take us anywhere"—"climb in back / Heaven's waiting on down the tracks." A heaven *with you*: this is the dream that powers these songs. Springsteen knows the dangers of running as well as the attractions, and he never hides them: "The highway's jammed with broken heroes on a last-chance power drive," he says in "Born to Run"; "Everybody's out on the run tonight but there's no place left to hide." But he also forces himself, with the sheer energy of his dozen guitar tracks if nothing else, to believe in the utopia that lies at the other end of the rainbow:

> Together Wendy we could live with the sadness
> I'll love you with all the madness in my soul
> Oh someday girl I don't know when
> We're going to get to that place where we really want to go
> And we'll walk in the sun but till then
> Tramps like us baby we were born to run

This utopian dream is unquestionably preferable to the repressive defense of the "death trap" as represented in *First Blood* by Sheriff Will Teasle. Still, as David Morrell knows, the road taken by both Rambo and Springsteen's hero in "Born to Run" is just as defensive, just as self-protective, as staying in town. The people who don't leave are afraid of being chewed up by the treacherous highway, which is, after all, jammed with broken heroes like Rambo on their last-chance power drive; but the "heroes" who do leave are afraid of being chewed up by the treacherous town, which, as Springsteen says here, "rips the bones from your back." *Both* the town and the road are death traps. It all depends on where you place yourself—or find yourself placed by economic or emotional powers beyond your control—with regard to the dreams of freedom and community. It all depends on what you are more afraid of, compromise or loneliness. And if, beneath the idealized facade of capitalist community, there is a deep-seated loneliness and alienation, there is also, beyond the idealized pale of mythic escape, the constant existential fact of self-compromise and self-hatred.[3]

In fact, ultimately there is very little difference between running away and staying put. Both are, as I started to say a minute ago, complementary expressions of capitalized manhood, of masculinity under conditions of capitalist patriarchy. There is the controlled good citizen, good father, good husband, good son, good employee, who regards his ideologically mandated-programmed-and-superbly-maintained self-control (that which keeps him a productive and obedient member of society) as a matter of personal autonomous choice, and carefully represses all rebelliousness in himself and his children along with the literal enactment of his escapist fantasies, so as to maintain what he thinks of as his freedom and integrity; and there is the controlled loner, pariah, wanderer, who knows how close he always stands to weakness, to the infantile desire for intimacy, sharing, belonging, love, cuddling, security, familiarity, protection, and carefully represses all that so as to maintain *his* freedom and integrity. They are two sides of the same ideological coin—or, perhaps, of the ideological capital only abstractly represented by coin.

The one important difference between running and staying put, as Springsteen began to discover out on the lonely road of *The Wild, The Innocent* and *Born to Run*, is that the "cautious man of the road" (as he would sing on *Tunnel of Love*) is typically more vulnerable to his own doubts and inner divisions than the man of the town. In town there are routines, rituals, well-worn social paths that protect you against awareness of self-doubt and division. (Will Teasle was better at repressing his torn feelings of love for and resentment of Orval

Kellerman than Rambo his need for love and approval and feeling of betrayal and abandonment.) Defensively naive as the "Born to Run" hero is, for example, dedicated as he is to solving all his problems with the madness of a wall of sound out of Phil Spector and Harley-Davidson, he does know that he and Wendy are going to have to live with sadness. For the road out of formulaic solutions and ritualized answers is paved with sadness. The road may begin in a defensive flight from the traps of community, belonging, limitation; but once you've started down it, it quickly becomes a road into the fear and the loneliness and the unfulfilled need we all carry around with us.

Springsteen's fourth and last album of the 1970s, *Darkness on the Edge of Town* (1978), was very much a transitional album for him. If we could think of these first four albums as Springsteen's tracing of the ground covered in *First Blood*, *Darkness* is the dark finale of that novel and movie, the night scene when Rambo has come back into town from the wilderness but is still not *of* the town, still lurks in the dark shadows of the town, and has to decide whether he is going to destroy everything, including himself, in a bang-up apocalyptic finish, or give himself up (the two alternatives presented to him, as to any outlaw, by a repressive society)—or, perhaps, whether he is going to find a third alternative. Springsteen came to the recording studio to make *Darkness* with fresh wounds from a bitter (no less bitter because victorious) court battle with his former manager Mike Appel, over the terms of the management contract (royalties, control of song rights); but the emotional fallout from the court battle has perhaps been exaggerated.[4] I read *Darkness* not as Springsteen's emotional response to an economic threat, nor even as a musical response to an emotional threat (economics personalized, legal control of song rights as metonymy for emotional control of self), but as a diving into a dark sea or street that had been waiting to swallow him up all along—pushed, as it were, by the very energy he had built up in *Born to Run* to fend off the terrors of the deep. Like Rambo throughout *First Blood*, Springsteen had been running from something all his life, especially, or perhaps only less and less unconsciously, throughout the successes of the 1970s (his 20s); and his running had been pushing him toward something, toward an abyss or an alienation deep inside himself, a darkness, that threatened (to melodramatize only slightly) his very sanity.

Part of it was his new fame, of course, and the isolation and bondage it almost irresistably brought. Ever since he was nine years old and saw Elvis on Ed Sullivan's show, he had known that he wanted to do for others what Elvis had done for him: redeem them from the hopelessness of their lives, fill their lives with meaning and direction. So when he was touted, after *Born to Run*, as the Rock and Roll Messiah, he must have felt some private twinge of satisfaction: that was, after all, what he got into the business for, saving souls, as it were, with a power the sisters who had taught him about Jesus had never heard of. But such acclaim is also insidious. Ironically, the man who was born to run is now run out of town—replaced by a clever double who gets his picture on the covers of *Time* and *Newsweek* and calls himself "Brucc" or, more irritatingly, "Boss." As he said much later of the whole period from the mid-1970s to the mid-1980s, "I really enjoyed the success of *Born in the U.S.A.*, but by the end of that whole thing, I just kind of felt 'Bruced' out.... You end up creating this sort of icon, and eventually it oppresses you" (Henke 41). The impostor gets all the attention, draws the stares and the crowds, and leaves you "lost and brokenhearted," as Springsteen would sing on *Darkness* ("Promised Land").[5]

On the one hand, he *can't* run, now; he has responsibilities to his fans, whom he has tacitly promised to save from their humdrum existences: he is a hero broken not out on the road, as he imagined himself in "Born to Run," but right there in town, on the wheel of his responsibility (like his father!). But on the other hand the man who is bound to those fans by iron bonds of responsibility is not even him, the little boy who wants to belong, but the impostor, whose imposture thus leaves him even more isolated than before.[6] Even more than the anonymous lonely road of the Western hero, the lonely road of fame in modern mass society "rips the bones from your back," peels off the protective layers with which you were hiding your own inner divisions from yourself and either drives you crazy or drives you sane—or rather, it drives you into that dark night of the soul from which you either protect yourself with chemical substances, mental illness, or suicide, or else emerge transformed.

In a 1987 BBC documentary on him called *Glory Days*, Springsteen (interviewed by David Hepworth) rehearsed the transitional period he went through around the time of *Darkness*:

*Springsteen*: After I got in the lawsuit, and I guess things had slowed down, and I began to write new music, and I guess at some point I realized some basic thing, that maybe you know I was the guy that gets the guitar, and I get the car, you know, and I get the girl, you know, and maybe I get to leave town, I get to get away, I get to escape, and I get to go down the highway. And you're scootin' down there, and everything's great, and you feel good, and then you realize that there's not a whole lot of other traffic on the road, you know, and that the cars that are passing you by have those real dark tinted windows, and you can't see in 'em too well. And then you realize that, like, that adds up to a big "So what?" You know, whatever you're doing, it just adds up to a big "So what?" And that what you are doing without a connection with the community, and with the people I grew up with, and with people who I hadn't met yet—what I was doing, it wouldn't have meant anything, it wouldn't have *been* anything.

*Hepworth*: Were you at the time looking at the example of people who'd gone before, from Elvis Presley to John Lennon to Mick Jagger, and thinking that by going that far and being that successful they were bound to lose some part of themselves?

*Springsteen*: I really don't think it was anything as conscious as that. I think it was just some, something, some survival instinct. I really do. I think that I knew that, that the most important thing to me was what happened when I walked out, whether it was in a little bar or on any stage, and how it made me feel. Because I wanted to find some way *in*, some way to be a part of, I guess, a community that I either, that was either really there or that I imagined, that I dreamt of. And that I knew that, not necessarily success, 'cause that's, that's just there, or it's not there, or, or—but that the things that can accompany it, you know, either the self-delusion, the distraction, the illusion, were things that, that felt threatening, they for some reason—which was why, when I was saying earlier, that, you know, *Time* and *Newsweek* and—I felt threatened at that time, I felt, those things felt threatening to some, some part of myself which would, which I felt was where I really lived, and what really made me want to live. And so, when I kinda, when I started to do *Darkness*, which, if you—most of the material on *Darkness* is confrontational, it's about somebody that, he turns the car around, and he heads back to town, you know, for better or for worse. It was something, it was something I felt I just had to do, you know, and that was where, I felt that there were so many people who had lost that part of themselves—great musicians, great artists, great singers, great—you know, a long line of them—and when they did, you know, much younger than they should have, they died essentially, or they died somewhere inside. That sorta cut them off from, from everything and everybody else that meant something. So I started to write songs about things that had happened to me, at one time or another, and I started to feel the reconnection.

Part of this process involved writing a different kind of song: less mythically integrated, less insistent on a fantasized Phil Spector unity, more inwardly divided both thematically and musically. *Darkness* is Springsteen's first determined exploration in inner division. It is unified, if at all, not by a striving for unity, a summoning of all physical and emotional strength behind a single-minded quest, as was *Born to Run*, but by Springsteen's willingness to lose unity, to be broken up—to *let go*. Three of the songs, "Adam Raised a Cain," "Streets of Fire," and

"Darkness on the Edge of Town," are musically divided between slow passages of self-control, trying to understand, trying to be reasonable, and sudden wild bursts of increasingly desperate energy, explosions of frustrated anger—the kind of erratic-tempoed songs you hated to dance to in high school (which is part of the point: Springsteen ain't in high school no more, adulthood is breaking up the dance, ruining his Saturday night). But *all* the songs are divided thematically, as Springsteen turns the power not only of his melodies but of his imagery and story-telling onto the problem of the abysses and alienations he feels within and without, inscribed on his body and in society at large.

The two songs on *Darkness* that perhaps most clearly reflect and enact (and perhaps help catalyze) Springsteen's crossing of the threshold from destructive anger into self-dispersal, self-surrender—that threshold that we saw Rambo crossing at the end of Stallone's movie, and that I want to show Springsteen moving beyond in the concluding chapters of this book—are "Promised Land" and "Darkness on the Edge of Town." "Promised Land" teeters both musically and thematically between the energy and the defensive self-assertion of *Born to Run* ("Mister I ain't a boy, no I'm a man / And I believe in a promised land") and the weariness of *Nebraska* ("I've done my best to live the right way / I get up every morning and go to work each day"); but now the energy is directed less at the maintaining of control and more at the slicing away of ego, of the repressive "self" placed in our bodies in infancy by a self-reproducing patriarchal society:

> But your eyes go blind and your blood runs cold
> Sometimes I feel so weak I just want to explode
> Explode and tear this whole town apart
> Take a knife and tear this pain from my heart

To "explode and tear this whole town apart" is Rambo's first solution; to "take a knife and tear this pain from my heart" is the second and redemptive solution Stallone gives him in the movie. Springsteen's words are desperate, here, because he is still only on the verge of the realization that the "town" and the "pain" that feel so real and so oppressive are not physical objects to be destroyed or excised, but ideological constructs, myths of the socius and the self that have been *programmed* politically into buildings and institutions and somatically into our flesh and blood, but that can only be removed by a subtler scalpel than either Rambo in *First Blood* or Springsteen here wields. He begins to move, again in desperately externalized images, toward a grasp of that subtler scalpel in the bridge:

> There's a dark cloud rising from the desert floor
> I packed up my bags and I'm heading straight into the storm
> Gonna be a twister to blow everything down
> That ain't got the faith to stand its ground
> Blow away the dreams that tear you apart
> Blow away the dreams that break your heart
> Blow away the lies that leave you nothing but lost
> and broken hearted

This is the storm that will twist his soul for the next decade or so, most devastatingly from late 1981 to late 1982, during the writing, producing, and release of *Nebraska*, and again after the *Tunnel of Love* tour from late 1988 to late 1989. It is the storm that Spenser, otherwise so brave, keeps running from, and that Rambo enters only when driven to it by external circumstances. Springsteen here begins to realize that there is no road around it, that he is going to have to drive right into the middle of it, and so starts making his plans, teaching himself to survive it.

The title cut on *Darkness* is a stumblebum song that perfectly enacts the kind of preparations Springsteen now increasingly realizes are the only ones that can do him any good. Its speaker is a bum who, having lost his money and his wife, stumbles around under Abram's Bridge out on the edge of town, alternately (in the first and second quatrains of each eight-line verse) muttering self-pityingly to himself and roaring with frustrated rage—and the music stumbles with him, slowing and racing, dropping to a simple hesitant, cautious melody line and drum beat (and almost stopping) and then cranking up the "Born to Run" wall of sound.[7] And what the alternations move us toward is release, surrender, the relinquishing of self-control, of the controlled and controlling masculine self, along with all its ideologically prescribed appurtenances (job, wealth, wife, children, house, cars...). The first quatrain of the first verse is filled with a carefully controlled sarcasm toward his ex-wife ("Now I hear she's got a house up in Fairview / And a style she's tryin' to maintain") that explodes in the second quatrain in a bitter rage at the discrepancy between his state and hers, or (and this is virtually the same thing) between his state and his one-time dreams:

> Well if she wants to see me
> You can tell her that I'm easily found
> Tell her there's a spot out neath Abram's Bridge and tell her
> There's a darkness on the edge of town

But something happens in the course of the song. The second verse is all about the destructive power of secrets—the sordid details of our private lives that we keep from each other, at one level, but at another the wall of repression by which we keep *everything* that threatens us at bay—and the frightening inevitability of letting them go ("Till some day you just let it loose / Let it loose or let it drag you down"). Maybe it's the open-endedness of this release, the fact that Springsteen's speaker just lets it loose, lets go of self-control without foreknowledge of the consequences, without knowing in advance whether letting go too won't "drag him down" (and the bitter fact is: it does). In any case, something happens; something changes. When in the soft quatrain that opens the last verse the speaker says that his lost wife and money "don't seem to matter much anymore," his words ring true. It is not sour grapes. He is isolated, as the "Born to Run" hero half-wanted to be (only half, because that hero still clung to a mother-substitute, his girlfriend Wendy); but his isolation is no self-protective escape. It is not something he even *wants* any more. It is something that has happened to him, something that has hit and ravaged him, the storm that Springsteen saw building up on the horizon earlier on side B. Once he finds himself there, he finds there is little room left for illusion—for the dreams that "tear you apart." He feels that his life is utterly hopeless—and that in that hopelessness lies his only hope. When he gets to the last (expanded) fierce quatrain, therefore, it is no longer anger that he is expressing; it is a passionate desire to go the whole route, to follow the dark street to its end and come out the other side. And the emotion he releases now becomes the fuel that powers his quest:

> Tonight I'll be on that hill 'cause I can't stop
> I'll be on that hill with everything I got
> Lives on the line where dreams are found and lost
> I'll be there on time and I'll pay the cost
> For wanting things that can only be found
> In the darkness on the edge of town

By rights, our culture's mythic stories tell us, this should be the darkness before the dawn: having divested himself of all his false hopes and dreams, even of ego, Springsteen's hero should regain his money and his wife (like Job, rewarded by a benevolent God for his faithfulness) and find true love and community back in society, in town. But Springsteen has no sense that "paying the cost" will buy him anything. Happiness is not for sale, even if the price you pay is almost unbearably high. It may even be, as John Berger argues, that happiness is only the lure capitalism holds out to *get* you to pay the price. By *Lucky Town* in 1992 Springsteen is beginning to feel his way tentatively to a happiness purged of the hype of publicity, so it may be possible. But in 1978 he is still far from even that tentative hope. He comes out of *Darkness* with a sense that you do have to pay and pay until you're broke and on the street, or under a bridge, *without hope of anything better*—without hope of monetary or emotional reward.

And in any case it is impossible for us, looking back on Springsteen's career in the 1980s, to make too large a claim for any therapeutic transformation he might have undergone. This was not only the decade in which he gained and lost a wife—he married Julianne Philips in 1985 and divorced her in 1988, exactly a decade after his speaker in the title cut on *Darkness*—and gained another, his lead vocalist Patti Scialfa, who helped him through the nightmares of the end of the decade; it was also the decade of both the dark, downbeat *Nebraska* and the 18-million-unit bestselling album (and supposedly upbeat) *Born in the U.S.A.*, most of the cuts on which were recorded originally in the same burst of desperate creative energy in late 1981 that produced *Nebraska*.

One of those songs, in fact, perhaps surprisingly, was the anthemic title cut that focused both the album and the incredibly successful 18-month world tour that followed and promoted it, "Born in the U.S.A." In retrospect, the origin of "Born in the U.S.A." in the recording session that produced "Johnny 99" and "Nebraska" is less surprising. Especially as it was recorded with the full band backing in May 1982, and released on the album in 1984, the song is heavy with the same world-weariness of the *Nebraska* songs: the leaden, almost spondaic beat like the heavy step of a weary boot; the tedious, repetitive chord progression, which in its refusal to progress at all (four bars of B, four bars of E) is closest to "Johnny 99"; the wild cracking of Springsteen's voice, half-singing, half-shouting, like a cross between the fierce intensity of "Johnny 99" and the deadness of "Nebraska"; and the despairing lyrics, telling the tale of a deadend life, just like the frustrated, stymied characters on the earlier album.[8] And maybe it's not so surprising either that the Vietnam vet Springsteen sings through is powerfully reminiscent of John Rambo, the Rambo of *First Blood*:[9]

> Come back home to the refinery
> Hiring man said, "Son if it was up to me"
> Went down to see my V.A. man
> He said, "Son, don't you understand now"

And especially:

> Down in the shadow of the penitentiary
> Out by the gas fires of the refinery
> I'm ten years burning down the road
> Nowhere to run, ain't got nowhere to go

Having been "born down in a dead man's town," all this speaker knows from his childhood is kicks and beatings, and "covering up." If you get in a "little home-town jam," there's no hope of working it out, patching it up, looking ahead to a better future; you get sent off "to a foreign land / To go and kill the yellow man." When you return, there is no job waiting for you at the refinery—shades of Johnny 99 and the Rambo who couldn't hold down a job. Understanding in this context specifically means adopting the viewpoint of management and realizing, in fatalistic appreciation of how hopelessly *everyone* is trapped in this economic system, that there is nothing they can do for you. (Do not vent your anger. Do not pick up a gun. Repress those instincts you were taught to release in Vietnam, or we will stick you in the penitentiary. Do not become a drifter, or we will pick you up for vagrancy, and perhaps provoke you into murder. Do not *do anything*—least of all become conscious of what exactly it is that has been done to you.)

"Born in the U.S.A."—a lot of good it did me. In the context of the whole song, the famous chorus is bitterly, almost obscenely, ironic. The land of the free. The land of opportunity. "From every mountainside, let freedom ring." In the country twang of Springsteen's holler, "Bawwwn in the Yew Ess Ayey," there lurks the howl of wolves.[10]

What I'm doing, of course, as anybody who was even semiconscious in 1984 and 1985 knows, is teasing out of the song precisely the dark side that nobody, at least nobody among the frenzied millions who came to hear Springsteen play on his world tour, seemed to be hearing. In concert the song became an explosively exciting stomp-and-shout piece: following Springsteen's lead, fans all around the world planted their foot on the heavy downbeat (no longer world-weary, no longer the sound of a boot trudging on toward nowhere) and shot their right fists hard into the air on the upbeat (on "Born").[11]

The politicians too jumped on the bandwagon. President Reagan himself, speaking in Hammonton, New Jersey, referred to the "message of hope" promoted by that Jersey boy, Bruce Springsteen:

All that we've done and all that we mean to do is to make this country freer still. America's future rests in a thousand dreams inside your hearts. It rests in the message of hope in songs of a man so many young Americans admire—

New Jersey's own, Bruce Springsteen. And helping you make those dreams come true is what this job of mine is all about.[12]

Reagan was patently trying to appropriate for himself some of Springsteen's enormous popularity, of course, especially with the massive ranks of Springsteen's audience: the working class and young adults, people in their 30s and 40s who grew up in the 1960s. If Springsteen sings the dreams and Reagan makes them come true, then the obvious place Springsteen fans should look for salvation is Reagan and the Republican machine.

Reagan's opponent Walter Mondale was quick to get in on the act, too: figuring that Springsteen's audience was probably made up of more Democrats than Republicans, he observed dryly that "Bruce may have been born to run, but he wasn't born yesterday." This too, of course, was appropriative, and only slightly more knowledgeable about Springsteen's music than Reagan's remark. *Born to Run* was Springsteen's hit album and title single in 1975, nine years before, and a familiarity with his most recent hit album and title single would have improved the forcefulness of Mondale's quip: "Bruce may have been born in the U.S.A., but he wasn't born yesterday." He may be an American, may be a voter, may be pumped up with the American Dream—but he's certainly no Reagan supporter.

Still, while Springsteen was careful not to endorse Reagan's opponent either, Mondale was certainly closer to the specifically political content of his message. As he told Kurt Loder in *Rolling Stone*:

I think what's happening now is people want to forget.... There was Vietnam, there was Watergate, there was Iran—we were beaten, we were hustled, and then we were humiliated. And I think people have a need to feel good about the country they live in. But what's happening, I think, is that that need, which is a good thing, is gettin' manipulated and exploited. And you see the Reagan reelection ads on TV—you know, "It's morning in America"—and you say, Well, it's not morning in Pittsburgh. It's not morning above 125th Street in New York. It's midnight and, like, there's a bad moon risin'. And that's why when Reagan mentioned my name in New Jersey, I felt it was another manipulation and I had to disassociate myself from the President's kind words.[13] (qtd. by Marsh *Glory* 285)

On the other hand—what *about* all those millions of Springsteen fans shouting out in total abandon, "Born in the U.S.A.!"? "Young people," as Reagan says, people young from his perspective—under 40, say—feeling in their guts what joy it is, or would have been, to be born in the U.S.A. All those anti-American Europeans, with their Green movements and their anti-nuke protests, wishing they'd been born in the U.S.A. What about them? Are they as wrong about Springsteen's song as Reagan was? And if they feel something that is truly there, some powerful hope despite the despair, could Reagan have been at least partly right too?

Maybe so. Gloomy lyrics notwithstanding, "Born in the U.S.A." is a powerful ode to America. The words may say there's no hope, but the music knows different. One is almost tempted to dichotomize the lyrics and the music, especially since Springsteen's famous gritty voice makes his lyrics hard to distinguish; musically speaking, what really stands out in the song as you listen to it is not the despair but the booming chorus, "Born in the U.S.A."

But of course it's more complex than that. The music doesn't contradict the lyrics; it places them in context. Things may be bad; I may have fought in a pointless war that killed my brother and seems to have killed my future; but I was still born here, and somehow, from somewhere, I feel power pumping into me. Hope, against all the evidence, against all odds.

What I'm getting at with all this, what this lengthy introduction to Springsteen's music is trying to say, is that Springsteen knows how to get past the impasse at which the collective creators of Rambo leave us: that hairline balance between suicidal despair (Morrell's Rambo) and therapeutic surrender (Stallone's Rambo) that we teeter on for a moment at the end of *First Blood* and then lose, perhaps forever, in the bloodthirsty sequels. Springsteen too stood on that balance at precisely the same time *First Blood* was being filmed, in late 1981, and has struggled with the same issues, the same dilemmas of holding on and letting go, being held onto and being let go of, as Parker, Morrell, and Stallone during exactly the same period, from the early 1970s till now—but for whatever reason (and I'm going to be exploring some possible explanations in this part of the book), he seems to me to have gone further, delved deeper, and found tentative, even cautious, but still truly *working* solutions to many of the problems that the other artists have only posed.

# Chapter Nine

# Healing the Father

"When I was really young, I don't remember thinkin' about it much." A brief pause. A sigh. "But as I got a little older, I watched my father...how he would come home from work and just sit in the kitchen all night. Like there was somethin' dyin' inside of him, or like he'd never had a chance to live." He emphasizes this last word ever so slightly, in such a way that you can't tell whether he is puzzled or bitter or both. "Until I started to feel there was somethin' dyin' inside of me. And I'd lay up in bed at night and feel like, if somethin' didn't happen...I was just gonna..." He takes a breath, squeezes it out; his voice is beginning to crack. "That someday I'd just..." Breathing harder now as if struggling with some massive weight that continues to press him down, he pushes on: "I felt like I was just gonna...If somethin' didn't happen, I was just...I felt like I was just..." Now he pants, pushing out his breath, gasping, gulping, forcing the words, "Like I was just gonna...just gonna..." (qtd. by Marsh *Glory* 80)

Perhaps the most striking thing about this concert monologue from Springsteen's "Born in the U.S.A." tour in 1985 is that, while it is the emotional equivalent of the monologue with which Stallone ends *First Blood*, for Springsteen it is consciously enacted autobiography, reenacted memory. It is, in fact, a kind of drama therapy, a replaying of emotional blockages that he has dealt with before, in his music and in his life, on stage and off, and that he will continue dealing with for the next few years—by the end of the decade with a professional therapist. Springsteen on stage in 1985 is past the worst, most stifling and suffocating feeling that he grew up with, that emotional sign or symptom of failure within the patriarchal system (the patriarchally successful man is *calm*, controlled, collected, maintains a determinedly even keel)—but only because he now increasingly knows what he feels. He still feels stifled and suffocated; but his deepening self-knowledge helps him live with the pain, and keeps generating in his musical and performative imagination therapeutic moments that move him toward health—him, and perhaps his fans as well.

And so in concert he plays at being 18 again, feeling trapped in his father's skin—plays for his fans very much the same kind of threshold scene that Stallone plays for his: "Breathing harder now as if struggling with some massive weight that continues to press him down, he pushes on: 'I felt like I was just gonna...'" Gonna what? In concert he breaks into "I'm on Fire"—"Sometimes it's like someone took a knife baby edgy and dull / And cut a six-inch valley through the middle of my soul," flooding into a plea for love—but it could have been any number of other transitional songs as well, songs in which Springsteen comes up to that threshold moment and then, decisively, *crosses* it, takes himself and his listeners over it en masse: "Sometimes I feel so weak I just want to explode / Explode and tear this whole town apart / Take a knife and cut this pain from my heart."

He can do it at will: this is the key, I think. If the sequels to *First Blood* are any indication, Stallone had little or no idea of what he was doing in writing that concluding monologue. It came to him out of nowhere—out of his unconscious, as Freud would say, or, as I would prefer, out of deep strata of body knowledge. This is the realm artists must be able to tap if they are to do more than repeat tired formulae; but *merely* to tap it, for purposes of artistic expression, say, as Stallone does in the writing and then in the acting of the scene, is finally to mire yourself in more tired repetitions. Repression and release, repression and release. Over and over. You don't know why you keep dredging this same material up from the depths of your somatic response ("Now he pants, pushing out his breath, gasping, gulping, forcing the words..."). You have no idea what it means, or what you might do with it. It's just there. It comes when you open yourself up to it; but because it is just more or less interchangeable artistic material, you don't go out of your way to open yourself up to it. When it comes time to write the concluding scene to *Rambo: First Blood Part II*, for example, you set up a similar scene—Rambo with M-16 strapped around his neck once more, angry once more at betrayal and abandonment—but the liberating emotional surrender doesn't pour out. What pours out instead is kneejerk patriotism: "I don't hate my country. I love my country." A tired repetitive formula. And by the end of *Rambo III* Stallone is John Wayne, handing the symbolic son a token of his paternal esteem and trudging off into the Afghanistani sunset. Nothing has been *gained* here. Stallone could summon up that magnificent transformative scene for the end of *First Blood*, but he couldn't hold onto it—couldn't stay with the transformation until it had remade him.

But Springsteen can, and this is perhaps his greatest strength as a man—perhaps also as an artist: a masculist artist. Springsteen's achievement is specifically that he has held tight to the turbulence of transformation, over and over again, in song after song and album after album, and that each song and each album has taken him a little further—into the darkness, into the storm, as we saw in chapter eleven, but also out of it again into the light, a light that, by *Tunnel of Love* (1987), and then *Human Touch* and *Lucky Town* (1992), will become increasingly mystical.

This does not necessarily mean that Springsteen knows exactly what he is doing when he writes one of his self-transformative songs. Springsteen seems to be, if anything, an even less conscious *creator* than Stallone: his band members have told interviewers that, when they are recording, Bruce will write five or six songs a day, day after day. There is no question of deciding *what* to write a song about; there is simply a need for a song, or five, and Bruce writes whatever is needed. This is not the mark of a painstaking artistic planner.

But Springsteen is a consummately conscious *listener* to his own songs, and herein may lie the difference. Springsteen pays attention to what his body—his musical body, the bodily knowing that writes his songs for him—is telling him. Part of it may be the fact that, unlike the novelist or the screenwriter/actor, the singer/songwriter typically performs his own songs over and over, hundreds and even thousands of times, first in the studio (10, 15, 20 takes, until you get it right), then for concert audiences; and to perform a song is to reinterpret it, to run it one more time through the channels of bodily knowing, to discover how it feels to time an entrance or a shout or a whisper differently, to slow a song way down (as he did with "No Surrender" on the "Born in the U.S.A." tour and with "Born to Run" on the "Tunnel of Love" tour) or to speed (or ham) it up, to change the words around, to beef up the backup or pare it down to a bare piano or acoustic guitar.[1] Springsteen says he grows with his songs as he plays them in concert, often—as with "Growin' Up," say—over what is now almost a 20-year period. He learns something new about his music every time he plays it; and because the music is *his*, he also learns something about himself. One wonders, in fact, had Stallone's version of *First Blood* been a Broadway hit instead of a movie, whether the repeated reliving and perhaps reinterpretation of that concluding scene on stage might not have taught him something about himself, about men and emotion and repression and letting go, before he tried to do a sequel.

## 190 No Less a Man

Ever since *Darkness* in 1978, the beginnings of his transformation, the recurring focus of Springsteen's musings about manhood, success and failure, belonging and isolation, defiance and surrender, anger and joy, has been his father. Doug Springsteen was a typical patriarchal father, withdrawn, taciturn, morose, always hovering on the verge of anger, always (or almost always) just barely under control; and one of Springsteen's concerns in his musical attempts to come to grips with his father is just what it means to be the son of such a man, to have modeled yourself on him, to have been denied love and warmth by him, indeed to have been taught to *taboo* love and warmth by him. Significantly, however, Springsteen sees in his father more than just a typical patriarchal man; he sees in him a typical *working-class* man. Gender and class both figure into Springsteen's explorations of his conditioning into patriarchal manhood. Doug Springsteen's "typical" masculine characteristics—emotional withdrawal, taciturnity, etc.—were exacerbated by his working-class living conditions, his reliance for a livelihood (and, in a culture nourished on the work ethic, for self-esteem, for his sense that he is a worthwhile person) on an indifferent capitalist economy that laid him off whenever he was perceived as surplus labor. "But as I got a little older, I watched my father...how he would come home from work and just sit in the kitchen all night. Like there was somethin' dyin' inside of him, or like he'd never had a chance to live." To be trapped in his father's skin, as Springsteen soon begins to realize he is, is to be trapped in the skin of a human being isolated by gender and class from everything that his body (flesh, blood, feeling) needs to stay alive, everything that is life-enhancing and life-supporting.

This notion of Springsteen being "inside his father's skin" may not be immediately clear. I will be coming back to it again and again throughout this chapter, but perhaps a few theoretical remarks might be in order here at the outset. The notion does in fact deviate in significant ways from reigning psychoanalytical assumptions about fathers and sons—assumptions that reign, need I add, outside the men's movement, in Freudian and even much feminist psychoanalysis. For Freud and his followers, including Lacan—indeed for patriarchal society as theorized and justified by Freud and his followers—the son is constituted as son (initiated into patriarchal masculinity) by distance from the father, by hierarchical fear of the father, or, as Lacan puts it, through the internalization of the alienating *nom du pere*, the Name of the Father that is also, in Lacan's French pun, the No of the Father: the paternal name or word as negation. By internalizing the negation that separates him (physically, emotionally, hierarchically, but above all, for Lacan, linguistically) from the father, the son is allowed to keep his penis—or rather (since Lacan is not really interested in real bodily organs, only in reified symbols) the phallic signifier—but only at the cost of recognizing it as not his own. His "phallus" (Lacan's symbolization of the penis as phallus only perpetuating the oedipal alienation) is under the sign of the father, marked by the No of the Father, loaned to him under the sufferance of paternal negation, and it will in fact betray him ("impotence") when his paternal introject disapproves of his sexual activity.[2] If anyone is inside another's skin, in this view, it is the father inside the son's skin, and then only under the sign of negation: the *Ideal-Ich* or superego is the father's proxy which, in Lacan's formulation, is the *Ideal-Nicht*, the differential negation that enables signification (the Symbolic) through alienation.

Feminist psychoanalysis, especially insofar as it merely revises Freud (Karen Horney, Nancy Chodorow) or Lacan (Luce Irigaray, Helene Cixous) from a feminist perspective, changes little of this. The major breakthrough in feminist psychoanalysis is the recovery of the mother, who in Freud and Lacan had been relegated to the undifferentiated preoedipal state, perceived (if at all) as a kind of faceless, featureless blob. For Chodorow, for example, the son is still constituted as son by negation, but the negation is now more complex (104-08). Since under patriarchy the mother is the prescribed primary caretaker, infant boys and girls both begin with a primary identification with her; in the oedipal stage, therefore (which Chodorow does not seriously challenge or modify), the father's negation prompts an even more powerful and potentially devastating negation: that of the little boy's identification with his mother. Rather than modeling himself on the father, then, who is frequently absent—either physically, as he was permanently for David Morrell, or emotionally, as is prescribed in patriarchal ideology, or both—and who in any case is *perceived*, normatively, as absent, whether he is there or not, in effect "absented"—the son is forced by a double negation to *de*model himself as son on the mother, lest he lose the negatively promised approval of the father. In this formulation men in patriarchal society are inwardly crippled by a double alienation: masculinity is founded on the negation of femininity (perceived or posited as primary and normal), and this negation is motivated and maintained by the No of the negated (absented) father.[3]

Now, much of this rings true. Certainly patriarchal society does program deeply tormented and tormenting double binds into our self-conceptions as men and women, and these psychoanalytical theories do offer a complex sense of those double binds. Nor are all of the proponents of this psychology as fatalistic about the oedipal and preoedipal "mechanisms" that "mold" gender identity as are Freud and Lacan; Chodorow, for example, believes that as fathers play an increasingly active role in child-rearing, as they share the role of primary caretaker with their wives, many of the worst aspects of the present system of engenderment will be eradicated.

The difficulty is, as I see it, that the entire edifice of the Oedipus complex *is* mechanistic and therefore fatalistic, unconducive to emancipatory change. Chodorow's uncritical acceptance of Freud's temporal preoedipal/oedipal split, for example—the notion that there is a preoedipal stage during which the child comes under the sign of the mother, and *then* an oedipal stage during which the child comes under the sign of the father—renders the hope she places in paternal child-rearing hollow. It means, if we take it seriously, that it doesn't really matter whether fathers attend the deliveries of their children, care for their newborn infants, bond with them at an early age. The oedipal period, the official period of paternal influence, doesn't start until the child turns one and a half or two or three, and all paternal presence before that age must be defined in terms of absence. The Freudian model, even in feminist revision, in effect fences the father out of infancy. Infancy belongs to the mother. If, as Chodorow hopes (and I believe), the increasing involvement of fathers in the parenting of infants and participation as equals in primary caretaking is beginning to have a beneficial effect on children, then the preoedipal/oedipal model must dissolve—must be perceived as an outmoded ideological construct that no longer has any explanatory power.

In fact I would argue that the model never did work—except insofar as it actively perpetuated the myth of the absent father that it was pretending to describe, and thus "worked" surreptitiously, by becoming a self-fulfilling prophecy. A parent is only truly "absent" when he or she is not only physically *never there* (Spenser's dead mother, Morrell's dead father, for example), but also *never mentioned* (even subvocally, subconsciously) as being potentially there. To mention the mother or the father a child never knew is to create the parent as *present*—if only by linguistic negation, as Lacan insists. But the father who is emotionally withdrawn, who shies away from child care, who spends most of the day at work and most of the time he is home in front of the television or behind a newspaper or under a car—in other words, the "normal" patriarchal father—is no more absent than the mother is when she leaves the child alone in its crib. What feminist psychoanalysts seem to be getting at when they perpetuate the myth of the preoedipal absent father is the frustrating sense that the normal patriarchal father is never emotionally available: never open, never loving, never physically demonstrative. There is a blockage that prevents human love from flowing back and forth between father and child. But this isn't absence; it's blockage. The normal patriarchal father may often be physically and emotionally absent, but that "absence" is itself a powerful presence in the small child's life from birth.

In fact, not only is the absent father a presence, he is a *positive* presence, in the sense of having an actual (not a virtual or negated) influence on the infant. To ignore someone, after all, is patently to *do* something to that person. To turn your back on someone, to shut someone out of your life, is to perform a real action. Emotional withdrawal is not the negation of emotion; it is the "positive" (real) channeling of an emotion that is only thematized as morally "negative," i.e. unpleasant, unacceptable. Cold indifference is not a lack of warmth; it is the active and vigilant repression of warmth, motivated by a fear of emotional vulnerability. And the ignored child feels that fearful repression as a real emotional force, as an impenetrable wall of defensive emotion, which batters his or her emotional needs until he or she builds his or her own wall, introjects the wall as his or her own positive emotional structure.

It is, in fact, a structure that boys and girls will introject in normatively opposite ways, and that will normatively *constitute* them as boys and girls, engender them into patriarchal sex roles, by that very opposition.[4] The daughter will normatively introject the paternal wall or emotional block as a withholding of love that she must seek to reverse later in life, with her dolls, her boyfriends, her husband, and especially her sons. The son, on the other hand, will normatively introject it as a withholding of love that he must seek to ignore, repress, especially since his mother's attempts to gain from him what she never gained from her blocked father render her "love" a smothering form of emotional blackmail, which he must learn to block precisely with the emotional tools he borrows from his father.

In this view the normal patriarchal father is just as "present" (*from birth*) as the normal patriarchal mother, and the presence of both is equally oppressive: the father's because he withholds what the child wants, the mother's because she demands what the child cannot give. This is the vicious circle of patriarchal parenting—and it proceeds not by negation and double negation, or by a succession of mutually exclusive stages, but by a complex reactive system that transmits crisscrossing patterns of emotional withdrawal and emotional demands from generation to generation.

This is the sense in which a son (or daughter) may be said to be "inside" a father's (or mother's) skin: what the child inherits from (or models on) its parents is the entire patriarchal complex as activated in a single body, a single set of feelings and reactions and defenses and needs. The son normatively "becomes" the father not, as Freud claimed, out of castration fear, but rather in an attempt to inhabit the father's masculine defenses against the mother's emotional demands; and he can be rescued from that destructive habitat only by realizing that it is built on—and therefore contains, concealed—his father's emotional vulnerability, the hurt needy little boy his father once was. Hence our slim but very real hope: by crawling inside our fathers' skins in search of protection, we have crawled inside the fearful needs that perpetuate the need for protection, and by discovering those needs we can be liberated from the deadening self-protective structures of traditional masculinity.

This model of the self-reproduction of patriarchal gender identity also makes it possible to allow for progressive change—for a gradual generational liberation out of the self-perpetuating cycle. If the mother's impossible emotional demands that bind her son to her are generated by her father's withholding of love, then every time a father learns to relax his defenses (developed partly to protect himself from his mother's emotional demands, partly through direct modeling on his blocked father) and release his love into open interaction with his daughter, he will increase the likelihood that his grandson will not be subjected to the same kind of manipulative smothering maternal "love" that infected his emotional life; and every time he relaxes his defenses with his son, he will increase the chances that his granddaughter will not be deprived of the love and warmth she needs from her father. Conversely, every time a mother learns to relax her fearful possessive grip on her son (developed partly in order to gain from him what she never got from her blocked father and husband, partly through direct modeling on her mother) and to open herself to him as a separate individual, she will increase the likelihood that her granddaughter will not be subjected to the same kind of paternal emotional withdrawal that crushed her emotional life; and every time she relaxes her demands on her daughter she will increase the chances that her grandson will not feel forced to retreat from his mother's impossible emotional demands behind an emotion-proof wall. This model, in other words, allows for the possibility of rendering the vicious patriarchal circle—gradually, perhaps, over a period of years, or

## Healing the Father 195

decades, or even generations, or even suddenly, as a result of a successful therapy or process of gender liberation—less vicious.

To put it succinctly: if the patriarchal dynasty of wounds entraps (and, however destructively, also empowers) both sexes, the gender liberation of either sex from dynastically wounded/normal masculinity or femininity will necessarily have the effect (however complexly, however mired it is in the anxiety that attends deviations from ideological norms) of instigating liberation in the other. Ample evidence is available for this claim in the very belatedness of the men's movement: women, just as victimized and traumatized by patriarchal society as men, were almost never given the social rewards for victimization and traumatization routinely granted men, and so initiated the process of *women's* liberation. Men, prodded into "crisis" by the imbalances generated by women's ideological "deviations," responded first with exaggerated authoritarianism (the "righteous father" reaction of the male supremacists) or liberal guilt (the "anxious son" reaction of the male feminists); but then, gradually—and, my model suggests, inevitably—we began to work toward liberation too.

Because by definition we all come to this liberatory process from a position within patriarchal programming, however—because men and women alike have been emotionally infected by the father's withholding of love and the mother's blackmail for love—gender liberation is no simple matter. It is emphatically not, as John Rowan points out (33), merely a matter of "consciousness raising," although that too is important. It is not enough simply to become aware of how men and women are victimized by the patriarchal system (even, in most men's and many women's cases, when they are trained to become victimizers). Awareness may be the first step—especially for the liberal libber, man or woman, who figures everything out in advance and then, with the help of a therapist or a support group, consciously sets out in quest of gender liberation—but it may come later, or last of all. Emotional trauma may begin the process, as it did at the end of *First Blood*: gender liberation may be the end result of a harrowing and seemingly endless battle with substance or emotional addiction (dependency on a physically abusive spouse, for example), posttrauma stress disorder after rape or war or other violent attack, the traumatic resurfacing of repressed incest memories from childhood, the empty nest syndrome, a heart attack or bout with terminal illness, or even, as in Springsteen's late 20s and early 30s, sudden success and acclaim. Not everyone, in other words, simply announces that he or she is a feminist or a masculist and sets about seeking liberation from gender programming; nor does everyone who undergoes a similar process call it, or even recognize it as, gender liberation.[5]

(I am not sure, for example, that Springsteen would identify himself as interested or engaged in men's liberation. Whether he is interested or not, however, my brief is that he is engaged in it.)

Also because most of us have already been emotionally infected by our fathers' withholding of love and/or our mothers' blackmailing for love, the difficult process of liberating ourselves from gender programming typically takes the form of reconstructing and in some deep sense reliving our relations with our parents: regressing back into childhood, becoming childish once again, allowing ourselves to experience once more the terrifying emotional vulnerability of childhood, that time when we were entirely at the mercy of often dysfunctional parents, and *living through it.* Surviving it. Emerging from the wreckage of our childhood defenses devastated but (often just barely) alive, and building anew—more specifically, letting our community build us anew, allowing social communion with friends and lovers to construct a new "self" that is not defensively autonomous like the old one, but complexly steeped in connection. (In fact, of course, the old "autonomous" self was steeped in connection too; the defensive illusion of autonomy was needed only because the connections channeled deadly double binds, mind and body games that were life-threatening and had to be defended against.)

To my knowledge, Springsteen has traversed only half of the transformative slope to date: he has "found" his father, and is only now beginning to realize that his mother may be lost as well. My sense is, in fact, that this is a not uncommon state of affairs: in patriarchal society fathers are *normatively* perceived as the main problem, mothers as the haven to which both sons and daughters flee when stymied in their approaches to their fathers. Fathers, as I said earlier, are normatively placed outside the circle of intimacy patriarchy prescribes between mother and children: placed outside both in the double sense (double bind) that they are at once ostracized and criticized for not being inside. Paul Olsen, for example, writes:

> While the father is out of it in this relationship, as he seems to be in so many of the encounters between mothers and sons—where the mother-son bond is so intense that he *must* stay out of it or lose face by being *chased* out of it—there is another sort of relationship which, if the top layers are peeled away, becomes quite obvious. This is where the boy perceives his father as the power, the chief, the dominant member of the household, and being frightened of him,

moves closer and closer to his mother, whom he sees as kind, soft, all-giving—and ultimately a victim.

But inside this familiar triangle, very often it is the mother who has constructed the myth of the father's control—which is a sort of opposite effect to the father telling his son to "do it for your mother." Here she cultivates an image of her husband's domination and power so as to stand free of, away from, her son's anger and bad feelings: they in essence form a united front against the "tyrannical" father.

"I wish you wouldn't do this because you know how your father will take it."

"Please don't say anything about this. You know how your father flies into a rage."

"I don't suppose it will do any good, but you should ask your father anyway."

Ad infinitum.

She and he will remain bonded, united, conspiratorial—and the boy will forever feel more comfortable in the presence of women, anxious and frightened in the presence of men. (135-36)

This is an important point, but it needs qualification. Mothers do often foster the myth of the tyrannical father; but they certainly do not construct it. Olsen means, of course, that within each family unit the mother may be the one to initiate and maintain the myth; but except in families where a "normal" patriarchal woman is married to a truly liberated man (a not unheard-of but relatively rare situation), this isolation of a single guilty party seems to me unrealistic. In a "normal" or traditional or ideologically conformist marriage both parents will contribute to the myth that the father is the feared but respected master and the mother is the lowly but beloved servant. This is partly, no doubt, for sheer pragmatic reasons—the arrangement yields both parents a certain amount of power—but to stop there would be shallow. The kind of power this arrangement yields, the satisfaction the wielding of that power provides, and the very *naturalness* of the power structures themselves all bespeak a deeper ideological origin of the myth of the tyrannical father. Both the mother and the father believe in it, foster it, transmit it to their children, because it was once transmitted to them, in their childhoods. It is an ideological norm. It is not a myth that they construct; it is a myth that constructs *them*, and victimizes them, as man and woman, father and mother.

This realization that the hated and feared tyrant who called himself your father was himself a victim is a powerful part of the transformative

## 198 No Less a Man

process Springsteen undergoes in the songs on *Darkness* and after. In "Adam Raised A Cain," for example, he says his father held him to his side when being baptized.

> In the summer that I was baptized
> My father held me to his side
> As they put me to the water
> He said how on that day I cried
> We were prisoners of love a love in chains
> He was standin' in the door I was standin' in the rain
> With the same hot blood burning in our veins
> Adam raised a Cain

The cautious memory of his *father's* memory of his baptism keeps his voice down, his tone controlled, throughout the first quatrain, the minor-key pendulum (Em-Am) ticking back and forth as he gradually works up the courage to feel the pain, the tears he shed in his father's arms as an infant; but then, as the second quatrain opens ("prisoners of love"), he touches the painful memory, the source of pain, the hidden wound, and begins to lose control. His voice goes ragged around the edges, rises in pitch and intensity, and he begins to feel his father's hands (holding him to his side) as a prison, as chains, as the block that he can't get past. The anger and the hurt and the betrayal swell up with a peripheral vision of himself and his father, just the two bodies, their physical placement in a dream or memory, his father in the door, neither out nor in but closer to being in than out—his father the married man, the homeowner, the working man, trying so hard to do things the socially approved way—himself out in the rain. *Why* do I have to be out in the rain? Why does it feel so impossible for me to come inside? *He* won't let me; but even if he would, I wouldn't go. Why not?

And then, with hard, spondaic emphasis, his voice rising to a screech of pain: "With the *same—hot—blood*—burning *in-our—veins*!" We've got the same blood, literally and metaphorically (he begins to sense, here, that his father feels the same way he does)—why then are we stuck in this old Biblical vicious circle of fathers and sons, Adam and Cain?[6] What is this painful bond between us, this bondage of pain, this attempt to bind up our wounds that wounds both of us and binds us together? Samuel Osherson writes in *Finding Our Fathers*:

The wounded father is the internal sense of masculinity that men carry around

## Healing the Father 199

within them. It is an inner image of father that we experience as judgmental and angry or, depending on our relationship father, as needy and vulnerable. When a man says he can't love his children because he wasn't loved well enough, it is the wounded father he is struggling with.

There are three aspects to our image of the wounded father, all linked but separable. The son may remember father as wounded, with father's deep sadness, incompetence, or anger dominating his image of the man. He may also remember father as wounding, evoking the lost and needy feelings the son experienced in having been rejected by or disappointing to the father. And thirdly, the son may introject and internalize distorted and idealized images and memories of father as he struggles to synthesize his identity as a man. (22)

He introjects the wound, in other words, and in his attempts to control or contain the pain, becomes his father. In the patriarchal dynasty of wounds, the son succeeds his father by inheriting the sign of his manhood, the emotional wound that mires him in protective fear of emotion and marks him outwardly as unemotional—cold, unfeeling, indifferent, withdrawn, at most bitter, resentful, but even then trying to put a good face on it—and stores up his patriarchal capital for the day when he will pass it on to his son.

> Daddy worked his whole life for nothing but the pain
> Now he walks these empty rooms looking for somthing to blame
> You inherit the sins you inherit the flames
> Adam raised a Cain

In the title image that forms his angry refrain, Springsteen links the dynasty of wounds (the "flames" that burn you when you inherit a taboo or "sin") with the mythic conflict between the first father and first son in the Bible, Adam and Cain; and implicitly, in fact, extends the dynasty of wounds backwards even from Adam, the "first father" who must, Springsteen seems to be suggesting, have inherited the sins from *someone*. Hidden in this image is a revisionary reading of Genesis that is even more radical than Freud's in *Totem and Taboo*. If Adam is Doug and Cain is Bruce, the implication is first that Cain inherited the "sins" and the "flames" from Adam, but then also (given the universalizing force of the "you") that Adam inherited the "sins" and the "flames" from God, the supposedly omniscient and benevolent deity who built into his paradise a prohibition that he must have known would lead to exile and shame: the insecure tyrant of a father who would later, at Babel, jealously guard his creaky and precarious superiority by scattering human languages; the scheming father who would still later "elect" a favorite son (the younger, Jacob, who became Israel, his chosen people) for the dubious and self-destructive honor of destroying the father's enemies and obeying the paternal commands; and the manipulative father who would finally incarnate his son to die for the sin that he himself instilled in his creatures, through the defensive prohibition in the Garden of Eden. The buck stops here: it would be hard to trace the dynasty of wounds any farther back than God the Patriarchal Father.

But note that, pragmatically, psychologically, in our historical situatedness, blaming the inherited wound on God is finally only a symbolic way of blaming nobody—of saying that the wound has always been there, that my father was no more to blame for it than I am, nor was his father, nor was his father's father. At no point (outside of futile theological speculation) can we stop the regression and say, "There is the cause of it all, there is the blow that caused the wound." All we can do is to name the wound, feel it, explore it, and seek to heal it, so that we don't pass it on to our children—so that the buck *will* stop somewhere, in a transformed future rather than in a uselessly projected past.

The therapeutic moment in "Adam Raised A Cain" and other songs about the father on *Darkness*, like "Factory," is the moment in which Springsteen feels the spiritual deadness or emptiness that his father has felt all his life, working "for nothing but the pain"—i.e., working for money and status and self-esteem, the trappings of patriarchal manhood, but gaining only pain—and, beyond even that, working *not to feel* the pain, trying in fact not to feel anything, and ending up in a state of not knowing what (or even whether) he feels. He begins to realize that his father is lost, confused, adrift—stymied and bound by the crosscurrents of an external world that humiliates him at every turning and an internal world that betrays him into feeling the humiliation.

"My father sat there every night for, I guess, about eighteen years," Springsteen told Dave Marsh, "and I never once asked him what he was thinking about, what was on his mind. I always felt he was cutting me short, and I guess in a lot of ways I was cutting him short. 'Cause I thought he didn't dream no more, and I was real wrong about that" (*Glory* 88). Probably Doug Springsteen thought he didn't dream no more too—that's one of the things we do to ourselves, to make the failure of our dreams more bearable: squelch the dreams, refuse to dream, repress the desire for something more.

One of the songs that Springsteen wrote for *Darkness* but held back for *The River* two years later was "Independence Day," a sad song that still can't imagine an actual reconciliation with his father—a warmth of

# Healing the Father 201

feeling, a closeness between them—but that now addresses him, and with new understanding. Danny Federici's high, fluty organ tracing out the F chord up to the second and third of the B-flat chord sets the mood for the song: the organ-flute sound *feels* feminine, feels like the tender, quavering channel of emotional authenticity that we men have been conditioned to repress and project onto women. As the intro rings out I feel shivers going up and down my spine, shivers of recognition and release, shivers of surrender to that feeling of emotional realness (and they recur throughout the song, especially when I play and sing it myself, letting the music not just bombard me from the outside but course through my body):

> Well Papa go to bed now it's getting late
> Nothing we can say is gonna change anything now
> I'll be leaving in the morning from St. Mary's Gate
> We wouldn't change this thing even if we could somehow
> 'Cause their darkness of this house has got the best of us
> There's darkness in this town that's got to us too
> But they can't touch me and you can't touch me now
> They ain't gonna do to me what I watched them do to you

There is some of the belligerent self-assertion of "Born to Run" in those words, and even when the speaker isn't being belligerent, he's resigned, fatalistic: "Nothing we can say is gonna change anything now." But the soft, almost pleading music tones all *verbal* belligerence down to a kind of begging of forgiveness: I'm leaving, but not because I hate you; don't feel I'm rejecting you.

In fact, as I feel it, the music even begins to transcend resignation, to move through the recognition that we *share* this fate, they did it to both of us, to an implicit possibility that is almost too audacious to voice: my bid for independence may save you too. If I can free myself from the "darkness of this house" (the darkness of the patriarchal dynasty of wounds), if I can break the chain that binds fathers and sons in the prison of patriarchal "love," maybe my escape will free you. What makes this hope (which may be mine; it's what I feel when I play the song) so audacious isn't just the reversal of father-son roles, the son rescuing the father; it's that the son is presuming to know that the father *wants* to be rescued, something that many fathers aren't yet willing to admit. "Nothing wrong with me. What do you mean, 'save me'?"

In any case, the song continues in this vein, lyrically insisting that the father is trapped and the son is getting out ("This is a town full of losers, I'm pulling out of here to win," as the Springsteen hero said back in "Thunder Road"), and accepting as immutable the father-son clash, while musically hinting at some possibility of true healing, until after the instrumental bridge, dominated by Clarence Clemons's mournful sax solo. Then the image of empty rooms from "Adam Raised a Cain" reappears, and with the repetition of this song's opening Springsteen begins to flesh out a new vision, an alternative to the beginning vision of a static father as a pathetic representative of a static town. Now *everybody's* leaving town, leaving the old familiar ways, the assumptions he and his father have shared—and though the second-person address to his father makes this sound like a loss, like something good and necessary being "swept away," as his father surely conceives it, again the implicit possibility is that this is a healing movement, a mass migration out of the old patriarchal vicious circles of father-and-son conflict, into something different. Maybe, finally, there's nothing to run *from*; the static town that "got the best of us" is itself on the move, disintegrating, and so no longer poses such a potent threat. Maybe, therefore, in this new situation the true escapism isn't running away, as in "Thunder Road" and "Born to Run," but clinging blindly to the old ways, refusing to desert a sinking ship:

> Now the rooms are all empty down at Frankie's joint
> And the highway she's deserted clear down to Breaker's Point There's a lot of people leaving town now
> Leaving their friends their homes
>     At night they walk that dark and dusty highway all alone
>
> Well Papa go to bed now it's getting late
> Nothing we can say can change anything now
> Because there's just different people coming down here now
> And they see things in different ways
> Soon everything we've known will just be swept away

And by the end of the song the powerful bond of sympathy, of shared pain, has taken over from the rebelliousness and the defiance, and Springsteen begins to cast around for the words that will take away the hurt: "Papa now I know the things you wanted that you could not say," he says (you don't have to pretend to be all right! I know that you hurt, and why!), and "I swear I never meant to take those things away."

Now the son's understanding of the father's wound, and his apology for exacerbating it before he understood what he was doing, is

## Healing the Father 203

out in the open. The music has brought Springsteen to a conscious awareness of his lyrics' emotional undercurrent: the muted rebellion of the first verse is outdated, he's past that now; what he feels now is no longer anger at rejection and rejection through anger, but sympathy. He knows what his father wanted without being able to say because he feels his father's hurt. In some important sense he is becoming his father—no longer in the repressive sense enforced by patriarchy, in which the son becomes the father by internalizing his defenses against pain (often, in fact, by refusing to become the father), but in a new transformative sense, in which the son is able to feel the father's wound inside his own body, to feel what his father had repressed and taught him to repress, and to *heal* it.

We aren't really doing it for our fathers, of course; we're doing it for ourselves. The possibility that healing the father's wound inside ourselves might have a transformative effect on our fathers is tantalizing, but that's not why we do it; we do it to reintegrate our own lives. In my own case, the restoration of close, warm relations between my father and myself (I say "restoration" because that's how it feels now, but *were* we ever warm and close?) that resulted from my surrender of defensive ego has had the effect of softening my father somewhat too, not only with me but with other people as well. It feels almost as if the removal of one frightening block in the world—the constant reproach of a rebellious son—has caused other defenses to crumble. My father has recently begun naming his own distress, discovering that he's not quite as self contained and happy as he long pretended to be. It feels to me like a miracle.

But for many fathers it's too late. Years of dulling, deadening, and above all *unrecognized* misery have clogged the arteries with defensive walls that block all healing, until they are struck down by their hearts, the organ whose futile attempts to signal the need for a change they've been repressing for so long, strikes them down. This happened to Doug Springsteen in June 1981, after the E Street Band had returned from the European leg of their "River" tour. Springsteen's father didn't die of his stroke, but came very close to it, and when Springsteen played "Independence Day" next, on home turf, at the Meadowlands in New Jersey over the Fourth of July weekend, he introduced the song by responding to the shock he had felt at the possibility of losing his father. Dave Marsh reports:

"I grew up in this house where nobody ever talked to each other," he began, sounding miserable. "We used to live on the left side of this little three-room house. There was a front room and then the kitchen and two bedrooms and a bathroom upstairs. With everybody livin' that close, it seemed that nobody ever sat down without being angry, tellin' each other what was on their mind. I could never talk to my old man, he could never talk to me, my mother couldn't talk to him...

"So I was glad when I finally got old enough and I started to live alone. Then, for about ten years I never saw my folks that much. And just recently, we came back from Europe.... If you get a chance, you gotta go there because you can't imagine it—it's not what you think it is or what you read in the papers. But we got back and I got a phone call a night or two later that my father had gotten sick. And I went out to California where he was in the hospital there.

"I started thinkin' on the way out about all the things that I always wanted to say to him that I never said and I always figured, well, someday we'll sit down and we'll talk about all this stuff—talk about why it was the way it was when I was young, talk about why he felt the way he did.

"But the years go by and it never comes up. I guess it feels like a dangerous subject or something. But he got sick and I realized that he was gettin' old and that...and that if I had somethin' to say to him, I should say it now...'cause family is forever and it's somethin' that..." Here he was drowned out by cheers but continued anyway, the audience all but irrelevant. "It's somethin' that don't ever go away, no matter how far you move away from each other or no matter what your feelin's are towards each other. It's just there in your blood all the time, in your blood.

"So if you got folks at home and have been waitin', waitin' to say stuff to 'em, don't waste too much time. 'Cause you'll always regret it." He said the last line in a mumble, so low and muttered that it was doubtful anybody ten feet from the mike heard him, although the listener who mattered most at that moment surely did. The song that night was nothing less than an act of contrition. (60-61)

The problem is, just *saying* the stuff isn't really enough. In order for the saying to make a difference, there has to be a readiness, a need, and a willingness to let the words flow out of that need. Otherwise it's just mouthing words, empty, ritualized words learned off TV, the words you know you're supposed to say to fathers whether you feel them or not. To put it in Osherson's words, you first have to feel your father's wound, and then speak to him out of the feeling of pain you know you share. *That* is healing—for you, and potentially, if it's not too late, for your father too.

By *Nebraska* Springsteen had made new progress with his father, with the internal, eidetic father ("paternal introject") who blocks integration far more effectively that the external one in the real world. His father is implicitly or fleetingly present in many of the songs, like "Mansion on the Hill," which recalls a childhood memory of Doug Springsteen taking Bruce and his sister Pam to look at a fancy house near where they lived, and "Used Cars," which traces the bitterness of a working-class childhood, your status judged by the car you drove, and the Springsteen family always having to buy some brokendown heap that the salesman sold to his father with ill-concealed contempt (I'll be returning to this song in chapter ten). But the cut that looks hardest at the emotional blocks separating father and son, in the context of what Springsteen called the "dark heart of a dream" in "Adam Raised a Cain," is "My Father's House."

It's a soft, dark folk tune written in the same three major chords (D-G-A) as "Nebraska" and "Highway Patrolman," but is closer in spirit (and in the actual progression of the chords) to the latter, which sets up a conflict of interests between love and duty and resolves it in favor of love. The "responsible" brother Joe Roberts tries to play the dual role of friend/equal and father/protector to his "wild" brother Franky, even when that means protecting Franky from the law he himself as a highway patrolman represents. Given a choice between a father-image as loving protector and a father-image as judgmental lawman, Joe chooses the former, and lets Franky escape his pursuit to Canada.

"My Father's House" sets up an entirely different situation, and moves in an entirely different direction, from a dream of total accepting love between father and son, through the empty-house image that keeps signaling his father's emotional absence, to a forlorn hope for the future; but somehow the song *feels* the same, has the same delicate balance between the despair of duty and the hope of love, as "Highway Policeman." "Last night I dreamed that," Springsteen starts out in slow, low-pitched 6/8 time—the mournful back-and-forth rhythm sounding less like a waltz than the rocking of a cradle—"I was a child." Out in the forest of the night, crashing through trees and hearing "the devil snappin' at my heels," looking for something:

> I broke through the trees and there in the night
> My father's house stood shining hard and bright
> The branches and brambles tore my clothes and scratched my arms
> But I ran till I fell shaking in his arms

This is a dream I've had too: between my discovery of a tender place inside me for my father, an empathetic sharing of his hurt and need, and the next time I saw him, I dreamed that he arrived at our house, and somehow the two of us tried to pass through a doorway at the same time, and our shoulders bumped. I reached out to steady myself on him, and found myself embracing him; his arms came up around me very tentatively, and I said in a small whisper, "I love you, Dad." I didn't think he'd heard me, but I could feel his arms tighten around me just slightly, and *knew* that everything was going to be all right.

And it was: when he arrived the blockages between us were gone. Springsteen, it seems, wasn't so lucky: "I woke and I imagined," he says, that "the hard things that pulled us apart / Will never again sir tear us from each other's hearts," but when he gets dressed and drives out to his father's house he finds it occupied by someone else. Desolate, he turns away and realizes that the reconciliation scene with his father was *just* a dream, a vision of reconciliation that may never be realized:

> My father's house shines hard and bright
> It stands like a beacon calling me in the night
> Calling and calling so cold and alone
> Shining 'cross this dark highway where our sins lie unatoned

The dark highway is the dark street he had been walking down for the past two or three years, of course; and if it is here illuminated coldly by the light shining from his father's house, it is also, I sense, itself a shadow *cast* by his father's house, the house of patriarchal repression. Men's ideologically normal need to repress love and warmth and closeness is precisely what darkens the street, precisely what makes both the house and the street (and everyone who lives or stands there, in the door or out in the rain) so "cold and alone." In this reading the unatoned sins *are* defenses, the inherited patriarchal walls that protect us from becoming frighteningly "at-one" with our wounded, withdrawn fathers.

Still, the dream is a powerful torch to shine into that darkness; and my guess is that the song's waking "reality," the vision of an unfamiliar woman turning him away (the nightmare mother protecting the absent father?), is not so much reality as an expression of Springsteen's own fears, the fear that the dream won't come true. What if I go to "fall shaking in his arms" and he goes cold on me, stiffens, pushes me away? Won't I then be doubly disappointed, fooled again—as I was in "Born to Run," as I swore I never would be again in "Promised Land"—by a dream?

What Springsteen has begun here, in fact, is a process of re-calling the past, calling and calling it back up from the darkness of self-protective forgetfulness. It means taking a new passage down the dark street of childhood in search of new lights—lights that were there all along but have been repressed and must now be rediscovered, *made* new. When the little boy's admiring love for his father is shut down by the father's inability to respond, it turns to anger, betrayal, hurt, resentment; as a result the boy soon begins to repress all the loving moments, all the times when father and son had fun together, laughed together, loved together. Those times start to feel wrong, false, delusory, in the bitterness of the adolescent boy's rebellious anger, and so they are actively forgotten, repressed. But now, in the adult son's attempt to reintegrate his father, to recover his "unfeeling" father first through defensive feeling (the angry father), next through vulnerable feeling (the hurt, scared father), and finally through openly positive feeling (the loving father), the good memories must be salvaged from the darkness of deliberate forgetfulness.

Thus on *Born in the U.S.A.* the one song that confronts the father, "My Hometown," begins with a loving memory of riding on daddy's lap in one of those "brand-new used cars":

> I was eight years old and running with a dime in my hand
> Into the bus stop to pick up a paper for my old man
> I'd sit on his lap in that big old Buick and steer as we drove
>     through town
> He'd tousle my hair and say son take a good look around
> This is your hometown

Now the music too begins to point toward resolution: where the *Nebraska* songs that were poised on that narrow line between love and duty, protection and legalism, caring and absence, were harmonically pure (straight major triads) but tonally flat, "My Hometown" insistently cracks across that line in eighth-note shifts from an unresolved-sounding E chord with an A bass to a resolved A chord, and from an F#m7 chord with an E bass to a resolved E chord. It's strange, but the major triads of "Highway Patrolman" and "My Father's House" sounded cautious, unwilling to commit (and the same chords in "Nebraska" sounded past all ability to commit); while the musical tensions of "My Hometown" express a new boldness, a new submerged *certainty* in Springsteen's feelings about his father. The song expands the father-son theme to the larger society in the second verse and bridge—the race tensions in the sixties, the closing down of the A and M Karagheusian rug mill that Springsteen's father had worked at—and then returns to the father-son theme, but now in the next generation:

> Last night me and Kate we lay in bed talking about getting out
> Packing up our bags maybe heading south
> I'm 35, we got a boy of our own now
> Last night I sat him up behind the wheel and said son take a good look around
> This is your hometown

Now the re-calling of childhood begins to bear fruit: the son who felt unloved by his father is able to recover a moment in which he did feel loved by his father, and by owning that moment is then able to pass the moment on to his own son. This handing-down—intensified by the two-bar delay between the last two lines, which in turn reflects and anticipates the 20-year delay (as it were) of Springsteen's own fatherhood—is the breaking-out that Springsteen was looking for back in "Born to Run": not the decision to move down South (which is going to fail so miserably in "Seeds," on the live album), but the ability to smash through the vicious circle of father-son unlove into little moments of caring and sharing like this.

But by far the most powerful moment in Springsteen's long process of father-recovery comes for me on the live album, in a concert recorded on my 31st birthday in my hometown, Los Angeles—and when I first heard it on the live album, in late fall 1986, just as I was beginning to open myself to the resentment and hurt I felt toward my own father, it *felt* like I was simultaneously being born and coming home. The moment isn't quite a song, nor quite *not* a song; it is the transition between the last words of the introduction to "The River" and the first strains of the song. Over Danny Federici's and Nils Lofgren's mournful Bm9-F#m organ-guitar backing, Springsteen tells a Vietnam story, a story about how his father exulted in the fact that he, Bruce, would have to go into the Army soon and become a "man"—meaning that he would have to cut his hair and learn some respect for authority.

This story's poignancy for me is that my father did more or less the exact same thing to me, and what I heard subliminally when he talked about the Army making a man out of me was that he wanted me dead—wanted me to go to Vietnam and be killed. Death with honor—a dead son is preferable to a rebellious one. When, two or three months past my 18th birthday, I came home from college with a beard and told my parents that I hadn't yet registered for the draft, they hit the roof. My mother shouted at me, "We'll come visit you in *prison!*" as if the shame of having a son in jail was worse than having him die in an evil war halfway around the world, and my father shouted at me to shave off my

## Healing the Father 209

beard. When I refused (summoning up all my courage to tell him no to his face), he wrestled me to the floor, pinned my arms down with his knees, and, panting, called for my mother to bring the razor—roughly the point at which Rambo explodes in *First Blood*.

So when Springsteen tells virtually the same story, with only a few variations along the way—his father has a barber cut his hair while he's helpless in the hospital, he actually gets called to take a physical—and then springs a surprise ending on me, I can't hold back the tears:

> When I was growin' up, me and my Dad used to go at it all the time, over almost anything. But, uh, I used to have really long hair, way down past my shoulders, and when I was seventeen or eighteen, oh man, he used to hate it. And we got to where we'd fight so much that I'd spend a lot of time out of the house. And in the summertime it wasn't so bad, 'cause it was warm and your friends were out. But in the winter, I remember standing downtown, and it would get so cold; and when the wind would blow I had this phone booth that I used to stand in, and I used to call my girl like for hours at a time, just talking to her all night long.
>
> And finally I'd get my nerve up to go home, and I'd stand there in the driveway, and he'd be waiting for me in the kitchen. And I'd tuck my hair down under my collar and I'd walk in, and he'd call me back to sit down with him.
>
> And the first thing he'd always ask me was, what did I think I was doing with myself. And the worst part about it was I could never explain it to him.
>
> I remember I got in a motorcycle accident once, and I was laid up in bed, and he had a barber come in and cut my hair. And man, I can remember telling him that I hated him and that I would never ever forget.
>
> And he used to tell me, "Man, I can't wait till the Army gets you. When the Army gets you they're going to make a man out of you. They're going to cut all that hair off and they'll make a man out of you."
>
> And this was in I guess '68, and there was a lot of guys from the neighborhood going to Vietnam. I remember a drummer in my first band coming over to my house with his Marine uniform on, and saying that he was going, and that he didn't know where it was. And a lot of guys went, and a lot of guys didn't come back. And a lot that came back weren't the same any more.
>
> And I remember the day I got my draft notice, I hid it from my folks. And three days before my physical, me and my friends went out and we stayed up all night. When we got on the bus to go that morning, man, we were all so scared.
>
> And I went—and I failed! And I came home—it's nothing to applaud about—but I remember coming home after I'd been gone for three days, and walking in the kitchen, and my mother and father were sitting there. My Dad says, "Where you been?" I said, "I went to take my physical." He says, "What

## 210  No Less a Man

happened?" I said, "They didn't take me."

And he said, "That's good."

And, as Dave Marsh says, reporting a slightly different version of this same introduction on another night of the LA stand, "The cheers rose almost to a scream, but Bruce said nothing, just uncradled the microphone and blasted into it with a harmonica wail so sharp it felt like a knife" (*Glory* 391-92). And the knife cuts me every time I hear it. His father said it was *good* that he didn't get drafted! His father didn't want him to go to Vietnam and be killed, didn't care about him becoming a "man" if that meant letting him get killed, didn't really care about anything so much as having his son stay alive, which means: he loved him after all! Since I first bought the album, I have discovered my father's love for me too, and the moment is no longer quite as powerful as it was back then; but for the first five or ten times I listened to the album this moment, the words "That's good" and the slicing harmonica intro to "The River," convulsed me, had me sobbing.

And in fact I am almost tempted to end this book right here. It would make a dramatic—and dramaturgically fitting—ending, tying together the softening of Spenser as my father (they're roughly the same age) and the breakdown of Rambo as myself in a cozy image of rediscovered father-son love. Spenser the Korean War veteran, Rambo the Vietnam War veteran who clashes with Will Teasle the Korean War veteran, and then Springsteen the kid who, like me, didn't have to go: there is an eloquent progression in these stories. Parker and Morrell/Stallone tell the ongoing story of the dynasty of wounds, passed on almost inexorably from fathers to sons, each generation fighting in a different war to prove its collective and individual manhood to the generation that went before, and dying (physically or emotionally) to protect the previous generation from its collective and individual fears. "Proving one's manhood," in these stories, *is* a matter of sealing off the emotional monsters that threaten one's father(s): not only are the horrors of war preferable to an open confrontation with anxiety and need, the horrors of war (killing, enduring pain and hardship) are the idealized seal for those feelings. At the end of the movie version of *First Blood*, Stallone seems to have broken Rambo out of the vicious patriarchal circle, the masculine dynasty of wounds; but in the sequels he is off to war again, suckered by the fathers once again in *Rambo II*, off to save and protect a father in *Rambo III*. In the narrative logic of my book, however, we can see Springsteen's "failure" to go to war, his 4-F failure to "become a man," to be (re)constituted as a patriarchal man, as the true sequel to *First Blood*: Springsteen is not only the man who was not destroyed by war, as Morrell's Rambo was, but the man who *never went*—who, we might say in a deliberately anachronistic reading, was saved from having to go to war by his father's relief that he didn't have to go. Springsteen's engagement with his father in song and story marks the possibility that the patriarchal dynasty of wounds can be broken—that the wounds can be healed and the dynastic succession brought shuddering to a stop.

But this utopian moment will not do. Attractive as such a narrative closure might be in song and story, it ill suits the ongoingness of real life. In fact Springsteen himself has been discovering as much since the mid-1980s: reconciled with his father, he finds himself finally, surprisingly, ready to marry, and does, in 1985; but something is still not right with his life, something is missing, there remains a snag somewhere, and by 1988 his marriage to Julianne Philips breaks up. Closure splinters and cracks; the "liberated" center will not hold. More work remains to be done.

# Chapter Ten

# Displaced Mothers

Like many rebellious boys, Springsteen always felt close to his mother. His father was inaccessible, locked into the taciturnity of his repressed anger, and no one—not his mother, none of the children—had the key; his mother was the emotionally available parent, the one, as he said in "Adam Raised a Cain," who called him by his "true name." Adele Springsteen was never a problem for Bruce. She and he could always talk. She was always on his side against his father, even if she rarely ventured to stand up for her son (Bruce knew that she would have if she had dared). Bruce gets his introversion, his desire for privacy, his loner tendencies, from his father, and his father's family; he gets his creativity from his mother. "What I am doing today is directly connected to my mother" (qtd. in *Glory Days* 87). Back in the late 1950s Adele loves music, especially Elvis; little nine-year-old Bruce discovers his life's direction watching Elvis on Ed Sullivan. In the Springsteen myth, as in many myths of childhood generated under conditions of patriarchy, the father is the angry, bitter, resentful, sullen, withdrawn, morose parent, the mother the happy, caring, sensitive parent, the source of stability.

"My mother is the great energy—she's the energy of the show," Springsteen tells Dave Marsh. "The consistency, the steadiness, day after day—that's her. And the refusal to be disheartened, even though she was really up against it a lot of the time" (86). And this is just the way she happened to be, right? Just her personality—a mere genetic or emotional accident of some sort. No: this is, of course, the way women are *supposed* to be in patriarchal society. This is the role they are normatively assigned, the role for which they receive ideological training, by parents, teachers, priests, advertisers. Women are the emotional beasts of burden, the load-bearers. Men withdraw; women bear up. Springsteen is partly aware of what bearing up cost his mother; but to his childlike eyes it all seems almost effortless: "My mother lived with an immense amount of stress and pressure all her life and she was a person of immense control. It was she who created the sense of stability in the family, so that we never felt threatened through all the hard times" (86). Immense control, yes—this is the sign of "normal" ideological behavior, and for the "normal" patriarchal woman it is control aimed at the rechanneling and transformation of "negative" (masculine) emotions for general familial use.

So Doug Springsteen is the problem, not Adele. The result is that, all through the late 1970s and early 1980s, when Springsteen is using his music and concert monologues to work through his relationship with his "parents," all he is really working on is his father. His relationship with his mother needs no work. It is only recently, in fact, spurred by complaints from his mother (of all people) that he never talks about her in his concerts, that he has begun talking about her at all, and then, as she probably half expected, in pure tones of glowing praise. She was "just like Superwoman, she did everything, everywhere, all the time" (qtd. by Kate Lynch, 16). Just what a mother wants to hear—*needs* to hear, since the patriarchal culture that programs women to be load-bearing emotional beasts also programs them to expect (and exact) praise only from their sons, nowhere else. The thanks for submerging yourself in your family, being Superwoman to them, comes when your son loves you, does what you want, lives up to your expectations, and tells the world what a wonderful mother he has. The worst thing that can happen to a mother—at least to one still under the sway of patriarchal programming—is to have an ungrateful son, one who "kicks her in the teeth,"

That there *is* a problem here, though, should be obvious. Mothers may be emotionally supportive, but their support has a price: gratitude. And the son's debt of gratitude is too great ever to be paid, which means paying a penalty, a secret one: guilt. The son owes his life to his mother. She carried him in her womb, delivered him, nursed him, raised him, loved him, comforted him when he was sad, rejoiced with him when he was happy. How can a debt like that be repaid? How, in other words, can a man ever escape the silken bonds of love with which his mother ties him to her?

The traditional answer is: he can't. So he puts up his defenses. He does the right thing by her, but never lets her inside his skin. He works hard to be a good son, obedient, supportive, encouraging, full of praise, but never lets her close to his most vulnerable areas. She knows exactly where they are, of course, and can jab him in them (*guilt!*) whenever she needs his "love" (needs him to build her up a little, make her feel good about herself, ease the weight of her defensive insecurity, her feeling of not being loved by her parents or her husband or herself); but he can insist that she exercise extreme discretion in those areas. A wife who ventures on that territory is subjected to total emotional shutdown.

One of the keys to this "normal" filial relation to the mother is its asymmetricality.[1] The son's "normal" relationships with father and mother are both dialectical; but the father-son relationship is dialectically symmetrical (imitative, reproductive, repetitive), while the mother-son relationship is dialectically asymmetrical (oppositional, reactive, inversive). Where the son reproduces his father's normative masculinity in a complex dialectical tension between challenging the authority that maintains their hierarchical distance and conforming himself to his father's behavioral strategies (the ideological repetition compulsion that Freud biologized as the Oedipus complex), he reacts against his mother's normative femininity in a complex dialectical tension between protecting himself against her emotional assaults (putting up the wall, donning the mask of unemotionality) and remaining totally open to her, being her boy, her confidant, her one boon companion in the world, idealizing her words for him as his "true name." The "normal" son's relationship with his mother is mired by patriarchy in a soggy field of pushes and pulls between acceptance and refusal of self-sacrificing "love," openness and defensiveness, gratitude and ingratitude, loyalty and guilt. As Paul Olsen puts it, it is a field of tension between infantile dependency, symbolized by the utterly contented baby at the breast, and a "mature" "independence" whose "normal" ideological facade—calm superiority and unemotionality, the smiling self-sufficiency of a man who has left his childhood far behind him—conceals a terrible longing for and fear of the dependent state:

The bond [between mother and son] is communicated—cemented and embellished—by the contact of body on body, skin on skin. And where this breaks down, so too does the bond—not only the bond, but the humanness, the ability to live. The presence or absence of possibilities in the life of a man will to a large extent be based on the quality of contact he has had with his mother's flesh, with the satisfaction or frustration derived from her flesh, from the degree of security and warmth and possibilities that her flesh offers him. [Note that this is true of little girls too; and the only reason Olsen places this much weight on *mothers*, on contact with mommy's body, is that patriarchy programs mothers to take this responsibility for the child's wellbeing, and fathers *not* to take it.] Without its positive, life-giving contact he becomes a living skeleton, soulless, pessimistic, depressed, frightened; with too much of it he becomes helpless, a perpetual child. But no one knows what is *enough*, what is the good and proper amount. (37-38)

And because we don't know, because we can never be sure whether we got enough love as infants or not enough, because we can therefore never know whether we are too attached to our mommies or too little, too infantile or not infantile enough, we repress the whole business. Infantile needs—me? Hah! "Mister I ain't a boy, no I'm a man," as Springsteen sings in "Promised Land." I believe in a, let's see, something harmless, something far away from here, something no one would think to tie back to mommy, yes, a—a *promised land*!

As Olsen makes clear, however, recognition of this tension, and a willingness to engage it, experience it, regressively relive it, can be therapeutic:

> At a meeting of psychotherapists, a very prominent Eastern guru is talking about detachment, about blanking out the thinking process. He maintains that in order to "see clearly" we must give up the images we carry within us, in essence free ourselves from inner content and return to a basic, perhaps "blissful" state in which all becomes one.
>
> The statement bothers, troubles, many of the psychotherapists present because they are related strongly to a materialistic world, strongly related to theories that stress outer, worldly reality as the only reality. And one says, "What he wants is the tit. He wants all of us to regress to the tit, like infants nursing."
>
> The psychotherapist doesn't see all of the picture, doesn't see that his theoretical bias against "regression" is merely a value judgment and not a truth, but he is on the right track. The blissful state so desired by proponents of Eastern disciplines (and so badly confused with "enlightenment" by their Western followers) is *precisely* the ability to regress, to return *at will* and for brief moments of time, to a primal state of bliss perhaps initially experienced at the mother's breast, but more likely within the womb itself. I stress *at will* because, unlike the sudden regression to earlier stages of life that can terrify and break apart a person in the throes of a psychosis or a "bad" LSD trip, this state of bliss or *samadhi* or whatever other term applies is achieved with attention and control, and can also be emerged from at will.... Damaged people experience great terror in this attempt and are apt to fragment from it: there is nothing "good" to return to.
>
> But you don't have to be damaged to fear this "return" or regression, even if it can be controlled.
>
> All you must be is a man—and that is enough to stand your hair on end at the mere possibility of being asked to retreat to a state so closely approximating the flesh-on-flesh contact with mother. It is creepy, frightening, anxiety-producing just in the thinking of it—and the first impulse is to run from any idea of it.

What a man is frightened of, more than anything else in the vast possibilities of living experience, is dependency, regression to a state in which he becomes an infant in the care of his mother—a mother later unconsciously symbolized by almost all women with whom he comes in contact.

A man may be able to *do* it, but the very thought of it terrifies him *because he knows it is possible,* because on some profound level he has never left the world of his mother. Because his unconscious *is* the unconscious of his mother and he has made frantic efforts to leave it, to become independent, to shake her.

A man spends most of his life running away from his mother's world through the pursuit of his masculine toys: he plays sports, jocks around in locker rooms, buys cars, spends his time learning how to wheel and deal financially, becomes sexually aggressive—all those driven activities which may turn a man into a parody. He can become intellectualized, using the "clean," "analytic," "logical" forms of thought and behavior to identify himself with "maleness," abandoning the intuition, sensitivity, and feeling that he defines as "female." And to cement his necessary avoidance of anything that may bring him closer to a way of being defined as feminine, society has provided him with a fear of homosexuality. To be tender is to be queer, to touch another man is to be queer, to kiss another man is to be queer—to be, that is, quintessentially feminine.

That is how far he wishes to travel from his mother. But he does it at the cost of incredible damage and waste: he buries at least half his life, lays to rest at least his potentiality as a full human being—and will live the rest of his life in conflict, like a self divided, like a socially acceptable schizophrenic. His so-called maleness always at war with his unconscious, with what is hidden from him, with what he does not know about the deeper regions of himself—but which always gets expressed in one way or another. (39-42)

This is, clearly, not yet a solution; it is really little more than a diagnosis and a sense that to overcome our "socially acceptable schizophrenia" we have to regress to infantile dependency, and emerge from that state renewed. Springsteen, who healed and broke the paternal dynasty of wounds by discovering his father's wound in himself, his need for love, his vulnerability, and feeling it, experiencing it, naming it, and so outgrowing it, has even less of a solution to the maternal dynasty of wounds than Olsen. Indeed, as far as I can tell, he has only just begun to realize that there is a problem to solve. Explicit references to the mother are, as I've said, extremely rare in his songs, and his recent references to her in concert monologues and interview remarks are almost invariably of the defensive Supermom variety.

## Displaced Mothers 217

An interesting exception to this rule is "Walk Like a Man" on *Tunnel of Love* (1987), his first album to deal openly and articulately with his ambivalences about women: there he addresses his father with love ("I remember how rough your hand felt in mine on my wedding day / And the tears cried on my shoulder I couldn't turn away"), but refers to his mother in a surprisingly terse third person, almost in the implacable tones of "Adam Raised a Cain" ("In the summer that I was baptized / My father held me to his side"):

> I remember ma draggin' me and my sister down the street to the church
> Whenever she heard those wedding bells
> Well would they ever look so happy again
> The handsome groom and his bride
> As they stepped into that long black limonsine
> For their mystery ride

Here Springsteen depicts his mother as a woman in love with love, in love with romance, weddings, happy endings, lived-happily-ever-afters—the ideologically prescribed addiction for "normal" women, as violent and pornographic images are for "normal" men—dragging her children along with her on her quests for vicarious satisfaction. Where ten years earlier, in his first approach to his father, Springsteen had portrayed him as looking for someone to *blame* or deidealize, someone onto whom to project his anger at masculine failure (the failure to gain total control over himself and his environment), now, in his first approach to his mother, he portrays her as looking for someone to idealize, someone onto whom to project her denial of feminine failure (the failure to gain total happiness through the love of the men in her life). Here, for the first time, Adele is no understanding angel who calls him by his "true name," but a kind of romance-robot who responds irresistibly, like Pavlov's dog, to the call of wedding bells from the nearby Catholic church. In fact, she responds irresistibly in two senses: she cannot resist the programmed stimulus herself (thus the power of Springsteen's "whenever"); and her insistence that her children experience the vision of perfect happiness through total love with her brooks no resistance from them (thus "draggin'").

Significantly, as these images flash across the screen of his memory the speaker of the song (whom I equate with Springsteen himself) is himself approaching the altar: the implication is, is Juli dragging me? Is this just some feminine stimulus-response thing, something she too is doing to me out of some programmed compulsion? Did I have no more say in this marriage than I did "whenever" my mother heard the wedding bells? Am I just a male pawn to be "dragged" "whenever" some romance-robot feels the programmed urge?

If these reflections awaken a gut-level voice of despair, the second line is more despairing still: "Well would they ever look so happy again?" What if the "happiness" that is so evident on everyone's face here at our wedding is only an image, an illusion, a programmed fantasy that only lasts long enough to trap you, then wears off to reveal the true depths of your imprisonment? That wearing off of the "look" of happiness would explain his mother's romantic projections, in fact—she represses the absence of romance in her own life by imagining it in the lives of strangers—and, combined with the force of being "dragged down the street to the church" by his mother, it would also explain (Springsteen may be imagined as thinking, or subliminally suspecting, as he walks down the aisle) why he fled marriage, romantic commitment of any sort, for so long, why he never wanted to own anything or be close to anyone, why he constantly dreamed of escape onto the highway of "Born to Run." Perhaps his frantic need to escape was motivated not—or not only—by a fear that what "they" did to his father "they" would do to him too, but by a sense that his mother was smothering him, holding him too close, demanding too much from him.

This is a beginning, but it is still only a hesitant and incomplete diagnosis. Springsteen is just beginning to access his anger toward his mother, his resistance to being "dragged" places, his unwillingness to be dependent on her emotionally—traditional male stuff that is usually kept strictly repressed—and it surfaces (so far) for only a fleeting moment in a single song. It surfaces again, *very* indirectly, on one of his most recent albums, *Human Touch* (1992), in the bridge of "The Long Goodbye," which I want to return to later:

> Well I went to leave twenty years ago
> Since then I guess I been packin' kinda slow
> Sure did like that admiring touch
> Guess I liked it a little too much

This doesn't give us much to go on. The only indication that this quatrain has anything to do with Adele Springsteen, in fact, is his association of "that admiring touch" not with his career since 1973 but with the shadowy, unnamed place he's been trying to leave, without much success, since the late 1960s and early 1970s—home, almost

## Displaced Mothers  219

certainly. This sounds like an attempt not only to leave his mother, to break away from his crippling emotional dependency on her "admiring touch," but also to bring that effort to consciousness, to name his maternal dependency as he once named his hurt anger at his father.

This sounds ungrateful, of course: now the mother is the villain for admiring and encouraging her son. Much of the rhetoric of "blaming the victim"—among both the men who blame their mothers and the women who defend them—is locked into this patriarchal mother-son symbiosis, even when it is most explicitly informed by feminist or masculist theory. It is, certainly, one of the hardest emotional bonds to break. But the real issue is not who the villain or victim is—whether the mother did terrible things to her son, or the son, in listing those things, is doing terrible things to his mother and her avatars. The real issue is a systemic one: how the patriarchy manipulates the mother-son relationship in order to satisfy the needs of neither the mother nor the son, in fact to keep both as miserable as possible while still enabling them to idealize the relationship. The relationship is, of course, like all patriarchal constructs, a sick one and must be broken, both retroactively, in the lives of adult men and women, and proactively, in the collective future of our culture. But the way to break it is not to assign blame to individual people, individual actants in the dysfunctional system.

When Judith Fetterley says of the mother in *The Resisting Reader*, for example, that "it is impossible for anyone to be this valuable" (77, quoted above), it is important to recognize that *both* the mother and the son have set the admiring mother (and, for that matter, the admired son) up to be more valuable than she or he can ever be, and that this idealization process was instilled in both (first in the mother, then, through her, in her son) by the patriarchy—and further, and most important, that attempts to deidealize that process should not necessarily be perceived as "ingratitude" (as it is normatively thematized by the patriarchal mother), "blaming the victim" (as it has come to be thematized by feminists), or "betrayal" (as it is normatively thematized by the patriarchal son). Breaking out of the patriarchal mother-son relationship is a step toward gender liberation for both parties, and by extension for all men and all women. Its perception and portrayal in negative terms (ingratitude, blaming the victim, betrayal) by both men and women are a tenacious survival of the patriarchal programming from which we would be free.

This begins to bring us full circle from Parker's search for the absent mother. Springsteen's first tentative steps toward an understanding of his mother, and of himself in relation to his mother, suggest that the overinvestment of the masculine self in a romantically idealized feminine other that Fetterley identified in connection with Gatsby and Daisy is the "normal" patriarchal product of maternal "love." The emotionally deprived daughter-as-grown-woman attempts to recuperate her loss by coaching her son to invest himself emotionally in her, or rather in an idealized image of her, a fantasy-mother whose very intangibility binds him more tightly to her (in the guilty fear that he has so far failed to grasp and be grasped by that mother-image because he hasn't tried hard enough, hasn't denied himself for her sufficiently) and her more tightly to him (in the desperate hope that his belief in her idealized self-projection will somehow transform her into the beloved daughter she never was).

Thus also "misogyny," that bitter accusation feminists have hurled at men, and have even, driven by those ideological survivals of patriarchal programming, identified as somehow "intrinsic" to biological maleness. Misogyny is what Fetterley calls the "divestment of moral indignation" that arises out of the illusory "investment of the romantic imagination" in the mother. Or, to put it as succinctly as possible: *misogyny is the return of the maternal repressed.* On one level, that most superficial level that patriarchy allows to reach our conscious awareness, it is the son's transference of anger at the demanding and self-withholding mother (too sacred—and too fragile—to be attacked) onto other women; but at a deeper and more insistently and defensively repressed level it is his transference onto other women of his maternal introject's repressed anger at her father for withholding love from her, and of her repressed demand that *her* paternal introject (projected in turn onto the son) give her the love she needs. Misogyny is displaced misandry, which is displaced misogyny. Around and around, back and forth: we pass patriarchal hatred from generation to generation and from gender to gender, mother to son to granddaughter, father to daughter to grandson, transforming it for the repressive use of the next and the other. Programmed by the "normal" mother (who was programmed by her "normal" father) to protect her against her own fears of not being loved, indeed to taboo the very possibility of ever venting his anger and frustration at her emotional demands and manipulations in direct confrontation with her (she would be devastated, his rage would be matricidal), the "normal" son must turn his anger elsewhere—and what better transferential target than his mother's avatars, his lovers, colleagues, and daughters?

This is not to defend "misogyny"; it is rather, I think, to place it in a context that is at once more personal, more subjective, and thus more potentially malleable, and more political, more systemic, and thus less potentially accusatory, than is often the case in feminist critiques of men or masculist critiques of women. Let me say it again: I am not blaming the mother for misogyny. I am arguing that misogyny is a horrendously "normal" function of the complex skein of patriarchal ideology—just as horrendously "normal" as the misandry that drives some feminists to launch a blanket attack on all men. And I am going to argue that the liberatory answer to "misogyny" or repressed mother-hatred is not to control it, as Spenser does, but to release it—not in controlled repressive and transferential doses, as in fact Springsteen does, and as patriarchy trains us to do, but in a transformative engagement with the experiences that first inscribed it on the son's infant body.

I repeat: Springsteen has not yet done this, and is just now beginning to sense the necessity of doing it. As a result, there is a powerfully misogynistic—or at the very least sexist—strain in his music. In "Mary Queen of Arkansas," for example, an almost universally despised cut on his first album, *Greetings* (1973), he portrays a mother-figure of ambiguous gender, a "queen" as quasimasculized mother, Mother Mary ("Queen of Heaven" is the submerged religious allusion, of course) as a transvestite who is, as Springsteen's speaker says, "not man enough for me to hate / Or woman enough for kissing." As for Will Teasle in the movie version of *First Blood*, these are the son's prescribed responses to men and women: you hate the former, kiss the latter. (Or, as Teasle implies, as father you kill the son, as mother you kiss him.) Given the sexual ambiguity of Mary in this song, this also implies an even more appalling criss-crossing prescription: charge the kiss (or the genital penetration) you give the woman with the hatred you feel for men (because she is not your idealized fantasy-mother, because she is too like the real mother whose reality you have fiercely repressed) and the hatred you feel for men with the emotional intensity of a kiss (because that hatred is a man's only permissible expression of emotional intensity for another man).[2] Then, to prove your ideological "manhood," repress the whole emotional complex: affect nonchalance, indifference. This is, after all, the distinctive mark of patriarchal masculinity: that you *don't care*. Here in Springsteen's song this programmed indifference in the speaker's approach to Mary is conceived or thematized in terms of both repressed homophobic revulsion for the male ("not man enough for me to hate") and repressed sexual desire for the female ("or woman enough for kissing")—both standard ideological inscriptions. The song itself suggests, however, that this "normal" thematization of indifference serves the crucial function of protecting the speaker from his true fear, infantile desire for flesh-on-flesh contact with the body of the mother: "Mary, my queen," he says, "your soft hulk is reviving."

The flip side of this tabooed desire for physical intimacy with the mother is the son's typical overt complaint: "I don't understand how you can hold me so tight," the speaker says, "and love me so damn loose." Let me go, this implies: let me be a separate person; or else, if you insist on holding me tight, at least *love* me, don't just make emotional demands on me. Best of all, let me loose *and* love me: love me unpossessively, undemandingly.

In fact, the accusations Springsteen's speaker levels at Mary in this song might be schematized into a diagnostic chart for sons' relations with their mothers: (1) your soft hulk revives me, but (2) whenever I let myself get too close to you you pull me *too* close, you smother me, which is oppressive precisely because (3) you don't let your love flow out to me, you expect mine to flow out to you, you expect me to give to you what you never gave to me, and so, to protect myself from those impossible demands, (4) I will pretend indifference to you, pretend that you are neither hatable man nor kissable woman and therefore entirely beyond my "normal" emotional repertoire. A depressing scenario, clearly—but one that just as clearly cannot be laid entirely at the son's feet (or, for that matter, at the mother's). The entire ideological web must be untangled, one strand at a time—or else (is this too much to hope for?) in one transformative release.

"Mary Queen of Arkansas" is one of Springsteen's most neglected songs, an embarrassment to his most partisan critics (it was never one of my favorites, either). Indeed musically it drags along, just barely mobile. Lyrically, however, it is full of early self-revelation; and we might even speculate that the song's musical inertia is a sign that Springsteen senses he's treading on sacred (tabooed) ground. This is, after all, back in 1972, when Springsteen is 23—not yet ready to deal with mommy and daddy, but still open to revelatory impulses that he would decisively shut down in *Born to Run*. It may even be that, as I argued was the case with the critical reception to Stallone in *First Blood*, the critics' negative response to "Mary Queen of Arkansas" has something to do with the unease her "soft hulk" causes us—that sense that we too are too close to a taboo, to a presexual desire for the soft hulk of our mother's body, for the breast, and possibly also (and here it really gets frightening) for the soft "maternalized" hulk of our father's body as well: for intimate physical contact with both parents in the first months of our lives.

This first album is in fact rife with complex and daring images of the son's need for and anger at his mother, which Springsteen will increasingly repress as he moves toward the macho synthesis of *Born to Run*. "Growin' Up," for example, has a subliminal movement from "I hid in the clouded wrath of the crowd" in verse one, suggesting his father's repressed anger, to "I hid in the clouded warmth of the crowd" in verse two, hinting at his father's repressed love, to "I hid in the mother breast of the crowd" in verse three. It is just a moment, all but occluded by Springsteen's gritty voice; but it is there, and I think it is a powerful one—all the more powerful for its contextual setting in a song full of adolescent vulnerability. Certainly the movement from "clouded wrath" through "clouded warmth" to "mother breast" seems to trace in advance the therapeutic progress Springsteen has himself made over the last 15 or so years of his singing career, beginning four or five years after he wrote this song (which has in fact remained one of his most popular concert pieces and a rich vehicle for various sketches and narrations).

Another song on *Greetings* that suggests Springsteen's ambivalent feelings about his mother is "For You," one of the most traditionally successful rockers on the album—though its lyrics, typically of the album, are modernistic and fragmentary in the extreme, not traditional at all. The suicidal female "you" to whom the song is addressed (a girlfriend in an ambulance, Springsteen told Dave Marsh) is clearly a mother-figure; the speaker's relation to her is steeped in precisely the mixture of affectionate intimacy and anger at distance that patriarchy prescribes for sons and mothers. He promises to "stand on file" to her "Cheshire smile," because "she's all I ever wanted"; but he also feels manipulated by her, used, as if she were creating him, "conceiving" him like a mother, and he denies her ability to do this to him ("Well take your local joker and teach him how to act / I swear I was never that way even when I really cracked"). He's there for her, heart and soul, like a good obedient son ("But I could give it all to you now if only you could ask"), but feels rejected, unneeded by her:

> I came for you, for you, I came for you
> But you did not need my urgency
> I came for you, for you, I came for you
> But your life was one long emergency
> And your cloud line urges me
> And my electric suges free

## 224 No Less a Man

She is not only, in his eyes, self-contained, self-sufficient; she is Supermom:

> Didn't you think I knew that you were born with the power
> of a locomotive
> Able to leap tall buildings in a single bound
> And your Chelsea suicide with no apparent motive
> You could laugh and cry in a single sound
> And your strength is devastating in the face of all these odds Remember how I kept you waiting when it was my turn to be the god?

On *The Wild, The Innocent & The E Street Shuffle* most of this maternal imagery is gone; we know little or nothing about Sandy or Diamond Jackie, and Rosalita, like Wendy in "Born to Run," is the mere female symbol of successful escape, living proof that her boyfriend is tough and masculine and ready to do anything to achieve his goals. Kitty in the song that bears her name, "Kitty's Back," is the desirable heartbreaker, the album's closest approach to a needed but unneeding motherfigure—unless it is the "Fat lady, big mama, Missy Bimbo" who "sits in her chair and yawns" in "Wild Billy's Circus Song," a mother-figure perhaps more along the lines of the mother in Harry Chapin's "Sniper" ("'You're ugly,' she said / 'You bug me,' she said / 'Please love me' I said / But she just sat there / With that same flat stare / That she saves for me alone / When I'm home / Take me home"). But neither song really gives us much to go on.

On *Born to Run* there is another Mary, the girlfriend in "Thunder Road" whom the Springsteen hero wants along on his flight from the "town full of losers" because she seems to have some sort of magical power to "make it real"—the kind of power the hero in "For You" attributed to his dying girlfriend, the kind of power sons attribute to their mothers—and certainly, as in "Mary Queen of Arkansas," there can be no denying the mythic resonances of *Mother* Mary for a lapsed Catholic like Springsteen (especially one who aspires to the title of Rock Messiah).

"She's the One" is probably *Born to Run*'s strongest mother song: she is, after all "the one," the one and only true love for this boy, even though he knows that she is all wrong for him, even though he knows that she has "secret places that no boy can fill," even though he says "I wish she'd just leave me alone"—who is this if not the mother? She is bigger than life, "the one" woman in the world (though he knows, undoubtedly, that there are millions of others) because he has transferred his feelings about his mother onto her. Like his father on *Darkness*, in "Adam Raised a Cain," the mother-figure here is shown "standing in the doorway like a dream"—a dream not of bitterness and exclusion and withdrawal, now, but of dangerous because tabooed delights, a dream of literally impossible promise that the speaker hopes against hope may be realized:

> With the thunder in your heart at night when you're kneeling in the dark
> It says you're never gonna leave her
> But there's this angel in her eyes that tells such desp'rate lies
> And all you want to do is believe her
> And tonight you'll try just one more time to leave it all behind
> And break on through

That is the hope: that you will one day "break on through" to the "real" mother whose ideal image looms just above or beyond the *real* real mother who withholds herself, and by withholding herself ties you to her ("you're never gonna leave her"). The very existence of this "real" mother who will satisfy all her son's desires if only he will give her what she needs—total love—is chief among those "desp'rate lies" she tells, and coaches her son to believe blindly; and the promise of complete satisfaction held out by this maternal fantasy is "The secret pact you made back when her love could save you from the bitterness."

The problem with these images, from an emancipatory point of view, is that they are all explicitly displaced images—images not of the mother but of the girlfriend. They are, therefore, still steeped in the repression that maintains them: because Springsteen directs his need for and rage at his mother away from her, projects those feelings onto her infinitely replaceable surrogates (and, whenever one begins to move from the promise-of-satisfaction mode to the punishment-for-transgression mode, from ideal love to real guilt, she *is* quickly replaced).

Springsteen's maternal imagery remains displaced on *Darkness* and after, but his new willingness to deal openly with his anger at his father does bring significant change: now, increasingly, the desired-but-dangerous mother-figure (who does figure in "Candy's Room") becomes the available-but-unhappy mother-figure. This shift is clearest in "Racing in the Street," where the racing hero drives that "little girl away" like a car, as he did Wendy in "Born to Run," but with his heightened awareness of what his father had done not only to him but to his mother, Springsteen now finds a new tone of sympathy for his patient, long-suffering mother:

> But now there's wrinkles around my baby's eyes
> And she cries herself to sleep at night
> When I come home the house is dark
> She sighs "Baby did you make it all right"
> She sits on the porch of her daddy's house
> But all her pretty dreams are torn
> She stares off alone into the night
> With the eyes of one who hates for just being born

This isn't Adele Springsteen, not literally; but my guess is that Springsteen's sudden sympathy for the woman who is won like a prize at a drag race comes out of his new sense of what his mother has had to put up with living with his father (her "daddy" as paternalist husband and *his* daddy). And when he imagines himself taking his "little girl" or "baby" down to the sea to "wash these sins off our hands," surely the implication is that the son is going to save the mother from the dulling, deadening father.

*The River* bombards us, for the first time in Springsteen's career, really, with men who desperately need love, desperately need a commitment from their lovers: "The Ties That Bind," "Two Hearts," "Out in the Street," "Crush on You," "I Wanna Marry You," "Fade Away," "The Price You Pay," and "Drive All Night" all plead for love, sometimes from an arrogated position of superiority, calling on things like duty and responsibility and the psychology of being alone and being together, sometimes desperately, from a position of fearful, insecure vulnerability ("Fade Away"), sometimes brashly, sometimes softly and romantically. Other songs defend against women's mother-power: "Sherry Darling" is a comic expression of frustration with a girlfriend's mother, the hero of "Hungry Heart" walks out on his wife and kids and never goes back, and women in "You Can Look (But You Better Not Touch)" become taboo objects (like the mother for her son) that are fatal to the man who touches them. In "The River" and "Point Blank" Springsteen brings the same sympathetic perception of his mother's suffering to bear as in "Racing in the Street," intensified, in "The River," by his sister's experience (on which the song was based) of getting pregnant and married and then having her husband lose his job.

The album ends on a powerfully personal note of loss: having witnessed a "Wreck on the Highway," the singer comes home to his lover and imagines himself as the man dying out on the highway, still lying broken out there in the rain, and also lying broken in here in bed, pulling his sleeping lover close to comfort him ("your soft hulk is reviving," as Springsteen sang back on *Greetings*), and in his mind's ear hearing a policeman arrive to tell her that her "baby"—the speaker himself—has died. This has the makings of a therapeutic regression: Springsteen as his mother's baby who dies to her, dies away from her, and by dying regains her as a separate adult, and thereby regains himself.

But how does that happen? Springsteen doesn't know, and in the following albums he continues to beat the imagistic bushes (continues to transfer his mother-feelings onto girlfriend-figures) in search of an answer. *Nebraska* is almost exclusively male, the only potentially significant woman being the stranger who meets him at the door at his father's house: as Springsteen turns full-time to the problem of his father, the mother is estranged.

Interestingly, however, one of the songs he wrote in that sudden burst of creative release in late fall, 1981, that got held over for *Born in the U.S.A.*, was "Downbound Train," which I read as the mother-version of "My Father's House." This song is almost as universally despised by rock critics and Springsteen fans as "Mary Queen of Arkansas," but I can't help it; along with "Born in the U.S.A." it is one of my favorite songs on the album, precisely because I find the dream sequence at the end so powerfully moving:

> Last night I heard your voice
> You were crying, crying, you were so alone
> You said your love had never died
> You were waiting for me at home
> Put on my jacket, I ran through the woods
> I ran till I thought my chest would explode
> There in the clearing, beyond the highway,
> In the moonlight, our wedding house shone
>   I rushed through the yard, I burst through the front door
> My head pounding hard up the stairs I climbed
> The room was dark, our bed was empty
> Then I heard that long whistle whine
> And I dropped to my knees, hung my head and cried

If this isn't a displaced dream of going home to mommy, I don't know what is. Change or drop one word—"wedding"—and you have all the elements of a potentially therapeutic regression to the mother-son bond. The song begins (in my subtextual reading: narratively it is about a man whose wife has left him) with a son who has been trying to wean himself emotionally from his mother, living apart, telling himself she no longer needs him and he no longer needs her. But then the dream comes, showing him his mother crying over her loss, his absence, her need for him, and before he has time to repress his own need his body acts for him, rushes out of the house onto a visionary moonlit landscape where the house he grew up in stands, and he tries to go home, tries to regress back to his childhood, but the room is dark—always dark, wherever Springsteen turns—and empty, like the rooms through which his embittered father once walked, and the singer hurls himself on the bed in tears. It is exactly the ending of "My Father's House"—except that Springsteen isn't yet ready to call it "My *Mother's* House." He is not ready yet to deal with the mother explicitly at all—but his unconscious is already dealing with it, through submerged symbols, through mother-surrogates. (Cf. also the plea for "a lover who will come on in and cover me" in the album's second song.)

And that brings us back to *Tunnel of Love*, with which I began this chapter: the album on which he finally (if still only hesitantly, and in passing) begins to deal openly with his feelings about his mother. Because it is still only a beginning, I cannot offer a therapeutic moment on it that will point the way for masculist liberation from the mother, as I did in chapter nine in regard to the father: Springsteen has not yet reached that far. I do, however, want to look at a song that deals transferentially with mother-need and mother-fear in a potentially therapeutic way, en route to what broken closure I can muster: "Cautious Man."

*Tunnel of Love* is Springsteen's first album written and recorded after his marriage to Julianne Philips, and one of the things he is manifestly trying to do throughout the songs on the album is to find a way to sink gracefully into married life, with his integrity intact. The stability of marriage is of course something that he has been running from for most of his adult life—and also, in some sense, something that he has been trying to talk himself into returning to since *The River*. Here he has returned to it, and tries to talk himself into believing that it's forever. Some of this is sheer determination, probably repressive determination, hoping against hope that this is the real thing, that he and Juli really have "made it real"; some of it is openly riddled with doubts, like the brilliant conclusion to "Brilliant Disguise":

> Tonight our bed is cold
> I'm lost in the darkness of our love
> God have mercy on the man
> Who doubts what he's sure of

And in fact the sexually restless last verse of "One Step Up"—"There's a girl across the bar / I get the message she's sending"—predicts pretty accurately the affair with Patti Scialfa that will wreck Springsteen's marriage not too many months after the album is released.

But Springsteen also senses, now, what it must feel like to come home. After 15 years of albums about darkness, he now realizes that coming home means light; and surprisingly, perhaps, given his fierce attacks on Catholicism throughout his career, the light is specifically a visionary light generated by God, or by some mystical force that a lapsed Catholic like Springsteen images as God. This light figures here and there on the album, on "Valentine's Day," for example ("And God's light came shinin' on through / I woke up in the darkness scared and breathin', born anew"), and it will return with renewed force on *Human Touch* and *Lucky Town*, transforming his concerts more than ever into rock-and-roll worship services, places of holy communion and salvation.³ Springsteen's finest exploration of this sacred impulse on *Tunnel of Love* is "Cautious Man," a song about a hobo who, by imagistic reversal—the man without a penny has to be as cautious with his life as the multimillionaire who wrote the song—becomes Springsteen himself:

> Bill Horton was a cautious man of the road
> He walked lookin' over his shoulder and remained faithful to his code
> When something caught his eye he'd measure his need
> And then very carefully he'd proceed

Here is the defensive "code" that Spenser and Rambo, too, cling to as a bulwark against a frightening world: masculine self-control as the only guarantee of survival. And, emotionally extravagant as he has been in his passionate attempts to get to the bottom of things through his music, bold as he has been in his willingness to face the monsters inside, Springsteen, too, is, has been, a cautious man, measuring his need and only then proceeding with care. But, like Bruce, Billy falls in love with a "young girl" (defensively, Springsteen continues to thematize women as "young girls," "little girls," "babies"—people as little like his mother as possible), and Springsteen's omniscient narrator remarks, rather dubiously, "It was there in her arms he let his cautiousness slip away." Perhaps what is happening here is that Springsteen feels Billy feeling *some* of his cautiousness slipping away—there is a relaxation of self-control, but only a very slight and probably imperceptible one, for:

> Billy was an honest man, he wanted to do what was right
> He worked hard to fill their lives with happy days and loving nights
> Alone on his knees in the darkness for steadiness he'd pray
> For he knew in a restless heard the seed of betrayal lay

He hasn't, clearly, let *all* his cautiousness slip away: he still has enough of it left to feel driven to "work hard" to do what's right, to be "honest" in the sense of self-controlled, "steady," mommy's obedient little boy, clinging defensively to his wife precisely because he knows how easy it would be for him to wander off, to hit the road again. This is Springsteen as his own father, broken on the highway of "Born to Run" and returned home to the father's house in "Adam Raised a Cain," trying again to make it work, make it good, make it real, but facing the deadening prospect of making it work through repression through the suppression of desire. I *don't* want to leave, I *don't*! Please let me not want to leave!

As he writes this song he is still married to Julianne Philips, but as he told James Henke in July, 1992, he didn't know how to be married, didn't know how to be a husband, and the whole album is full of his restless cautiousness, his simultaneous desire to be gone and not to be gone. He did leave Juli, of course, during the *Tunnel of Love* tour, but just exchanging one wife for another didn't solve his problem—which, he began to realize around this time, lay much deeper, in his own failure to leave home "twenty years ago" ("The Long Goodbye"). Hitting the road on tour felt like leaving home, but wasn't; as he told James Henke, it was just another, more mobile form of isolation:

> I tend to be an isolationist by nature. And it's not about money or where you live or how you live. It's about psychology. My dad was certainly the same way. You don't need a ton of dough and walls around your house to be isolated. I know plenty of people who are isolated with a six-pack of beer and a television set. But that was a big part of my nature.
>
> Then music came along, and I latched onto it as a way to combat that part of myself. It was a way that I could talk to people. It provided me with a means of communication, a means of placing myself in a social context—which I had a tendency not to want to do.
>
> And music did those things but in an abstract fashion, ultimately. It did them for the guy with the guitar, but the guy without the guitar was pretty much the same as he had been.
>
> Now I see that two of the best days of my life were the day I picked up the guitar and the day that I learned how to put it down. Somebody said, "Man

how did you play for so long?" I said, "That's the easy part. It's stopping that's hard."

*When did you learn to put the guitar down?*

Pretty recently. I had locked into what was pretty much a hectic obsession, which gave me enormous focus and energy and fire to burn, because it was coming out of pure fear and self-loathing and self-hatred. I'd get onstage and it was hard for me to stop. That's why my shows were so long. They weren't long because I had an idea or a plan that they should be that long. I couldn't stop until I felt burnt, period. Thoroughly burnt.

It's funny, because the results of the show or the music might have been positive for other people, but there was an element of it that was abusive for me. Basically, it was my drug. And so I started to follow the thread of weaning myself. (42)

In "Cautious Man" we see the first strands of this thread. Bill Horton is addicted to the road as Bruce Springsteen is addicted to music, to concerts—to the road as touring, to not coming home to the house he had finally bought, against every grain in his body, in Rumford, New Jersey.[4] But that life is making him miserable. He knows deep down that he is going to leave Juli, and the thought terrifies him. What if he can never love and be loved? What if there is no home for him? In "Cautious Man" he imagines the happy ending to the story, the therapeutic discovery that smashes through the restlessness and lets him settle down without inner pressures; and if this is still just a hopeful image of future health, it is still grounded in a deeply felt self-awareness, an increasing sense that this is how it *will* be, someday:

> One night Billy awoke from a terrible dream callin' his wife's name
> She lay breathing beside him in a peaceful sleep, a thousand miles away
> He got dressed in the moonlight and down to the highway he strode
> When he got there he didn't find nothing but road
>
> Billy felt a coldness rise up inside him that he couldn't name
> Just as the words tattooed 'cross his kunckles he knew would
>     always remain
> At their bedside he brushed the hair from his wife's face,
>     as the moon shone on her skin so white
> Filling their room in the beauty of God's fallen light

Billy takes the plunge, surrenders his caution, leaves himself vulnerable. He realizes that a life of suppressed dreams is a life of quiet desperation, a life like Doug Springsteen's, but also, frighteningly, like Bruce Springsteen's as well; realizes that he must put love to the test, must risk losing everything, by going out to the highway, by exposing himself to what he's most afraid of: the call of the open road. This is the plunge that Spenser never got up the courage to take; that Rambo in *First Blood* and the desperate killers on *Nebraska* only took when driven to the end of their rope by angry, repressive father-figures or an indifferent capitalist society. Bill Horton takes the plunge out of an inner compulsion. Like Springsteen during the writing of *Nebraska*, he dives into the darkness and looks around, tries to find something that won't disappear out from under him. Like Joe Roberts in "Highway Patrolman," he lets his defensive brother-image slip off into the darkness, over the border, without guarantees of what will happen without defenses. This is the beginning of masculist transformation: letting go. Billy goes out to the road, the path of his earlier defensive escapes from compromise, from limitation, knowing that path is so well worn through his head, through his body, through his emotional responses, that taking off down it would be the easiest thing in the world. Would be—and will be, if when he gets to the highway the need to defend is still there, the need to protect that dark inner sanctum. If the childhood image of the spiritually destroyed father is still potent: dad as the representative of domesticated masculinity. If the childhood image of the all-powerful mother is still in force, demanding, taking, like a black hole imploding with defensive love.

But he gets to the highway and all those old bogeymen and bogeywomen are gone, vanished into the dark, across the border like Franky Roberts. There is nothing there. "Nothing but road." Road as an asphalt surface painted with lines—a place for cars to drive. The other road, the defensively alluring road, road as that inner path to a vague place of freedom where we can "walk in the sun," is gone. It is like the alcoholic discovering that booze is just liquid, or the peep show addict discovering that nudity is just skin. The snake in the garden was just a garden snake. He didn't *need* his defenses. He was defending against the fear of defenselessness. To learn that, he had to expose himself to his inner defenseless state, to vulnerability, to that darkness of inner night which his wandering and his code both defended against and maintained. Defending against inner darkness does maintain it: keeps it locked up, keeps the inner sanctum dark.

This song traces, in fact, a three-part transformation roughly adumbrated in the three parts of my book, to which I will be returning in the conclusion: the discovery that the old way, the defensive masculine way, doesn't work (Spenser); the descent into symbolic death, beyond defenses, into that dark inward place where there *is nothing*, where the world disappears (Rambo); and then the return to society, marked by a heightening of the senses to visionary reality (Springsteen). Billy returns from the road to find the moonlight bathing his wife's face and the entire bedroom with a mystic splendor, "God's fallen light." This is no religious conversion in the traditional sense; Springsteen is not returning to the Catholic fold. It is simply a potent sign of his (ongoing) transformation—an overwhelmingly new awareness of the beauty of life once what William Blake called the doors of perception have been cleansed. The hero has descended from the world of artificial light into the world of total darkness, and returned from there to find the old world suffused with a new light.

The music confirms this return. We're back to the soft folk-country sound of *Nebraska*, just a voice and an acoustic guitar, but without the anguish; or rather, moving *through* the anguish to a whole new range of feelings. Springsteen's raspy voice subtly traces the transformation: beginning tight, controlled, cautious; loosing some of the fierce, pent-up anguish of "Adam Raised a Cain" or "Darkness on the Edge of Town" in the third verse ("On his right hand Billy'd tattooed the word love and on his left hand was the word fear," with a tenuous, fearful fall-off on "fear"); regaining control in the fourth verse ("Now Billy was an honest man"); but then, with "restless heart" and "seed of betrayal," control and cautiousness begin to slip away, as the *lyrics* said they did back in the second verse. The fifth verse, Billy's encounter with the "road," summons up the anguished energy of the love-and-fear tattoos again, but this time directs it into transformative action; and when Billy goes out to the highway, Springsteen's voice dies, goes flat, as in "Nebraska," only to be reborn with a mystic wonder, an edge of awe, in the last verse, which closes with Springsteen sounding close to tears.[5] Springsteen's voice has always been an incredibly expressive instrument; here in "Cautious Man" he surpasses himself.[6]

Both artistically and therapeutically, "Cautious Man" is a tremendous achievement; but it marks no plateau of gender liberation, no utopia where Springsteen can "walk in the sun." Certainly its structural position on the album, in the middle of unresolved self-doubts, fears that the marital center will not hold, severely qualifies Billy Horton's claims to have been transformed, liberated once and for all from his restlessness. And its biographical position in Springsteen's life, a few months before he leaves his wife for his female vocalist, makes it look like sheer wish-fulfillment. In "Cautious Man" Springsteen deals with many of his blockages, but one of them is not his mother—as in fact the thematization of Billy's wife as a "young girl" suggests. This song, which I would so like to present as an ending to Springsteen's (and this book's) quest, is only a beginning—the beginning of a therapeutic process that may even lead through the darkness of *Nebraska* one more time.

Springsteen has said of *Human Touch* and *Lucky Town*, the twin albums he released in April 1992, that they trace his dark path since *Tunnel of Love*—or rather, specifically, that *Human Touch* traces the dark path and *Lucky Town* explores the calm place he has reached at the end of it. But I don't know. He seemed to have reached a calm place in *Tunnel of Love*, too, in "Cautious Man" and "Valentine's Day," and yet the end of the tour that promoted that album precipitated one of his worst crises yet. It seems to me that he's still in the tunnel, with more love than he's had before, certainly—the love not only of Patti but of his two children as well, Evan and Jessie—but no closer to the light at the end than before. Both albums (even *Lucky Town*, which supposedly signifies the calm place) feel uneasy and unsettled to me, at once flat and explosive, uninflected and desperate—in fact very like the transitional albums from the late 1970s and early 1980s. Much that is formulaic and derivative on them results from the same defensive emotional needs as the similar cuts on *The River*, say; much that is transitional and revisionary on them results from the same sense of inner upheaval as the comparable cuts on *Darkness* and *Nebraska*. Almost certainly the much-publicized "failure" of both albums—as of this writing, just over three months after they appeared, they had "only" sold 1.5 million copies each—is wrapped up in this willingness of his to be broken again, to smash through the protective icons not only of *Born in the U.S.A.* but of *Tunnel of Love* as well, and return to the fragmented spiritual place that generated *Nebraska*.

There is much that is old on both albums. There is the old defensive machismo in "Gloria's Eyes," "Roll of the Dice," "All Or Nothin' At All," "Man's Job," and "Real Man" on *Human Touch*—most of the album, in fact—though it is almost invariably broken or problematized in subtle ways on the album, more powerfully in concert.[7] In "With Every Wish" on the same album Mark Isham's mournful muted trumpet guides Springsteen across the river to a dim vision of the displaced mother calling from the other side:

> These days I sit around and laugh
> At the many rivers I've crossed
> But on the far banks there's always another forest
> Where a man can get lost
> Well there in the high trees love's bluebird glides
> Guiding us 'cross to another river on the other side
> And there someone is waitin' with a look in her eyes
> And though my heart's grown weary
> And more than a little bit shy
> Tonight I'll drink from her waters to quench my thirst
> And leave the angels to worry
> With every wish...

There is also much that is undeniably new, some of it arising out of Springsteen's own shifting life experiences: his wife Patti, who has forced him to look more closely at his impulse to walk away from difficult relationships,[8] injects a new boisterous energy into his love songs ("You shouted 'jump' but my heart faltered / You laughed and said 'Baby don't you understand?'" in "Leap of Faith" on *Lucky Town*), and in "Living Proof," also on *Lucky Town*, his son Evan injects a new poignancy into his quest for meaning by "swallowing" or incarnating "God's fallen light" on *Tunnel of Love*:

> Well now on a summer night in a dusky room
> Came a little piece of the Lord's undying light
> Crying like he swallowed the fiery moon
> In his mother's arms it was all the beauty I could take

"Pony Boy," which closes *Human Touch*, is a song his grandmother used to sing to him: "I made up a lot of the words for the verses," Springsteen told James Henke; "I'm sure there are real words, but I'm not sure they're the ones I used. It was the song that I used to sing to my little boy when he was still inside of Patti. And when he came out, he knew it. It's funny. And it used to work like magic. He'd be crying, and I'd sing it, and he'd stop on a dime" (70). The song makes me envision a Springsteen album of children's songs; I sit and listen to it raptly even though I didn't hear him singing it in the womb, and am not (at least outwardly) a squalling infant.

But for me the most interesting songs on the albums are not new in this way, or even very new in any way—are steeped, in fact, in the old, in the past, in past efforts to make sense of his life. I want to begin to

## 236  No Less a Man

conclude this chapter, and the body of the book, with a look at two such songs: "The Long Goodbye" on *Human Touch* and "Book of Dreams" on *Lucky Town*.

The title "The Long Goodbye" alludes to the Raymond Chandler novel,[9] of course, and Robert Altman's 1973 movie version—both of them studies in betrayal that by implication charge the song with a haunting bleakness, which Springsteen then sets about transforming in the direction of new hope. Musically the song seems a reprise of "Born to Run" as crossed with "Johnny 99"—the back-and-forth pendulum swing of the latter's chord progression (reversed and dropped a third here from B-F# to C-F and relieved by a ninth-bar escape into B-flat) trapping the singer in a "chain of my own lies," and the hard-rock wall of sound from the former driving him to the emotional brink one more time, this time, maybe, in order to cross over to what "With Every Wish" has just identified as "the other side":

> My soul went walkin' but I stayed here
> Feel like I been workin' for a thousand years
> Chippin' away at this chain of my own lies
> Climbin' a wall a hundred miles high
> Well I woke up this morning on the other side
> Yeah Yeah this is the long goodbye

The out-of-body image in that first line is new to Springsteen, and will recur in the last three songs on *Lucky Town*: most obviously, as we'll see in a moment, in "Book of Dreams," but also, in the striking bodily form of birds, in "Souls of the Departed" ("At night in dreams he sees their souls rise / Like dark geese into the Oklahoma skies") and "My Beautiful Reward" ("Tonight I can feel the cold wind at my back / I'm flyin' high over gray fields my feathers long and black"). Most of the rest of this, however, is vintage Springsteen imagery, especially the work exhaustion and the sense of being trapped.

What is interesting about this return to the old images, however, is that now for the first time he feels trapped *because* he is trying to break free, rather than the other way around—and that the work exhaustion that he had always before associated with his father (what complaints could a rock star have in comparison with a factory-worker?) is now explicitly tied to Springsteen's own liberatory labor, the emotional work of breaking free of his inner chains. In fact, if as I suggested earlier this song's bridge points to an emotional engagement with the "admirin' touch" of his mother, an attempt to break free of that old dependency

## Displaced Mothers 237

through a new awareness of its existence and its harmfulness, then we might say that Springsteen is conflating his father's normative *physical* exhaustion as a working-class man with his own normative *emotional* exhaustion as a patriarchal son, and pushing toward a liberation from both, now under the aegis not of his father but of his mother.

To be sure, the song only adumbrates—only hopes. There is no solution here, despite that wishful ninth-bar drop into B-flat, that would-be escape from the shuttle movement. There is at once an old/new weariness in Springsteen's voice, here, up in the higher tenor ranges (E and F in the verses, A and B-flat in the bridge), and a new assurance, a new confidence in his ability to "let the hammer fly" and smash "that last link in the chain"—a simultaneous sense that it's the "Same old faces it's the same old town / What once was laughs is draggin' me now" (a familiar plaint from everything Springsteen's done before) and that "The moon is high and here I am / Sittin' here with this hammer in hand."

I'm not sure "Book of Dreams" offers a solution either, but there is, at least, a new peace, an acceptance, as the singer stands "drinkin' in the forgiveness / This life provides":

> I'm standing in the backyard
> Listening to the party inside
> Tonight I'm drinkin' in the forgiveness
> This life provides
> The scars we carry remain but the pain slips away it seem
> Oh won't you baby be in my book of dreams

The party is a pre-wedding celebration of some sort; Patti and her girlfriends are inside, Bruce on the outside looking in; then suddenly Bruce has a mystical experience, an out-of-body experience very much like the one in "The Long Goodbye" ("My soul went walkin' but I stayed here") and "My Beautiful Reward" ("Down along the river's silent edge I soar"):

> In the darkness my fingers slip across your skin
> I feel your sweet reply
> The room fades away and suddenly I'm way up high
> Just holdin' you to me
> As through the window the moonlight streams
> Oh won't you baby be in my book of dreams

Here the mystical moonlight streaming through the window recalls "Valentine's Day" and "Cautious Man" from *Tunnel of Love*—the "God's light" that begins to glow in Springsteen's inner darkness on all three albums, the previous one and these two, through both windows and little Evan—but the transcendence of body and physical surroundings is new, and significant. Taken in isolation, that third verse sounds like mystical sex, Bruce and Patti in bed but being transported by their love into a higher sphere; but the narrative movement of the song as a whole suggests that it is in fact bigger than that, more transformative a mystical *and* a sexual experience. If in the first two verses Bruce is standing outside the window looking in, the first line of the third verse suggests that he caresses her *from outside*, not only "through" the window but *without* the window, as if the window and the distance between them were not there. We have seen Springsteen trapped outside doors and windows before, in the transitional songs of the late 1970s and early 1980s—especially "Adam Raised a Cain" on *Darkness* and "My Father's House" on *Nebraska*[10]—and we have seen him brought back into the house, into community, into the domestic tunnel of love, especially in "Cautious Man." What we seem to see here is Springsteen transcending windows, transcending the architectural and other barriers between people through a visionary out-of-body experience that joins him with his lover despite the physical spaces that separate them.

But even this does not approach the full complexity of the song's event, for it ignores the music—a very *Nebraska* music, in fact, soft and slow, with voice and acoustic guitar augmented by understated bass and drums (and at some points organ and a synthesized glock), the voice, as on *Nebraska*, down at the bottom of the tenor range, the instrumental backing playing a soft A/D/E chord progression (dropped a fourth from the many D/G/A progressions on *Nebraska*). To be precise, musically the song is a reprise of "Used Cars," whose first line it repeats melodically almost note for note—though as I say, transposed down a fourth, from A to E (from the fifth of the D major triad to the fifth of the A major triad).[11] "Used Cars" was one of the most bitter songs on *Nebraska*, full of the pain of poverty that Springsteen still feels years later, after the runaway success of *Born to Run*; and interestingly, if its melody and harmony and imagery tie it to "Book of Dreams," its imagery knits both those songs together with "Thunder Road" on that earlier album.

Specifically what begins to take shape as we trace these melodic, harmonic, and imagistic strands through Springsteen's work over two decades is a variously tonalized scene that is probably most fully imagined in "Thunder Road": a scene that highlights front and back doors, yards, and carseats in order to explore the tension between leaving and staying home, breaking free and settling in, standing on your own two feet and accepting the compromises of community and love. Here are the relevant lines:

> The screen door slams, Mary's dress sways
> Like a vision she dances across the porch as the radio plays...
>
> Don't run back inside, darling, you know just what I'm here for...
>
> Well I got this guitar, and I learned how to make it talk
> And my car's out back if you're ready to take that long walk
> From your front porch to my front seat
> The door's open but the ride it ain't free
>
> ("Thunder Road," *Born to Run*)
>
> My little sister's in the front seat with an ice cream cone
> My ma's in the back seat sittin' all alone
>
> ("Used Cars," *Nebraska*)
>
> I'm standing in the backyard
> Listening to the party inside...
>
> I'm watchin' you through the window
> With your girlfriends from back home
>
> ("Book of Dreams," *Lucky Town*)

In the negative image of the family, from "Used Cars," Pam Springsteen sits in the front seat of the car, Adele in the back, while Doug "steers her slow out of the lot / For a test drive down Michigan Avenue." Where is Bruce? Outside the car, of course: "Me, I walk home on the same dirty streets where I was born / Up the block I can hear my sister in the front seat blowin' that horn." He feels trapped in the car with his family, watching his mother finger her wedding band and the "salesman stare at my old man's hands"—trapped not only in the car but in the poverty that keeps them driving broken-down used cars, in the certainty that, short of a winning lottery ticket, there is no escape from all this. He walks home to give himself a sense of hope, of possible escape; but the only place for him to walk is "the same dirty streets where I was born."

By the time he writes this song, of course—and even more by the time he writes "Book of Dreams"—he has in a sense won the lottery: as he says in "Ain't Got You" (*Tunnel of Love*), as a megastar he gets "paid a king's ransom for doin' what comes naturally." But in another sense he hasn't, and never will; there is no lottery that can produce the magical state of happiness that he dreams of as a boy and young man. His boyhood dream is never having to drive a used car again; a few years pass, and he dreams of not having to "sweat the same job from mornin' to morn" like his father; then of escaping the town and its chains, first alone, later with a woman like Mary, whose ambivalence about leaving and staying reflects (and allows him to repress) his own. Mary dances on her front porch "like a vision," almost like a wraith or a ghost, halfway between Adele's problematic reality inside the house and the romanticized reality of his own front seat—or, to expand that image slightly, halfway between the deadend sight of his mother sitting all alone in the back seat of their "brand-new used car" and the openended mystical embrace with Patti in "Book of Dreams."

And it is that halfway point that Springsteen himself most insistently occupies all through his work, and that he returns to, after a cautious attempt to place himself firmly inside the happy home on *Tunnel of Love*, in "Book of Dreams." Strangely, perhaps, but significantly as well, Springsteen situates his mother in that middle ground as well, sharing with him the desire to get the hell out *and* the desire to go back in and make things better: sitting on the front porch in "Racing in the Street," all her pretty dreams torn; dragging Bruce and Pam "down the street to the church whenever she heard those wedding bells" in "Walk Like a Man." His mother is the centripetal force that ties him to his family, but also, it seems to me, at least subliminally, the centrifugal force that tears him away, thrusts him out into the world. And if this tension builds into Bruce a double bind of home and the world, love and freedom—"go away closer"—that tension has also been enormously productive in his work, both the work of writing hit songs and the work of breaking free of the dysfunctional relationships that warp his life.

Paul Olsen has a wonderful theory, in fact, that the "good" mother isn't the obedient matron who trains her children too to obedience; it is the "unsafe" mother who gives her children mixed messages, like the good Catholic mother he describes who suddenly yells at her son for unthinkingly obeying the priest. (The priest had asked all the teenagers to stand up and take the Legency of Decency pledge—they were to swear not to go see movies declared objectionable by the Church—and he was about to walk forward reflexively when his mother snapped at him, "No one's going to tell you what movies you can see" [100]). Let me quote Olsen at length:

> Now it is precisely the "good ["unsafe"] mother" who contributes significantly to this dissolution [of social stability]. She does not preach rebellion or anarchy on a soapbox; she does not tell everybody in the family that the revolution has come. What she does is to take her repressive and stifling tradition of compliance, submission, and unconsciously throw it to the winds. For the American and European woman, it has been her sacred duty to produce worthwhile male members to keep society not balanced but stable—stable and hence stagnant. Given a period of time with this stagnation and we have the phenomenon of senators and congressmen urging a President to rattle some sabers internationally—in essence, just for the hell of it.
>
> But when a mother begins to subvert the sacred family group by communicating to her son (which she will do more powerfully, even though subtly, than to her daughter, because most women still have the feeling that rebellion is masculine) that something is wrong, that many more things are possible, that life really has no rules—in short, when she subliminally conveys to her son that rebellion is possible, yet gives him enough opposition that he can *effect* the rebellion—then the rebellion takes place through an act of intense and vibrant imagination.
>
> In other words, she makes it possible for her son to break their symbiotic bond, permitting him to become his own man in the only way that a man can—through a rebellion and moving away from dependency and familial stagnation and control.
>
> Note that I said she *permits* him. He does it by himself, but she has laid the groundwork for the possibility. You can be free, she lets him know. Take your freedom. Yet most of the time she does not even know she is doing this, and will react badly when her son begins to take the freedom she has subtly, and unknowingly, allowed him to take.
>
> So that the good mother, as I am describing her in this way, is a mother who can also be depriving. Depriving to the point of not allowing her son to become swallowed by her ever-flowing breast. And she is dominating too, dominating enough to give her son something against which to rebel, to break free of—but not dominating to the point of robbing his soul and perhaps sending him to the madhouse. She gives him always a bit less than he needs, she makes him reach, so that he can see that there are possibilities in the world greater than she can offer him.

This may *seem* like a double message: the conscious, waking-life message is given that the son should be a good boy, love his mother, listen to her and obey her rules—while her inner life is subtly propelling him and at times not so subtly propelling him, toward rebellion, freedom. But it isn't really a double message at all, not if the underlying message is listened to—as it always is. The conflict is necessary; it is the only thing that propels one toward growth—and in the conflict is *enormous* pain. But without the pain there is no differentiation, no separation from the mother, and one becomes a frightened, dependent social vegetable.

Such a mother does *not* want to destroy her son. The inconsistency of the message shows this. She is merely giving him something to overcome, to fight against; for if she were to remove the obstacle, the fight would be over and there would be no freedom ever. Because every time she gives her son opposition and resistance, the underside of the coin appears—the side of rebellion and manhood. Her behavior immediately calls up its opposite because she has laid the groundwork for precisely that response. Her posture of dominance immediately triggers off the necessity of revolt; her criticism can immediately let her son focus on his own strengths, and her attacks can also stimulate a knowledge of his own strengths.

It is all in the doing, in the *being*. The son will for years remain in a state of anger at his mother because of her lack of acceptance and approval—and that anger is the key to whatever liberation will be achieved. The context of anger keeps the separation from mother going on, until one day the relationship with mother will be seen more clearly for what it is. (112-15)

It may well be that this description has nothing to do with Adele Springsteen—that her astonishing love for Elvis in the late fifties, say, the period in which Bruce, too, learned the magic of music by watching Elvis on Ed Sullivan, can be explained in some other way. It may even be that Olsen is off track: that the "unsafe mother" is not fruitful for her son's later therapeutic process, that her inner conflicts are simply the patriarchal double binds that keep him tied to her and unaware of it. Still Olsen's image can, I suggest, be fruitful in another way.

The son's greatest obstacle to the full cathartic exploration of his anger at his mother, or even to his recognition that he feels anger at her and therefore has a problem that must be addressed, is a fear that his anger will "kill" her: that, as I said earlier, his rage will be matricidal, either physically or emotionally. The myth of the fragile mother is a normative patriarchal fantasy that protects mothers and their sons from transformative encounters with emotional realities: because the slightest negative response to the "normal" mother's actions sends her into

## Displaced Mothers 243

paroxysms of tears, the son must work to control his response, to conform it to idealized standards of positivity, which requires that he exclude from it all felt realities that might upset her emotional balance. He must, he learns early on, protect her from psychic disintegration. This implants a taboo deep inside his own emotional economy that blocks access to repressed feelings—precisely those feelings which must be released if he is to be freed.

The mother learns to manipulate this fantasy, of course, early in her childhood, through direct modeling on her own mother; but it is not only a weapon. It is also a victimization. The woman who believes in and exploits the myth of her emotional fragility is herself made fragile by it. She truly believes that she will be devastated by anger—precisely because she was trained to believe that her anger would devastate *her* mother. If her son (or daughter) ever released the full torrent of his anger at her, what would happen in fact is not that she would be destroyed, but that her self-control (the walls that keep her own mother-anger in) would be so powerfully undermined that she would *rather* be destroyed than exposed to those repressed feelings. The dynasty of wounds is a dynasty of walls protecting each generation's parents from their own repressed feelings; to heal the wounds and break the dynasty we must smash the walls in a domino effect that sends walls crashing back into the past, first our parents', then their parents', and so on, until at last God's walls fall too, and he allows Adam and Eve to eat from the trees of knowledge and life—allows them, and us, at last to know and to live.

The implication for the son's liberation from his mother is that somewhere, somehow, he must summon up the courage to explore his repressed feelings of anger at his mother—overcome the programmed terror he feels at even entering the areas in his body in which those feelings are stored—and then name them, release them, purge them. This may in fact be devastating: as I say, the myth of feminine fragility does generate *real* feminine fragility. An outburst of deep-seated filial anger—not the carefully controlled and masked anger that mothers are used to hearing from their sons but the emotional deluge that results from the release of repression—might well put a mother in the hospital. The trouble is that this knowledge keeps not only us, the sons, in prison—it keeps our mothers in prison too. We cannot delude ourselves into believing that the release of repression will automatically heal her too—it may, at worst, frighten her into psychotic reaction—but neither can we go on deluding ourselves into believing that, if we just put our childhoods behind us, let bygones by bygones, dwell in the present instead of morbidly harping on the past, everything will be all right.

It is, I suggest, in this context that Paul Olsen's image of the "unsafe" mother can be fruitful. For if the son finds in his mother's behavior indications that she too might be conflicted, might herself be leaning toward rebellion and liberation, he may well take heart: he may be able to convince himself that his confrontation with his own repressed feelings of anger at her might even have the effect of liberating her as well as him. I know of several families in which sons, daughters, and mothers are undergoing radical liberatory processes all at the same time, leaving only the father to buttress up the structures of patriarchal ideology (and to feel abandoned by everyone he loves). In this sort of situation, every advance in one person is an advance for all (except, alas, the father): the mother's self-discoveries empower her children, the children's self-discoveries empower their mother. Indeed, the possibility that the fragile mother is not so fragile after all—that she possesses great reserves of emotional strength that she has long drawn on but never recognized—may make it possible for the grown son to risk inflicting great hurt on her by naming his grievances, whether by shouting at her or by singing an angry or accusatory song about her. Then he can rest assured that, however deeply he hurts her, she will recover—and may even "recover" something that she had not known she had, a sense of her own toughness.

It may also be that the mother is truly strong enough to withstand her son's anger, but that the son is also far enough along in his own therapeutic process to see that the mother he is angry at is not the living person on the other phone but the mother-image in his head. This is the bottom line in any transformative reconciliation with a parent—you can't change them, you can only change your image of them—but deep-seated mother-images are enormously more difficult to transform than father-images.

The strongest explanation of this relative difficulty is that, as I began to suggest in chapter four, the infant first begins generating a "mother-image" of some inchoate somatic sort in the womb, at conception, through sympathetic somatic responses to, or introjective imitations of, the mother's anxieties and other feelings; hence the image's serene untouchability for linguistic therapies (Freud's "talking cure").[12] It is probably safe to say that for fetal/infantile traumas, linguistic therapies aren't therapies at all, for they have no therapeutic power over prelinguistic formations; indeed even as analyses, as attempts to know rather than to cure, they are somewhat suspect in the treatment of infantile traumas, since they can work on infantile material only inferentially (retroductively), by postulating a prelinguistic "cause" or "source" for a later linguistic formulation (like the retelling of an adolescent or adult dream).

A slightly weaker version of this explanation (if the fetus's "feeling" or somatic imitation of its mother's emotional states is disputed) is that the infant first begins generating a mother-image at birth, through the intimate bonding channeled by repeated care and particularly by breastfeeding—that intensely pleasurable and also conflictual relation in which the infant alternates between beatific incorporation of the breast and anxious loss of the breast.[13] If the mother is afraid of or anxious about her own sexuality (and in a repressive patriarchal culture like our own this fear or anxiety is ideologically normal), the nursing infant will also imbibe with the milk the mother's anxious reaction to the pleasurable feelings produced by his or her sucking. The infant will then internalize (as a component of, and in some sense a constitutive force in, the pleasure of sucking at the breast) the mother's guilty fear of feeling good, the terror that the good feelings are sexual and that the mother is therefore somehow sexually attracted to her infant, the doubly bound perception of the infant as at once the innocent victim of illicit desires and the guilty perpetrator of those desires, and the need to repress not only that attraction and the good feeling that generates it but the resulting doubly bound perception of the infant as permanently as possible.[14]

The weakest version of the explanation (if, say, the mother never breastfeeds and both parents or other caretakers share the bottle-feeding and other caretaking more or less equally, or if the father or other male caretaker cares for the infant exclusively) is that motherhood is ideologically far more heavily and conflictedly invested in Western culture than is fatherhood, and that the new mother's anxious preconscious need to live up to cultural ideals for motherhood will shape her infant's emotional development far more powerfully than the new father's need to be a good father.

(This conflicted ideological investment is of course a factor in the stronger explanations as well: it is precisely this investment, not some biological code, that is passed from mother to child in the womb and/or at the breast. What characterizes this third explanation is not, in other words, its emphasis on the ideological investment of motherhood, but rather its attempt to isolate the mother-to-infant transmission of that investment from the specifically physiological processes of gestation and lactation.)

However we explain the difficulty we have accessing our maternal "inscriptions," it seems clear that those inscriptions do defy traditional linguistic therapy and yield only to various regressive therapies that recreate the fetal or infantile experience in the adult sufferer's body, such as primal scream therapy, drama and imagery therapy, or rebirthing. All three are closer to music and art and religion, in fact, than they are to Freudian psychoanalysis; and all three have striking counterparts in Springsteen's musical career.[15] His concerts in particular strike me as public therapy sessions combining image and drama (Springsteen's song scenarios and skits), primal screams and shrieks and shouts of all sorts, and the connective breathing of all ritual music and dance, an ancient mystical/monastic technique that is used in rebirthing therapy to bypass cortical control of the limbic system and to recover the experiences carefully hidden there. Connective breathing is in fact originally an ancient *musical* technique for stepping outside of repressive psychosocial "normality" into a potentially liberating visionary state (the trance music of the Brazilian umbanda or candomble, for example). The transrational power of rock music to move a hundred thousand fans to ecstasy is a dim remembrance of an earlier ritual power, the power invoked by the shaman with his drums and his chants, by the witch with her ritual invocations of higher spirits. It is probably this atavistic survival of primitive ritual magic in rock music that leads some religious conservatives to brand it satanic: if careful rational (cortical) control of all behavior is "godlike," and anything that deviates from the godly norm is satanic, then indeed rock music is "satanic."

But of course "satanic" is only mainstream Christianity's fearful label for experience that escapes its rational net (mystical Christianity has always been in "tune" with ritual music and connective breathing—and, not coincidentally, has often been persecuted by the mainstream Church). What is truly at stake in the connective breathing of various mystical prayers and invocations, ritual songs and dances, and rebirthing therapy is the power to transform a person from within, to *be reborn*, by tapping a primitive part of the brain that authoritarian civilization has worked hard and long to repress: "lay there in the darkness scared and breathing," as Springsteen gasps in "Valentine's Day"—"born anew." That new birth may be Springsteen's truest musical quest, his deepest mystical desire; certainly his increasing use of mystical light and out-of-body imagery points strongly in that direction. Perhaps it should be everyone's; even yours, and mine.

# The Giant

2. Well if the forest ever knew that the giant was there
   They surely no longer care
   Elk munch moss from the giant's beard
   Squirrels scamper through his hair
   The winds and snows chap and batter his frame
   His cheeks glisten in the rain
   Oh the giant is dead, yes the giant is dead
   Will he ever rise again?
   Will he ever rise again?

3. But there's a hand of fear that crawls like a crab
   Dragging a rusty knife
   Beneath dank coffins of crumbly skin
   The giant feels a stab of life
   I lie in ambush like a termite's jaws
   He feels my stirring as a pain
   Oh the giant is dead, but his blood pumps red
   Will he ever sleep easy again?
   Will he ever sleep easy again?

4. The dance of dread rives me to my roots
   Lightning burns my body clean
   Relieved of its coffin of blood run cold
   My heart waves a flag of green
   My body lives but it's the body of a reed
   Bending to a need or a pain
   Oh the giant is dead, but I raise my head
   And slip into my life again
   Yes I slip into my life again

Copyright 1993 Doug Robinson.

# Conclusion

# The Hero Myth

The heroic male. Man as hero. We are coached by the subvocal prompting of ideology to conceive of men in heroic terms: the strong, silent warrior who ignores pain, cold, and hunger to vanquish the enemy, to penetrate the fortress, to save (and win) the maiden. The hero, in our restrictive idealizations of him, is precisely someone who suppresses emotion (fear, anxiety, need, even anger) and stands alone (becomes "self-reliant" and "self-sufficient"—i.e., shuns human society, isolates himself from a network of caring people) in order to overcome impossible odds and rise from success to success.

This is a myth, clearly, a "normal" or normative ideological construct that we are taught by society to introject and seek to realize in our own lives. Our heroism may be small, almost insignificant compared with the heroes of the glorious past (Samson, Achilles, St. George); but it feels important to us. Suppressing feeling and shunning the company of loved ones may be just a matter of neglecting our families and pushing ourselves to work 14- or 16-hour days seven days a week—to "get ahead," to "make it," to make a go of a private business or even to impress the boss. It may be no more than blocking the physical demands of our bodies for sleep and nutrition and the emotional demands of our wives and children for connection and caring, so as to maintain the mythic image of the strong, self-sufficient hero.

Put this way, the hero myth seems antiquated, obsolete, ripe for the dungheap of history. This particular ideological reduction of the hero myth may help perpetuate male hegemony in business and politics and the family, but it does so at an enormous cost. It is destructive of human community: the self-made "hero" is impossible to communicate with, let alone compromise with. Wives, children, and colleagues despair of ever getting far enough past his ironclad defenses to engage a human being in conversation. It remains one of the most dehumanizing aspects of both capitalism and socialism. It sucks all vitality and flexibility out of communal life. It is destructive of the next generation: the blockage of emotion frustrates sons into imitating it and daughters into escalating the blockage in their fathers, and later in their husbands, male friends, and sons, through increased demands on it. And above all it is destructive of the "hero" himself: the typical modern hero dies in his fifties of a massive coronary, precisely because he has denied his body's demands all his life, and suppressed the symptoms of physiological rebellion with tranquilizers and other pharmaceuticals.

The problem is that our intuitions are so deeply structured by this myth that it is difficult, almost impossible, to imagine alternatives. In fact, as far as I can tell our culture gives us only two, which may or may not be versions of the same thing: negating masculinity and imitating femininity. (These are of course the reverse of women's conventional alternatives for "change": negating femininity and imitating masculinity.) We can, like John Stoltenberg, call ourselves effeminists and systematically assimilate our behavior to that of traditional women (at precisely the historical moment when women are trying to liberate themselves from that behavior). Or we can try to generate a "new" masculinity by systematically eradicating (which usually means repressing) all traces of the old, leaving a blank to be filled in later. Neither alternative seems particularly attractive, effective, or even attainable. Simple negation or eradication is probably impossible, and would get us nowhere even if it were possible. Mimicking the normative myths of patriarchal femininity, exchanging one destructive gender identity for another, is ludicrous.

What we need, it seems to me, is a new myth, a heuristic narrative if you prefer, to help us structure our emancipatory progress out of the old and toward the new. This is not an original idea of mine, of course, and certainly not my sole concern; not only have feminists been working on the problem as it applies to women's liberation for some time now (especially through Wicca, the return to witchcraft, and various animistic and polytheistic goddess-religions), it is the focus of much recent work in the mythopoeic men's movement as well, inspired in large part by feminist models. Since there is no reason to assume that a new masculinity should differ absolutely from a new femininity—while differences will undoubtedly remain, they will certainly not be grounded in polar opposition and repressed mutual hatred—there is much we can learn from women's work in this area.

John Rowan's 1987 book *The Horned God* and Robert Bly's 1990 book *Iron John* are probably the best examples of this tendency in the men's movement, and I want to return to both books in a moment. First, however, I want to suggest a larger context for the remythification of masculinity, specifically a return to a earlier form of the hero myth, one that was deeper, less reductive, also considerably less defensively success-oriented. I am thinking of Joseph Campbell's work in *The Hero With a Thousand Faces* and *Myths to Live By*, where, drawing on vast anthropological materials and Jungian psychoanalysis, he sets up a "universal" hero myth that probably is not universal but may be heuristically useful for men's liberation. In Campbell's reading (or construction) of this myth, the hero first receives a call to adventure, a summons out of the flow of ordinary day-to-day experience, and sets out on a path; at the consummation of his quest undergoes an initiation, often a symbolic death; and then returns to the ordinary world transformed, in possession of the knowledge or other boon that is needed to save society from impending disaster.

What I find salutary about this myth is that it places central emphasis on the symbolic death that transforms the hero: the "going under," in Nietzsche's phrase, the dark night of the soul that we saw Rambo going through (and possibly emerging from) in the movie version of *First Blood*, and heard Springsteen going through in the late 1970s and early 1980s, and coming out of in the early nineties. This is no prettified success manual for business majors. It is a profoundly frightening path through utter ego-destruction, the complete dissolution of the defensive self, to a regeneration that can be redemptive only insofar as it is *new*, which is to say discontinuous with the patriarchal "I" that seeks liberation. Here is Campbell's description of the hero's ego-surrender or symbolic death, which he images as the descent into the belly of the whale, from *The Hero With a Thousand Faces*:

This popular motif gives emphasis to the lesson that the passage of the threshold is a form of self-annihilation. Its resemblance to the adventure of the Symplegades is obvious. But here, instead of passing outward, beyond the confines of the visible world, the hero goes inward, to be born again. The disappearance corresponds to the passing of a worshiper into a temple—where he is to be quickened by the recollection of who and what he is, namely dust and ashes unless immortal. The temple interior, the belly of the whale, and the heavenly land beyond, above, and below the confines of the world, are one and the same. That is why the approaches and entrances to temples are flanked and defended by colossal gargoyles: dragons, lions, devil-slayers with drawn swords, resentful dwarfs, winged bulls. These are the threshold guardians to ward away all incapable of encountering the higher silences within. They are preliminary embodiments of the dangerous aspect of the presence, corresponding to the mythological ogres that bound the conventional world, or to the two rows of teeth of the whale. They illustrate the fact that the devotee at the moment of entry into a temple undergoes a metamorphosis. His secular character remains without; he sheds it, as a snake its slough. Once inside he may be said to have died to time and returned to the World Womb, the World Navel, the Earthly Paradise. The mere fact that anyone can physically walk past the temple guardians does not invalidate their significance; for if the intruder is incapable of encompassing the sanctuary, then he has effectually remained without. Anyone unable to understand a god sees it as a devil and is thus defended from the approach. Allegorically, then, the passage into a temple and the hero-dive through the jaws of the whale are identical adventures, both denoting, in picture language, the life-centering, life-renewing act. (91-92)

This hero-path seems to me precisely the path that needs to be followed by men today, in one form or another. John Rowan points out the pitfalls of consciousness-raising, showing that you can raise your consciousness without affecting your behavior, and calls for *unconsciousness*-raising in its stead. But this raising of the unconscious mind is, "allegorically," to use Campbell's term, exactly what the hero-myth is all about: a descent into the dark world of the unconscious, where the true monsters live and must be overcome, and then a return to conscious life with new and deepseated answers. The "liberated" liberal man, who talks like a feminist but is only partly, through strict but never entirely successful self-control, able to bring his behavior into line with his words, is no solution to male sexism. Men must be transformed. And to achieve that transformation we might do worse than to look to mythology.

John Rowan's book, and the pagan movement he advocates, constitutes one highly influential and worthwhile attempt to do just this. The pagan Great Goddess and Horned God in all their specific mythological incarnations (Ishtar and Tammuz, Isis and Osiris, Inanna and Dumuzi, Cybele and Attis, Demeter and Dionysus), are repressed mythic figures of great archetypal power, power reaching to us from beneath centuries of patriarchal repression, and calling us specifically to a new gender unconscious. The Goddess has been of central importance to feminists in the Wicca movement, the modern return to witchcraft; Rowan suggests that the Goddess's male companion, the Horned God, might play an equally powerful role in men's transformation. He quotes from Starhawk's 1979 book *The Spiral Dance*:

For both women and men, the [Horned] God is also the Dying God. As such, He represents the giving over that sustains life: Death in the service of the life force. Life is characterized by many losses, and, unless the pain of each one is fully felt and worked through, it remains buried in the psyche, where, like a festering sore that never heals, it exudes emotional poison. The Dying God embodies the concept of loss. In rituals, as we enact his death over and over again, we release the emotions surrounding our own losses, lance the wounds, and win through to the healing promised by his rebirth. This psychological purging was the true purpose of dramatic tragedy, which originated in Greece out of the rites of the dying god Dionysus. (qtd. in Rowan 87)

"He is difficult to understand," Starhawk writes, "because He does not fit into any of the expected stereotypes, neither those of the 'macho' male nor the reverse-images of those who deliberately seek effeminacy. He is gentle, tender and comforting, but He is also the Hunter.... He is untamed sexuality—but sexuality as a deep, holy, connecting power. He is the power of feeling, and the image of what men could be if they were liberated from the constraints of patriarchal culture" (qtd. in Rowan 85-86).[1]

I find this new paganism intriguing and potentially powerful; but I also see two problems in it. One is the depth and tenacity of our programmed skepticism. The deadening Calvinist/capitalist demystification of reality has over the last 200 or 300 years left us profoundly suspicious of anything that cannot be easily reduced to empirical proof. Never mind that, as Gilles Deleuze and Felix Guattari show in *Anti-Oedipus*, capitalism has not so much *de*mystified reality as *re*mystified it, so that, say, the mythology of the hero's descent into the whale's belly is replaced with the psychological mythology of the little boy wanting to make love to his mother but being frightened by his perception of his mother's castration into bowing to the father's will. The remystification only confirms our skepticism about myth.

The result of both scientific demystification and psychoanalytical remystification is specifically that, when our lives are shattered by emotional crises, we are powerfully attracted to the "scientists" who will sedate us and/or lock us up in an Oedipal institution—psychoanalysts, psychiatrists—and remain suspicious of the archetypal figures once (a thousand years ago) programmed into our social unconscious (and still there, deep down) that might help us swim through the seas that would drown us. The problem is, perhaps the help *is* there; but how do we get through to it? The very patriarchal programming that makes us sick also makes us suspicious of myth. We need to overcome the programming to be able to turn to myth for help; but we need the help of myth to overcome the programming. This is not an insurmountable difficulty, but it is a serious and widespread one.

The other problem is that, as Campbell makes clear in *Myths To Live By*, the function of a "properly operating mythology" is not only "to waken and maintain in the individual a sense of awe and gratitude in relation to the mystery dimension of the universe...so that he recognizes that he participates in it" (221), but "to offer an image of the universe that will be in accord with the knowledge of the time, the sciences and the fields of action of the folk to whom the mythology is addressed" (221). The difficulty with that latter function is that the "knowledge" of our time is still almost exclusively patriarchal knowledge, which gives patriarchal Freudian psychoanalysis, with its paternal control of little boys through the agency of castration fear and of little girls through the agency of penis envy, a powerful position. Since hero mythology has largely served patriarchal societies, it is easy enough to transform it into a tame ancillary to our own patriarchal society as well: the boy-hero sets out to redeem the wasteland ruled by the ailing Fisher King, and in killing-cum-healing the Fisher King *becomes* the Fisher King. This is Freud's Oedipus myth all over again. I have the same qualms about Robert Bly's emphasis on the warrior in *Iron John*; for while Bly is careful to distinguish the true warrior from the mere macho killer, the line between the two is culturally vague and extremely difficult to hold in focus, and it is all too easy to reidealize male violence using Bly's book—which may, in fact, partially account for its runaway popularity.

An example from my own experience: my father traumatizes me at age 18 by jumping on top of me, pinning me down, sneering at my tears, and shaving my beard off, and in order to make sure that that sort of experience will never recur, I put distance between myself and my father. I build the kind of walls that Bly says the true warrior must erect and defend, lest he become a "soft man." I develop a prickly but polite detente-mode that allows me to be "different" from my father (allows me to maintain what I think of as my "integrity") without antagonizing him into repressive violence. But of course the "prickly but polite detente-mode" is not my own invention at all; it is repressive traditional masculinity. In order to be different from my father I become exactly like him. I become a "man."

So how are we to be transformed?

If, as Campbell insists, a myth can only be powerful if it ends by confirming shared values, obviously the first step in achieving a masculist transformation must be the formation of a countersociety. This is the function of the men's movement, as it has been of the women's movement. Then there is communal support not only for the traumatic process of self-transformation, but also for the transformed man who emerges from it. Without that kind of support, transformation can lead to, or be interpreted as, psychosis—and the end result of both eventualities is the same, incarceration in an institution.

The second step—and *only* second step, arising gradually and integrally out of the first—is to develop our own hero-mythology, our own modern masculist version or versions of the hero-path, by which to guide ourselves past patriarchal programming to a new masculinity. The trouble with the new paganism is that it seeks simply to *ignore* modernity, rather than engaging and incorporating it into a renewed myth. This may involve repression (early on), and it may involve a legitimate purging of modernity (later on); but however the pagan retreat from modernity is effected, a simple retreat doesn't seem to me the strongest base for a complex social transformation, a gradual *transition* from the current patriarchal culture to something else. I have the same reservations about radical readings of the New Testament, in which Jesus now calls us to "follow" him not to church and institutionalized obedience, but to the Cross as ego-surrender and resurrection of the body (the body that patriarchy taught us to kill with self-control and tranquilizers). Since for the last millennium or so we have been a Christian civilization, this gives us more current, and thus more effective, archetypal tools for the transformation of self and society; but Christianity too is an old, outdated religion. We need a *new* hero-myth, a specifically modern masculist hero-myth that can appeal to the vast majority of men.

The one element of Robert Bly's book that I do very much like is his reconstruction of ritual initiation: a process by which older men "steal" the adolescent boy from his mother and the other women and initiate him into manhood.[2] The problem with this, as Bly is ruefully aware, is that we have all too few older men capable of initiating young men into a transformed, life-enhancing manhood. Such a state is what we are striving for; in our current striving his vision is attractive precisely because it acts like a resplendent city on the horizon, drawing us onward. Bly's schema of ritual initiation works best, in fact, *in* his book: he is the older man who offers to initiate us younger men into the manhood he has found. His book (and the many popular workshops and seminars he has given) serves as a kind of proleptic masculine model for the utopian community toward which the women's and men's movements strive.

A less attractive because more realistic possibility, I suggest, might lie in a reconstruction of schizophrenia, that frighteningly radical alternative to capitalist patriarchy that R.D. Laing first, Joseph Campbell and Gilles Deleuze and Felix Guattari after, set up as *the* modern hero-experience. Because it is the defenseless person's natural response to an insane ideology like patriarchy, and because it therefore becomes the bogeyman with which we scare ourselves into developing repressive defenses, schizophrenic imagery provides a powerful mythological countermyth to patriarchy. I cannot resist quoting at length from Campbell's discussion of a schizophrenic experience he takes from one of Laing's books:

> The first experience is of a sense of splitting. The person sees the world going in two: one part of it moving away; himself in the other part. This is the beginning of the regressus, the crack-off and backward flow. He may see himself, for a time, in two roles. One is the role of the clown, the ghost, the witch, the queer one, the outsider. That is the outer role that he plays, making little of himself as the fool, a joke, the one kicked around, the patsy [cf. the strategic importance for straight men's liberation of gay liberation, of assuming the gay role therapeutically]. Inside, however, he is the savior, and he knows it. He is the hero chosen for a destiny....
>
> The second stage has been described in many clinical accounts. It is of a terrific drop-off and regression, backward in time and biologically as well. Falling back into his own past, the psychotic becomes an infant, a fetus in the womb. [Cf. primal therapy, a guided tour into and out of this healing phase in schizophrenia that has become centrally important in recent therapeutic transformations.] One has the frightening experience of slipping back to animal consciousness, into animal forms, sub-animal forms, even plantlike....
>
> "Show me the face you had before your father and mother were born!" We have had occasion before to refer to this meditation theme of the Japanese Zen masters. In the course of a schizophrenic retreat, the psychotic too may come to know the exaltation of a union with the universe, transcending personal bounds: the "oceanic feeling," Freud called it. Feelings arise then, too, of a new knowledge. Things that before had been mysterious are now fully understood. Ineffable realizations are experienced; and in fact, as we read about them, we can only be amazed....
>
> There may come next, according to a number of accounts, the sense of a terrific task ahead with dangers to be met and mastered; but also a presentiment of invisible helpful presences that may guide and help one through. These are the gods, the guardian demons or angels: innate powers of the psyche, fit to meet and to master the torturing, swallowing, or shattering negative forces. And if one has the courage to press on, there will be experienced, finally, in a terrible rapture, a culminating overwhelming crisis—or even a series of such culminations—more than can be borne.

# Conclusion 257

These crises are mainly of four typical sorts, according to the kinds of difficulty that will have conduced to the regressus in the first place. For instance, a person who in childhood has been deprived of essential love, authority, rigor, and commands, or in a house of tumult and wrath, a drunken father raging about, or the like [extreme versions of the "normal" patriarchal father], will have been seeking in his backward voyage a reorientation and centering of his life in love. Accordingly, the culmination (when he will have broken back to the start of his biography and even beyond, to a sense of the erotic first impulse to life) will be a discovery of a center in his own heart of tenderness and of love in which he can rest. That will have been the aim and meaning of his entire backward quest. And its realization will be represented through an experience, one way or another, of some sort of visionary fulfillment of a "sacred union" with a wifely mothering (or simply a mothering) presence.

Or if it had been a household in which the father had been nobody, a nothing, of no force in the home at all; where there had been no sense of paternal authority, no one of masculine presence who could be honored and respected, but only a clutter of domestic details and disordered feminine concerns [Campbell's sexist portrait of woman-centered life such as many feminists have sought], the quest will have been for a decent father image, and that is what will have to be found: some sort of symbolic realization of supernatural daughterhood or sonship to a father.

A third domestic situation of significant emotional deprivation is that of the child who feels itself to have been excluded from its family circle, treated as though not wanted; or with no family at all. In cases, for example, of a second marriage, where a second family has come along, a child of the first may feel and actually find itself excluded, thrown away, or left behind. The old fairy-tale theme of the wicked stepmother and stepsisters is relevant here. What such an excluded one will be striving for in his inward lonely journey will be the finding and fashioning of a center—not a *family* center, but a *world* center—of which *he* will be the pivotal being. (*Myths* 225-28)

The important feminist/masculist point to add to Campbell's account is that, under conditions of patriarchy, all childhoods are more or less conducive to this sort of "psychosis." You do not need a drunken, raging father or a physically absent father to be driven toward a transformed experience of masculinity; all you need is a father or father-figure who was programmed by society to defend himself against the world's assaults on his scared, hurt little inner core with authoritarian anger and withdrawal—which is to say, just about any father at all. The other side of that, which Campbell does not explore, is that you do not need a neurotically possessive and manipulative mother or a physically absent mother to be driven toward a transformed experience of femininity either; all you need is a mother or mother-figure who was programmed by society to defend herself against the world's cold denial of her self-worth by demanding from her children the love she never got from her parents, which is to say, again, just about any mother at all. (More women have been changed by feminism than men by masculism, which means that women now have a better chance of being mothered by a feminist than men do of being fathered by a masculist; but rather than taking statistical averages, our task should be to work toward a time when mothering and fathering will have been radically transformed by the changes we bring about in our own lives.)

On the other hand, powerful as this schizophrenic experience is as a model for a modern antipatriarchal hero-myth, it may also be extreme. Not everybody is willing to undergo traumatic transformation, and there are different gradations of traumatic transformation. My own experience was of being broken emotionally in a bitter verbal fight, and discovering, in the pit of my post-fight depression, that a whole defensive wall had been torn down inside me; that I was more defenseless than I was before. In that state I found it easier to relate to my wife, and she to me; the uneasiness, the defensiveness, was largely gone. Unprepared to engage the world without my defenses, I started to build them back up again, but my wife's immediate negative reaction signaled to me that something *wrong* was happening; and somehow I found the courage not to repair the damaged walls but to leave myself open.

The result was a sequence of increasing descent, over a period of several months, into a foggy world where nothing existed, not even myself. (I thought of it not as *me descending*, but as a "sequence of increasing descent"—there just *was* a descent.) It sounds counter-intuitive to call this a mild form of schizophrenia (a clinician might have described it as a severe depression); but compare Rollo May's 1958 description of what he called the "schizoid disturbance," which makes my "fog" sound like a much more common experience than is commonly thought:

Many psychotherapists have pointed out that more and more patients exhibit schizoid features and the "typical" kind of psychic problem in our day is not hysteria, as it was in Freud's time, but the schizoid type—that is to say, the problem of persons who are detached, unrelated, lacking in affect, tending towards depersonalization, and covering up their problems by means of intellectualizations and technical formulations....

There is also plenty of evidence that the sense of isolation, the alienation of one's self from the world is suffered not only by people in pathological conditions, but by countless "normal" persons as well in our day. (56)

If this were true in 1958—and it rings true 35 years later—then the problem facing us is not schizophrenia, but the intellectual and technical defenses against schizophrenia that keep us from experiencing the "schizoid disturbance" in therapeutic, transformative ways.

I felt neither depression nor panic; neither elation nor anticipation. Somehow, for about a two-month period, I went about my day-to-day business, including my teaching and writing; but I have no memory of it. I do remember gradually emerging from it by feeling a light entering the fog, a warmth, that gradually took on the features of my six-month-old daughter Anna; as I fixed on her, more lights entered, my wife, my older daughters, and then, weeks later, my father. It was only after I had, in a therapeutic regression to my early childhood, *become* my father, become him not as "father," not as authoritarian tyrant, not as the cold man who I felt had never loved me, but as "little boy," as the hurt, scared little boy he had been when he was growing up, that I was able to recover my "self"—although it was such an unfamiliar self that for a long time I didn't recognize it as mine. But that self-recovery at least made it possible for me to continue the self-therapeutic process in a more deliberate way, leading to a complete reconciliation with my father and, about a year later, to an engagement with my feelings of being engulfed by my mother. Dealing with that generated the numbing dread I felt in the later Spenser novels as he gradually made his way into the vicinity of his mother's disappearance; so terrifying was that dread that I lived with it, fought it, suppressed it for two years before I finally found the courage to begin to enter into that dark pre- and postnatal world that Spenser sought in *A Catskill Eagle*—that world that is without language, without mind, and virtually without light.

My experience, I suspect, though much less devastating than the process Joseph Campbell describes—I was never outwardly psychotic, no one ever suggested that I check into a hospital—is also more traumatic than many men would willingly undergo. And that is fine. I am not interested in imposing my experience, or any single experience held up as "the" model for masculist transformation, on all men. But I think it is important for us to start collecting these experiences, discussing them, considering their various gradations and applications, and above all discovering their underlying "myth."

And I structured the argument of this book up so as to take one step in that direction. Based on my own experience and my adaptive reading of Campbell, I linked each of my three popular heroes with a single phase of a modernized hero myth of masculist transformation: *Spenser* with what Campbell calls the "road of trials," which for the modern masculist hero involves the symptomatic failure of "correct" masculine behavior (its destructive effects on others, the feminist withdrawal of approval for traditional masculinity) leading to self-analysis, self-reappraisal, a search for a new self in purely intellectual terms; *Rambo* with symbolic death, the descent into the belly of the whale, or in modern terms the surrender of programmed defensive ego in personality disintegration; *Springsteen* with "regeneration," the gradual restructuring or rebirth of masculinity in a potentially redemptive transformation.

It is important to remember, I believe, that the mythic hero does not simply *determine* to "attain moral perfection," in the Franklinesque ascesis idealized by (and as) the liberal ideology of personal autonomy. Setting off down the mythic "road of trials" toward transformation is not a matter of enrolling in a seminar or entering psychoanalysis, something you decide might be worthwhile. It is tempting to say that we are "summoned"—by feminists perhaps, or by our male or female lovers and friends, the people around us who push and pull us toward health, and certainly that does happen—but in fact the usual scenario is that we awaken from the sleep of ideological mystification to find ourselves already trudging down (or mired in) the road of trials, already caught up in the double binds of our patriarchal programming, already lost when we were not even aware that we were en route. "Men's crisis," the catch phrase of the popular press, *is* the road of trials. We are already on it. Even our fathers and brothers (even sons!) who refuse to recognize the changed and changing world we live in, who refuse to admit that feminists may be right, who insist on living by the values and assumptions that worked 100, or 50, or 20 years ago, and on repressing the intense frustrations that this course generates—even they are already on the road of trials. They are simply blinded by ideological programming to what is happening all around them.

Those of us who are aware that something in us has to change, that we have to be transformed, have very little agreement as to what that transformation needs to be or how to bring it about. My suggestions for a "going-under," a schizophrenic night of the soul, may seem extreme to some. The notion that men's liberation involves no more than a little consciousness-raising seems hopelessly superficial and naive to me. Much work needs to be done, both in masculist theory and in the therapeutic practice of masculist transformation. But it seems to me that the push of the first stage of the hero myth and the pull of the third stage are something we can all agree on now, at least in a rough, heuristic way. We are already on the way, and we cannot turn back. We do not know where we are headed, or how to get there, but the urge to keep pushing forward is, however frightening, in some sense irresistible. We may be "broken heroes on a last-chance power drive," as Springsteen sings in "Born to Run"; but we have seen all too clearly what happens to our fathers and brothers who refuse to admit that they are being broken, and to realize that empowerment comes through a relinquishing of power. We cannot know what will come of our letting go, our surrendering the reins of power; we do know that whatever it is, we must risk it.

Part of this, too, is our vague sense of the third stage, regeneration, rebirth. This is not merely a personal need; it is a collective one. Patriarchy, in the varying forms of anxious politicians who respond to uncertain international situations by maintaining or escalating hostilities; of anxious manufacturers who strive for success by exploiting the working class and the Third World and raping the environment; and of anxious criminals who mimic the legalized exploitations and victimizations of the ruling classes in their murders, thefts, rapes, swindles, and production and distribution of physically destructive chemicals—patriarchy in all these forms is threatening the survival of the human race. We know that we cannot go on polluting the environment or pushing the Third World over the brink into mass starvation. We know that the human race is seriously threatened by ecocatastrophe in the next 20 to 100 years. We know this; it is not a science-fiction fantasy or alarmist exaggeration. If anything is a science-fiction fantasy, it is the fond hope that scientists will invent some miraculous remedy to the world's problems—a cheap and easily producible source of food or medicine for world hunger and disease, a technique for harnessing solar power for the energy shortage, a chemical to purify the polluted water and air or to enrich the deforested and depleted soil—which will relieve us of the pressure to make drastic changes in our political and psychological structures.

It is, I believe, dangerously naive to think that we can survive as a race without some form of collective regeneration, at least in the West, which directs the majority of the destructive power; and that regeneration must come from within if it is to make any significant difference without. If it is naive to entertain the utopian dream that such regeneration is in fact possible, it is nevertheless one of the very few chances we have.

# Notes

*Introduction*

[1] Jeffords defines the "masculine point of view" as "the disembodied voice of masculinity, that which no individual man or woman can realize yet which influences each individually" (xiii)—the somatized voice of normal masculine gender programming, or what I have called elsewhere the ideosomatics of masculinity (see *The Translator's Turn*).

[2] For useful historical summaries of the men's studies work in the fields of social psychology and history, see Tim Carrigan, Bob Connell, and John Lee's article "Toward a New Sociology of Masculinity," especially as first published in *Theory & Society* (a shorter version, lacking the critical review of "men's liberation" studies on 564-78, was collected in Harry Brod, ed., *The Making of Masculinities*), and Peter Filene's article on men's history, also in Brod's collection (esp. 112-19). Other sociological and social-historical studies include Dennis P. Hogan's *Transitions and Social Change* (1981), Clyde W. Franklin, II's *The Changing Definition of Masculinity* (1987), and Jack Balswick's *The Inexpressive Male* (1988). More popular books on the subject, which I'll be using in the course of this study, include Herb Goldberg's *The Hazards of Being Male: Surviving the Myth of Masculine Privilege* (1976), *The New Male: From Macho to Sensitive But Still All Male* (1979), *The New Male-Female Relationship* (1983), and *The Inner Male: Overcoming Roadblocks to Intimacy* (1987), Andrew Tolson's *The Limits of Masculinity* (1977), Paul Olsen's *Sons and Mothers* (1981), and Samuel Osherson's *Finding Our Fathers* (1986). John Rowan's *The Horned God* (1987) offers not only an excellent history of the men's movement in Britain since he joined it in 1972, but draws on pagan archetypes to help men first truly feel, then truly heal the wounds left in us by feminist attacks. Robert Bly's *Iron John* (1990) is another powerful attempt to redefine masculinity in ancient terms, by recalling the ritual structure of initiation: we must not only be liberated from the dehumanizing masculinity of capitalist patriarchy, we must be initiated by a community of older men into a new rehumanized masculinity.

[3] Minnesota books include David Savran's *Communists, Cowboys, and Queers* (1992), Constance Penley and Sharon Willis's forthcoming collection *Male Trouble*, and, in their popular culture series, Paul Smith's forthcoming *Clint Eastwood: A Cultural Production*. NYU books include Kevin White's *The First Sexual Revolution: The Emergence of Male Heterosexuality in Modern America* (1992) and Peter F. Murphy's forthcoming collection *The Fiction of Masculinity: Literary Constructions of Manhood*. Oxford books include my own *Ring Lardner and the Other* and Scott Coltrane's *Family Man: The Social Implications of Shared Domestic Labor*. Other books on men

## 264   No Less a Man

published by university presses include David D. Gilmore's *Manhood in the Making: Cultural Concepts of Masculinity* (Yale, 1990), Mark C. Carnes and Clyde Griffen's collection *Meanings for Manhood: Constructions of Masculinity in Victorian America* (Chicago, 1990), Dennis Bingham's *Masculinities, Male Spectatorship and Hollywood Stars* (Rutgers, forthcoming), Thais Morgan's collection *Men Writing the Feminine* (SUNY, forthcoming), Martin Green's *The Adventurous Male: Chapters in the History of the White Male Mind* (Penn State, forthcoming), and Peter Lehman's *Running Scared: Masculinity and the Representation of the Male Body* (Temple, forthcoming). A few academic trade presses have gotten into the swim too. Beacon Press has brought out Michael S. Kimmel and Thomas E. Mosmiller's collection *Against the Tide: Pro-Feminist Men in the United States, 1776-1990, A Documentary History* (1992) and Michael A. Messner's *Power at Play: Sports and the Problem of Masculinity* (1992). BasicBooks has done E. Anthony Rotundo's *American Manhood: Transformations in Masculinity from the Revolution to the Modern Era* (forthcoming), Robert L. Griswold's *Fatherhood in America: A History* (forthcoming), and Kathleen Gerson's *No Man's Land: Men's Changing Commitments to Family and Work* (forthcoming). HarperCollins has done Michael Kimmel's *Manhood: The American Quest* (forthcoming). This list, already incomplete, will be outdated by the time this book takes its place on it.

   I draw much of this information on new books and trends in men's studies from Scott Heller's piece "Scholars Debunk the Marlboro Man: Examining Stereotypes of Masculinity" in the February 3, 1993, *Chronicle of Higher Education.*

   [4]The equivalent derivation from "feminine" would be "femininism," which might, I suppose, be used to attack the reactionary politics of Phyllis Schlafly. No feminist would allow it to be applied in a blanket sense to *women*, but that is precisely what many feminists do with the term "masculinist."

   I have myself been "victimized," if inadvertently, by the blanket application of that term: in my article "The Trivialization of American Literature" in *American Quarterly* I wrote that the emancipatory critic's project "may be feminist, or masculist, or whatever else, whatever seems most pressing" (219)—but after I had returned the corrected page proofs a copy editor at *AQ* happened upon my coinage and, not recognizing it, changed it to "masculinist," in which form in eventually appeared in the journal. The change makes rather appalling hash of my sentiment: the implication is that it doesn't really matter whether you are a feminist or a male chauvinist, just so long as you are committed to social change.

   [5]Classic male-feminist books are Michael Korda's *Male Chauvinism* from 1972, Marc Feigen Fasteau's *The Male Machine* from 1975, and Stephen Heath's *The Sexual Fix* from 1982; a male-feminist essay collection, *Men in Feminism*, edited by Alice Jardine and Paul Smith, was published in the same year as the three masculist collections, 1987, and several new collections have appeared or are appearing in the nineties, notably Boone and Cadden's *Engendering Men* and Morgan's *Men Writing the Feminine.*

⁶Note, however, the problematic relation of these last three works to men's studies. In my frustrations with editors who refused to believe there might actually be a market for men's studies—this was before Robert Bly's *Iron John* convinced even the hardiest skeptics—I made few overt claims of "masculism" in my reading of Lardner; men's studies is an almost (not quite) hidden agenda in that book.

Lentricchia, too, conceives his reading of Stevens (to which my reading of Lardner was heavily indebted) not as a masculist project, though it manifestly is, but rather as the critical extension and correction of a feminist project, that of Sandra Gilbert and Susan Gubar, which he portrays as essentialist (in the sense of treating gender as if it were an essence, and as if it were not powerfully qualified by race and class). If he is aware of the increasing body of masculist writing, he doesn't show it.

Leverenz, on the other hand, is aware of that work, but oddly misreads it and distances himself from it. In his introduction he writes that his "basic thesis" is "that any intensified ideology of manhood is a compensating response to fears of humiliation," and comments:

I've come to question the psychoanalytic view, now adopted by many feminist critics, that manhood compensates for various fears of women and mothering. I think male rivalry is a more basic source of anxiety, though the language of manhood makes ample use of maternal scapegoating. Nor has my discussion of manhood been much influenced by recent works in men's studies, primarily because those histories tend to accept feminist views of manhood as patriarchy. Such views are probably accurate in describing women's experience of men in the home, but they don't reflect men's experience of each other at work, where most American men measure themselves. If women writers portray manhood as patriarchy, male writers from Melville to Sam Shepard, David Mamet, and David Rabe portray manhood as a rivalry for dominance. (4)

This is an incredible web of half-truths. I would understand his characterization of "men's studies" if he cited male-feminist works in his footnote, but the works he cites include Brod's excellent masculist anthology and Pleck's critique of the "negative" conception of masculinity as grounded in the denial of femininity, and several other historical works that explore masculinity as a psychosocial construct. None "tends to accept feminist views of manhood as patriarchy," which I take to be an awkward way of saying what I said some feminists polemically imply: that patriarchy is fundamentally male (constructed and maintained by men for male gratification), which is, as far as I can see, quite a different proposition from the notion of "manhood as patriarchy." As I read it his book *is* men's studies; why this rhetorical gesture distancing himself from it?

As for the surprisingly reactionary claim that masculinity is based on "rivalry for dominance," the obvious question is what causes this rivalry. Biology? Then we are very close to the ideology of male supremacy. Society? Ideology? Then the roots of rivalry go deeper, the fear of humiliation stems from earlier childhood or infantile anxieties than men's experience of each other at work, and halting the inquiry at rivalry only serves to mystify the working of ideology. It was, in any case, Freud's theory that manhood was primarily a rivalry for dominance (*Totem and Taboo*); feminist psychoanalysis gets the oedipal/preoedipal division from Freud, not the notion that little boys develop manhood by defending against their mothers (a later sociological theory, not a psychoanalytic one). I will be discussing these issues in greater detail in chapter ten.

Other books on men and literature are forthcoming as I send this to press, by Thais Morgan, Peter F. Murphy, and others.

[7]And is there already some connection between these "Kilgore Trout novels," as I think of them, these sketchily outlined book ideas, and the book I did write? Kinsella's narrator Ray goes to the University of Iowa library in Iowa City to research J.D. Salinger, whom the announcer's voice has told him to take to a Red Sox game, and discovers a rare interview with Salinger that says the eremitic writer is an avid Red Sox fan. "As I read," the narrator says, "I discovered some uncanny coincidences. Or are there ever coincidences?" (30). The same thing occurs to me: Iowa City is where David Morrell lived too, until moving to Santa Fe in 1993, and the University of Iowa library is where he used to research his books (though not *First Blood*, which he wrote at Penn State). Come to think of it, it was at an Iowa Writers' Workshop in Iowa City that Robert Scholes encouraged Kurt Vonnegut to write metafiction in the late 1960s, and the result, *Slaughterhouse Five*, included Kilgore Trout.

[8]And, as George Lipsitz begins to show in *Time Passages*, there is a powerful dialectic in the social process of "covering" another singer's song, a dialectic that moves toward hegemony in the big record labels' attempts to coopt rock and roll in the late 1950s and early 1960s by releasing, distributing, and aggressively marketing (including payola to disc jockeys) tamer cover versions of popular singer-songwriters distributed by independent labels (123-24), but, as the Folkways album shows, in a counterhegemonic direction as well. (Lipsitz's examples are from the British Invasion's covering of ethnic working-class songs from America; there are of course hundreds of others.) Rock music, as Lipsitz stresses, is a powerfully dialogical medium in the Bakhtinian sense of being saturated with past voices and inclined or oriented toward a future (and potentially emancipatory) response. Three Springsteen covers that I will not be dealing with in part three and might mention here are explicitly political concert pieces: Woody Guthrie's "This Land is Your Land" from the "River" tour in 1980, Barrett Strong and Norman Whitfield's "War" from the "Born in the U.S.A." tour in 1985, and Bob Dylan's "Chimes of Freedom" from the Amnesty International tour in 1988. (The first two were released on the live album in 1986, the third on a maxi-single in late 1988.) In his introduction to "This Land is Your Land" at the Nassau Coliseum, December 28, 1980, he grounded his interpretation of the song in his recent reading of Joe Klein's *Woody Guthrie: A Life*, and stressed that it was originally intended as an "angry song," a protest song, a rebuttal to Irving Berlin's "God Bless America," a way of saying that the disenfranchisement of the poor and various ethnic groups was and is contrary to the spirit of American democracy. In his introduction to "War" at the Los Angeles Coliseum on September 30, 1985, Springsteen was even more explicit:

If you grew up in the sixties, you grew up with war on TV every night, a war that your friends were involved in. And I want to do this song tonight for all the young people out there. If you're in your teens—'cause I remember a lot of my friends, when we were seventeen and eighteen, we didn't have much of a chance to think about how we felt about a lot of things. And the next time they're gonna be looking at you. And you're gonna need a lot of information to know what you're gonna wanna do. Because in 1985, blind faith in your leaders—or in anything—will get you killed. 'Cause what I'm talking about here is—

And the band explodes into "War! / What is it good for? / Absolutely nothing, say it again!" Here Springsteen's cultural memory of what it was like to be a 17- and 18-year-old boy in the late 1960s, with the threat of going to Vietnam hanging over your head, is "imported" into the ostensibly peaceable era of the mid-1980s, suffused as it was with Reagan's Cold War rhetoric of bombing the Soviet "evil empire" back into the Stone Age, the commitment of Marines to Beirut and Grenada (later Iraq and Somalia) and half a dozen less well publicized trouble spots around the world, and the low-key but unceasing talk of reinstating the draft.

[9]Sometimes I wonder about my evaluations of these works. I find in Leonard Maltin's *TV Movies and Video Guide* this review of Peckinpah's movie: "Boredom reigns supreme in retelling of Sheriff Garrett's pursuit of ex-crony Billy the Kid. The many familiar character actors can't breathe life into inexplicably dull film; Dylan's score (and small role) are equally unmemorable" (755). I will be quoting a similar Maltin attack on *First Blood* in part two.

## Part One

### *Chapter One: The Hardboiled Hero*

[1]Though of course they too are idealized in significant ways. Sara Paretsky told me in a telephone conversation that her understanding of V.I. Warshawski's toughness is filtered through her own life situation of being confined to a wheelchair: her detective does the things (like defending herself in a dangerous city, Chicago, in a dangerous world) that she herself cannot. Still, Vic Warshawski has the gritty *feel* of reality: she is powerfully convincing.

[2]The first Travis McGee novels are from the mid-1960s, and show it: "Trav," the indolent Florida boat bum who helps friends out of jams and keeps half the take, is a philosopher in these early books, but his philosophy tends to be uncritical of male supremacy. (In fact, I find him almost insufferably priggish and self-satisfied.) Gradually, however, through the mid-1970s, Macdonald begins to respond sympathetically to feminism—to introduce stronger, more articulate and competent women into his novels, to smite Travis McGee down with deep emotional divisions and doubts whenever he starts feeling smug, and to put into Trav's mouth long, sensitive, and increasingly searching explorations of his own masculinity, its dark, hidden sides as well as

the public sides that he relies so heavily on in his work. He also introduces Meyer, a kind of male prototype for the post-patriarchal future: big, heavy, hairy, Neanderthaloid, Meyer is nevertheless uncannily aware of the emotional complexities of human interactions and situations; he has the knack of instant rapport with almost anyone, usually by listening closely to what people are saying; and, a world-class economist, he manipulates capitalist society just enough to make a comfortable living and spends the rest of his time on his boat (or Trav's) with other people.

[3]Note, however, that while reader-response theorists openly flout the affective fallacy in their work, following the neo-Kantian phenomenological tradition in their emphasis on the individual's subjective processes rather than a reified "text," they do not actually commit it. Norman Holland reduces reader response not to affect, but to liberal "transactions" grounded in static "identity themes." David Bleich understands the reader's intersubjective engagement with the writer in terms not of emotional identification and transformation, but of a largely intellectual two-stage process he calls symbolization and resymbolization. Stanley Fish grounds individual readers' subjective constructions of meaning in an institutional context that he calls the "interpretive community," which, he says, shapes and controls every aspect of our interpretive activities.

The most interesting and I think fruitful reader-response theory in recent years has been allied with feminist concerns for gender liberation: Elizabeth A. Flynn and Patrocinio Schweickart's essay collection *Gender and Reading*, for example, which has strongly influenced my thinking about the critical endeavor. See also my discussion of this book and the utopian practice of "reading beyond the ending" in chapter six of *Ring Lardner and the Other*.

[4]See e.g. Freud's *Jokes and Their Relation to the Unconscious*, *The Psychopathology of Everyday Life*, *The Interpretation of Dreams*, *Civilization and its Discontents*, and *Totem and Taboo*; Horney's *Self-Analysis* and *The Neurotic Personality of Our Time*; Miller's *Thou Shalt Not Be Aware*; and Goldberg's *The New Male*, *The New Male-Female Relationship*, and *The Inner Male*.

[5]The bulk of my biographical information on Parker is taken from Maria Karagianis's *Boston Globe* piece on him.

[6]In *Poodle Springs* (1989) he completed an unfinished Chandler manuscript, and in *Perchance to Dream* (1991) he wrote a sequel to *The Big Sleep*.

[7]Note that, while Iris is a "broad" here and "Mrs. Milford" (70), by the third Spenser novel, *Mortal Stakes* (1975), he is saying "Ms. Utley" (83), and by *Looking for Rachel Wallace* (1980) he has Spenser correct a smalltime hood who refers to Rachel as "the broad": "You mean Ms. Wallace, scumbag" (157). For a tough-guy writer, Parker is sensitive to feminist linguistic innovations.

[8]Parker seems to have purged most of his disgust at the university in this first novel; he doesn't attack academia again in the Spenser series until *Playmates* (1989). His two non-Spenser novels do feature anti-academicism, in Aaron Newman's bitter remark to his academic wife Janet that "You're doing committee work and loving it in there in your asshole department with all the

asshole academics pretending to care about Chaucer and Andrew Marvell when all they really want is tenure and promotion" (*Wilderness* 117), and he portrays Jennifer Grayle's husband John Merchent in *Love and Glory* as a timid, ineffectual, but pompous and self-important English professor who is proud of being a Sara Teasdale specialist, saying, "I was really quite fortunate to find a whole area of literature like that in which little work had been done" (163). When Boone returns to college to win back Jennifer, he is (like his creator) fairly dismissive of the work done in English departments: "Literature's interesting," he says. "It's good to read, fun to talk about." "That's all?" (158) Jennifer says.

*Chapter Two: The Liberal Hero*

[1] For a broader historical analysis of this social change, see T.J. Jackson Lears, *No Place of Grace*, especially chapter two on the artisan ideology. For useful discussions of the shift in the context specifically of changing conceptions of masculinity in the decades around the years 1700 and 1900, see Michael S. Kimmel's "The Contemporary 'Crisis' of Masculinity in Historical Perspective," esp. 137-43, and for 1800-1940, see the essays collected by J.A. Mangan and James Walvin in *Manliness and Morality*. The essays collected by the Plecks in *The American Man* offer another series of useful perspectives on this social history, as do, from another perspective, the essays collected by Lloyd de Mause in *The History of Childhood*.

[2] See John G. Cawelti's *Apostles of the Self-Made Man*, esp. ch. 3 on Parkman and Emerson, and Irvin G. Wyllie's *The Self-Made Man in America*, for further discussion.

[3] The best book I know on the negative sides of this halfway liberation—this treatment of symptoms without concern for the patriarchal disease itself—is Betty Friedan's *The Second Stage*.

[4] See also Joel Porte's chapter "The Protest" in *Representative Man: Ralph Waldo Emerson in His Time* for a useful discussion of Emerson's fears about his own masculinity.

[5] Emerson's wife Ellen Tucker died at the age of 19, in 1831. It was to be some years before her estate cleared probate, but by the late 1830s and early 1840s he had $23,000 invested, yielding him a comfortable annual income of about $1200.

[6] Leverenz finds the significant parallels to Thoreau's position in Emerson as well:

Emerson's attitude toward workers has something of Thoreau's contempt for the Irish, though without *Walden*'s puckish mockery. He takes them more seriously, with a more profound contempt. They are the herd, the mob, the mass, "bugs and spawn," at best a kind of larvae. In the two broad groupings into which Emerson usually divides society, the workers will forever be inert, unless a few self-reliant men bring them to intellectual vitality. "The life of labor does not make men, but drudges," he writes in May of 1843. "The German and Irish millions, like the Negro," he says in "Fate," "have a great deal of guano in their destiny." Toward the end of "Nature" Emerson goes so far as to say, "you cannot freely admire a noble landscape, if laborers are digging in the field hard by" (*CW* 1:39). (58)

⁷Socrates begins by establishing that "one, Love is always the love of something, and two, that that something is what he lacks" (200e), but then goes on to envision, through a lesson taught him by a Mantinean woman named Diotima (a female persona of Socrates himself, at least in Plato's rhetorical strategy), a state of perfect love in which the gap between desire and fulfillment, lack and plenitude, is no more:

And if, my dear Socrates, Diotima went on, man's life is ever worth the living, it is when he has attained this vision of the very soul of beauty. And once you have seen it, you will never be seduced again by the charm of gold, of dress, of comely boys, or lads just ripening to manhood; you will care nothing for the beauties that used to take your breath away and kindle such a longing in you, and many others like you, Socrates, to be always at the side of the beloved and feasting your eyes upon him, so that you would be content, if it were possible, to deny yourself the grosser necessities of meat and drink, so long as you were with him.
  But if it were given to man to gaze on beauty's very self—unsullied, unalloyed, and freed from the mortal taint that haunts the frailer loveliness of flesh and blood—if, I say, it were given to man to see the heavenly beauty face to face, would you call *his*, she asked me, an unenviable fate, whose eyes had been opened to the vision, and who had gazed upon it in true contemplation until it had become his own forever? (211de)

⁸In fact, during the course of the novel Spenser spends something like $1000 of his own money on Paul, for no better reason than that nobody has ever done that for Paul before, bought him nice clothes that fit right, taken him out to dinner, taken him to the ballet. Parker occasionally pays lip-service in his novels to the hardboiled convention that the detective must be just barely getting by—for a long time Spenser drives a car with a taped vinyl roof, and he always insists on doing the *right* job the *right* way, even if that means not getting paid for it—but mainly his hero spends money as if he were independently wealthy. Since Spenser's tastes (and spending habits) get gradually more expensive as the series progresses, my guess is that Spenser's wealth reflects Parker's wealth: that as Spenser's success increasingly frees Parker from financial worries, Spenser's important gestures of largess—the autonomous "love" that gives out of self-sufficient integrity—become increasingly magnanimous.

*Chapter Three: Violence and Need*
¹In *Love and Glory,* in place of his wisecracking middle-aged private eye Spenser, Parker gives us a wisecracking college kid from the 1950s (the book is semi-autobiographical, its hero is semi-Parker) who wisecracks his way into conflict with his professors and ultimately right out of college and into the Army. It is the Korean War, and Boone is shipped out—not into battle, into the radio corps (like Parker himself and the hero of his other non-Spenser novel,

*Wilderness*). While Boone's in Korea his girlfriend Jennifer gets pinned, engaged, and married, and Boone's life starts to come apart at the seams.

"She knew it would hurt me," Boone summarizes for us the letter in which Jennifer tells him all this, "but she could never quite deal with my intensity, with my totality. She was a little afraid of it. She felt, finally, overpowered, possessed, and she couldn't live like that" (65). It's a familiar complaint. That's why Susan Silverman leaves Spenser. Janet Newman says the same thing about Aaron in *Wilderness*, and lives with it only by withdrawing into a protective shell of her own. Parker feels the effect of the "intensity" and "totality" of his masculine self-control on the woman he loves more than anything else in his life, his wife Joan, and in his novels keeps wondering what the hell to do about it.

In *Love and Glory*, he tries letting Boone break down—something that, apart from drinking and risking his life a bit more than usual, Spenser can never do. There ensues a gradual disintegration that takes ten years out of Boone's life (too drunk to remember) and ends on the beach in Southern California, where he remembers a line from *The Great Gatsby*— " 'Conduct,' Scott Fitzgerald had written, 'may be founded on the hard rock or the wet marshes' " (107)— and decides to put his life back together, with the ultimate objective of winning Jennifer back. He gets a job, begins lifting weights, meets a librarian that he talks about books with, and finally returns to Boston, enrolls in the university where Jennifer's husband is a professor and Jennifer herself is a grad student. "*The scary thing is*," he wrote to Jennifer before he went down and out, "*that I don't see how I'll be able to care about anything, ever, except you, and you're gone. What will I do? I don't want to get ahead. I want to go back*" (93). Can't repeat the past? Of course you can.

The key is—and here's where Parker throws away what he gained in Boone's breakdown—control. By making Jennifer his rock, Boone makes himself a rock. Unlike many men, Parker and all of his alter egos know that they feel, and feel passionately; but they also know that their passion frightens everyone around them, and so they learn to control it, to keep it under lock and key. When they let it out, they let it out in controlled ways; they let tiny trickles of it seep out under the door, so that no one will be overwhelmed. That's the way to get Jennifer back: don't scare her off with overpowering intensity.

> Jennifer laughed her thrilling laugh. "Oh, Boonie. It's good to have you around again. Can we be friends?"
> 
> "Sure," I said. "It's one of the reasons I came back."
> 
> "Like we were? You really were the best friend I ever had."
> 
> "You were that to me," I said.
> 
> "And you really were, still are, like nobody else. I still haven't met anyone like you."
> 
> "And I was just a kid then," I said. "Wait till you see how much better I've become. You may tear off all your clothes and pounce on me." [*She's* going to be the one to lose control now—not him.]
> 
> "Gee," Jennifer said, "we could never eat at the faculty club again."

## 272  No Less a Man

> The sexual reference made my throat tighten. I had to force my voice out, but it sounded normal enough once out. I thought of her and Merchent waiting before they had the baby, taking precautions, and having intercourse carefully, sleeping together each night, being naked together often. I thought of the casual and intimate possession that people develop when they've been married a few years, a possession that excludes the rest of the world, that sets them apart regardless of their passion for each other, that marks *us* and differentiates from *them*. It was almost too much. It almost overwhelmed me. Almost drove me backward into the despair I'd worked so fiercely at overcoming. For a moment everything swam in front of me, and ran together, and I clasped my hands beneath the table as hard as I could, swelling the muscles in my arms and then my chest and back. *Control*. I had come this far. I was with her. Talking of being friends. I could look at her, and if I reached out and touched her, she wouldn't flinch. "Time is but the stream I go fishing in." The time she's been with Merchent, the kid, the press of nakedness, the life they led, was downstream from where I fished. The stream kept going and the water I fished in was always new. When I had her again, the others who had had her wouldn't matter. Except as obstacles they didn't matter now. (152-53)

This Emersonian (here specifically Thoreauvian, from the end of the "Where I Lived, and What I Lived For" chapter of *Walden*) will to power over time is Gatsby through and through: "The stream kept going and the water I fished in was always new," but of course the newness he desires is one that has already incorporated the oldness and pastness of Jennifer's love for him, back before Korea. It is a Platonic newness that has transcended time.

When Boone goes out to lunch with Jennifer, he dresses with a sensuous attention to detail that recalls Gatsby's parading of his shirts before Daisy; Jennifer, like Daisy, "could entrance people and so she did. It was a power she used neither for good nor evil, but for the simple, unexamined pleasure of its exercise.... She loved being central. There was nothing malign in this, or even selfish" (150). Parker gives us Gatsby's bumping his head up against the stubborn fact of Daisy's child: " 'I've been married eight years, Boonie. ...I have a daughter,' she said. 'A home, a life' " (160). And when Jennifer gets to know him better and alludes, like so many of the Spenser characters, to the high price Gatsby paid for living too long with his dream, Boone answers with the standard pitch for autonomy and self-control:

> "You're too closed in, Boonie," Jennifer said. "You're the most entirely autonomous person I've ever met, but you pay a high price for it."
> "Not as high a price as I paid when I wasn't autonomous," I said. "When you married Merchent I nearly went under. By the time I bottomed out in L.A. a derelict, I was dying. If autonomy means being in control of your life, I had none. Now I do. And I will never lose it again." (174)

Parker gives us a lot more of the conversations between his two star-crossed lovers than Fitzgerald ever did: this is a most self-conscious rewrite of *Gatsby*. Jennifer, for one thing, is much more articulate than Daisy, and Parker has his Gatsby character narrate the story, with much attention to the signals his body is giving him when he feels threatened:

> It was thrilling to talk with her about myself. It was too exciting for me. It threatened my control. But it was irresistible. I wanted her to go on.
> "In some ways you're right," I said. "I grew up in the years after I bottomed out in L.A., and I had to learn what mattered. I'm clear on that now. I know what I care about. I know what I need to control and what I can control and what I can't. It's a kind of freedom."...
> "What do you need to control, Boonie?"
> "Me. My feelings. I feel very strongly. If I don't keep them clamped all the time, they run to excess. They're destructive of me and other people. If I combine them with drink, it's a mess."
> "Humor," Jennifer said.
> "It's one way," I said. "It's a distancing trick. Another way is to stay inside."
> "Inside yourself," Jennifer said.
> "Yes." (188)

This explains the uneasy humor of the Spenser novels as well: it's a defense. By *Love and Glory* Parker has discovered that for himself. Staying inside works for his male characters, but writing novels is a way of *not* staying inside, of exploring the effect of various outside forces on his masculine self-control. The standard (liberal masculine) wisdom that Boone parrots here is that the only alternative to the "freedom" of strict self-control is self-destructive excess; but in fact the process of writing the novels also offers a third alternative, a therapeutic process of experimenting with controlled surrender and release, a search for the deepseated needs that drive the self-destructive plunge into excess and that, once exposed to the light of day, might be rendered harmless.

In any case, the Gatsby story works, here: Jennifer comes around, realizes she's still in love with Boone, realizes also that she is now strong enough and mature enough to withstand the pressure of his controlled intensity, and leaves her husband for Boone. No Myrtle dies; no Wilson murders Boone; no Nick retreats to visions of "a fresh, green breast of the new world." Happy ending without reservations. The success of the liberal hero beyond Emerson's wildest dreams.

### *Chapter Four: The Missing Mother*

[1]Parker's most overt exploration of the cold, distant mother-figure is in his first non-Spenser novel, *Wilderness*, where Aaron Newman's wife Janet is portrayed as locked into a defensive fortress that awakens all of Aaron's anxieties and insecurities. By giving this wall to the woman, Parker leaves open a tiny window through which to explore the man's fear and vulnerability. This means a kind of experimental reversal of traditional gender roles, as if Aaron were the woman begging her cold husband for a little love and being called childish in return:

> "You ever wonder how that would make me feel?"
> "Being scared, you mean?"

"Yeah, being scared. You ever think, maybe, 'Gee, the poor guy must be really down and feeling bad, how can I make him feel better?' You ever have any thoughts like that?"

"I don't know what I'm supposed to say."

"Jesus Christ. It's not 'supposed to.' Don't you have any instincts, any fucking heart? Can't you see I'm hurting? Don't you have any impulse to help me. To put your arms around me and say 'I love you. I don't care what you do, I love you'?"

"Aaron," she said. And stopped. And took a deep breath. It shook in a slight vibrato as it went in. "Aaron, grow up."

"What's that supposed to mean? Only little kids need love and compassion?"

"I love you. But if you feel bad about yourself and how you acted I can't fix that. You have to fix that."

"While I'm fixing it, it might help to know you're caring about me."

"Aaron, I've lived with you for twenty-three years. Doesn't that suggest I care about you?" (116)

That, of course, is traditionally the man's line: you don't have to show love by being open, vulnerable, trusting, caring; all you have to do is stick around. In some sense *Wilderness* is a novel about the effect of feminism on men: as women become empowered by the women's movement, by political and emotional advances, by that new feeling of competence that women's successes in the world have engendered, men begin to fall back into women's traditional role, pleading for more love and compassion, and getting only cool contempt in return: "Grow up." The scene continues:

"Sure, you care about me, but not like I care about you. You don't look forward to coming home and seeing me. You don't get a thrill when I walk through the door. You don't get a thrill from touching me."

"And don't you resent it," Janet said. "Don't you take every opportunity to make me feel guilty that I don't feel like you do. Is there only one way to love? Does everybody have to love the way you do or be not loving?"

"How can you love someone and not feel as I do?" he said.

"One can. One does. The trouble with you is that you're over-invested. You dwell on me too much. Every encounter. Every event. Every exchange of words or ideas is charged as if it were a moment of high passion."

"True. I care only about you. I care only for your approval or disapproval. I have achieved an autonomy in my life that only you violate. Only you and the girls, and the girls are growing and going away. Now it's all turned on you. And you're turning out. You're doing committee work and loving it in there in your asshole [university English] department with all the asshole academics pretending to care about Chaucer and Andrew Marvell when all they really want is tenure and promotion."

"Aaron..."

"I know it's hard. I know you feel the pressure. I try and change. I try and love you less." His voice thickened. "But think what I lose if I love you less. The central meaning of my life. At forty-six I have to change it?"

"Goddamn," she said. (117)

The plot of the novel is that Aaron has witnessed a murder, and the murderer and his gang are threatening him and his family to keep him from testifying. The police promise to protect them, but Adolph Karl, the murderer, seems to have a cop in his pocket, and knows Newman's every move. While Newman is reporting the murder and ID-ing Karl, Karl is already sending two thugs around to strip and tie up Janet, and carve "A.K." into the skin above her pubic hair with a knife. Aaron goes in the next day to cancel the ID, and is both mortified when the cops call him a coward and terrified when they predict that Karl may well snuff him anyway, just to play it safe. So the Newmans decide to kill Karl, with the help of their neighbor Chris Hood, who is himself something of a hood—a white Hawk. They discover that Karl likes to go fishing up in the Maine woods, and go up there to wait for him. Getting up in the woods, loading their guns, reviewing their plans, Aaron starts to change, to "grow up," to become what society thinks of as a "man":

"You seem better, Aaron" [Janet says].
"How so?"
"Less—what?—ambivalent, I guess. Less tied in a knot, more ready, looser."
"If rape is inevitable, lay back and enjoy it," Newman said.
"Meaning?"
"Meaning I'm committed. It's too late to agonize. I'm scared, but I'm not uncertain, you know."
"I guess so."
"You're kind of nice yourself," he said.
"Like what?"
"Like not so bossy, not so controlling. Softer, maybe."
"I just react to you," she said. "If you don't push at me, I don't have to push back."
Newman made a harsh, derisive sound. "Family that kills together stays together," he said. (162)

They continue the discussion a ways down the trail, after Chris Hood has been killed and they've taken out one of Karl's men:

"You really mean that," Newman said, "about being tough because you had me to back you up?"
"Yes."
"I never fully got that sense, or the sense that you were aware of it."
"I don't know why," she said. "It seems perfectly clear."
"But you're always so manage-y. You're so..." He stopped and stared out at the rain-soaked trail beyond his screen of white-pine boughs, "so separate. You never seem at all dependent."
"Because I don't hold your hand or lean on your arm or run on about how much I need you?"
"Some of that wouldn't hurt," he said.
"It's not the way I am."

"Why not?"

"I suppose it has something to do with fear, fear that if I'm dependent on anything or anyone I can't control my life. It's a control issue, as they say at the consciousness groups."

"You can control me," he said.

"That scares me too. It's like the old Groucho Marx joke. I wouldn't want to depend on anyone I can control."

"Would you be more affectionate if you couldn't control me?"

"Maybe."

"But if you couldn't control me, wouldn't that scare you and make you hostile?"

"Maybe."

"Jesus Christ," he said. (197-98)

[2]That Spenser's emotional dependence on Susan is largely autobiographical is clear from Parker's interview remarks to Maria Karagianis: "If you want a key point in my life, it was 1950 at the freshman dance, when I met Joan Hall. She is the central metaphor for existence. So that if it's good for her, it's good, and if it's bad for her, it's bad, and if it takes me away from her, it's bad, and if it takes me close to her, it's good. It makes life much simpler" (1).

[3]*Playmates* is a tired playback of *Mortal Stakes* with none of the complex identifications Parker set up in that earlier novel between the squeezed athlete and Spenser himself. Parker returns to the attacks on academia of his first novel, but not even this seems deeply felt (he has, in any case, been out of academia for 15 years: the wounds have largely healed). *Stardust* is a story about protecting a woman who doesn't want Spenser to protect her and disappears, but the woman is more like Candy Sloan of *A Savage Place* than Rachel Wallace in *Looking for Rachel Wallace*—not a feminist, not a "new woman," dependent for self-esteem on the approval of men she despises—and Spenser never allows himself to become emotionally invested in her as he does in the earlier novels. He goes through the motions of finding the father who tried to murder her and bundling her off to his Henry David Thoreau cabin in Maine to recover from her ordeal; but he has become a Spenser-machine, something like the Hawk who, Spenser thinks, never feels anything.

## Part Two

*Chapter Five: From* First Blood *to* First Blood

[1]A very good case could be made for Barth's sensitivity to the very same issues of masculine redemption-through-surrender that I am going to be showing Morrell exploring, especially in a novel like *Giles Goat-Boy* written in Barth's early 30s. This is not the case Morrell himself made for the novel in his dissertation, where he read the ending of *Giles* in terms of the generic expectations aroused by tragedy:

Tragic heroes have tragic flaws, and his [George Giles's] is a trait of character we have seen before in Barth's fiction: the passionate urge to know. It gives to Giles his chance for glory and also brings about his downfall, because, although the unexamined life for him is not worth living, his examined life is not capable of being lived. And thus to date [up through *Chimera* in 1972] this book is Barth's most optimistic, and that because it is mystical or perhaps "optimystic": a person with the proper attributes can, if he tries desperately hard, achieve ultimate knowledge. Thus too the book is pessimistic, though it does not approach the pessimism of an earlier book like *The End of the Road*, or even *The Sot-Weed Factor*. Ebenezer Cooke learns something of what Giles learns, that he is doomed to fail, that things never work out as hoped, that the best he can do is try to atone for his past mistakes. But Eben never has any compensation for his knowledge, no joy to offset his pain and sorrow. Giles does. That instant of illumination seems worth all that comes after. Hence the reader feels both elated and depressed by Giles's extra-brilliant rhetoric as he foresees his destruction in the lightning on the hilltop—which is how the reader ought to feel at the consummation of a tragedy. Yet the reader is elated and depressed in no common wise. His emotions are caused not only by sympathy for Giles but as well because the reader has seen how high a person can go and because he knows the odds are he himself will never get that high. (79)

Morrell's academic depersonalization of his own response to *Giles Goat-Boy* as something happening to "the reader" (who is both generically and factually a "he"), along with the emotional charge he just barely manages to conceal in his academic rhetoric, suggests to me that Morrell is identifying strongly with George Giles at this point—that he too longs for illumination, and mourns with George the dissipation of that revelatory moment into decline, the ordinary falling off of triumph and success. I think Barth too, at this point in his life, may be mourning George's decline; but he is closer to George's own tragic view of life, which Barth will settle into more calmly in his later novels (beginning in *LETTERS* in 1979), than Morrell. One fairly trivial way of explaining this is that Morrell is still, at this writing, a young man: determinedly optimistic himself, ambitious, bent on fame and fortune (which he has since achieved, and found to be empty), and wants George Giles's story to end at its heroic climax in his early 20s—doesn't want Barth to add the posttape in which George recounts the next (and last) decade of his life, with its disappointments, disillusionments, failures, resignations.

A less trivial way of saying the same thing is that Morrell has not yet worked out his morass of hope and despair and determination and fear, his complex of optimism and pessimism, in his own novels. George Giles at the end of Barth's novel is not so very different from Saul Grisman at the end of Morrell's *Brotherhood of the Rose*, for example: melancholy, maybe even a little bitter at how far he has fallen from the height of his glory, but also increasingly able to recognize that his fall was, as the title of the concluding chapter indicates, a redemption. As I read both *Giles* and *Brotherhood*, the "instant of illumination" is not "worth all that comes after," i.e., all the painful compromises of ordinariness; it is only valuable as a transformative, therapeutic *pathway* to what comes after, the extraordinary acceptance of ordinary life, which is what truly does have human value. George's heroism lies partly in the courage he summons to undergo symbolic death and rebirth (Saul doesn't; he just kills his foster father); but that transformation is no end in itself. It is a catalytic gateway to ordinary, post-patriarchal manhood. Morrell seems close to this realization when he returns to Saul in *The Fraternity of the Stone*; Barth likewise, when he returns to Ambrose Mensch from *Lost in the Funhouse* in *LETTERS*. But neither writer seems willing to embrace that deprogrammed state as a positive ideal; for both it feels like lying fallow, resting up for the next heroic enterprise, a "loss" of masculine self that can only be justified on the grounds that it may be put to good use later.

*Giles Goat-Boy* has been a critical favorite of mine since I wrote my M.A. thesis on it in 1975: see my book on the novel, my discussion of it at the end of *American Apocalypses* (226-32), and my article on it in relation to Wolfgang Iser and Bernard Bergonzi.

[2]It is at least open to question whether Morrell's fourth novel with a the-something-of-the-something title, *The Covenant of the Flame* (1991), is part of the series—whether it makes the trilogy into a tetralogy. It does share with the previous novels a plot revolving around fanatically militant religious organizations at war with one another, but none of the characters from the previous novels carries over. It is also unusual among Morrell's novels in its creation of a female protagonist, Tess Drake, and its total lack of dead fathers and rankling resentment over abandonment and betrayal.

[3]It is interesting also that the name he chose for his hero was inspired by a French poet who was one of the first to transform the social status of being "disaffected" into a badge of bohemian honor, Arthur Rimbaud. Morrell describes the process of naming Rambo in the *Playboy* article: "One of my graduate school languages was French, and on an autumn afternoon, as I read a course assignment, I was struck by the difference between the look and the pronunciation of the name of the author I was reading, Rimbaud. An hour later, my wife came home from buying groceries. She mentioned she'd bought some apples of a type she'd never heard about before, Rambo. A French author's name and the name of an apple collided, and I recognized the sound of force" (134).

[4]At Columbia, Lawrence Turman gave the movie to Richard Brooks to direct; Brooks liked the story but didn't like the stereotyped sheriff, and wrote 115 pages of a screenplay based on his vision of the story. He never finished it, but planned to end it with Rambo surrendering and being killed by an unidentified shooter in the sheriff's force. Brooks, a Marine veteran, wanted to explore changing attitudes toward American soldiers—much as the film that was finally produced did. He had the screenplay open with Rambo coming into town on Memorial Day, with shots of the townspeople laying wreaths on graves. "And then Rambo comes into town," Brooks told Pat Broeske. "And the townspeople who are honoring the men who fought in World War II hate him, because he was one of those who fought in Vietnam" (33). Brooks wanted Lee Marvin or Burt Lancaster for the sheriff, but never had a particular actor in mind for Rambo. According to Brooks, Columbia waffled on the project,

expecting the war to be over any day, worrying about the American public's reaction to it, and when they finally wanted him to do it, he no longer wanted to.

The rights were then sold to Warners, who tried to get Robert de Niro and Clint Eastwood interested in it—de Niro, of course, later starred in *The Deer Hunter*, Eastwood in the Grenada-Korea picture *Heartbreak Ridge*. It was finally given to Martin Ritt, a pacifist who wanted to blame the military for what happened to Rambo: Colonel Trautman was going to be the true villain of the piece. He wanted Paul Newman to play Rambo, but never got a commitment. "I can never condone murder," Ritt told Pat Broeske. "So I cannot think of Rambo as a hero. I saw him as a poor, unfortunate guy who was put upon—and who had been taught to use extraordinary gifts in a destructive way" (33).

The project next went to Sydney Pollack, who wanted to cast Steve McQueen as Rambo and Lancaster as Sheriff Teasle. He was concerned that the theme was "too dark," but "What I liked about the project was that it says, 'You can go to the brink of madness and then recover from it'—and you can't. In many ways I thought it was a powerful investigation into what a war mentality can create.... And I remember thinking that the book was something of a cheat.... That it was finally there more as an excuse for violence rather than to explore what made the violence happen" (33). This "cheat" is, of course, how the movie's (and the novel's) detractors have seen it: more violence. Certainly that's probably a big part of its incredible success.

In 1975, Martin Bregman started working on the movie, with Al Pacino as Rambo and David Rabe writing the script. Pacino eventually backed out of the project, but not before Rabe had written a script with Trautman and Teasle combined as a kind of composite repressive father-figure and a maniacal Rambo. "People would have understood the character," Rabe told Broeske, "but they wouldn't have had empathy for him. There is a kind of violence that excites an audience and makes them feel that it's a lot of fun. Mine was not" (36). Rabe's Rambo would not, he says, have become a pop hero.

The movie took its first significant step toward actual production in 1977, when producer William Sackheim got involved. Sackheim and Michael Kozoll, who later co-created *Hill Street Blues* for television, wrote the script that was ultimately produced, with later revisions by Larry Gross, David Giler, and, most significantly, Sylvester Stallone, who shares the script credit with Sackheim and Kozoll. Sackheim and Kozoll saw Rambo and Teasle as doomed characters who were "made for each other" (36), a line from the end of the script that was later cut. John Frankenheimer was going to direct, Brad Davis was cast as Rambo (after considering Powers Boothe, Michael Douglas, and Nick Nolte), financing was available from Cinema Group, and Rambo—the first time this had been proposed in the film's Hollywood wanderings—was going to live. They weren't thinking of a sequel at that point, according to Carter de Haven, who was producing. "We wanted him to come out of that building knowing there was a place for him" (36). But then the film's distributor, Filmways, was taken over by Orion, and *First Blood* was killed.

Andrew Vajna and Mario Kassar bought the rights both to the film and to the Sackheim/Kozoll script as their first project for their new production company, Carolco. Vajna and Kassar had been successful distributors in the Orient, and sensed that, even if Americans didn't like the movie, it would sell well abroad. Besides, Vajna told Pat Broeske, "Our whole thought process, at the time, was that the Vietnam Era was not as unpopular as it had been for the past 10 years. We thought there might be a place for the movie—and the character" (36). They were also the first ones to think of Stallone, who by 1981 had really only had one hit, *Rocky*, and was perceived as being on a downward slope. Stallone also revised the Sackheim/Kozoll script, adding a long monologue at the end where Rambo cries out his anguish. It was, David Giler remembers, something like 18 pages long in Stallone's first version; Giler cut it down to one. Larry Gross wanted Rambo to die—he wanted more tragedy in the piece—and in fact this question wasn't settled until a very late stage in the production. Trial audiences were shown two versions, one with Rambo living, one with him dying, and they were divided 50-50. In the end the production team decided to let him live—and added hundreds of millions of dollars to Rambo revenues.

⁵Stallone, Vajna told Pat Broeske, "was the No. 1 choice. Because in a way, this was a kind of Rocky picture—although nobody saw it that way except perhaps Mario and me. This was an underdog who was mistreated and mishandled and was fighting for the right to survive" (36).

⁶The song is written in Cm, which the lyrics and Dan Hill's voice intensify at the end, and passes through B-flat, Ab, G, and C, which the horns and strings and pastoral photography intensify at the beginning. Significantly enough, the same melodic theme will be rendered symphonically in *Rambo: First Blood Part II* as heroic action music, most of the cries and whimpers gone. (Not all; the mournful strains of the end of *First Blood* sound briefly in the sequel when Rambo briefly recaps the events of the earlier movie for Co, his native contact and fleeting love interest, played by Julia Nickson.)

⁷We don't know what year it is, and in fact never do find out; all we learn is that Rambo has been back for seven years. In *Rambo: First Blood Part II* we are read to from Rambo's file: "Rambo, John J., born 7/6/47...joined the Army 8/6/64, accepted Special Forces specialization, black weapons, cross-trained as medic, helicopter and language qualified, fifty-nine confirmed kills, two Silver Stars, four Bronze, four Purple Hearts, Distinguished Service Cross, and Medal of Honor." If he joined the Army in August of 1964, he would not have arrived in Vietnam until 1965, which would make it impossible for him to have been back for seven years in 1972, the year the novel was released. (And in any case in the novel he had only been back six months.) A reasonable guess is that he kept returning to Vietnam right up till the last year of U.S. involvement, 1974, which would set the movie in 1981, the year it was filmed. It is, perhaps, strange that Rambo should just be looking his good buddy up now, seven years after he returned from Vietnam; but that is one of the adjustments the producers had to make as a result of the movie's ten-year production process.

## Chapter Six: The Hurt, Betrayed Son

[1] Visually the scene is striking: the helicopter circles nervously overhead, first trying to land, then receiving the order to abort and playing out conflicting responses to the order (Trautman orders the pilot to land anyway but is countermanded by Murdock's man in the back of the chopper, who pulls a gun on Trautman and warns him not to be a hero); 30 or 40 feet below, at the vortex of its tight circles, stands an obedient and suppliant Rambo, looking about six inches tall, the good little boy who did what he heard his daddy tell him to do and now wants to be rewarded with love, or at least with rescue. He holds an exhausted POW at his side; Vietnamese soldiers are advancing on him, firing on him with Kalashnikovs. The camera angles make us first identify with the father on high, fleshed forth in the metal body of the helicopter thirty feet up and the three men torn by internal conflicts over the treacherously cold voice in their ears; then with Rambo down on the ground, as the chopper pulls away and the Vietnamese troops close in on him.

[2] A more recent image-parallel to Stallone than Davy Crockett, as he walks down the road behind the opening credits, is in fact Bill Bixby as David Banner in the TV series *The Incredible Hulk*—and that hero's radiation-caused transformation into a raging green-skinned monster who is, finally, *nice*, a good guy, is entirely congruent with the *First Blood* movie image of Rambo. Significantly enough, Spenser identifies with the Incredible Hulk in *Valediction* (74), when he has been abandoned by Susan. It is an attractive image for the macho loner: the "nothing kid" who, when pushed hard enough by external circumstances, when pushed to the edge of his tolerance, is suddenly transformed into a violent monster whose violent powers have been *conditioned* by society (radiation, Special Forces training) but are *channeled* by the macho hero into a force for good. The movie Rambo doesn't actually get a chance to do much good in this first episode, of course (and it is largely an ideological question whether what he does in the second and third episodes is good); but he is so clearly a *good person*, a nice guy in a bad situation, that our hearts go out to him.

[3] One of the contemporary American popular writers who know this best is Stephen King—not only in his horror fiction but in his wonderful critical book on horror, *Danse Macabre*. I was, in fact, sorely tempted to include a discussion of King's novels in this book, but, for reasons of economy, in the end didn't. Next time. But I can't forebear pointing out here that, in the King novel I take to be his most explicitly emancipatory, *Firestarter*, he creates a Rambo-like character called John Rainbird, who uses a carefully tailored story about a POW experience in Vietnam to gain the sympathy of the novel's eight-year-old heroine, Charlie McGee. King is on record as a major fan of Morrell's—he once taught a writing course based around *First Blood* and one other novel, saying that if apprentice writers could learn how to build and maintain suspense like Morrell, they'd be set for life—and it seems clear to me that in the "Blackout" chapter of *Firestarter* he is specifically (though maybe only unconsciously?) alluding to *First Blood*. Rainbird sounds like Rambo, of course; and both are Vietnam vets who were highly trained in warfare. Rainbird has made the

transition back to civilian life by becoming a hit man for a clandestine government agency called the Shop—very much like the heroes of Morrell's "Brotherhood" series. Still, though he does well in espionage, better than any of his employers, to the point of absolute contempt for them, he shares with Rambo a mystical fascination with dying, and is ultimately satisfied when Charlie kills him with her fire—he loves her, admires her, and her fire is a kind of psionic enactment of female sexuality, fiery passion—just as Rambo is satisfied by his violent death at Trautman's hands. Two odd similarities: both Rambo and Rainbird are named John, but Rambo didn't get a first name until 1982, when the movie was released, and *Firestarter* was published in 1980; and both Rambo and Rainbird are half-Indian, but Morrell didn't give Rambo Indian blood until the novelization of *Rambo: First Blood Part II*, in 1985. Could King have seen the Sackheim-Kozoll script before writing *Firestarter*, and could Morrell have borrowed Rambo's Indian blood from King's novel—or were both mere coincidences? Or were both writers tapping into a collective myth?

Note that, despite the moral differences between the two heroes—Rambo is driven, a man doing his best in a bad situation, while Rainbird is devious, evil, a man in the service of paternal repression—both represent for their creators deadends to a certain programmed form of masculinity who therefore *must* die and be superseded by a new generation with a new potential for emancipation. The new "generation" in Rambo's case may well be Stallone's Rambo ten years later; in King's novel the new generation is more obvious: it is little Charlie McGee, the pyrokinetic girl who transforms the evil accident that programs her genetically into liberating empowerment.

It's also worth noting that King, like Morrell, cannot remember his father: Don King left his wife and children when little Stevie was two. (He discusses his fatherlessness in chapter four of *Danse Macabre*, "An Annoying Autobiographical Pause." I recommend *Danse Macabre*, by the way, as an absolutely delightful romp through not only horror but popular culture, based on much the same premise about repression and release as Fiedler's *What Was Literature?* but with a good deal less vestigial elitism.)

[4]There is no full-scale biography of Stallone; I take this biographical information from St. Pierre's brief pictorial life.

[5]I should note that Jerry Goldsmith's music contributes enormously to the sense I get of Rambo's emotional vulnerability. Stallone doesn't do it all—although it's also possible that Stallone's acting encourages me to feel the impact of Goldsmith's music as emotionally congruent. (It is also possible that I'm projecting my own feelings of vulnerability onto Stallone's acting and Goldsmith's music.) I want to draw particular attention to a recurring running bass line played by synthesized cellos, which first begins when Rambo turns back toward town in blatant defiance of Teasle's orders; then starts up again (after some fright chords while Rambo is breaking free of his captors) when he escapes the police station and jumps on the motorcycle; again when Teasle and Orval Kellerman and the deputies and Orval's dogs are chasing Rambo in the dark; again when the National Guard chase him into the mine; and finally, at half-tempo, when Rambo is plunging through the mine in search of a back way

Notes    283

out. The base line is modified throughout the movie, sometimes running in straight (hopeful) 4/4 time, sometimes stumbling into a torturous 10/8 or 14/8 time; sometimes modulating up a half-tone from the basic C-Bb-sus chord progression. But the base pattern seems to be something like this:

It sounds to me like the beating of a heart under stress, fibrillating perhaps—the heartbeat of fear, excited fear, the fear that follows great adventure, but it is not a heady excitement, a glorified, manly adventure, certainly not something Rambo enjoys or wants to be involved in. Significantly, again, this melodic theme is reworked (often counterpointed with the similarly transformed "It's a Long Road" theme) in *Rambo: First Blood Part II* to signify precisely the heroic adventure that the earlier movie avoided.

Andrew Laszlo's photography, too, plays its part in the first movie's expression: his blending of stark colors with black shadows, the dark green of the Canadian evergreens and the misty gray of dusk; the orange of Rambo's body illuminated by the torch in the mine and the blackness around him, the cold blue of his body against the blackness as he drops his torch and climbs up the ladder out of the mine.

*Chapter Seven: Surrender*

¹For a good discussion of this repressed desire for passivity in patriarchally programmed men, see Herb Goldberg's chapter "Sleeping is Feminine" in *The New Male*. Goldberg lists eight related aspects of this masculine resistance to "healing, recuperative, life- and health-sustaining attitudes and processes" (35):

1) Emotional expression is feminine.
2) Giving in to pain is feminine.
3) Asking for help is feminine.
4) Alcohol abstinence is feminine.
5) Self-care is feminine.
6) Dependency is feminine.
7) Touching is feminine. (35-38)

And conversely:

1) The less sleep I need,
2) The more pain I can take,
3) The more alcohol I can hold,
4) The less I concern myself with what I eat,
5) The more I control and repress my emotions,
6) The less attention I pay to myself physically, *the more masculine I am*. (38)

## 284   No Less a Man

[2]And in fact, though the mythic tenor of the movie makes this easy to miss, Rambo's familiarity with pain, frustration, weakness, and failure resurfaces in the second movie, not so much in the jungle or the camp as at the end, when he is making his patriotic speech to Trautman. Not only are his words far less macho and jingoistic than they seem on the surface—they are, after all, a plea for *love*, not emotionally frozen respect or recognition—but his voice cracks with hurt, and he is close to tears. Stallone will no longer let him sink through the hurt anger into the cleansing tears, this time (and in *Rambo III* the hurt anger never even surfaces); but the pain and the vulnerability are still there. Here is the exchange:

> Trautman: The war, everything that happened here may be wrong, but dammit, don't hate your country for it.
> Rambo: Hate! I'd die for it!
> Trautman: Then what is it you want?
> Rambo: I want what they [the POWs he saved] want, and every other guy who came over here and spilt his guts and gave everything he had—*once* for our country to love us as much as we love it. That's what I want.

[3]In the 1988 edition of the *TV Movies and Video Guide*, for example, Leonard Maltin sneers at the implausibility of the movie and then adds: "And a kewpie doll to anyone who can understand more than three words of Sly's final monologue" (318). Leonard, please send me my kewpie doll care of the publisher.

[4]There is a similar but I think diametrically opposed encounter with this PTSD imagery in Bobbie Ann Mason's wonderful novel *In Country*, which confronts the problems faced by the Vietnam vets from a triply distanced standpoint: Mason's 17-year-old protagonist Sam Hughes not only didn't go to Vietnam (like Morrell and me), she is young and female. Her father died in the war and her uncle, whom she lives with, is a vet who copes with the "hole" in his imagination with more "successful" self-control than the Rambo of *First Blood* can muster (with the kind of self-control Morrell gives Rambo in the third installment of the series):

> She felt the way Emmett must feel when he watched birds. It was as though the most ordinary thing had opened up into a thousand meanings. Emmett had told her of a Zen exercise for controlling the mind. It was a way of grabbing it and bringing it back every time it started to wander. She hadn't been interested at the time, but maybe, she thought now, when Emmett watched birds he was trying to keep his mind from wandering. That was like an old song, the Beatles singing "I'm fixing a hole where the rain gets in/And stops my mind from wandering." That was what Emmett was doing with his hole, trying to stop the rain. If he concentrated on something fascinating and thrilling, like birds soaring, the pain of his memories wouldn't come through. His mind would be full of birds. Just birds and no memories. Flight. (139)

His *conscious* mind: there's the rub. Concentrating on a replacement image controls the flood of traumatizing memories through the hole (between conscious and unconscious?) but it doesn't plug it, and it doesn't defuse the memories themselves. The birds and the Beatles are a stopgap, not a solution. Interestingly, Mason's protagonist becomes obsessed with Vietnam in the summer of 1984, after the release of Springsteen's *Born in the U.S.A.*, and lyrics and tunes off the album keep playing on the radio all through the novel, from its epigraph ("Ten years burning down the road / Nowhere to run ain't got nowhere to go") to its conclusion at the Vietnam Veterans Memorial in Washington, D.C., which Sam encounters with Springsteen's album clutched like a talisman in her hand.

## Part Three

### Chapter Eight: The Dark Street

[1] For a good discussion of Springsteen's politics in the context of popular music, see John Street's *Rebel Rock*, esp. 194-96. Simon Frith's *Sound Effects* is another useful study of "youth, leisure, and the politics of rock 'n' roll" (his subtitle), but one that I find disagreeably tainted with an elitist distaste for his subject matter. Lipsitz's chapter on rock music (99ff) is another excellent treatment of the political thrust of rock; see esp. 104-07 for a persuasive critique of Frith, and 35 and 105-06 for discussions of Springsteen's politics.

[2] And Springsteen tells Dave Marsh that he was writing out of a deeply felt emotion, here, out of his gut: "The *Nebraska* record sounds a lot like me, in the sense of the feeling. I don't mean in the particular details of the stories, but the emotional feeling feels a lot like my childhood felt to me, a lot of the people I grew up with, the tone.... The whole thing is, when you tell a story, a story is only good if it's your story in some fashion. Even *Nebraska*, which is extreme emotionally, the thing that makes it real is knowing what that feels like. In a funny way I feel it's my most personal album" (*Glory* 148). I would guess, in fact, that it feels not only like his childhood, but like his present: like the desolation he feels when he lets something go, lets his defenses go, lets the heady sound of "Born to Run" go. You hope there's something beyond that, some new meaning, some new joy—but what if there isn't? What if this is it?

[3] Dave Marsh reports Springsteen's feelings from that time, and his feelings now, in *Glory Days*:

"I throw out almost everything I ever own," he'd told *Melody Maker*'s Ray Coleman during his first visit to England [on the "Born to Run" tour]. "I don't believe in collecting anything. The less you have to lose, the better you are, because the more chances you'll take. The more you've got, the worse off you get." And Bruce's philosophy applied to a lot more than houses. When his friend George Theiss, the lead vocalist of their first band, the Castiles, got married in 1969, Bruce told him flat out, "Man, you'll never make it now."

It was an icy comment, but in those days Bruce could be equally cold about himself. "You know, you have to be self-contained," he proclaimed in the mid-1970s.

"That way you don't get pushed around. It depends on what you need. I eat loneliness, man. I feed off it. I live on a lotta different levels, y'know, because I've learned to cope with people, which is—be cool all the time. I can roll with the punches. It's a way of getting along."

That idea helped make Bruce self-sufficient in his 20s. But he was entering his 30s now, and some of his dogmatism seemed dubious, even to himself. Unlike Clarence, his shyness of marriage applied exclusively to himself. But there were still blocks and barricades about the possibility of domesticity in his life, and he'd put them there himself.

The contrast with the ideals of his concerts and songs was unmissable. Even Bruce knew that.

"All my houses seem to have been way stations," he said many months later. "Which is funny, because the things that I admire and the things that mean a lot to me all have to do with roots and home, and myself, personally, I'm the opposite. I'm very rootless in that sense. I never attach myself to any place that I am.

"I always felt most at home when I was like in the car or on the road, which is, I guess, why I always wrote about it. I was very distant from my family for quite a while in my early twenties. Not with any animosity; I just had to feel loose. Independence always meant a lot to me. I had to feel I could go anywhere, anytime, in order to get my particular job done. And that's basically the way I've always lived." (*Glory Days* 83-84)

[4]His only passing (and disguised) reference to the lawsuit in his music, in fact, comes in a single that he released in 1980, on the B side of "Hungry Heart" (*The River*), "Held Up Without A Gun":

> Some damn fool with a guitar, watch him on the street;
> Ain't got nowhere to go, ain't got nothing to eat.
> Man with a cigar says, "Sign here son."
> Held up without a gun, held up without a gun.

The implication is that Mike Appel robbed him by getting him to sign (on the hood of a car) an exploitative contract.

[5]See his remarks to Dave Marsh:

"I know this is idealistic," he once said, "but part of the idea our band had from the beginning was that you did not have to lose your connection to the people you write for. I don't believe that fame or success means that you lose that connection, and I don't believe that makin' more money means you lose it. That's not what separates people. What separates people are things that are in their heart. So I just can never surrender to that idea. Because I know that before I started playing, I was alone. And one of the reasons I picked up the guitar was that I wanted to be part of something. And I practiced and I studied and I worked real hard to do that, and I ain't about to give it up now."

More than that, maintaining his connections was a form of self-protection. "One of the things that was always on my mind to do was to maintain connections with the people I'd grown up with, and the sense of the community where I came from," Bruce remarked a couple of years later. "That's why I stayed in New Jersey. The danger of fame is in *forgetting*, or being distracted. You see it happen to so many people...The type of fame Elvis had, and that I think Michael Jackson has, the pressure of it, and the isolation that it seems to require, has gotta be really painful. I wasn't gonna let that happen to me. I wasn't gonna get to a place where I said, 'I can't go in here. I can't go to this bar. I can't go outside'." The only sure way—the only way at all—to keep things in perspective was to keep a visceral connection with everyone else. (*Glory Days* 75)

⁶As Dave Marsh comments in *Born to Run*: "The weirdest anomaly of success is that it requires compromises never demanded of failure. It isn't just the minor infringements on one's humanity—such as signing autographs at meals, which reduces the very act of eating to a promotional event. It's also the expectations, and the possibility, that one will do *anything* to keep from losing what's been gained. And this, of course, is antithetical to the rock and roll dream, which says that the only way to possess anything of true importance is to risk losing all" (201).

See also Springsteen's uneasy exploration of the rift between image and person on *Lucky Town*, in "Local Hero":

> I was driving through my hometown
> I was just kinda killin' time
> When I seen a face staring out of a black velvet painting
> From the window of the five and dime

It's Bruce, and it isn't; it's a local hero—"he used to live here for a while"—and thus both the "Boss" (a nickname Springsteen hates) and a dim analogue of the boy who used to live there. In the rest of the song Springsteen retraces his steps into the bitter trap of herohood:

> There's a big town 'cross the whiskey line
> And if we turn the right cards up
> They make us boss the devil pays off
> And them folks that are real hard up
> They get their local hero...

⁷Springsteen reflects this oscillation in his chord progressions as well, slipping in the soft first quatrains from the tentative resolve of a straight G major triad into the hesitations of C chords over a G base, the G base at once providing a continuity of emotion and taking the edge off the C chord (as if to say "Maybe—maybe not"), and then letting the chord changes whip loose in the second quatrains, slamming from G to C and then from G to Em and finally, on the refrain, to a solid D major triad that underlines the one thing the speaker is positive of: "There's a darkness on the edge of town."

⁸Springsteen released another bleak Vietnam song on the B side of his "Born in the U.S.A." single, "Shut Out the Light," which points ahead most strongly, in fact, to the dark personal songs on *Lucky Town* (1992) eight years later. Johnson Linnier lies awake at night, staring at the ceiling, unable to move

his hands, unable to feel anything when his wife wants to make love; "He stares across the lights of the city and dreams of where he's been."

'This connection between Springsteen's weary, wandering vet and Morrell's and Stallone's is something that Springsteen's devotees have been eager to deny: witness Dave Marsh saying, in the passage I quoted earlier, that Springsteen was no Rambo. He also insists that Springsteen is no Stallone:

> Comparisons between Springsteen and Stallone were easy; they were bandied about everywhere, from casual conversations to the editorial page of the *Chicago Tribune*. The discrepancies were less instructive, given that Stallone's Rocky and Rambo were such obvious jingoistic stooges, with no depth, no humanity, and, in the end, a following that lasted only as long as the thrills were as fresh as the rivulets of stage blood that fueled them. If there was any purpose in comparing Springsteen to such brainless trash, it was primarily because *Rocky IV* and *Rambo* pointed up how completely the political and cultural right dominated all attempts to define "American" qualities, which suggests something of what Springsteen risked by daring to offer a separate vision. (*Glory Days* 362)

The first thing to say about this is that Marsh is obviously right about the cultural dominance of the right during the Reagan presidency, and also, perhaps, about *Rocky IV* and *Rambo: First Blood Part II*, both of which came out during the heyday of Springsteen's "Born in the U.S.A." tour. But he's wrong about there being no other reason to compare Springsteen and Stallone than to list their differences. In the first place, judging Stallone's artistry as a writer and actor on the basis of his overly mythologized sequels to *Rocky* and *First Blood* is very much like judging Springsteen's artistry as a writer and singer on the basis of his overly mythologized *Born in the U.S.A.* Say what you want, that record, too, had a jingoistic veneer that appealed strongly to the American political and cultural right. Just a veneer, just things like yelling the chorus of "Born in the U.S.A." with passionate abandon; but the veneer is all Marsh is reacting to in Stallone as well. The myth. The public image of Rocky and Rambo—which really isn't all that different from the public image of Springsteen in 1984 and 1985. The real difference, at this level, is that Marsh has been a fan and friend of Springsteen's since 1974, and sees past the public image, but has never been a fan or friend of Stallone's, and so sees only the myth.

At a deeper level—the level I insisted on in part two—it should be obvious that Stallone's characters do have depth and humanity (and that he conveys them with a subtle artistry that the public often misses), and that the depth of his characters' humanity lies precisely in a profound personal confrontation with the darkness of weakness and failure and despair that Springsteen has explored so insistently in his music. I agree that this humanity is nowhere near as deep in the Rocky and Rambo sequels as it is in *Rocky* and *First Blood*; but then I would insist that Springsteen's humanity is nowhere near as deep on *Born in the U.S.A.* as it is on *Darkness* or *Nebraska*, either—and on both *Nebraska* and *Darkness* (as we've just seen) Springsteen, too, is drawn to exactly the same visions of explosive retributive violence as the Rambo of *First Blood*. And if I found the ideology of *Rambo: First Blood Part II* (and *Rambo III*) abhorrent, I also find the ideology of "You Can Look (But You Better Not Touch)" abhorrent. I happen to believe that Springsteen has found the nerve of his own fears more consistently than Stallone, and traces its contours, feels the pain, more bravely; but I don't think there's much justification for Marsh's simplistic polarization of the two, Springsteen on the left, Stallone on the right, Springsteen creating art, Stallone brainless trash.

[10] In concert Springsteen has worked variously, over the years, to underscore the bleak message of this song; during his *Human Touch/Lucky Town* tour in 1992-93 he began segueing into "Born in the U.S.A." out of a frighteningly harsh, almost savage rendition of "Souls of the Departed" (*Lucky Town*, 1992), complete with sounds from the L.A. riots (police sirens and radios), searchlights, and a Hendrix-inspired "Star Spangled Banner" that linked the two wars—Vietnam in "Born in the U.S.A." and the Persian Gulf in "Souls"—with the political repressions of the Reagan/Bush years. When I saw him in Atlanta in November, 1992, he used the sirens and searchlights and a raspy police radio to transform "57 Channels (And Nothing On)" into a similar indictment of the cult of wealth that typified and symbolized those years, the American upper classes' isolationist withdrawal into various empty forms of "home entertainment."

[11] In the 1987 BBC documentary on Springsteen from which I quoted earlier the interviewer asked him how many people he thought misunderstood "Born in the U.S.A." to be just a kind of patriotic, flag-waving song, and he replied:

It was interesting, because I read somewhere they did a high school survey, and they asked kids, "What was 'Born in the USA' about?" And they said, "Well, it's about my country." Well, that's pretty good, it's a good start, right? I mean, that *is* one of the things it's about, you know. But I think one of the problems that we have is that, it's not that people aren't taught to think, but they're not taught to think hard enough. I mean, "Born in the USA" is not ambiguous. All you've got to do is listen to the verses. If you don't listen to the verses, you're not going to get the whole song.... That song had an enormous amount of pride in it, pride in being an American, but what they missed was they missed the shameful part. I mean, the guy in that song—he's just proud he lived. He survived. I think that people felt that character's sense of pride and misinterpreted it, certainly in the spirit of the times, like, you know, "America, my country right or wrong," and all the bullshit that gets sold to you and thrown at you over the TV and in political campaigns, and with the whole manner of the Reagan presidency. And I realized at the time that that was okay. Because that what you do if somebody doesn't understand your song, is you keep singing your song. And you'll sing it again down the road, and somebody who didn't understand it before, they're gonna understand it then.

[12] On Sept. 19, 1984, four days before Springsteen's 35th birthday. For a more detailed discussion, see Marsh's *Glory Days* (254-66, also ff).

[13]Even as he has grown more articulate politically, in fact, Springsteen has continued to shy away from overt pronouncements on presidential politics. During the 1992 presidential campaign, for example, on his *Lucky Town/Human Touch* tour, he politicized his love ballad "If I Should Fall Behind" (*Lucky Town*) only obliquely, saying that neither Bush nor Perot seemed interested in helping others "stay in stride"; when I saw him in Atlanta, three weeks after the election, he dedicated the song to Bill Clinton, who he said is going to need a lot of help from all of us.

### Chapter Nine: Healing the Father

[1]For the slow version of "No Surrender," see the live album; for the acoustic version of "Born to Run," see the Springsteen *Video Anthology*.

[2]For an excellent masculist discussion of "the wisdom of the penis," and a persuasive argument that the term "impotence" is sexist, see Herb Goldberg's *The Hazards of Being Male*, chapter three.

[3]For an excellent, solidly researched and carefully reasoned masculist critique of this view of masculinity, see Joseph Pleck's *The Myth of Masculinity*.

[4]For a fuller discussion of this model, see my *Lardner* (22ff).

[5]Nor is everyone, for that matter, who calls herself a feminist or himself a masculist necessarily liberated. Indeed, as I suggested in my discussion of Parker in connection with *The Great Gatsby* and Judith Fetterley, most of the residual anger of both the women's and the men's movements stems from unliberation, from ongoing transferences from the little girl's anger at her withdrawn father to the grown woman's anger with "all men," or from the little boy's anger at the demanding mother to the grown man's anger with "feminists."

[6]It is, of course, not just Biblical but a patriarchal circle of fathers and sons: remember Laius and Oedipus.

### Chapter Ten: Displaced Mothers

[1]The reciprocal engenderment model I am fleshing out both here and in the father chapter incorporates, but I believe brings a larger social perspective to bear on, the "mother domination" theory of masculinity developed in the late nineteenth and early twentieth century (in order to engineer a remasculinization of liberal society) and recuperated by some early members of the profeminist men's movement in the 1970s (in order to defend against blanket feminist associations of masculinity with oppressive patriarchy). Joseph H. Pleck summarizes the argument:

The male child, the argument goes, perceives his mother and his predominantly female elementary school teachers as dominating and controlling. These relationships *do* in reality contain elements of domination and control, probably exacerbated by the restriction of women's opportunities to exercise power in most other areas. As a result, men feel a lifelong psychological need to free themselves from or prevent their domination by women. The argument is, in effect, that men oppress women as adults because they experienced women as oppressing them as children.

> According to this analysis, the process operates in a vicious circle. In each generation, adult men restrict women from having power in almost all domains of social life except child-rearing. As a result, male children feel powerless and dominated, grow up needing to restrict women's power, and thus the cycle repeats itself. It follows from this analysis that the way to break the vicious circle is to make it possible for women to exercise power outside of parenting and parent-like roles and to get men to do their half share of parenting. (419)

Pleck admits that this model has some basis in fact, but "has been quite overworked. This theory holds women themselves, rather than men, ultimately responsible for the oppression of women—in William Ryan's phrase, 'blaming the victim' of oppression for her own oppression" (420).

While agreeing with Pleck that the theory has often been "overworked" in the sense of being used defensively by men who feel emotionally threatened by feminist charges of sexism and oppression, I find his reading overcautious. There is no reason to equate the vicious circle of patriarchal engenderment with "blaming the victim," for example: if it is a vicious circle prescribed by patriarchal ideology, then no one is to blame, neither the mother nor the son (and, from a feminist point of view, neither the father nor the daughter). The reciprocally self-reproducing engenderment system is to blame. It programs all of us to perpetuate the oppressive system. The model has been used by defensive men, but it is not an inherently defensive model.

Indeed my sense is that Pleck's overcautiousness is itself the flip side of defensiveness, a way of bending over backwards so as not to offend feminists, not to seem to be accusing women of anything, *not* blaming the mother—an injunction that, as I will be suggesting in a few pages, is part of our patriarchal programming, part of the patriarchal double bind. Men's accusations of women (the mothers did this to us!) and of ourselves (we did this to ourselves!) are parallel ideological/emotional/somatic straitjackets that we must learn to take off. I think my model can help both to explain how this happens—we are taught by our fathers to blame our mothers and by our mothers to blame ourselves (and our fathers)—and also to show us how to remove the straitjacket.

[2] For a useful counterpoint to my "straight" reading of Springsteen, see Martha Nell Smith's persuasive "gay" reading of him in *SAQ*—a reading that underscores the powerful homoerotic movement of Springsteen's imagination. A student of mine at the University of Mississippi, Doug Branch, is also working on a dissertation on butch icons in American culture, and reads Springsteen in that tradition, along with James Dean, baseball players, and the actors in Lee jeans commercials.

[3] Part of this impression arises out of Springsteen's new band, especially his back-up singers, who sound more like a gospel choir at a black Baptist revival than rock singers: Bobby King, whom Springsteen introduces onstage as "the king of soul" and who serves as a kind of iconic replacement for Clarence Clemons; Cleopatra Kennedy, who used to sing back-up vocals for Diana Ross; Angel Rogers, who used to sing with Stevie Wonder and Paula Abdul; Carol Dennis, who sang with Dylan for years; and Gia Ciambotti from the Graces.

## 292  No Less a Man

With the addition of Crystal Taliafero on lead guitar, percussion, and sax (the Big Man's tiny female replacement on "Born to Run"), also back-up vocals, Springsteen has pushed his onstage sound toward gospel/soul in a big way; the old joke that there were more blacks onstage at a Springsteen concert than in the audience is four times truer now than it was when it was only Clarence Clemons up there. (The best source of information on Springsteen's band changes—and much more—is Bill Flanagan's interview/article in *Musician*.)

But Springsteen too works the crowd like a revival preacher, crooning over and over, piously, "Tonight I need your precious love, tonight I need your sacred love, tonight I need your precious love to lead me into the real world" during "Real World" (*Lucky Town*, 1992), and, prayerfully, down on his knees, "Have you ever felt so lonely? Have you ever felt so lost inside?" during "Just Another Roll of the Dice" (*Human Touch*, 1992). "Light of Day," a song he wrote for Paul Schrader's movie of the same name, has become a focal number for audience participation on the new tour, features a shouted preacherly harangue, almost an altar call, in which Springsteen (sounding more than ever like a black Baptist preacher—or James Brown) asks his fans whether they know why he came tonight. The implicit answer is: to save our miserable souls (and I can't speak for others, but it feels a lot more efficacious to me than any church service I ever attended). As Springsteen grows more comfortable with the soteriological power of human spirituality, his role as Rock-n-Roll Messiah assumes more and more of the outward trappings of institutionalized Christianity, especially the more charismatic and socially marginal forms of it— indeed the very low-church forms, white and black, whose music (country and soul) converged to generate rock and roll in the first place. A useful introduction to the white low-church "backdrop to Bob Dylan," and thus to Springsteen as well, is Wilfrid Mellers' *A Darker Shade of Pale*.

[4]As he told Henke:

> Yeah, it started after I got back from the *River* tour. I'd had more success than I'd ever thought I'd have. We'd played around the world. And I thought, like, "Wow, this is it." And I decided, "Okay, I want to have a house." And I started to look for a house.
>
> I looked for two years. Couldn't find one. I've probably been in every house in the state of New Jersey—twice. Never bought a house. Figured I just couldn't find one I liked. And then I realized that it ain't that I can't *find* one, I couldn't *buy* one. I can find one, but I can't buy one. Damn! Why is that?
>
> And I started to pursue why that was. Why did I only feel good on the road? Why were all my characters in my songs in cars? I mean, when I was in my early twenties, I was, I was always sort of like "Hey, what I can put in this suitcase, that guitar case, that bus—that's all I need, now and forever." And I really believed it. And really lived it. Lived it for a long time. (41-42)

[5]Actually, just to show how subjective these readings of the "tone" or emotional charge of Springsteen's songs are, let me note that I just went back and listened to "Nebraska" again, after the experience of writing this chapter, of tracing Springsteen's growth from *Greetings* through *Nebraska* to *Tunnel of*

*Love*, and this time his voice no longer sounded flat and dead. It had a powerful, haunting tenderness to it, a feel of love and wonder, very much as on "Cautious Man." And this makes sense: even while Springsteen is exploring the extremes of his own fears, the deadening effect of isolation, the darkness of not being loved, he also feels a tenderness for the scared little boy inside of him that is feeling these things. Without that tenderness, without a deep, hidden, but powerful self-love, there could be no healing: Springsteen would *be* Charles Starkweather. Feeling like Charles Starkweather, he writes a song about emotional deadness and discovers in that deadness new life, something that he finds he *cares* about, cherishes, wants to nourish. Bill Horton is Charles Starkweather with the courage to leave himself defenseless to what he's afraid of (not just restlessness but meanness, lovelessness); instead of protecting his fears by spreading death inside and out, he surrenders himself to life.

⁶Springsteen's guitar gives us some new chord voicings, too, that point tentatively ahead to victory, to homecoming. The song is written in G, and, like so many of the *Nebraska* songs, plays G off D (also Em and C); but now critical (transitional) D-chords have a new F# bass to fill them with wonder. (For example, Billy awakes from a terrible dream—the dream of "Downbound Train"—on C, then calls his wife's name on D/F#.) This D/F# sounds to me like the equivalent to the E/G# on "Born to Run," the song that "Cautious Man" most conspicuously overturns. Using the third as a bass note has the effect of suspending a chord, or making it sound suspended, charging it with reservations or misgivings. Where on "Born to Run" the E/G# qualifies the energy Springsteen is pouring into escape, as if to say, "Is this what you really want?", on "Cautious Man" the D/F# qualifies the vocal and harmonic caution with which he is holding back the flood of emotion, of awe and joy, as if to say, "Wait a minute, isn't there more to this than you're saying, aren't you stemming some kind of inner tide?"

⁷"Gloria's Eyes" undermines the macho posing most overtly, revealing the macho poseur's dread of the woman's otherness; in "Man's Job," too, all his "illusions slip away" as he watches his "girl" dance with another man (the scene of "I Wish I Were Blind" as well). "Real Man" redefines masculine courage as "the guts to give you all my love," which is close to the old chivalric cliche but actually edges just past it, into an awareness of just how terrified macho men are of their own emotions, of the vulnerability of falling in love. "Roll of the Dice" is pretty blindly macho, but interestingly enough the gambling image recurs in the next cut, "Real World"—"And we're goin' with the tumblin' dice"—in a context that explodes the macho front.

⁸He told James Henke:

She had a very sure eye for all my bullshit. She recognized it. She was able to call me on it. I had become a master manipulator. You know, "Oh, I'm going out of the house for a little while, and I'm going down..." I always had a way of moving off, moving away, moving back and creating distance. I avoided closeness, and I wouldn't lay my cards on the table. I had many ways of doing that particular dance, and I thought they were pretty sophisticated. But maybe they weren't. I was just doing what came naturally. And then when I hit the stage, it was just the opposite. I would throw myself forward, but it was okay because it was brief. Hey, that's why they call them one-night stands. It's like you're there, then *bang*! You're gone. I went out in '85 and talked a lot about community, but I wasn't a part of any community.

So when I got back to New York after the Amnesty tour in '88, I was kind of wandering and lost, and it was Patti's patience and her understanding that got me through. She's a real friend, and we have a real great friendship. And finally I said I've got to start dealing with this, I've got to take some baby steps. (44)

[9]The one, in fact, that introduces the woman whom Marlowe will marry in *Poodle Springs*, which Robert Parker finished for Chandler.

[10]But note also the connection with the "empty rooms" imagery from "Adam Raised a Cain" ("Daddy worked his whole life for nothing but the pain / Now he walks these empty rooms looking for something to blame") and "Independence Day" ("Now the rooms are all empty down at Frankie's joint / And the highway she's deserted clear down to Breaker's Point"), which is recapped strikingly, along with the "house on the hill" imagery from "My Father's House" and "The Mansion on the Hill," in "My Beautiful Reward," Springsteen's closing song on tour:

> From a house on a hill a sacred light shines
> I walk through these rooms but none of them are mine
> Down empty hallways I went from door to door
> Searching for my beautiful reward.

[11]Also, "Used Cars" is rhythmically more complex, switching from 4/4 time in the first bar to 2/4 in the middle bar and back to 4/4 in the last; "Book of Dreams" sticks with 4/4 throughout.

[12]Close to this explanation is Springsteen's own claim that his son Evan heard him singing "Pony Boy" to him in the womb, and "remembered" it after he was born—remembered it somatically rather than cognitively, in his body's relaxation response.

[13]On this relation, see especially Kristeva's "Place Names," in *Desire in Language*.

[14]As Alice Miller has argued forcefully, it is to this sort of guiltily repressed sexual feeling in the *parent* that any signs of infantile sexuality or the "Oedipus complex" must be attributed: if the son feels sexually attracted to his mother, it is because she unconsciously generated that sexual attraction in him; if the son feels a murderous hatred for his father, it is because he unconsciously generated that hatred in him. See *Thou Shalt Not Be Aware*, esp. "Oedipus: The 'Guilty' Victim."

[15]And this ad hoc "therapy" has in fact taken him a long way down the dark path. It is only recently, at the end of the 1980s, that he has turned to a professional therapist to help him past some blockages that his music couldn't negotiate: "The best thing I did was I got into therapy. That was really valuable. I crashed into myself and saw a lot of myself as I really was. And I questioned

all my motivations. Why am I writing what I'm writing? Why am I saying what I'm saying? Do I mean it? Am I bullshitting? Am I just trying to be the most popular guy in town? Do I need to be liked that much? I questioned everything I'd ever done, and it was good" (Henke 44).

*Conclusion*

[1] See also chapter five of Starhawk's later book *Dreaming the Dark*, on "Goddesses and Gods: The Landscape of Culture," which contains some of the most sensitive and insightful writing on male psychology that I've ever read.

[2] My colleague Sherrie Gradin asks, in her marginal comments to an earlier draft of this book: "But if a new transformation for males does take place, will it be necessary to 'steal' the boy?" I don't know. I take her to be asking whether the utopian transformation of all patriarchal engenderment—of both masculinity and femininity—might not render all parenting, including mothering, less destructive, so that both men and women would work together to raise boys and girls in harmonious, life-affirming ways, making it unnecessary for boys of a certain age to be raised by men in isolation from women (and for girls to be raised by women in isolation from men). I find this utopian vision attractive, and think it a goal worth striving for; but I also find some value in Bly's attempt to re-envision the "primitive" past in positive ways. The point about "stealing" the boys from their mothers is that it is not stealing at all, but a ritualistic drama staged by the men and the women to underscore the transfer of pedagogical responsibility from the women to the men: to dramatize the society's belief that boys should be raised by women until a certain age (around puberty, presumably) and by men after that time. I have grave reservations about this model of childrearing, since it seems to be just a more overt staging of Freud's Oedipus complex (present mother/absent father = preoedipal stage; present father/displaced mother = oedipal stage); but, given the destructive and almost unbreakable power of the patriarchal mother-son bond, I find it attractive as a transitional mode from the present childrearing schema to something like the utopian moment Sherrie seems to be projecting.

# Works Cited

Abbott, Franklin, ed. *New Men, New Minds: Breaking Male Tradition. How Today's Men are Changing the Traditional Rules of Masculinity.* Freedom, CA: Crossing P, 1987.

Althusser, Louis. "Ideology and Ideological State Apparatuses (Notes Toward an Investigation)." Trans. Ben Brewster. *Lenin and Philosophy and Other Essays.* London: New Left Books, 1969. 121-73.

Attali, Jacques. *Noise: The Political Economy of Music.* Trans. Brian Massumi. 1977. Minneapolis: U of Minnesota P, 1985.

Bakhtin, Mikhail. "Discourse in the Novel." Trans. Caryl Emerson and Michael Holquist. *The Dialogic Imagination: Four Essays.* Ed. Michael Holquist. Austin: U of Texas P, 1981. 259-422.

Balswick, Jack. *The Inexpressive Male.* Lexington, MA: Lexington Books, 1988.

Banner, Lois. "In Response to Douglas Robinson." *American Studies Association Newsletter* 11.3 (Sept. 1988): 7-6.

———. "Margaret Mead, Men's Studies, and Feminist Scholarship." *American Studies Association Newsletter* 11.1 (Mar. 1988): 2-6.

Bannister, Robert. "Gender and American Culture: The Masculinization of American Thought, 1910-1950s." Unpub. book manuscript.

Barth, John. *The End of the Road.* Garden City, NY: Doubleday, 1958.

———. *The Floating Opera.* New York: Appleton-Century-Crofts, 1956.

———. *Giles Goat-Boy.* Garden City, NY: Doubleday, 1966.

———. *LETTERS.* New York: Putnam, 1979.

———. *Lost in the Funhouse.* Garden City, NY: Doubleday, 1972.

———. *Sabbatical.* New York: Putnam, 1982.

———. *The Sot-Weed Factor.* Garden City, NY: Doubleday, 1960.

———. *Tidewater Tales.* New York: Putnam, 1987.

Berger, John. *Ways of Seeing.* Harmondsworth: Penguin, 1972.

Bingham, Dennis. *Masculinities, Male Spectatorship and Hollywood Stars.* New Brunswick: Rutgers UP, forthcoming.

Bleich, David. *Subjective Criticism.* Baltimore: Johns Hopkins UP, 1978.

Bly, Robert. *Iron John: A Book About Men.* Reading, MA: Addison-Wesley, 1990.

Boone, Joseph A., and Michael Cadden, eds. *Engendering Men: The Question of Male Feminist Criticism.* New York and London: Routledge, 1990.

Bouton, Jim. *Ball Four.* New York: Shector, 1970.

Brod, Harry, ed. *The Making of Masculinities: The New Men's Studies.* Boston: Allen & Unwin, 1987.

Broeske, Pat H. "The Curious Evolution of John Rambo." *Los Angeles Times/Calendar* 25 Oct. 1985: 31-38.

Campbell, Joseph. *The Hero With a Thousand Faces*. 1949. Princeton: Princeton UP, 1973.

―――. *Myths to Live By.* 1972. New York: Bantam, 1978.

Carnes, Mark C., and Clyde Griffen, eds. *Meanings for Manhood: Constructions of Masculinity in Victorian America*. Chicago: U of Chicago P, 1990.

Carrigan, Tim, Bob Connell, and John Lee. "Toward a New Sociology of Masculinity." *Theory and Society* 5.14 (Sept. 1985). Brod, ed., 63-102.

Cawelti, John G. *Adventure, Mystery, and Romance: Formula Stories as Art and Popular Culture*. Chicago: U of Chicago P, 1976.

―――. *Apostles of the Self-Made Man: Changing Concepts of Success in America*. Chicago: U of Chicago P, 1965.

Chodorow, Nancy. *The Reproduction of Mothering: Psychoanalysis and the Sociology of Gender*. Berkeley: U of California P, 1978.

Cohan, Stephen, and Ina Rae Hark, eds. *Screening the Male: Exploring Masculinities in Hollywood Cinemas*. New York: Routledge, forthcoming.

Cohen, Ed. *Talk on the Wilde Side: Toward a Genealogy of a Discourse on Male Sexualities*. New York: Routledge, 1993.

Coltrane, Scott. *Family Man: The Social Implications of Shared Domestic Labor*. New York: Oxford UP, forthcoming.

Crompton, Louis. "Byron and Male Love: The Classical Tradition." Brod, ed., 325-32.

Crowley, John W. "Howells, Stoddard, and Male Homosocial Attachment Victorian America." Brod, ed., 301-24.

de Mause, Lloyd, ed. *The History of Childhood*. New York: Psychohistory P, 1974.

Deleuze, Gilles, and Felix Guattari. *Anti-Oedipus*. Trans. Robert Hurley, Mark Seem, and Helen R. Lane. 1972. Minneapolis; U of Minnesota P, 1983.

Douglas, Ann. *The Feminization of America*. New York: Alfred A. Knopf, 1978.

DuPlessis, Rachel Blau. "For the Etruscans." *The New Feminist Criticism: Essays on Women, Literature, Theory*. Ed. Elaine Showalter: New York: Pantheon, 1985. 271-91.

―――. *Writing Beyond the Ending: Narrative Strategies of Twentieth-Century Women Writers*. Bloomington: Indiana UP, 1985.

Elshtain, Jean Bethke. *Women and War*. New York: Basic Books, 1987.

Emerson, Ralph Waldo. *The Journal and Miscellaneous Notebooks of Ralph Waldo Emerson*. Ed. William H. Gilman et al. Cambridge, MA: Harvard UP, 1960.

―――. "Self-Reliance." *Essays: First Series*, 43-90. Vol. 2 of Edward Waldo Emerson, ed., *The Compete Works of Ralph Waldo Emerson*. Boston: Houghton Mifflin, 1903.

Faludi, Susan. *Backlash: The Undeclared War on American Women*. 1991 rpt. New York: Anchor/Doubleday, 1992.

Farrell, Warren. *The Liberated Man*. New York: Bantam, 1975.

Feigen Fasteau, Marc. *The Male Machine.* New York: Dell, 1975.
Fetterley, Judith. *The Resisting Reader: A Feminist Approach to American Fiction.* Bloomington: Indiana UP, 1978.
Fiedler, Leslie. *What Was Literature?* New York: Simon & Schuster, 1982.
Filene, Peter. "The Secrets of Men's History." Brod, ed., 103-20.
Fish, Stanley. *Is There a Text In This Class? The Authority of Interpretive Communities.* Cambridge: Harvard UP, 1980.
Fitzgerald, F. Scott. *The Great Gatsby.* New York: Scribners, 1925.
Flanagan, Bill. "Ambition, Lies, and the Beautiful Reward: Bruce Springsteen's Family Values." *Musician* 169 (Nov. 1992): 58-76.
Flynn, Elizabeth A., and Patrocinio P. Schweickart, eds. *Gender and Reading: Essays on Readers, Texts, and Contexts.* Baltimore: Johns Hopkins UP, 1986.
Franklin, Clyde W., II. *The Changing Definition of Masculinity.* New York: Plenum, 1984.
Freud, Sigmund. *Civilization and Its Discontents.* Trans. James Strachey. 1930. New York: Norton, 1961.
———. *Jokes and Their Relation to the Unconscious.* Trans. James Strachey. 1905. New York: Norton, 1963.
———. *The Psychopathology of Everyday Life.* Trans. Alan Tyson. 1901. New York: Norton, 1965.
———. *Totem and Taboo.* Trans. James Strachey. 1913. New York: Norton, 1950.
Friedan, Betty. *The Second Stage.* New York: Summit Books, 1981.
Frith, Simon. *Sound Effects: Youth, Leisure, and the Politics of Rock 'n' Roll.* New York: Pantheon, 1981.
Frost, Robert. *Complete Poems of Robert Frost.* New York: Henry Holt, 1949.
Gambaccini, Peter. *Bruce Springsteen.* 1979. New York: Perigree/Putnam, 1985.
Gerson, Kathleen. *No Man's Land: Men's Changing Commitments to Family and Work.* New York: Basic Books, forthcoming.
Gilmore, David D. *Manhood in the Making: Cultural Concepts of Masculinity.* New Haven: Yale UP, 1990.
Gingold, Alfred. *Fire in the John: The Manly Man in the Age of Sissification.* New York: St. Martin's, 1991.
Goldberg, Herb. *The Hazards of Being Male: Surviving the Myth of Male Privilege.* 1976. New York: Signet, 1977.
———. *The Inner Male: Overcoming Roadblocks to Intimacy.* New York: NAL, 1987.
———. *The New Male: From Self-Destruction to Self-Care.* New York: Signet, 1980.
———. *The New Male-Female Relationship.* 1983. New York: Signet, 1984.
Goodman, A., and P. Walby. *A Book About Men.* London: Quartet, 1975.
Green, Martin. *The Adventurous Male: Chapters in the History of the White Male Mind.* College Park: Pennsylvania State UP, forthcoming.

Griffin, Susan. *Woman and Nature: The Roaring Inside Her*. 1978. New York: Harper & Row, 1980.
Griswold, Robert L. *Fatherhood in America: A History*. New York: Basic Books, forthcoming.
Heath, Stephen. *The Sexual Fix*. London: Macmillan, 1982.
Heller, Scott. "Scholars Debunk the Marlboro Man: Examining Stereotypes of Masculinity." *The Chronicle of Higher Education* 3 Feb. 1993: A6-8, A15.
Hirsch, E.D., Jr. *The Aims of Interpretation*. Chicago: U of Chicago P, 1976.
_____. *Validity in Interpretation*. New Haven: Yale UP, 1967.
Hogan, Dennis P. *Transitions and Social Change: The Early Lives of American Men*. New York: Academic P, 1981.
Holland, Norman. *5 Readers Reading*. New Haven: Yale UP, 1975.
_____. *Poems in Persons*. New York: Norton, 1973.
Horney, Karen. *The Neurotic Personality of Our Time*. 1937. New York: Norton, 1964.
_____. *Self-Analysis*. 1942. New York: Norton, 1968.
Hyrde, Richard. Dedicatory letter to Margaret More Roper, *A devout treatise vpon the Pater noster/ made fyrst in latyn by the moost famous doctour mayster Erasmus Roterodamus/ and tourned into englishe by a yong vertuous and well lerned gentylwoman of .xix. yere of age*. London: Thomas Berthelet, c. 1525. Rpt. in *Erasmus of Rotterdam: A Quincentennial Symposium*. Ed. Richard L. DeMolen. New York: Twayne, 1971. 97-104.
Jameson, Fredric. "Postmodernism and Consumer Society." *The Anti-Aesthetic: Essays on Postmodern Culture*. Ed. Hal Foster. Port Townsend, WA: Bay Press, 1983. 111-25.
_____. "Reification and Utopia in Mass Culture." *Social Text* 1 (1979).
Jardine, Alice, and Paul Smith, eds. *Men in Feminism*. New York: Methuen, 1987.
Jeffords, Susan. *The Remasculinization of America: Gender and the Vietnam War*. Bloomington: Indiana UP, 1989.
Kahn, J.H. *Job's Illness: Loss, Grief, Integration: A Psychological Interpretation*. New York: Pergamon P, 1975.
Karagianis, Maria. "The Parker Code." *The Boston Globe Magazine* 12 Apr. 1981: 1, 41-44.
Kaufman, Michael, ed. *Beyond Patriarchy: Essays by Men on Pleasure, Power, and Change*. Toronto: Oxford UP, 1987.
Keen, Sam. *Fire in the Belly: On Being a Man*. New York: Bantam, 1991.
Kimmel, Michael S. "The Contemporary 'Crisis' of Masculinity in Historical Perspective." Brod, ed., 121-54.
_____. *Manhood: The American Quest*. New York: Harper Collins, forthcoming.
Kimmel, Michael S., and Thomas E. Mosmiller, eds. *Against the Tide: Pro-Feminist Men in the United States, 1776-1990, A Documentary History*. Boston: Beacon P, 1992.
King, Stephen. *Danse Macabre*. Rev. ed. New York: Berkley Books, 1985.

———. *Firestarter*. 1980. New York: Signet, 1981.
Korda, Michael. *Male Chauvinism*. London: Coronet, 1972.
Kovic, Ron. *Born on the Fourth of July*. New York: McGraw-Hill, 1976.
Kristeva, Julia. "Place Names." *Desire in Language*. Ed. Leon Roudiez. Trans. Thomas Gora, Alice Jardine, and Leon Roudiez. New York: Columbia UP, 1980. 271-94.
Lacan, Jacques. *Speech and Language in Psychoanalysis*. Trans. Anthony Wilden. 1968. Baltimore: Johns Hopkins UP, 1981.
Lehman, Peter. *Running Scared: Masculinity and the Representation of the Male Body*. Philadelphia: Temple UP, forthcoming.
Lentricchia, Frank. *After the New Criticism*. Chicago: U of Chicago P, 1980.
———. *Criticism and Social Change*. Chicago: U of Chicago P, 1983.
———. *Ariel and the Police: Michel Foucault, William James, Wallace Stevens*. Madison: U of Wisconsin P, 1988.
———. "Andiamo!" *Critical Inquiry* 14 (Winter 1988): 407-13.
Leverenz, David. *Manhood and the American Renaissance*. Ithaca: Cornell UP, 1989.
Lipsitz, George. *Time Passages: Collective Memory and American Popular Culture*. Minneapolis: U of Minnesota P, 1990.
Lynch, Kate. *Springsteen: No Surrender*. 1984. New York: Bobcat Books, 1986.
Mailer, Norman. *The Prisoner of Sex*. Boston: Little, Brown, 1971.
Maltin, Leonard, ed. *TV Movies and Video Guide/1988 Edition*. Rev. ed. New York: Signet/NAL, 1987.
Mangan, J.A., and James Walvin, eds. *Manliness and Morality: Middle-Class Masculinity in Britain and America, 1800-1940*. New York: St. Martin's, 1987.
Marsh, Dave. *Born to Run: The Bruce Springsteen Story*. Rev. ed. New York: Dell, 1981.
———. *Glory Days: Bruce Springsteen in the 1980s*. New York: Pantheon/Random House, 1987.
Mason, Bobbie Ann. *In Country*. New York: Harper & Row, 1985.
May, Rollo. "Contributions of Existential Psychology." *Existence: A New Dimension in Psychiatry and Psychology*. Eds. Ernest Angel and Henri F. Ellenberger. New York: Basic Books, 1956. 37-91.
Mellers, Wilfrid. *A Darker Shade of Pale: A Backdrop to Bob Dylan*. New York: Oxford UP, 1985.
Messner, Michael A. *Power at Play: Sports and the Problem of Masculinity*. Boston: Beacon P, 1992.
Middleton, Peter. *The Inward Gaze: Masculinity and the Postmodern Subject*. New York: Routledge, 1992.
Miller, Alice. *The Drama of the Gifted Child: The Search for the True Self*. Trans. Ruth Ward. 1979. New York: Basic Books, 1986.
———. *For Your Own Good: Hidden Cruelty in Child-Rearing and the Roots of Violence*. Trans. Hildegarde and Hunter Hannum. 1980. New York: Meridian/NAL, 1983.

―――. *Thou Shalt Not Be Aware: Society's Betrayal of the Child.* Trans. Hildegarde and Hunter Hannum. 1981. New York: Meridian/NAL, 1986.

Modleski, Tania. *Feminism Without Women: Culture and Criticism in a "Postfeminist" Age.* New York and London: Routledge, 1991.

Morgan, Thais, ed. *Men Writing the Feminine.* New York: SUNY P, forthcoming.

Morrell, David. *Blood Oath.* 1982. New York: Fawcett Crest/Ballantine, 1985.

―――. *The Brotherhood of the Rose.* 1984. New York: Fawcett Crest/Ballantine, 1987.

―――. *The Covenant of the Flame.* New York: Warners, 1991.

―――. *The Fifth Profession.* New York: Warners, 1990.

―――. *First Blood.* 1972. New York: Fawcett Crest/Ballantine, 1988.

―――. *The Fraternity of the Stone.* 1985. New York: Fawcett Crest/Ballantine, 1986.

―――. *John Barth: An Introduction.* University Park: Pennsylvania State UP, 1976.

―――. *The League of Night and Fog.* 1987. New York: Fawcett Crest/Ballantine, 1988.

―――. "The Man Who Created Rambo." *Playboy* 35.8 (Aug. 1988): 88-89, 134-37.

―――. *Rambo: First Blood Part II.* 1985. New York: Berkley/Jove, 1988.

―――. *Rambo III.* New York: Berkley/Jove, 1988.

Murphy, Peter F., ed. *The Fiction of Masculinity: Literary Constructions of Manhood.* New York: New York UP, forthcoming.

Nichols, Jack. *Men's Liberation: A New Definition of Masculinity.* Kingsport, TN: Kingsport P, 1975.

Nichols, John. *American Blood.* 1987. New York: Ballantine, 1988.

Olsen, Paul. *Sons and Mothers.* 1981. New York: Ballantine/Fawcett Crest, 1982.

Osherson, Samuel. *Finding Our Fathers: The Unfinished Business of Manhood.* New York: Macmillan/Free, 1986.

Parker, Robert B. *A Catskill Eagle.* 1985. New York: Dell, 1986.

―――. *Ceremony.* 1982. New York: Dell, 1983.

―――. *Crimson Joy.* New York: Delacorte, 1988.

―――. *Double Deuce.* New York: Delacorte, 1992.

―――. *Early Autumn.* New York: Delacorte/Seymour Lawrence, 1981.

―――. *God Save the Child.* 1974. New York: Dell, 1983.

―――. *The Godwulf Manuscript.* 1973. New York: Dell, 1983.

―――. *The Judas Goat.* 1978. New York: Dell, 1983.

―――. *Looking for Rachel Wallace.* 1980. New York: Dell, 1985.

―――. *Love and Glory.* 1983. New York: Dell, 1984.

―――. *Mortal Stakes.* 1975. New York: Dell, 1983.

―――. *Pale Kings and Princes.* New York: Delacorte, 1987.

―――. *Paper Doll.* New York: Putnam, 1993.

―――. *Pastime.* New York: Delacorte, 1991.

―――. *Perchance to Dream.* New York: Putnam, 1991.

———. *Playmates*. New York: Delacorte, 1989.
———. *Promised Land*. 1976. New York: Dell, 1985.
———. *A Savage Place*. 1981. New York: Dell, 1983.
———. *Stardust*. New York: Delacorte, 1990.
———. *Taming a Sea-Horse*. 1986. New York: Dell, 1987.
———. *The Widening Gyre*. 1983. New York: Dell, 1984.
———. *Wilderness*. 1979. New York: Dell, 1983.
———. *Valediction*. 1984. New York: Dell, 1985.
Parker, Robert, and Joan Parker. *Three Weeks in Spring*. New York: Dell, 1977.
Penley, Constance and Sharon Willis, eds. *Male Trouble*. Minneapolis: U of Minnesota P, forthcoming.
Plato. *Symposium*. Trans. Michael Joyce. *The Collected Dialogues of Plato*. Eds. Edith Hamilton and Huntington Cairns. 1961. Princeton: Princeton UP 1980. 526-74.
Pleck, Joseph H. *The Myth of Masculinity*. 1981. Cambridge, MA: MIT P, 1984.
Pleck, Elizabeth H., and Joseph H. Pleck, eds. *The American Man*. Englewood Cliffs, NJ: Prentice-Hall, 1980.
Porte, Joel. *Representative Man: Ralph Waldo Emerson in His Time*. New York: Oxford UP, 1979.
Radway, Janice. *Reading the Romance: Women, Patriarchy, and Popular Literature*. Chapel Hill: U of North Carolina P, 1984.
Reagan, Ronald. Campaign Speech in Hammonton, NJ, Sept. 19, 1984. *Weekly Compilation of Presidental Documents* 20.38 (24 Sept. 1984): 1314.
Reimer, James D. "Rereading American Literature From a Men's Studies Perspective: Some Implications." Brod, ed., 289-300.
Riesman, David, with Revel Denney and Nathan Glazer. *The Lonely Crowd: A Study of the Changing American Character*. New Haven: Yale UP, 1950.
Robinson, Douglas. *American Apocalypses: The Image of the End of the World in American Literature*. Baltimore: Johns Hopkins UP, 1985.
———. *John Barth's Giles Goat-Boy: A Study*. Jyväskylä, Finland: U of Jyväskylä, 1980.
———. "Reader's Power, Writer's Power: Barth, Bergonzi, Iser, and the Modern-Postmodern Period Debate." *Criticism* 28.3 (Summer 1986): 307-22.
———. *Ring Lardner and the Other*. New York: Oxford UP, 1992.
———. "To the President." *American Studies Association Newsletter* 11.3 (Sept. 1988): 8-7.
———. *The Translator's Turn*. Baltimore: Johns Hopkins UP, 1991.
———. "The Trivialization of American Literature." *American Quarterly* 40.2 (June 1988): 205-23.
Robinson, Lillian S. *Sex, Class, and Culture*. Bloomington: Indiana UP, 1978.
Rotundo, E. Anthony. *American Manhood: Transformations in Masculinity from the Revolution to the Modern Era*. New York: Basic Books, forthcoming.
Rowan, John. *The Horned God: Feminism and Men as Wounding and Healing*. London: Routledge and Kegan Paul, 1987.

Savran, David. *Communists, Cowboys, and Queers*. Minneapolis: U of Minnesota P, 1992.
Schweickart, Patrocinio P. "Reading Ourselves: Toward a Feminist Theory of Reading." *Gender and Reading: Essays on Readers, Texts, and Contexts*. Eds. Elizabeth A. Flynn and Patrocinio P. Schweickart. Baltimore: Johns Hopkins UP, 1986. 31-62.
Schwenger, Peter. *Phallic Critiques: Masculinity and Twentieth Century Literature*. London: Routledge & Kegan Paul, 1984.
Silverman, Kaja. *Male Subjectivity at the Margins*. New York: Routledge, 1992.
Smith, Martha Nell. "Sexual Mobilities in Bruce Springsteen: Performance as Commentary." *SAQ* 90 (Fall 1991): 833-54.
Smith, Paul. *Clint Eastwood: A Cultural Production*. Minneapolis: U of Minnesota P, forthcoming.
Snodgrass, Jon, ed. *A Book of Readings for Men Against Sexism*. New York: Times Change Books, 1977.
Springsteen, Bruce. *Born in the U.S.A*. New York: CBS, 1984.
_____. *Born to Run*. New York: CBS, 1975.
_____. *Bruce Springsteen & the E Street Band Live/1975-1985*. New York: CBS, 1986.
_____. *Darkness on the Edge of Town*. New York: CBS, 1978.
_____. *Greetings from Asbury Park, N.J*. New York: CBS, 1973.
_____. *Human Touch*. New York: CBS, 1992.
_____. *Lucky Town*. New York: CBS, 1992.
_____. *Nebraska*. New York: CBS, 1982.
_____. *The River*. New York: CBS, 1981.
_____. *Tunnel of Love*. New York: CBS, 1987.
_____. *Video Anthology/1978-1988*. New York: CBS Music Video Enterprises, 1989.
_____. *The Wild, The Innocent, & The E Street Shuffle*. New York: CBS, 1973.
St. Pierre, Roger. *Sylvester Stallone: An Independent Story in Words and Pictures*. Bridge Close: Anabas, 1985.
Starhawk. *Dreaming the Dark: Magic, Sex and Politics*. Rev. ed. Boston: Beacon P, 1988.
Stark, John. "Forget Stallone: A Peaceful Prof From Iowa Put Rambo on the Map." *People* 30.2 (11 July 1988): 103-07.
Stevens, Wallace. *The Collected Poems*. 1954. New York: Random House, 1982.
Stoltenberg, John. *Refusing to Be a Man: Essays on Sex and Justice*. New York: NAL/Dutton, 1990.
Street, John. *Rebel Rock: The Politics of Popular Music*. Oxford: Basil Blackwell, 1986.
Theweleit, Klaus. *Male Fantasies*. Vol. 1, *Women Floods Bodies History*. Trans. Stephen Conway, collabs. Erica Carter and Chris Turner. Minneapolis: U of Minnesota P, 1987. Vol. 2, *Male Bodies: Psychoanalyzing the White Terror*. Trans. Erica Carter and Chris Turner, collab. Stephen Conway. Minneapolis: U of Minnesota P, 1989.

Thoreau, Henry David. *Walden*. 1854. Ed. J. Lyndon Shanley. Princeton: Princeton UP 1971.
Tolson, Andrew. *The Limits of Masculinity: Male Identity and the Liberated Woman*. New York: Harper & Row, 1977.
Verny, Thomas, with John Kelly. *The Secret Life of the Unborn Child*. 1981 rpt. New York: Delta/Dell, 1988.
White, Kevin. *The First Sexual Revolution: The Emergence of Male Heterosexuality in Modern America*. New York: New York UP, 1992.
Wilkinson, Rupert. *American Tough: The Tough-Guy Tradition and American Character*. Westport, CT: Greenwood P, 1984.
Wimsatt, W.K., and Monroe C. Beardsley. "The Affective Fallacy." *The Verbal Icon*. Lexington: U of Kentucky P, 1954.
———. "The Intentional Fallacy." *The Verbal Icon*. Lexington: U of Kentucky P, 1954.
Wolf, Naomi. *The Beauty Myth: How Images of Beauty Are Used Against Women*. New York: Morrow, 1991.
Wyllie, Irvin G. *The Self-Made Man in America: The Myth of Rags to Riches*. New York: Free, 1954.

# Index

*A Book About Men* (Goodman/Walby), 24
Abbott, Franklin, 24
Abdul, Paula, 291
Achilles, 249
Adam, 198-200, 243
"Adam Raised a Cain" (Springsteen), 172, 179, 198-200, 202, 205, 212, 217, 225, 230, 233, 238, 294
Adams, Boone (*Love and Glory*), 87, 100, 157, 269, 270-73
*Adventure, Mystery and Romance* (Cawelti), 48-49
*Adventurous Male, The* (Green), 264
affective fallacy (Wimsatt/Beardsley), 42, 268
*Against Our Will* (Brownmiller), 80-81
*Against the Tide* (Kimmel/Mosmiller), 264
"Ain't Got You" (Springsteen), 240
Albright, Billy, 7
"All or Nothin' At All" (Springsteen), 234
Allister, Mark, 7
Althusser, Louis, 17
*American Apocalypses* (Robinson), 278
*American Blood* (Nichols), 158-60
*American Man, The* (Pleck/Pleck), 24, 269
*American Manhood* (Rotundo), 264
American Studies Association (ASA), 27
Amnesty International, 168, 294
Amygism, 13
"Anecdote of the Jar, The" (Stevens), 95
*Anti-Oedipus* (Deleuze/Guattari), 253
*Apostles of the Self-Made Man* (Cawelti), 269
Appel, Mike, 286
*Ariel and the Police* (Lentricchia), 30, 95-98
*ASA Newsletter*, 27
Attis, 252

backlash, antifeminist, 2, 11-16, 23
*Badlands* (Malick), 173
Bakhtin, Mikhail, 266
Balboa, Rocky (*Rocky*), 127
*Ball Four* (Bouton), 32
Balswick, Jack, 263
Bancroft, Barbara, 7
Banner, Lois, 27-28
Banner, David (*The Incredible Hulk*), 281
Bannister, Robert, 13-14
Barrows, Anita, 43
Barry, Delmar (*First Blood*), 127-28
Barth, John, 109-10, 276-78
Bartlett, Kevin/Marge/Roger (*God Save the Child*), 65
Beardley, Monroe C., 42
Beatles, 284
Belson, Sgt. Frank (Parker), 46, 47
belying device (Wilkinson), 51-52
Berger, John, 62, 182
Bergonzi, Bernard, 278
Berlin, Irving, 266
*Beyond Patriarchy* (Kaufman), 24
*Big Sleep, The* (Chandler), 268
Billy the Kid, 32-33, 267
Bingham, Dennis, 264
Birdy (*Birdy*), 160-62
*Birdy* (Wharton/Parker), 160-62

307

Birkin, Rupert (*Women in Love*), 43
Bixby, Bill, 281
Black, Rose Mary (*Crimson Joy*), 99-103
Blake, William, 233
blaming the victim, 219-21, 291
Bleich, David, 42, 268
*Blood Oath* (Morrell), 114-20
Bly, Robert, 25, 250, 263, 265; and initiation, 255, 295; and the warrior, 254
Bodkin, Robin, 7
Bond, James, 127
*Book of Readings For Men Against Sexism, A* (Snodgrass), 24
"Book of Dreams" (Springsteen), 236-40, 294
Boone, Daniel, 110
Boone, Joseph A., 25, 264
Boothe, Powers, 279
*Born on the Fourth of July* (Kovic), 31, 167
*Born on the Fourth of July* (Stone), 31
"Born in the U.S.A." (Springsteen), 128, 183-86, 227, 285, 287-89
*Born in the U.S.A.* (Springsteen), 174, 183, 189, 207, 227-28, 266
*Born to Run* (Marsh), 287
"Born to Run" (Springsteen), 174, 175-77, 181-82, 189, 201-2, 206, 208, 218, 222, 230, 261, 290, 292, 293
*Born to Run* (Springsteen), 170, 174-78, 180, 185, 223-25, 239, 285
*Boston Globe*, 53, 268
"Bourgeois Blues" (Leadbelly), 32
Bouton, Jim, 32
Branch, Doug, 7, 291
Brandstetter, Dave (Hansen), 39-40
Brangwen, Ursula (*Women in Love*), 43
"Breathing Again" (Robinson), 164-65

Bregman, Martin, 279
"Brilliant Disguise" (Springsteen), 228
Brod, Harry, 24, 30, 263, 265
Broeske, Pat H., 6, 123, 151, 278-80
Brooks, Richard, 278
*Brotherhood of the Rose, The* (Morrell), 112-13, 114, 133-34, 277-78
"Brotherhood" series (Morrell), 112-13, 134, 282
*Brothers*, 24
Brown, James, 292
Brownmiller, Susan, 79-81
Broz, Joe (Parker), 54-55
*Bruce Springsteen and the E Street Band Live 1975/1985* (Springsteen), 208, 290
Buchanan, Daisy (*The Great Gatsby*), 88-89, 220, 272
Bunyan, Paul, 110
Bush, George, 33, 150, 289, 290

Cadden, Michael, 25, 264
Cain, 198-200
Calvinism, 34
Campbell, Joseph, 251-52, 254-60
candomble, 246
"Candy's Room" (Springsteen), 225
capitalism, 20, 34
Carnes, Mark C., 264
Carolco, 123, 280
Carp, Tom (*American Blood*), 160
Carraway, Nick (*The Great Gatsby*), 87, 273
Carrigan, Tim, 263
Carson, Kit, 110
Carter, Jimmy, 120, 150
Castiles, 170, 285
"Cat's in the Cradle, The" (Chapin), 33
*Catcher in the Rye, The* (Salinger), 92
*Catskill Eagle, A* (Parker), 60, 91, 93,

95, 97-99, 104-5, 114, 259
Caulfield, Holden (*The Catcher in the Rye*), 92
"Cautious Man" (Springsteen), 176, 228-34, 238, 293
Cawelti, John G., 48-49, 269
*Ceremony* (Parker), 61-63, 71, 74, 76
Chamorro, Violeta, 121
Chandler, Raymond, 40, 45, 53, 105, 268, 294
*Changing Men*, 24
*Changing Definition of Masculinity, The* (Franklin), 263
Chapin, Harry, 31, 33, 168, 224
Chaucer, Geoffrey, 269
Chee, Jim (Hillerman), 40
*Chimera* (Barth), 109, 277
"Chimes of Freedom" (Dylan), 266
Chodorow, Nancy, 191-92
Christie, Agatha, 39, 60
CIA, 33, 113
Ciambotti, Gia, 291
Cimino, Michael, 31
*Civilization and Its Discontents* (Freud), 268
Cixous, Helene, 191
Clemons, Clarence, 202, 291-92
*Clint Eastwood* (Smith), 263
Clinton, Bill, 290
Co (*Rambo: First Blood Part II*), 280
Coburn, James, 33
Cohan, Stephen, 25
Cohen, Debra Rae, 7
Cohen, Ed, 25
Coleman, Ray, 285
Coltrane, Scott, 263
Columbato, Al (*Birdy*), 160-62
Columbia Records, 174
Columbia Pictures, 278
*Coming Home*, 123
*Communists, Cowboys, and Queers* (Savran), 263
Connell, Bob, 263

Connelly, Cathy (*The Godwulf Manuscript*), 55
"Contemporary 'Crisis' of Masculinity in Historical Perspective" (Kimmel), 269
Cooke, Ebenezer (*The Sot-Weed Factor*), 277
Costigan, Jerry (*A Catskill Eagle*), 98
Costigan, Russell (*A Catskill Eagle*), 91, 98
Country Joe and the Fish, 31
*Covenant of the Flame, The* (Morrell), 113, 278
"Cover Me" (Springsteen), 228
Crenna, Richard, 143, 145
*Crimson Joy* (Parker), 60-61, 99-103, 104
*Critical Inquiry*, 44
Crockett, Davy, 110, 128, 281
Crompton, Louis, 30
Cronenberg, David, 31
Cronkite, Walter, 121
Cross, Amanda, 39
Crowley, John W., 30
"Crush on You" (Springsteen), 226
"Curious Evolution of John Rambo, The" (Broeske), 123
Cybele, 252

Danforth (*First Blood*), 152, 154
*Danse Macabre* (King), 281-82
*Darker Shade of Pale, A* (Mellers), 292
"Darkness on the Edge of Town" (Springsteen), 180-83, 233
*Darkness on the Edge of Town* (Springsteen), 170, 172, 177-83, 198, 200, 225-26, 234, 238, 288-89
Davis, Brad, 279
de Beauvoir, Simone, 43
de Haven, Carter, 279
de Mause, Lloyd, 269

de Niro, Robert, 279
*Dead Zone, The* (King/Cronenberg), 31
Dean, James, 291
*Deer Hunter, The* (Cimino), 31, 279
Deleuze, Gilles, 253, 256
Demeter, 252
Dennehy, Brian, 132, 139, 142
Dennis, Carol, 291
*Desire in Language* (Kristeva), 294
Diamond Jackie ("New York City Serenade"), 224
Dimmesdale, Arthur (*The Scarlet Letter*), 30
Dionysus, 252
Diotima (*Symposium*), 270
Di Palma, Laura (Matera), 40
disintegration, 5, 44, 251-52
*Dixie Association, The* (Hays), 31
Donne, John, 57
*Double Deuce* (Parker), 61, 95, 105
Douglas, Ann, 13
Douglas, Michael, 279
"Downbound Train" (Springsteen), 227-28, 293
Doyle, Jim A., 25
Drake, Tess (*The Covenant of the Flame*), 278
drama therapy, 246
"Dream On," 25
*Dreaming the Dark* (Starhawk), 295
"Drive All Night" (Springsteen), 226
Dumuzi, 252
Dunlap, Susan, 39
DuPlessis, Rachel Blau, 43
Dylan, Bob, 32-33, 174, 266-67, 291, 292

E Street Band, 203
*Early Autumn* (Parker), 61, 65, 74
Eastwood, Clint, 279
Edwards, Jonathan, 65
"effeminate rich man" (Emerson/Thoreau), 68-70
effeminism (Stoltenberg), 26
Eliot (*The Brotherhood of the Rose*), 133, 145
emancipation: in gender politics, 22-23, 43; in literary criticism, 17, 29, 30-31, 116; in music, 33
Emerson, Ralph Waldo, 66-72, 78, 88, 97, 170, 269-70, 272, 273
*End of the Road, The* (Barth), 109, 277
*Engendering Men* (Boone/Cadden), 25, 264
Eve, 243
Exley, Frederick, 31

"Factory" (Springsteen), 200
"Fade Away" (Springsteen), 226
Faludi, Susan, 11-16
*Family Man* (Coltrane), 263
*Fan's Notes, A* (Exley), 31
Fansler, Kate (Cross), 39
Farrell, Warren, 24
"Fate" (Emerson), 269
*Fatherhood in America* (Griswold), 264
fathers: and killing, 143-44; and the constitution of the son, 190-98; masculist, 258
Federici, Danny, 201, 208
Feigen Fasteau, Marc, 264
Felton, Gordon (*Crimson Joy*), 99-103
feminism, 8, 18, 120; and critiques of men and masculinity, 21-22, 33, 79-81, 124-25; and the decline of the middle class, 61, 64-65; and the hardboiled detective novel, 39-40; impact on men, 274; and liberation, 290; and masculism, 26; in Parker, 40
*Feminization of America, The* (Douglas), 13
Fetterley, Judith, 43, 88-89, 103, 219-

Index    311

20, 290
*Fiction of Masculinity, The* (Murphy), 263
Fiedler, Leslie, 282
*Field of Dreams* (Robinson), 32
*Fifth Profession, The* (Morrell), 113-14
"57 Channels (And Nothing On)" (Springsteen), 289
Filene, Peter, 263
Filmways, 279
*Finding Our Fathers* (Osherson), 198-99, 263
*Fire in the Belly* (Keen), 25
*Fire in the John* (Gingold), 25
*Firestarter* (King), 33, 281-82
*First Blood*, 31, 232; critical responses to, 156-57, 222, 267; and emotional trauma, 195; movie version of, 17-19, 210-11, 221, filming 123-28, 166, 278-80; original novel, 18, 34-35, 109, 121-27, 266; and Springsteen, 176-77, 180, 183, 186-89, 209
*First Sexual Revolution, The* (White), 263
Fish, Stanley, 268
Fisher King, 254
Fitzgerald, F. Scott, 30, 86-89, 271-73
"Fixin' to Die Rag, The" (Country Joe and the Fish), 31
Flanagan, Bill, 292
*Floating Opera, The* (Barth), 109
"Flowers Are Red" (Chapin), 33
Floyd, Lester (*Mortal Stakes*), 79, 84
Flynn, Elizabeth A., 268
Folkways, 32, 266
"For You" (Springsteen), 223-24
"Fourth of July (Sandy)" (Springsteen), 175, 224
Frankenheimer, John, 279
Franklin, Benjamin, 260
Franklin, Clyde W., II, 263

*Fraternity of the Stone, The* (Morrell), 113, 134, 278
Freud, Sigmund, 44, 115, 188, 190-92, 199, 244, 246, 258, 268; and Oedipus, 111, 192, 214, 254, 266, 295; and the writer as neurotic, 112
Friedan, Betty, 269
Frith, Simon, 285
Frost, Robert, 57, 58, 70-74, 78, 97, 170

Galt (*First Blood*), 146
Gambaccini, Peter, 174
Gardiner, Ellen, 44
Garrett, Pat (*Pat Garrett and Billy the Kid*), 267
Gatsby, Jay (*The Great Gatsby*), 87-89, 220
Gawain, Sir, 39, 46
gay males, 39, 97
*Gender and Reading* (Flynn/Schweickart), 268
George, St., 249
Gerson, Kathleen, 264
Giacomin, Patty (Parker), 104
Giacomin, Paul (Parker), 41, 44, 65-66, 74, 77-78, 87, 270
"Giant, The" (Robinson), 247-48
Gilbert, Sandra, 44, 265
Giler, David, 151, 279-80
*Giles Goat-Boy* (Barth), 109, 276-78
Giles, George (*Giles Goat-Boy*), 277-78
Gilmore, David D., 264
Gingold, Alfred, 25
"Gloria's Eyes" (Springsteen), 234, 293
*Glory Days* (BBC), 178-79, 289
*Glory Days* (Marsh), 35, 166, 170, 178-79, 185-86, 200, 210, 212, 285-89
*God Save the Child* (Parker), 47, 60-61, 65, 92-93

"God Bless America" (Berlin), 266
*Godwulf Manuscript, The* (Parker), 35, 45-59, 60, 137
Goldberg, Herb, 45, 263, 268, 283, 290
Goldsmith, Jerry, 127, 282
Goodman, A., 24
Gorbachev, Mikhail, 110
Graces, the, 291
Gradin, Sherrie, 1-3, 7-8, 295
Grafton, Sue, 39
Grayle, Jennifer (*Love and Glory*), 269, 271-73
*Great Gatsby, The* (Fitzgerald), 30, 86-89, 271-73, 290
Great Goddess, 252-53
Green, Martin, 264
*Greetings from Asbury Park, N.J.* (Springsteen), 35, 174, 221-24, 227, 292
Grenada, 11, 150, 279
Griffen, Clyde, 264
Grisman, Saul (*The Brotherhood of the Rose*), 112-13, 133, 145, 277-78
Griswold, Robert L., 264
Gross, Larry, 145, 279-80
"Growin' Up" (Springsteen), 174, 175, 189, 223,
Guattari, Felix, 253, 256
Gubar, Susan, 44, 265
Guthrie, Arlo, 32
Guthrie, Woody, 32, 266

"Halfway to Heaven" (Chapin), 33
Hammer, Mike (Spillane), 52
Hammett, Dashiell, 40, 45, 53, 105
Hammond, John, 174
Hansen, Joseph, 39
Hark, Ina Rae, 25
Harris, Emmy Lou, 32
Harroway, Vic (*God Save the Child*), 90

Harry Chapin Foundation, 168
Hawk (Parker), 41, 44, 82, 93, 97, 102, 105; anticipated by Iris Milford, 52; and balance, 76-79; compared to Chris Hood, 275
Hawthorne, Nathaniel, 30
Hayden, Judy (*The Godwulf Manuscript*), 55-56
Hayden, Lowell (*The Godwulf Manuscript*), 46, 54-59
Hays, Donald, 31
*Hazards of Being Male, The* (Goldberg), 263, 290
health, movement toward, 6, 137, 187
Healy, Lt., (Parker), 47
*Heartbreak Ridge*, 279
Heath, Stephen, 264
Heilbrun, Carolyn, 39
"Held Up Without a Gun" (Springsteen), 286
Heller, Scott, 264
Hemingway, Ernest, 30, 147
Hendrix, Jimi, 289
Henke, James, 230-31, 235, 292-95
Hepworth, David, 178-79
*Hero With a Thousand Faces, The* (Campbell), 251-52
*Heroes* (Kagan), 31
"Highway Patrolman" (Springsteen), 205, 207, 232
Hill, Dan, 127, 280
*Hill Street Blues* (Sackheim/Kozoll), 279
Hillerman, Tony, 39
*History of Childhood, The* (de Mause), 269
Hobbs, Roy (*The Natural*), 31
"Hobo's Lullaby" (Guthrie), 32
Hogan, Dennis P., 263
Holiday, Billie, 174
Holland, David, 42, 268
Hollister, Cap (*Firestarter*), 33
Hood, Chris (*Wilderness*), 275

*Horned God, The* (Rowan), 250, 252-53, 263
Horney, Karen, 45, 191, 268
Horton, Bill ("Cautious Man"), 229-34, 293
Houston, Charles (*Blood Oath*), 120
Houston, Carol (*Blood Oath*), 117-19
Houston, Jan (*Blood Oath*), 114, 115
Houston, Pete (*Blood Oath*), 114-20
Houston, Stephen (*Blood Oath*), 117-19
Hughes, Emmett (*In Country*), 284
Hughes, Sam (*In Country*), 284-85
*Human Touch* (Springsteen), 189, 218, 229, 234-40, 289-90, 292
"Hungry Heart" (Springsteen), 226, 286
Hussein, Saddam, 11
Hyrde, Richard, 26

"I Wanna Marry You" (Springsteen), 226
"I Wish I Were Blind" (Springsteen), 293
"I'm on Fire" (Springsteen), 188
ideological analysis (Jameson), 20-22
"If I Should Fall Behind" (Springsteen), 290
imagery therapy, 246
*In Country* (Mason), 284-85
Inanna, 252
*Incredible Hulk, The*, 134, 281
"Independence Day" (Springsteen), 200-3
*Inexpressive Male, The* (Balswick), 263
*Inner Male, The* (Goldberg), 263, 268
inner-direction (Riesman), 48-49, 72
*Interpretation of Dreams, The* (Freud), 268
*Inward Gaze, The* (Middleton), 25
Iran hostage crisis, 35, 124-25, 150
Iraq, 11, 150

Irigaray, Luce, 191
*Iron John* (Bly), 25, 250, 254, 263, 265
Iser, Wolfgang, 278
Isham, Mark, 234
Ishtar, 252
Isis, 252
"It's a Long Road" (Goldsmith/Shaper), 127, 283

*Jacknife* (Jones), 31
Jackson, Michael, 287
Jagger, Mick, 179
James, Henry, 39
Jameson, Fredric, 20, 31, 43
Jardine, Alice, 264
Jeffords, Susan, 11, 13, 16, 150, 263
Jesus, 19; radical readings of, 255
Job, 182
*John Barth* (Morrell), 109
*John Barth's Giles Goat-Boy* (Robinson), 278
"Johnny 99" (Springsteen), 171-73, 183
*Jokes and Their Relation to the Unconscious* (Freud), 268
Jones, David, 31
*Journal of Men's Studies, The*, 25
*Judas Goat, The* (Parker), 60-61
Jung, C. G., 251
"Jungleland" (Springsteen), 168
"Just Another Roll of the Dice" (Springsteen), 234, 292-93

Kagan, Jeremy Paul, 31
Kant, Immanuel, 56, 268
Karagianis, Maria, 53, 268, 273
Karl, Adolph (*Wilderness*), 275
Kassar, Mario, 127, 279-80
Kaufman, Michael, 24
Kaul, Bill, 7-8
Keats, John, 57
Keen, Sam, 25

Kellerman, Orval (*First Blood*), 140-42, 176-77, 282
Kennedy, Cleopatra, 291
Khan, Genghis, 80-81
Khomeini, Ayatollah, 125
Kilmoonie, Chris (*The Brotherhood of the Rose*), 113, 133-34, 145
Kimmel, Michael S., 264, 269
King, Bobby, 291
King, Don, 282
King, Stephen, 31, 33, 281-82
Kinsella, W.P., 31-32, 266
Kinsella, Ray (*Shoeless Joe*), 266
Kitty ("Kitty's Back"), 224
"Kitty's Back" (Springsteen), 224
Klass, Philip, 109
Klein, Joe, 266
"Knocking on Heaven's Door" (Dylan), 33
Korda, Michael, 264
Korean War, 210, 270-71, 279
Koufax, Sandy, 78
Kovic, Ron, 31, 167
Kozoll, Michael, 145, 150, 279-80, 282
Kristeva, Julia, 294
Kristofferson, Kris, 33
Kyle, Harry (*Ceremony*), 62-63
Kyle, April (*Ceremony*), 74, 98
*L.A. Times*, 6, 123, 151
Laakso, Tarvo, 7
Lacan, Jacques, 190-92
Laing, R.D., 255-59
Laius (*Oedipus Rex*), 290
Lancaster, Burt, 278-79
Landau, Jon, 166
Lardner, Ring, 265
Lasch, Christopher, 120
Laszlo, Andrew, 283
Lawrence, D.H., 43
Leadbelly, 32
*League of Night and Fog, The* (Morrell), 113

"Leap of Faith" (Springsteen), 235
Lears, T.J. Jackson, 269
Leary, Timothy, 54
Lee, John, 263
Lehman, Peter, 264
leisure, 58; and liberal values, 33, 68-74
Lennon, John, 179
Lentricchia, Frank, 30, 44, 95-98. 265
*LETTERS* (Barth), 110, 277-78
Leverenz, David, 30, 44, 67, 265-66, 269-70
Levinson, Barry, 31
liberalism, 52; and the decline of the middle class, 60; and men, 21; and self-reliance, 65-72
*Liberated Man, The* (Farrell), 24
*Light of Day* (Schrader), 292
"Light of Day" (Springsteen), 292
*Limits of Masculinity, The* (Tolson), 263
Linnier, Johnson ("Shut Out the Light"), 287-88
Lipsitz, George, 31, 266
"Living in Paradise" (Robinson), 7, 38
"Living Proof" (Springsteen), 235
"Local Hero" (Springsteen), 287
Loder, Kurt, 35, 185
Loder, Kurt, 185
Lofgren, Nils, 208
"Long Goodbye, The" (Springsteen), 218-19, 230, 236-37
*Looking for Rachel Wallace* (Parker), 39, 54, 60, 61, 81, 99, 268, 276
*Lost in the Funhouse* (Barth), 109, 278
love: and masculine self-control, 85-86; and need, 70-74
"Love Song" (Robinson), 7, 9-10
*Love and Glory* (Parker), 86, 270-73
Lowell, Amy, 13
*Lucky Town* (Springsteen), 182-83, 189, 229, 234-40, 287, 289-90, 292

Lynch, Kate, 213

Macdonald, John D., 31, 40, 45, 267-68
machismo, 16; and macho code, 76-78, 84-86, 229; and macho pride, 89-91
MacLane, Drew (*The Fraternity of the Stone*), 113, 134
Maguire, Liz, 7
Mailer, Norman, 30, 124-25, 147
*Making of Masculinities, The* (Brod), 24, 30, 263
Malamud, Bernard, 31
*Male Chauvinism* (Korda), 264
*Male Fantasies* (Theweleit), 24-25
male feminism, 18, 21, 26-27, 67, 195, 264, 265
*Male Machine, The* (Feigen Fasteau), 264
*Male Subjectivity at the Margins* (Silverman), 25
male supremacy, 20, 33, 150, 195
*Male Trouble* (Penley/Willis), 263
Malick, Terence, 173
Maltin, Leonard, 267, 284
Mamet, David, 265
Mangan, J.A., 269
*Manhood* (Kimmel), 264
*Manhood and the American Renaissance* (Leverenz), 30, 44, 67
*Manhood in the Making* (Gilmore), 264
*Manliness and Morality* (Mangan/Walvin), 269
*M_nnerphantasien* (Theweleit), 24-25
"Mansion on the Hill" (Springsteen), 205, 294
"Man's Job" (Springsteen), 234, 293
Marlowe, Philip (Chandler), 45, 294
Marsh, Dave, 35, 166, 169-70, 185-86, 200, 203, 210, 212, 223, 285-89
Marvell, Andrew, 269

Marvin, Lee, 278
Mary ("Mary Queen of Arkansas"), 221-22
"Mary Queen of Arkansas" (Springsteen), 221-22, 224, 227
Mary ("Thunder Road"), 175, 224, 240
masculinism, 26, 264
*Masculinities, Male Spectatorship and Hollywood Stars* (Bingham), 264
masculinity: and ideological norms, 31; and machismo, 16, 21, 39, 56, 234; and macho primitivism, 147; and macho violence as self-creation, 81-84; patriarchal, 5; and social class, 70-74; and self-reliance, 65-75; utopian, 21; and vulnerability, 137-38
masculism, 23-29, 260, 265; and the hero path, 255; and liberation, 228, 290; in literary criticism, 30-31, 44; and Stallone's ending to *First Blood*, 150-51; in Springsteen, 189; and transformation, 45, 259-61; and violence, 79-82
Mason, Bobbie Ann, 284-85
Matera, Lia, 39
May, Rollo, 258-59
McCone, Sharon (Muller), 39
McGee, Andy (*Firestarter*), 33
McGee, Charlie (*Firestarter*), 281-82
McGee, Travis (Macdonald), 30-31, 267-68
McLiam, John, 140
McQueen, Steve, 279
*Meanings for Manhood* (Carnes/Griffen), 264
Mellencamp, John, 32
Mellers, Wilfrid, 292
*Melody Maker*, 285
Melville, Herman, 265
*Men Writing the Feminine* (Morgan), 264
*Men in Feminism* (Jardine/Smith), 264

men's liberation, 14
*Men's Liberation* (Nichols), 24
men's movement, profeminist, 1-2, 5, 23-26, 150-51
men's studies, 24-25, 263, 265; subsumed in feminism, 27
Men's Studies Association, 24
Mensch, Ambrose, 278
Merchent, John (*Love and Glory*), 269, 272
Messner, Michael A., 264
Meyer (Macdonald), 268
middle class, decline of, 33, 60
Middleton, Peter, 25
Milford, Iris (*The Godwulf Manuscript*), 52, 268
Mill, John Stuart, 26
Miller, Alice, 45, 115-17, 268, 294
Millett, Kate, 30, 43
Millhone, Kinsey (Grafton), 40
Mishima, Yukio, 30
misogyny, 22, 49, 119, 220-21
Missy Bimbo ("Wild Billy's Circus Song"), 224
Mondale, Walter, 185
Morgan, Thais, 264, 266
Morrell, David, 6-7, 16, 18, 34-35, 147, 150, 153, 157, 168, 172-73, 176, 186, 210-11, 266; and abandonment, 132-36; and genesis of Rambo, 121-26, 139; and John Barth, 109-10, 276-78; and King's *Firestarter*, 281-82; and the missing father, 111-19, 155, 191-92; and self-therapy, 112, 120
Morrell, George (father), 114
*Mortal Stakes* (Parker), 60-61, 64, 70, 78-79, 84, 86, 99, 268, 276
Mosmiller, Thomas E., 264
mothers: feminist, 258; and love, 143-44; and sons, 213-16, 242-46; and Spenser, 92-105; unsafe, 240-42, 244

*Ms.* Magazine, 63-64
Muller, Bob, 166
Muller, Marcia, 39
Murdock (*Rambo: First Blood Part II*), 132, 137, 281
*Murphy Brown*, 25
Murphy, Peter F., 263, 266
*Musician*, 292
"My Beautiful Reward" (Springsteen), 236-37, 294
"My Father's House" (Springsteen), 204-7, 227-28, 238, 294
"My Hometown" (Springsteen), 207-8
mysticism, 189; and connective breathing, 246; and light, 229, 233, 237-38; and sex, 238, 240
*Myth of Masculinity, The* (Pleck), 290
*Myths To Live By* (Campbell), 251, 254-58

Napier, Charles, 132
National Organization for Changing Men, 24
National Organization for Men Against Sexism (NOMAS), 24
*Natural, The* (Malamud/Levinson), 31
"Nature" (Emerson), 269
"Nebraska" (Springsteen), 171-72, 183, 205, 233, 292-93
*Nebraska* (Springsteen), 169-73, 181, 183, 204-7, 227, 232-34, 238-39, 285, 288-89, 292-93
need, 86; and love, 70-74; and Spenser's self-control, 91-92
negative hermeneutic (Jameson), 20, 43
Nelson, Willie, 32
*Neurotic Personality of Our Time* (Horney), 268
New Criticism, 42
*New Male, The* (Goldberg), 263, 268, 283
*New Male-Female Relationship, The*

(Goldberg), 263, 268
*New Men, New Minds* (Abbott), 24
New Right, 18
"New York City Serenade" (Springsteen), 224
Newman, Aaron (*Wilderness*), 100, 268-69, 271, 273-76
Newman, Janet (*Wilderness*), 268-69, 271, 273-76
Newman, Paul, 279
*Newsweek*, 174, 178, 179
Nichols, Jack, 24
Nichols, John, 158
Nickson, Julia, 280
Nietzsche, Friedrich, 251
*No Man's Land* (Gerson), 264
*No Place of Grace* (Lears), 269
"No Surrender" (Springsteen), 174, 189, 290
Nolte, Nick, 279
Nye, David, 7

O'Connell, Martin, 12
Oedipus (*Oedipus Rex*), 290; and the Oedipus complex, 111, 192, 214, 254, 294-95; and oedipal institutions, 253; and the preoedipal phase, 266
O'Hara, Scarlett (*Gone With the Wind*), 131
O'Shaughnessy, Kiernan (Dunlap), 40
Olsen, Paul, 196-97, 214-16, 240-42, 244, 263
"On the Road to Kingdom Come" (Chapin), 33
"One Step Up" (Springsteen), 228
Orchard, Marion (*The Godwulf Manuscript*), 48-51, 137
Orchard, Roland (*The Godwulf Manuscript*), 48-50, 53-54, 137
Orchard, Terry (*The Godwulf Manuscript*), 46-48, 53-54, 137
Orion Pictures, 279

Ortega, Daniel, 121
Osherson, Samuel, 198-99, 204, 263
Osiris, 252
other-direction (Riesman), 48-49, 72
"Out in the Street" (Springsteen), 226
*Over the Top*, 137

Pacino, Al, 279
*Pale Kings and Princes* (Parker), 60, 61, 94-96
Panza, Sancho (*Don Quixote*), 32
*Paper Doll* (Parker), 61, 66, 105
Paretsky, Sara, 39, 267
Parker, Alan, 160
Parker, Robert B., 6, 16, 18, 21, 35, 157, 170, 186, 210, 268, 270-73, 290, 294; and academia, 53-59; and autonomy, 66-74; and *The Great Gatsby*, 86-89; and the hard-boiled detective tradition, 39-42, 45-59; and liberal values, 60-65, 168; and the missing mother, 92-105, 219; and the problem of Spenser, 40, 103-5; and self-therapy, 40-45, 112
Parker, Joan (n_e Hall), 271, 276
Parkman, Francis, 66, 269
*Pastime* (Parker), 60-61, 93, 104
*Pat Garrett and Billy the Kid*, 32-33
patriarchy, 1, 265-66; and the battle of the sexes, 6, 22; and the double bind, 80-81; and the hero myth, 249-50; ideology of, 16; as men, 26; and protective ideal, 134
Peckinpah, Sam, 32, 267
Penley, Constance, 263
*People* Magazine, 6, 109, 112, 119
*Perchance to Dream* (Parker), 268
Perot, Ross, 290
Persian Gulf War, 289
*Phallic Critiques* (Schwenger), 30
Phil (*The Godwulf Manuscript*), 55-56

Philips, Julianne, 183, 211, 228, 230-31
"Place Names" (Kristeva), 294
Plato, 270
*Playmates* (Parker), 60-61, 103-4, 268, 276
Pleck, Joseph H., 24, 265, 269, 290-91
Pleck, Elizabeth H., 24, 269
"Point Blank" (Springsteen), 226
*Political Unconscious, The* (Jameson), 20
Pollack, Sydney, 279
"Pony Boy" (Springsteen), 235, 294
*Poodle Springs* (Chandler/Parker), 268, 294
popular culture, 15-23; and men's art, 31-33; as mythic, 110-11
Porte, Joel, 269
positive hermeneutic (Jameson), 20, 43
post-trauma stress disorder (PTSD), 123-25, 160, 195
postmodernism, 45
Pound, Ezra, 13
Powell, Dennis (*The Godwulf Manuscript*), 46-47, 55
*Power at Play* (Messner), 264
Presley, Elvis, 174, 177, 179, 212, 242, 287
"Pretty Boy Floyd" (Guthrie), 32
"Price You Pay, The" (Springsteen), 226
primal scream therapy, 246, 256
Prine, John, 31
*Prisoner of Sex, The* (Mailer), 30
Program for the Study of Women and men in Society (USC), 24
*Promised Land* (Parker), 60-61, 63, 65, 82, 92, 99
"Promised land" (Springsteen), 178, 180-81, 188, 206, 215
psychoanalysis: feminist, 266; Freudian, 246, 254; Jungian, 251

*Psychopathology of Everyday Life, The* (Freud), 268
Puritanism, 65
Pynchot, Herman (*Firestarter*), 33
Quirk, Lt. Martin (Parker), 47-48
Quixote, Don, 32

Rabb, Linda/Marty (*Mortal Stakes*), 78-79, 86
Rabe, David, 265, 279
"Racing in the Street" (Springsteen), 225-26, 240
Rainbird, John (*Firestarter*), 281-82
*Rainbow, The* (Lawrence), 43
Raines, Jackie (*Double Deuce*), 105
Ralph ("Johnny 99"), 171-73
Rambo, (John), 1, 6-7, 19, 23, 34, 114, 210, 229, 232; myth of, 16-18, 109-11; genesis of, 121-25, 278; and the hero's symbolic death, 251, 260; and King's John Rainbird, 281-82; in movie version of *First Blood*, 137-39, 144-46, 150-58, 186, 278-80, 281; in *First Blood* the novel, 129-38, 147-50, 172, 211; and Springsteen, 166, 170-73, 176-77, 180-81, 183, 187-88, 209, 288-89; in sequels, see *Rambo: First Blood Part II* and *Rambo III*
*Rambo: First Blood Part_II*, 110, 132, 137, 150, 153, 158, 188, 210, 280, 281-84, 288-89
*Rambo III*, 110, 112, 134, 135, 150, 153, 188, 210, 289
rape, 80-81
"Reader's Power, Writer's Power" (Robinson), 278
reader-response theory, 42, 268
Reagan, Ronald, 7, 12, 19, 33, 35, 121, 123, 150, 184-85, 267, 288-89
"Real Man" (Springsteen), 234, 293

"Real World" (Springsteen), 292-93
*Rebel Rock* (Street), 285
rebirthing, 246
"Reborn" (Robinson), 7, 108
Redford, Robert, 31
*Refusing To Be a Man* (Stoltenberg), 26
Reimer, James D., 30
*Remasculinization of America, The* (Jeffords), 11-16, 150
*Representative Man* (Porte), 269
"Resistance to Civil Government" (Thoreau), 74
*Resisting Reader, The* (Fetterley), 219-20
"Rich Boy, The" (Fitzgerald), 30
Riesman, David, 72
Rimbaud, Arthur, 278
*Ring Lardner and the Other* (Robinson), 30, 32, 44, 80, 263, 265, 268, 290
Ritt, Martin, 279
"River, The" (Springsteen), 208, 210, 226
*River, The* (Springsteen), 200, 203, 226-28, 234, 266, 286, 292
Roberts, Franky/Joe ("Highway Patrolman"), 205, 232
Robinson, David, 8
Robinson, Phil Allen, 32
Rock and Roll Messiah, 19, 178, 224, 292
*Rocky IV*, 288
Rogers, Angel, 291
Rogers, Chief (*Pale Kings and Princes*), 47
*Rolling Stone*, 35, 185
romantic investment/divestment of self in opposite sex (Fetterley), 88-89, 103, 219-20, 290
Rosalita ("Rosalita (Come Out Tonight)"), 224
"Rosalita (Come Out Tonight)" (Springsteen), 224
*Roseanne*, 62
Ross, Diana, 291
Rotundo, E. Anthony, 264
Rowan, John, 26, 195, 250, 252-53, 263
*Running Scared* (Lehman), 264
Ryan, William, 291

*Sabbatical* (Barth), 110
Sackheim, William, 145, 150, 282, 279-80
Salinger, J.D., 266
"Sam Stone" (Prine), 31
Samson, 249
Savage (*The Fifth Profession*), 113-14
*Savage Place, A* (Parker), 60-61, 91, 276
Savran, David, 263
*Scarlet Letter, The* (Hawthorne), 30
schizophrenia, 255-59
Schlafly, Phyllis, 264
"Scholars Debunk the Marlboro Man" (Heller), 264
Scholes, Robert, 266
Schrader, Paul, 292
Schweickart, Patrocinio P., 43, 268
Schwenger, Peter, 30
Scialfa, Patti, 183, 229, 235, 240, 293-94
*Screening the Male* (Cohan/Hark), 25
*Second Stage, The* (Friedan), 269
*Secret Life of the Unborn Child, The* (Verny), 95
"Seeds" (Springsteen), 208
Seeger, Pete, 32
*Self-Analysis* (Horney), 268
self-made man, 66
*Self-Made Man in America, The* (Wyllie), 269
self-reliance, 65-72
"Self-Reliance" (Emerson), 66-69
self-therapy: in Morrell, 112, 120; in

Parker, 40-45, 112; in Springsteen, 187-89
*Sexual Politics* (Millett), 30
*Sexual Fix, The* (Heath), 264
Shakespeare, William, 53, 57, 58
Shaper, Hal, 127
"She's the One" (Springsteen), 224-25
Sheen, Martin, 173
Shepard, Sam, 265
Shephard, Harvey (*Promised Land*), 63
"Sherry Darling" (Springsteen), 226
*Shoeless Joe* (Kinsella), 31-32
"Shut Out the Light" (Springsteen), 287-88
Silverman, Kaja, 25
Silverman, Susan (Parker), 39-41, 44, 74, 84, 88, 93, 98-99, 105, 131, 271, 276; and feminism, 62-64; and Spenser's need, 90-92; and Spenser's self-control, 76-78
*Slaughterhouse Five* (Vonnegut), 266
Sloan, Candy (*A Savage Place*), 91, 276
Smith, Martha Nell, 291
Smith, Michael P., (*American Blood*), 158-60
Smith, Paul, 263-64
"Sniper, The" (Chapin), 33, 224
Snodgrass, Jon, 24
Snow, Stephen, 31
Socrates, 71, 270
*Sons and Mothers* (Olsen), 263
*Sot-Weed Factor, The* (Barth), 109, 277
"Souls of the Departed" (Springsteen), 236, 289
*Sound Effects* (Frith), 285
Spacek, Sissy, 173
Spector, Phil, 177, 179
Spellman, Sherry (*Valediction*), 103
Spenser, 1, 6-7, 16, 18-19, 21, 23, 34-35, 131, 137, 170-71, 210, 221, 229, 232, 270-71; and autonomy, 65-66, 141; and balance, 76-79; and the descent into darkness, 259; and fixation on Susan, 76-79, 90-92, 276; and Gordon Felton, 99-103; and the hardboiled detective tradition, 40-41, 45-59; and the hero's road of trials, 260; and inner-direction, 49-52; as the Incredible Hulk, 281; and liberal values, 60-75; and the missing mother, 92-105, 111, 117, 192; and nonsexist discourse, 268; and self-control, 155; and self-therapy, 40-45; and taboo, 98-99, 114; and violence, 79-84; and Wallace Stevens, 95-98
*Spenser: For Hire*, 18
Spillane, Mickey, 49, 52
*Spiral Dance, The* (Starhawk), 252-53
Springsteen, Adele (mother), 226, 239-40, 242; addiction to romance, 217-19; as source of stability and energy, 212
Springsteen, Bruce, 1, 6-7, 16, 18-19, 23, 32, 35, 128, 120, 162; and Adam and Cain, 198-200; and ambivalence about mother, 221-27; and drama therapy, 187-89; and the dream of reconciliation, 204-7; and the father, 190, 203-4; and *First Blood*, 232; and the hero's regeneration, 260; and homoeroticism, 291; and gender liberation, 196; in *In Country*, 285; and letting go, 179-83, 231-34; and marriage, 228-34; and mother's addiction to romance, 217-19; and the need for community, 177-83; and own son, 207-8; and Rambo, 166, 170-73, 176-77, 180-81, 183, 187-88, 209, 229, 232,

233; and Reagan's appropriation, 184-85; and romantic escape, 174-77; and Stallone, 288-89; and Vietnam, 166-68, 183-84, 208-11
Springsteen, Doug (father), 190, 199-200, 203-5, 232, 239; at the A and M Karagheusian rug mill, 207; and making a man of his son, 209-10; as source of bitter isolation, 212
Springsteen, Evan (son), 235, 238
Springsteen, Pam (sister), 205, 239, 240
St. Laurent, Pierre de (*Blood Oath*), 114, 118
St. Pierre, Roger, 282
Stallone, Jacqueline (mother), 137
Stallone, Frank (father), 137
Stallone, Sylvester, 6, 16, 18, 109-10, 121, 125-30, 139, 156-57, 166, 168, 186-89, 210, 282; as actor, 137-38, 222; and concluding monologue, 284; and movie ending, 150-51, 153; and revision of Sackheim-Kozoll script, 279-80; and Springsteen, 288-89
Stanley, Julia Penelope, 43
"Star-Spangled Banner" (Hendrix), 289
*Stardust* (Parker), 61, 103-4, 276
Starhawk, 252-53, 295
Stark, John, 6, 109, 112, 119
Starkweather, Charles, 173, 293
Stevens, Wallace, 30, 57, 95-98, 102
Stoltenberg, John, 26, 250
Stone, Oliver, 31
*Strange Snow* (Snow), 31
Street, John, 285
"Streets of Fire" (Springsteen), 179
Strong, Barrett, 266
*Subjection of Women, The* (Mill), 26
Sullivan, Ed, 177, 212
"Sunday Morning" (Stevens), 95-98, 102

Superman, 18
Sweet Honey in the Rock, 32
"Sylvie" (Leadbelly), 32
*Symposium* (Plato), 71

Taj Mahal, 32
Taliafero, Crystal, 292
*Talk on the Wilde Side* (Cohen), 25
*Taming a Sea-Horse* (Parker), 61, 62, 98
Tammuz, 252
Tarr, Cathie/Janine (*American Blood*), 158-60
Teasdale, Sara, 269
Teasle, Will (*First Blood*), 130, 132, 137, 146, 153, 210, 221, 279, 282; and the death trap of the town, 176; and ESP with novel Rambo, 147-50; and the fathers, 138-44
Tenn, William, 109
Theiss, George, 285
Theweleit, Klaus, 24-25
"This Land is Your Land" (Guthrie), 32, 266
Thomas, Marlo, 63-64
Thomas, Linda (*Valediction*), 91
Thoreau, Henry David, 57, 170, 269-70, 272, 276; and social class, 69-70
*Thou Shalt Not Be Aware* (Miller), 115, 268, 294
"Thunder Road" (Springsteen), 175, 201-2, 224, 239
*Tidewater Tales* (Barth), 110
"Ties That Bind, The" (Springsteen), 226
*Time Passages* (Lipsitz), 31, 266
*Time*, 174, 178-79
*Time Passages*, 266
Tolson, Andrew, 263
*Totem and Taboo* (Freud), 199, 266, 268

"Toward a New Sociology of Masculinity" (Carrigan/Connell/Lee), 263
transformation, 5; masculist, 45, 259-61
*Transitions and Social Change* (Hogan), 263
*Translator's Turn, The* (Robinson), 263
Trask, Chief (*God Save the Child*), 47
Trautman, (Captain/Colonel) Sam, 112, 125, 128, 132-34, 151-54, 279, 281-82; and the fathers, 138, 141-46; in *Rambo: First Blood Part II*, 284
Trout, Kilgore (Vonnegut), 266
Tucker, Ellen, 269
*Tunnel of Love* (Springsteen), 176, 181, 189, 217, 228-35, 238, 240, 292-93
Tupper, Martin (*Dream On*), 25
Turman, Lawrence, 278
*TV Movies and Video Guide* (Maltin), 267, 284
"Two Tramps in Mud-Time" (Frost), 70-74
"Two Hearts" (Springsteen), 226

umbanda, 246
Urich, Robert, 18
"Used Cars" (Springsteen), 205, 238-40, 294
utopian vision (Jameson), 20-23; and the sixties, 35

Vajna, Andrew, 127, 279-80
*Valediction* (Parker), 60-61, 78, 83-84, 86, 91, 99, 102-3, 281
"Valentine's Day" (Springsteen), 229, 234, 238, 246
Verny, Thomas, 95
*Video Anthology* (Springsteen), 290
Vietnam, 11, 13, 31, 34-35, 110, 121-25, 135-36, 142-43, 145, 158, 160, 208-11, 278, 280-81, 287, 289
Vietnam veterans, 16, 123-25, 151, 158, 166-68, 288
Vietnam Veterans of America, 166-68, 169
violence, 79-84; and masculinity, 39; and narcissistic rage, 119
*Vision Shared, A* (Folkways), 32
Vonnegut, Kurt, 266

Walby, P., 24
*Walden* (Thoreau), 269, 272
"Walk Like a Man" (Springsteen), 217, 240
Wallace, Rachel (Parker), 39-41, 44, 61, 88-91, 105, 268, 276
Walvin, James, 269
"War" (Strong/Whitfield), 266-67
Warner Brothers, 123, 279
Warshawski, V.I. (Paretsky), 40, 267
Watergate scandal, 35, 110, 120
Wayne, John, 121, 127, 188
Wendy ("Born to Run"), 175, 177, 182, 224-25
Wharton, Edith, 39
Wharton, William, 160
*What Was Literature?* (Fiedler), 282
White, Kevin, 263
Whitfield, Norman, 266
Whitman, Walt, 57
*Why Are We In Vietnam?* (Mailer), 124
Wicca, 250
*Widening Gyre, The* (Parker), 60-61, 63, 65, 77, 86-87, 99, 103
*Wild, The Innocent, and the E Street Shuffle, The* (Springsteen), 35, 174-75, 224
"Wild Billy's Circus Song" (Springsteen), 224
*Wilderness* (Parker), 271, 273-76
Wilkinson, Rupert, 51

Willis, Sharon, 263
Wilson, George (*The Great Gatsby*), 273
Wilson, Myrtle (*The Great Gatsby*), 273
Wimsatt, W.K., 42
"With Every Wish" (Springsteen), 234
Wolf, Naomi, 11-13, 14
Wolfe (Robbins), Susan J., 43
Wolfe, Tom, 11
*Women in Love* (Lawrence), 43
women's movement, 1-2, 6, 43; as promasculist, 23; and women's writing, 30

Wonder, Stevie, 291
Woodstock, 31
*Woody Guthrie* (Klein), 266
work, 58; and liberal values, 33, 68-74
World War II, 114
"Wreck on the Highway" (Springsteen), 226-27
Wyllie, Irvin G., 269

Yates, Chief (*The Godwulf Manuscript*), 47
"You Can Look (But You Better Not Touch)" (Springsteen), 226, 289